SELF-HANDICAPPING
THE PARADOX THAT ISN'T

THE PLENUM SERIES IN
SOCIAL / CLINICAL PSYCHOLOGY

Series Editor: C. R. Snyder
University of Kansas
Lawrence, Kansas

SELF-DEFEATING BEHAVIORS
Experimental Research, Clinical Impressions, and Practical Implications
Edited by Rebecca C. Curtis

SELF-HANDICAPPING
The Paradox That Isn't
Raymond L. Higgins, C. R. Snyder, and Steven Berglas

A Continuation Order Plan is available for this series. A continuation order will bring delivery of each new volume immediately upon publication. Volumes are billed only upon actual shipment. For further information please contact the publisher.

SELF-HANDICAPPING

THE PARADOX THAT ISN'T

RAYMOND L. HIGGINS
AND
C. R. SNYDER

University of Kansas
Lawrence, Kansas

AND
STEVEN BERGLAS

McLean Hospital/Harvard Medical School
Belmont, Massachusetts

PLENUM PRESS • NEW YORK AND LONDON

Library of Congress Cataloging-in-Publication Data

Higgins, Raymond L.
    Self-handicapping : the paradox that isn't / Raymond L. Higgins
and C.R. Snyder and Steven Berglas.
        p.   cm. -- (The Plenum series in social/clinical psychology)
    Includes bibliographical references and index.
    ISBN 0-306-43540-3
    1. Self. 2. Psychology, Pathological.   I. Snyder, C. R.
II. Berglas, Steven.   III. Title.   IV. Series.
RC455.4.S45H54   1990
616.89--dc20
                                                                90-36519
                                                                CIP

© 1990 Plenum Press, New York
A Division of Plenum Publishing Corporation
233 Spring Street, New York, N.Y. 10013

Printed in the United States of America

To my wife, Sarah, and son, Ian, for
collaborating with my positive self-
illusions.
—R.L.H.

To Alfred Adler and Fritz Heider, who
drew the blueprints.
—C.R.S.

To those teachers who have selflessly
fostered my success.
—S.B.

CONTRIBUTORS

STEVEN BERGLAS, McLean Hospital/Harvard Medical School, Belmont, Massachusetts 02178

RAYMOND L. HIGGINS, Department of Psychology, University of Kansas, Lawrence, Kansas 66045

FREDERICK RHODEWALT, Department of Psychology, University of Utah, Salt Lake City, Utah 84112

ELIZABETH A. SELF, Department of Psychology, University of Kansas, Lawrence, Kansas 66045

C. R. SNYDER, Department of Psychology, University of Kansas, Lawrence, Kansas 66045

FOREWORD

The concept of self-handicapping can be legitimately anchored in a variety of intellectual contexts, some old and some newer. As this volume reminds us, Alfred Adler was perhaps the first to articulate the significance of various self-defeating claims and gestures for protecting the self-concept. Thus the apparent paradox of "defeat" in the interests of "protection." More recently (but still more than 30 years ago), Heider's "naive psychology" added attributional rhetoric to the description of self-defeating strategies. While predominantly cognitive in its thrust, the attributional approach incorporated several motivational influences—especially those involving egocentric concerns. Heider hardly violated our common sense when he suggested that people are inclined to attribute their performances in a self-serving manner: the good things I caused; the bad things were forced upon me.

The notion of self-handicapping strategies, proposed by Berglas and myself a little more than a decade ago, capitalized on these homely truths while adding a particular proactive twist. We not only make excuses for our blunders; we plan our engagements and our situational choices so that self-protective excuses are unnecessary. In doing so, we use our attributional understanding to arrange things so that flawed and failing performances will not be interpreted in ways that threaten our self-esteem.

But do all of us do these things? Surely, the topics of excuse making—in the forms of procrastination, of distraction, of preparation failures, of headaches, colds, and hangovers—are so much a part of cultural lore that we can acknowledge our (occasional?) use of such explanations for failure in a self-mocking manner. A prominent concern of this volume are those points of transition between healthy egocentrism and pathological internalizations of self-handicapping styles. Indeed, the topic of self-handicapping is particularly intriguing (and instructive) because it lies at the intersection of social, personality, and clinical psychology. Self-handicapping phenomena are cognitive, motivational, and interpersonal. They are strategic while eluding conscious awareness. They may be intensely private, but they depend on shared cultural understandings that define the symbolic meaning of action. They are ultimately controlled by a society that defines the rank ordering of stigmatizing labels. The chapters that follow nicely document the importance of these intersecting contexts in helping us understand how people can defeat their long-range purposes in the short-range interests of promoting them.

In particular, a full understanding of self-handicapping undermines any distinction between person-caused and situation-caused performances. Our conventional understanding is that situations constrain us in various ways, making certain acts more or less likely. More specifically, situations facilitate some performances and inhibit others. A certain rough consensus about the constraint potential of commonly experienced situations provides the soil for the growth of self-handicapping strategies. Self-handicappers trade on the consensual understanding of situational constraint.

Situations constrain behavior, but people choose situations. Thus each of us can play a role in deciding how to be constrained. Individual differences in making these decisions are thus joined to the reality of constraining situational forces. It is at the various daily choice points that personality and social psychology merge and overlap. In the most commonly featured examples, the self-handicapper, in the interests of protecting a fragile competence image, chooses to place him or herself in a situation that inhibits successful performance. The "situation" may be obviously external (as in choosing among levels of task difficulty), a mixture of external and internal (as in deciding to take a drink), or exclusively internal (as in withdrawing effort or cultivating a somatic symptom). The self-handicapper thus tries to control the conditions of performance to provide a built-in protective attribution for failure or, if fortune smiles, an augmented self-esteem attribution deriving from success under constraint. In choosing among these conditions, one is struck with the importance of explanatory priorities, which again are derived from either explicit or implicit cultural understandings of preferred attributional labels. It is better to fail because one is lazy than because one is stupid. Though "test anxiety" may be preferred over obvious alternatives as a label for a low SAT score, most would prefer the label of "depressed" to the label "anxiety neurotic" when suffering through a period of distress. Similarly, the stigma of "psychotherapy" or "psychiatric disorder" is shunned in favor of being "in analysis." And so on.

The apparent paradox of self-handicapping is that the choice of inhibiting conditions makes failure more likely. Though failure can perhaps be more conveniently explained with reference to the inhibiting constraint, it is still failure. And failing or flawed performances can have a devastating long range effect on the very competence image that self-handicapping is designed to protect. Sooner or later, the underachiever and the alcohol abuser reach a point where the self-saving, self-confirming performance is no longer an option. *Manana*, it turns out, was yesterday.

Finally, even when we focus on the more successful instances of self-handicapping (and surely the phenomenon is too ubiquitous to be consistently pathological), the perils of deception and self-deception are always present. For self-handicapping to be effective, it would appear that the right hand must not be fully aware of what the left hand is doing. I must think I am choosing a handicap for some other, more acceptable reason, or the attributional significance of the handicap loses its appeal. To put it another way, the salience of situational constraint must exceed the salience of my choosing to so constrain myself. The issue of credibility is ever-present whether the self or others are the target of one's attempts to merit a self-protective attribution.

These and many other considerations are lucidly discussed in the chapters that follow. Although I am somewhat chagrined that my own contributions to the self-handicapping literature have been scarce since our original formulation more than a decade ago, I am positively delighted that the concept has received so much research attention since then. Because of this attention, and recently reported studies, the publication of this volume is indeed timely. Welcome to the labyrinth of self-handicapping strategies. May you see a little—but not too much—of yourself in the pages to follow.

Edward E. Jones

Princeton, New Jersey

PREFACE

Late in the summer of 1987, when the idea for this book first took shape, the self-handicapping concept was approaching the tenth anniversary of its introduction into the public domain. A rapidly growing literature on the topic suggested the timeliness of mounting a comprehensive examination of this young and somewhat fractious field.

In this volume, we develop an historical perspective that emphasizes the convergence of theoretical traditions from both clinical and social psychology to yield the "modern" self-handicapping concept. This emphasis reflects our belief that research and theory relating to self-handicapping, a major means of coping with negative life events, resides squarely at the fulcrum of the interface between clinical and social psychology.

In addition, we present what is currently known about the variables that influence self-handicapping; we explicate the effects of self-handicaps; we outline frameworks for understanding how self-handicapping "lifestyles" may be developed and maintained over time; and we detail some of the treatment issues facing those involved in helping self-handicappers. Lastly, in the final chapter of the book, we present a balance-theory analysis of self-handicapping: the goal being to provide an overarching perspective on how self-handicapping is imbedded within our ongoing struggle to negotiate palatable interpretations of events that threaten our self-esteem and feelings of personal control.

There are a number of individuals who have contributed to the present book, but whose names do not appear on the author line. First and foremost are those students (most now graduated) who have worked with us on research projects associated with self-handicapping: Robert Augelli, JoAnn Basgall, Craig DeGree, Mitch Handelsman, Robert Harris,

Jon Farrell-Higgins, Rick Ingram, Craig Neumann, Cheryl Newburg, Suzanne Perkins, Allen Sherman, Jennifer Shrag, Tim Smith, and Rita Stucky. Next are colleagues and friends who have offered us encouragement and helpful critiques: Gerald Alder, Edward Jones, Mark Leary, Philip G. Levendusky, James Shepperd, and Beatrice Wright. Finally, we would like to express our special appreciation to Elizabeth A. Self and Frederick Rhodewalt for contributing chapters to the book; to Edward E. Jones for providing the foreword; and to Eliot Werner at Plenum for lending his backing to our effort.

Raymond L. Higgins
C. R. Snyder
Steven Berglas

Lawrence and Belmont

CONTENTS

Chapter 2

Elizabeth A. Self

Chapter 3

Frederick Rhodewalt

Steven Berglas

Chapter 6

The Maintenance and Treatment of Self-Handicapping:
  From Risk-Taking to Face-Saving—and Back

Raymond L. Higgins and Steven Berglas

Chapter 7

Self-Handicapping from a Heiderian Perspective: Taking Stock of "Bonds" 239

Raymond L. Higgins and C. R. Snyder

CHAPTER 1

SELF-HANDICAPPING
HISTORICAL ROOTS AND CONTEMPORARY BRANCHES

RAYMOND L. HIGGINS

The patient selects certain symptoms and develops them until they impress him as real obstacles. Behind his barricade of symptoms the patient feels hidden and secure. To the question, 'What use are you making of your talents?' he answers, 'This thing stops me; I cannot go ahead,' and points to his self-erected barricade.
(Alfred Adler, 1929, p. 13)

The self-handicapper, we are suggesting, reaches out for impediments, exaggerates handicaps, embraces any factor reducing personal responsibility for mediocrity and enhancing personal responsibility for success. One does this to shape the implications of performance feedback both in one's own eyes and in the eyes of others.
(Edward E. Jones & Steven Berglas, 1978, p. 202)

INTRODUCTION

From time to time in the history of science an idea emerges "before its time" and is destined to languish in relative obscurity until the way somehow is prepared for it to assume its rightful place in the order of things. Sometimes, the idea is so precocious that there is no basis in contemporary science or cultural development for its significance to be

RAYMOND L. HIGGINS • Department of Psychology, University of Kansas, Lawrence, Kansas 66045.

1

comprehended or evaluated. Perhaps the most dramatic example of this was Democritus's fifth-century B.C. proposal that the atom was the fundamental building block of matter. It wasn't until the twentieth-century A.D. that physical science had advanced to the point that Niels Bohr was finally able to describe the atom as we now understand it. There are other times when an idea "submerges" because there are repressive cultural or ideological forces at work. As an instance of this, consider that Copernicus's heliocentric (sun-centered) model of the then-known universe was actively suppressed by the Catholic church, based on theological convictions that God's earth *must* be the center of the universe. Moreover, Copernicus's later advocates (e.g., Galileo) were zealously persecuted by the Inquisition.

It would be folly for me to presume that the subject of this book, the self-handicapping concept, represents an intellectual achievement of the magnitude or historical importance of those noted above. I will, however, be so bold as to suggest that, like them, it is an idea that appeared and then suffered relative obscurity before "finding its time." Also like them, its ultimate (recent) reemergence as a topic of active inquiry owes to the advancement of science (cf. atomic theory) and to the weakening of ideological repression (cf. heliocentric conceptions of the solar system).

There is, moreover, yet another analogy from the history of science that seems pertinent to the subject of self-handicapping. On rare occasions, parallel ideas or insights spring forth from what appear to be totally independent sources. A fascinating example of this was the simultaneous publication of theories of evolution by Charles Darwin and Alfred Wallace in the late 1850s. It was Darwin's later publication of his book on the origin of species that led to his subsequent, near-exclusive identification with evolution in the minds of most people. As an evolution theorist (Edward Wiley) recently said to me, it really didn't matter who came up with the idea first—what mattered more was who managed to "put the idea over."

I am proposing here that this latter type of pragmatic reality has also played a role in the case of the self-handicapping concept. It would be specious for me to imply that Alfred Adler's notion of "safeguarding," somehow "died aborning" or failed to have a significant impact of its own. However, certain accidents of history have clearly led his idea that people protect themselves from failure by taking steps that seem to risk insuring defeat to be more closely associated with Edward E. Jones and Steven Berglas in the minds of contemporary social scientists.

Perhaps the most important of these historical accidents is the fact that Adler conceived his safeguarding notion virtually *de novo* at a time when experimental psychology was in its infancy and in an intellectual context that emphasized the building of grand psychodynamic theories rather than empirical investigation. In contrast, Jones and Berglas's self-handicapping concept represented a creative *extension* of firmly established social psychological theory at a time when the intellectual commitment of a burgeoning number of academic psychologists, who were under pressure to "publish or perish," was to empiricism. Moreover, the publication of the book *Excuses: Masquerades in Search of Grace* (Snyder, Higgins, & Stucky, 1983) made a significant contribution to the quickening pace of inquiry into the self-protective processes associated with excuse tactics. Without doubt, the modern zeitgeist greatly assisted Jones and Berglas in their contemporary effort to "put the idea across."*

Jones and Berglas (1978; Berglas & Jones, 1978) first coined the term *self-handicapping* in order to describe a process wherein people protect their competence images by *proactively* arranging for adversity in specific performances. Although this was the first published use of the term, it was not their first recognition of the phenomenon (e.g., Berglas, 1976; Jones & Berglas, 1975). As early as 1975, for example, Jones and Berglas were referring to such ploys as "strategies of externalization." Also, as my preceding comments and the opening epigraph from Alfred Adler indicate, the paradoxical idea that people safeguard their images by undermining their success already had a long, preexisting tradition in clinical thought.

In the following pages, I will outline the history of thinking about self-handicapping (safeguarding) behaviors within both the clinical and more recent social psychological traditions, and I will draw contrasts between the resulting concepts. Subsequently, I will shift my attention to providing an overview of contemporary areas of empirical and theoretical work within the self-handicapping domain.

THE CLINICAL TRADITION

In 1902, Sigmund Freud invited Alfred Adler, Wilhelm Stekel, Rudolf Reitler, and Max Kahane to his home to discuss psychoanalysis. He thus initiated the precursor of the Vienna Psychoanalytic Society (Jones, 1955). He also unwittingly provided Adler with encouragement to develop and articulate his increasingly competitive alternatives to Freud's thinking. By

---

*To say that the zeitgeist was "kinder" to Jones and Berglas than it had been to Adler is not to say that the self-handicapping concept was warmly received by all. According to E. E. Jones (personal communication, August 1988), an earlier version of the Jones and Berglas (1978) discussion of the use of alcohol consumption as a self-handicapping strategy was "rejected summarily" by a prominent journal of the American Psychological Association.

1911, Adler's political usefulness to Freud had waned, and his independent views could no longer be construed as useful elaborations on accepted Freudian dogma (Stepansky, 1983).

In two special-request addresses to the Vienna Psychoanalytic Society on January 4 and February 1, 1911, Adler elaborated his ideas regarding the relationship of his theory of masculine protest to Freud's theory of libidinal repression. In the wake of these meetings and Freud's spirited rejection of Adler's provocative new ego psychology, Adler resigned as chairman of the Vienna Psychoanalytic Society and, later, from the society itself. Freud's enmity toward Adler's rivalry and his desire to impose a greater degree of theoretical purity on his society were such that, in the October 11, 1911, meeting of the society, he engineered a purge of Adler's remaining supporters (Nunberg & Federn, 1974). Freud subsequently moved to deepen his relationship with Carl Jung, the next major dissenter from his notion that the sexual instincts were fundamental psychological bedrock (Stepansky, 1983).

THE MASCULINE PROTEST

As Adler's ideas evolved over the course of his association with Freud and beyond, the role he ascribed to instinctual (libidinal) forces in the development of personality diminished, and the role he ascribed to *subjective* evaluations of both organic and environmental influences increased. A physician, he was acutely interested in accounting for the manner in which people's lives were shaped by their reactions to physical weaknesses or disabilities (organ inferiorities). Over time, however, he recognized that other weaknesses, including those produced by adverse environmental conditions (e.g., pampering, neglect), had a profound influence on personality development.

During and following the time of their split, Freud repeatedly characterized Adler's views as too biological for his own tastes, apparently still referring to Adler's earlier work on organ inferiority (Stepansky, 1983). In actuality, however, Adler was mounting the first major social psychological challenge to the supremacy of Freud's own objectivist biological determinism (Ansbacher & Ansbacher, 1967). Indeed, Adler's characterization of the sexual drive and its effects (e.g., the Oedipus complex) as mere artifices of a perspectivistic ego's efforts to safeguard itself from feelings of inferiority must have perturbed Freud mightily.

In place of Freud's psychology of repression, Adler offered a psychology of self-esteem. At the time of his split with Freud, Adler regarded the driving force behind personality as the struggle to compensate for subjective feelings of weakness and inferiority by nurturing

attributes and feelings of strength and power (i.e., the "masculine protest"). As his thinking evolved, however, Adler left homeostatic mechanisms behind and introduced teleological perspectives into his theory.

THE GOAL OF SUPERIORITY

Deeply influenced by Vaihinger's (1925) philosophy of "as if" (Ansbacher & Ansbacher, 1967), Adler emphasized the role of fictional goals
in providing integration and direction for people's lives (Adler, 1926). As
Adler saw things, people literally fashion their life goals out of the fabric
of their constitutional makeups and personal experiences. They are
guided in their efforts to achieve those goals by their subjective *self's*
(ego's) appraisals of the obstacles and opportunities encountered.

Despite the future orientation provided by the fictional goal, however, the goal was still seen as idiosyncratic to the individual as well as
largely compensatory in nature. At one level, for example, Adler held
that the guiding fiction provided the individual with a tool for overcoming inferiorities.

> Nevertheless, we can say that the guiding image of the child must be con-
> structed 'as if' it were able, by influencing the direction of his will, to bring
> him greater security and orientation. (Adler, in Ansbacher & Ansbacher,
> 1967, p. 98)

At yet another level, the guiding fiction was itself regarded as a compensation for felt inferiorities.

> In each mind there is the conception of a [fictional] goal or ideal to get beyond
> the present state and to overcome the present deficiencies and difficulties by
> postulating a concrete goal for the future. By means of this concrete goal, the
> individual can think and feel himself superior to the difficulties of the present
> because he has in mind his success of the future. (in Ansbacher & Ansbacher,
> 1967, p. 100)

Adler was not finished with his theory, however. He later advanced
his teleological perspective even further by positing the existence of a
universal guiding motive—the struggle to achieve superiority. By superiority, Adler meant the overcoming of external obstacles and a kind of
self-actualization or personal completion similar to that articulated by
Kurt Goldstein (1939). Normal individuals in this scheme sought to
achieve superiority by overcoming their felt deficiencies (inferiority *feelings*) in a largely task-oriented and socially contributory manner. Neurotic individuals, in contrast, were thought to be so impressed with the
magnitude of their perceived inferiorities, and so discouraged about
their chances of overcoming them in socially useful ways, that they

developed an *inferiority complex*. The inferiority complex, in turn, fostered the development of a *superiority complex*. For neurotic individuals, then, superiority striving became directed toward protecting their prestige, avoiding defeat, and sustaining the esteem-giving *illusion* of working toward true superiority (Ansbacher & Ansbacher, 1967).

THE CONCEPT OF PSYCHOLOGICAL DEFENSE

With the preceeding review of some of the major features of Adler's theory in hand, we can begin to see how his ideas played a major (many would say corrective) role in influencing thinking about the nature of psychological defenses. The notion that people engage in defensive behavior was first introduced by Freud in his 1894 work, "The Defence of Neuro-psychoses" (Freud, 1953). Freud's psychology, however, was essentially an "id" psychology in which the fundamental threat to psychological stability was the possibility that unacceptable libidinal impulses would intrude into consciousness.

The ego's role in the psyche was primarily a reactive and, for Freud, apparently uninteresting one. For many years after he introduced his notion of defense, Freud neglected the concept and regarded the unconscious *repression* of libidinal promptings as the wellspring of neurotic behaviors (Munroe, 1955). Symptoms merely represented substitute expressions of repressed material (Freud, 1943).

As noted above, Adler's rejection of Freud's emphasis on the libidinal determinants of behavior formed part of the basis for their split in 1911. A second factor was Adler's insistence that symptoms were unconsciously created by the ego (self) in order to safeguard itself from the esteem losses that might attend failures to face and overcome life's challenges (Stepansky, 1983). For Adler, the self was the center of and the prime mover within the psyche: Freud's repression was only one of many possible safeguarding strategies the self could muster in its defense. Although Freud later revised his own theory to include ego defenses as an important arena for psychoanalytic study, and even went so far as to demote repression to being only a special form of ego-defensive operation (e.g., Freud, 1936), he steadfastly maintained that such defenses were aimed at protecting the ego from instinctual threats (Ansbacher & Ansbacher, 1967).

Subsequent dynamic theorists were more willing than Freud to recognize the ego's need to defend against environmental threats. In her classic 1936 treatise on the ego defenses, for example, Anna Freud (1948; also see Sandler & Freud, 1985) acknowledged the role that ego defenses play in deflecting external as well as instinctual threats. Moreover, as other influential psychodynamic theorists began to extol the formative importance of environmental forces on personality (e.g., Horney, 1950; Sullivan, 1953), thinking about the nature of psychological defenses assumed a distinctly Adlerian flavor in the sense that they were viewed as "safeguarding the subjective self and self-ideal from threatening outside situations" (Ansbacher & Ansbacher, 1967, pp. 265).

Withdrawal as a Safeguarding Strategy

In their edited version of Adler's writings, Ansbacher and Ansbacher (1967) identify two primary forms of safeguarding strategies, aggression and withdrawal (seeking distance). Of the two, the strategy of seeking distance through the *construction of obstacles* is most relevant for our current discussion. Interestingly, Adler regarded this strategy as a relatively positive one: Although the individual was involved in creating obstacles to his or her success, the strategy, nevertheless, entailed attempts to face the threatening tasks. According to Adler, the benefit of using this safeguarding strategy was that

> the patient's self-esteem is protected in his own judgment, and usually also his prestige in the estimation of others. If the decision falls against him, he can refer to his difficulties and to the proof of his illness which he has himself constructed. If he remains victorious, what could he not have done if he were well, when, as a sick man, he achieved so much—one handed, so to speak. (in Ansbacher & Ansbacher, 1967, p. 276)

Adler's Legacy

The list of Adler's contributions to psychology is impressive, despite the fact that he is only infrequently credited by those who have followed in his steps. He was a pioneer in promoting holistic views of the personality, in advancing teleological views of psychological life as movement toward a goal, in developing subjectivistic and phenomenological orientations to understanding human behavior, and in championing self-esteem maintenance as a central dynamic underlying behavior (Ansbacher & Ansbacher, 1967; Stepansky, 1983). He has also been recognized as the first person in Western civilization to advocate the use of paradoxical treatment strategies (Mozdzierz, Macchitelli, & Lisiecki, 1976; Weeks & L'Abate, 1982).

The legacy of Adler's view of symptoms as having excuse-making functions is clearly apparent in the work of later writers. Horney (1950), for example, also saw self-esteem maintenance as a primary aim of neurotic symptoms. In her view, the neurotic individual's self-esteem hinged on his or her ability to maintain an overly idealized self-image.

Because the idealized image was realistically unobtainable, however, Horney believed that neurotics use a number of face-saving devices that strongly resemble the aggression and distance-seeking strategies described by Adler. In the face of threats to their neurotic pride, for instance, Horney believed that neurotics engage in such tactics as attacking their detractors and avoiding potentially humiliating situations. More directly relevant here was Horney's belief that, "since all these measures are more a camouflage than a remedy for his pride, he may start to cultivate his neuroses because the neurosis with a capital N then becomes a precious alibi for the lack of accomplishment" (p. 107).

Somewhere along the line, Adler's idea that symptom-based performance impediments serve to generate esteem-saving attributions for performance failures seems to have moved into the "public domain" and largely ceased being specifically associated with him outside of Adlerian circles. Berne (1964), for example, described a transactional game called "wooden leg," in which the protagonist gains esteem-saving distance from threatening performances by alluding to some handicapping condition (including insanity or neurosis), but he provides no reference to Adler's work. Similarly, Adler's idea that psychiatric symptoms and deviant behaviors have value as interpersonal influence and control (including excuse) strategies has recurred repeatedly, but usually without reference to him, in the works of Ludwig and Farrelly (1966, 1967), Goffman (1959, 1961), Braginsky, Braginsky, and Ring (1969), Haley (1963), Artiss (1959), Coyne (1976), Shaw (1982), Belknap (1956), Sarbin and Mancuso (1980), Fontana, Klein, Lewis, and Levine (1968), MacAndrew and Edgerton (1969), Schlenker (1980), Scheff (1971), Zimbardo and Radl (1981), and Kaplan (1980), among others (see Snyder *et al.*, 1983, for notable exception).

Although Adler's idea regarding the ego-defensive erection of barriers to adequate performance never disappeared from the clinical literature (viz. Berne, 1964), it has not enjoyed the empirical and theoretical attention that has been associated with his notion that symptoms may be used to secure important "secondary gains." Indeed, it was not until 1978, following the publication of two articles by Jones and Berglas (1978; Berglas & Jones, 1978), that the problem of strategic self-defeatism in the service of self-esteem began to receive widespread notice.

Jones and Berglas described the "self-handicapping" use of drugs and underachievement to preemptively confound attributions to lack of competence in the face of potential failures. There is no evidence, however, that this self-handicapping idea was derived conceptually from Adler's work or from more recent Adlerian discussions of the excuse value of alcohol and drug abuse (e.g., Steffenhagen, 1974). Rather, the self-handicapping concept appears to have evolved from virtually independent theoretical considerations.† In the following section, then, my attention will be directed toward reviewing the development of Jones and Berglas's self-handicapping concept and toward tracing its theoretical lineage within the field of social psychology.

THE SOCIAL PSYCHOLOGY TRADITION

The 1950s witnessed the presentation of two major orientations for thinking about the meaning of human behavior. In his book *The Presentation of Self in Everyday Life*, for example, Goffman (1959) articulated his views concerning *impression management*, a process whereby people manage their overt behaviors in order to manipulate the impressions that others form of them. Almost simultaneously, Heider (1958) published *The Psychology of Interpersonal Relations*, thereby presenting a framework for thinking about the manner in which people perceive and attempt to make sense of behavior. It is my thesis here that the self-handicapping idea, as ultimately articulated by Jones and Berglas (1978; Berglas & Jones, 1978) represents a synthesis of these two theoretical orientations. In effect, self-handicappers accomplish their impression-management goals by capitalizing on a "naive" awareness of the processes through which people form causal explanations. In the following discussion, I will briefly outline the development of the impression-management and causal attribution literatures with the aim of describing their ultimate convergence in the self-handicapping concept.

IMPRESSION MANAGEMENT

Although Goffman (1959) was the most influential early proponent of the impression-management perspective on behavior, the phenomenon wherein psychiatric patients appear to purposefully manipulate the presentation of their symptoms in order to achieve their personal goals had been and was being recognized by others (Artiss, 1959; Belknap, 1956; Dunham & Weinberg, 1960; Szasz, 1961). It was not until the

†In written comments concerning a prepublication draft of this chapter, E. E. Jones (personal communication, August 1988) wrote: "As you may know, I am a clinical psychologist by training and was naturally aware of Adler's contributions. Somewhere back in the dark recesses of my youth I was fully exposed to Karen Horney, Anna Freud, the debates about secondary gain, and many other historical streams and tributaries that undoubtedly found their way into the self-handicapping concept. You are absolutely right, however, that we never made explicit reference to Adler and that his writings were much more pertinent than we ever recognized at the time."

mid-1960s however, that empirical demonstrations of strategic symptom presentations appeared.

In the initial study, Braginsky, Grosse, and Ring (1966) examined the prediction that psychiatric newcomers (hospitalized for less than 3 months) would be more motivated to gain release from the hospital than would oldtimers (hospitalized for more than 3 months). The authors varied whether a self-report questionnaire was labeled the "Mental Illness Test" or the "Self-Insight Test." Patients completing the "Mental Illness" version were told that "true" answers would signify a need for continuing hospitalization, while patients completing the "Self-Insight" version were told that "true" answers would be predictive of early release. As expected, the oldtimers answered "true" more often on the "Mental Illness" version than on the "Self-Insight" version, while newcomers did the opposite. The authors concluded that the patients had manipulated their responses in order to achieve their goals.

Shortly on the heels of the Braginsky et al. (1966) study, a number of other studies demonstrated the ability of psychiatric patients to impression manage (e.g., Braginsky & Braginsky, 1967; Braginsky et al., 1969; Braginsky, Holzberg, Ridley, & Braginsky, 1968; Fontana & Gessner, 1969; Fontana & Klein, 1968; Fontana et al., 1968). These studies provided compelling evidence that psychiatric symptoms are more than a manifestation of mental illness—they can be a means for achieving important personal benefits.

Although the early impression-management literature was primarily concerned with the ability of psychiatric patients to strategically modify their symptoms, subsequent research in this area has focused more on the self-presentational concerns and tactics of "normal" (typically college student) populations. Moreover, this latter literature served to direct researchers' attention toward a somewhat different class of self-presentational goals. Goffman's (1959) central concern was with the use of impression-management tactics to define the nature of interpersonal relationships, and the work on symptom presentation largely emphasized the securing of tangible benefits (e.g., hospital privileges; Braginsky & Braginsky, 1967). Beginning with the work of Jones (1964), impression management came increasingly to be seen as serving important social approval, self-esteem, and interpersonal control or power needs (see also, Jones & Wortman, 1973). Moreover, it was soon recognized that, in order for people to achieve their self-presentational goals, it is necessary for them to be able to adopt the perspective of (i.e., to predict the response of) their target audience (e.g., Weinstein, 1968). This insight provides a key link between the self-presentation and causal attribution literatures.

Causal Attribution

Heider's (1944, 1958) work on person perception and attributional processes eventually made a major impact on the field of social psychology. His "naive" theory of causal attributions provided a useful framework for thinking about the conditions that provide observers with information concerning the dispositional characteristics of actors and, relatedly, for thinking about the conditions under which people are seen as responsible for outcomes. The importance of these processes was such that, by 1967, two additional theories relating to the formation of causal attributions had been advanced. Both built upon the principles detailed by Heider.

In 1965, Jones and Davis advanced their theory of correspondent inferences to account for the conclusions that observers draw from other people's actions. Specifically, their theory was concerned with how people arrive at inferences about the intentions and dispositional characteristics of others. Such inferences are based on judgments of the desirability and uniqueness of the effects produced by them. For example, if it is concluded that an actor foresaw and had the ability to produce the consequences of an action (e.g., harm to another person), the probabilities are high that he or she will be regarded as having *intended* to produce the harm and, depending on the circumstances, it may be also concluded that the actor is "callous" (a *dispositional* attribution). By the same token, to the extent that an action has unique consequences, in comparison to those of other possible actions, or has only one desirable consequence or a small number of them, the probability increases that those consequences will be regarded as the goal of the action.

In contrast to Jones and Davis's correspondent inferences model, Kelley's (1967) analysis of covariance theory of attribution focused on the assignment of causality to all aspects of the environment, including objects and conditions as well as people. Kelley proposed that attributions concerning causes are most likely to center on those aspects of the environment that covary with the outcomes. For example, an actor is most likely to be seen as the cause of an outcome if the actor is associated with similar outcomes under differing circumstances (low distinctiveness), if the actor is routinely associated with the outcome (high consistency), and if other people are only rarely (or never) associated with the outcome (low consensus).

In 1971, Kelley added the principles of discounting and augmentation to his theory. In effect, the discounting principle signifies that, when an outcome is associated with more than one plausible cause, the attribution to any one of those causes will be weaker than if it stands alone. In contrast, the augmentation principle indicates that the attribution of causality to a given agent is strengthened if the outcome occurred despite the presence of inhibiting influences.

SELF-SERVING ATTRIBUTIONS

The attributional theories advanced during the 1950s and 1960s stimulated a large body of research. In the main, the accumulated evidence has served to validate the basic attributional principles. Of particular relevance here, however, is the turn that a portion of this literature took toward examining the role of subjectively motivated biases in attributional phenomena.

From the time of Heider's (1958) seminal work, it had been recognized that personal wishes and needs might influence attributions. Given the prestige that esteem maintenance motives have historically enjoyed in the field of psychology (e.g., Allport, 1937; James, 1890; Maslow, 1954; Rogers, 1965; Sullivan, 1953), it was only natural that these attributional biases should be formulated in terms of self-esteem maintenance motives. In the words of Hastorf, Schneider, and Polefka (1970), for example, "We are prone to alter our perception of causality so as to protect or enhance our self-esteem. We attribute success to our own dispositions and failure to external forces" (p. 73).

As empirical studies began to focus on the attributions that people make for outcomes with which they are associated, it was, in fact, observed that subjects attribute greater causality to themselves for positive than for negative outcomes (see Bradley, 1978; Miller & Ross, 1975; Zuckerman, 1979, for reviews). From the perspective of the attributional theories outlined above, one of the central esteem-saving goals of such egoistic asymmetries in the attribution of causality is the avoidance of unsavory dispositional attributions (e.g., attributions to incompetence following failure). In line with Kelley's (1971) discounting principle, for example, emphasizing the role of external factors (e.g., luck, task difficulty) in producing a negative outcome should serve to discount the role of such internal (and esteem-determining) factors as ability (Miller, Norman, & Wright, 1978; Schlenker, 1980; Wortman, 1976).

The demonstration that esteem motives contaminate and distort the reporting of information-processing cognitions associated with the attribution of causality provided a firm empirical justification for theoretical links between the attribution and self-presentation (impression-management) literatures (Snyder et al., 1983). This was particularly true in light of evidence that the tendency toward self-protective attributions is heightened when performances are subject to the scrutiny of others (see Bradley, 1978, for review).

SELF-HANDICAPPING

In 1975, Jones and Berglas described a variety of self-presentational tactics (strategies of externalization) that they believed were characteristic of certain drug users (see also Berglas, 1976). These strategies presumed that people not only have implicit knowledge of attributional principles, but that they also actively manipulate the environment (including their own behavior) to shape the attributions made about their behavior. In a subsequent, similar discussion of the motivations underlying drug–alcohol use and underachievement, Jones and Berglas (1978) relabeled the phenomenon "self-handicapping." Almost simultaneously, they (Berglas & Jones, 1978) reported two empirical investigations of the use of drugs as a self-handicapping strategy.

Among the more significant aspects of Jones and Berglas's self-handicapping notion was the idea that people *proactively* arrange circumstances to capitalize on Kelley's (1971) discounting and augmentation principles. By emphasizing the preemptive quality of self-handicapping, Jones and Berglas veered away from the established self-serving attribution literature which emphasized the *retrospective* application of attributional principles. (See Snyder *et al.*, 1983, for extended discussion of the distinctions between anticipatory and retrospective excuse processes.)

Also significant was their suggestion that self-handicapping derives from "an *abnormal* investment in the question of self-worth" (emphasis added; Jones & Berglas, 1978, p. 205). The self-handicapper's self-regard was represented as being so exquisitely vulnerable to debasement that ego-defensive motives (i.e., to avoid responsibility for failure) come to outweigh achievement motives. Thus, a kind of neurotic paradox was born: Although the self-handicapper's ultimate goal is the maintenance (or enhancement) of a competence *image*, the self-protective method involves undermining the likelihood of mastery. In the words of Berglas and Jones (1978), self-handicappers "do not primarily set out to insure failure; they are willing to accept (probable) failure if it can be explained away *and* if (possible) success will have augmented value for self-esteem" (p. 406).

Although Jones and Berglas (1978) acknowledged that the anxiety relief associated with being protected by a self-handicap might occasionally result in enhanced performance, their emphasis was on viewing handicapping as defensive and as directed toward warding off threats to self-esteem (as opposed to public esteem).

As defined by Berglas and Jones (1978), self-handicapping involves "any action or choice of performance setting that enhances the opportunity to externalize (or excuse) failure and to internalize (reasonably accept credit for) success" (p. 406). According to them, this behavior is particularly characteristic of individuals "who have a precarious but not entirely negative sense of self-competence" (Jones & Berglas, 1978, p. 200). The manner in which people come to develop a "competence complex" (p. 204) and to defensively avoid unconfounded (diagnostic) assessments of their competence can be understood via a brief summary of some of the burdens of positive feedback.

Jones and Berglas (1978) discussed two primary avenues through which people may come to have precarious competence images and inordinate concerns about putting those images to the test. The first relies on an analysis of the *exchange* and *signifying* value of positive reinforcement (cf. Jones, 1964). In simplified terms, Jones and Berglas suggested that people (especially children) may have difficulty in establishing a confident sense that they are unconditionally valued and loved because of confusion concerning whether the social reinforcements they receive are contingent upon adequate performance (i.e., exchanges) or whether they signify unconditional love and caring. Once the individual believes (or suspects) that love and esteem derive from his or her ability to gratify others, unambiguous failures may be too threatening to allow. As Jones and Berglas put it, "He who tries and fails loses everything. He who fails without trying maintains a precarious hold on the illusion of love and admiration" (1978, p. 204).

The second major avenue for developing a competence complex (and the one most attended to in subsequent theoretical and empirical work) is a history of noncontingent positive reinforcement. Jones and Berglas suggested that noncontingent success experiences result in a generally positive, *but insecure,* self-concept. The insecurity flows from the person's inability to confidently discern the basis for his or her success. According to this reasoning, the self-handicapper is motivated to maintain his or her image of competence, but is reluctant to put it to a clear test because of fears that it is insubstantial. Moreover, Jones and Berglas suggested that the confidence-eroding consequences of noncontingent success may be exacerbated by the tendency for successes to generate heightened expectations for future performances (cf. S. C. Jones, 1973; Peter & Hull, 1969). For the affected individual, then, self-handicapping becomes a means for simultaneously resisting the coercive effects of positive feedback and avoiding (in)competence attributions for failures to live up to expectations.

Although Jones and Berglas (1978) hypothesized the existence of at least two etiological pathways for the development of self-handicapping as a defensive style, the only empirical studies of the phenomenon published by either author exclusively emphasized the critical role of noncontingent success experiences. In both studies, Berglas and Jones

(1978) predicted that subjects would self-handicap by electing to use a (bogus) performance-inhibiting drug (Pandocrin) rather than a (bogus) performance-enhancing drug (Actavil) prior to a retest on an intelligence task for which they had previously received noncontingent success feedback. It was thought that, relative to contingent success feedback, giving subjects noncontingent success feedback would promote self-handicapping by arousing performance uncertainty and by stimulating motives to avoid disconfirmation of their (noncontingent) success images. Some of the subjects in both studies, then, were first tested on largely insolvable problems and given (noncontingent) success feedback. Other subjects were tested on largely solvable problems and given (contingent) success feedback. All subjects were then allowed to elect to use Pandocrin or Actavil in anticipation of being retested. In support of their theory, both studies found that noncontingent success subjects were more likely than contingent success subjects to select Pandocrin (they did not actually ingest it). However, this was only true for their male research subjects.

In 1981, Tucker, Vuchinich, and Sobell reported two experiments examining the use of alcohol to self-handicap. In a procedure nearly identical to that of Berglas and Jones (1978), male college social drinkers were tested on solvable or insolvable problems, given success or no feedback, and led to anticipate a retest following alcohol consumption. In the second study, but not the first, noncontingent success subjects consumed more alcohol than contingent success subjects. Tucker *et al.* concluded that their subjects did use alcohol to self-handicap, but that this effect was eliminated when they were given access to a familiar performance-enhancing strategy (i.e., in the first study subjects were given study materials).

In 1982, Kolditz and Arkin presented a further replication and extension of Berglas and Jones's (1978) Pandocrin findings. These authors varied whether subjects' drug selection (i.e., Actavil vs. Pandocrin) and retest performances were public or private. Noncontingent success subjects chose Pandocrin more often than contingent success subjects, but only when their drug choice was public. The basic self-handicapping phenomenon was affirmed, but Kolditz and Arkin suggested that it was motivated by *public* esteem (impression-management) motives rather than by the private esteem motives that had been emphasized by Jones and Berglas (1978; Berglas & Jones, 1978).

By 1982, then, the self-handicapping theory of drug and alcohol use had received important empirical support, albeit with some relatively minor caveats, from three different laboratories. In that same year, however, Snyder and Smith (1982) proposed a major revision and expansion of the self-handicapping concept in an effort to integrate Jones and Berglas's ideas about self-handicapping with Adlerian notions regarding the safeguarding functions of psychological symptoms.

THE CLINICAL–SOCIAL INTERFACE

"UPDATING" THE SELF-HANDICAPPING CONCEPT

C. R. Snyder and Timothy Smith (1982) were the first to highlight the similarities between Adler's ideas about the use of symptoms to safeguard self-esteem and Jones and Berglas's thinking about self-handicapping. Although Jones and Berglas (1978) had acknowledged that sick-role behavior and manifestations of "mental illness" could serve as self-handicaps (see pp. 201–202), they, nonetheless, heavily emphasized tactics that could deflect the search for causal explanations toward external factors (e.g., alcohol or drugs) or, at minimum, toward transient personal variables (e.g., lack of effort or preparation) that preserve the illusion of personal competence and control. Snyder and Smith (1982) sought to revise the self-handicapping construct to explicitly include tactics that place the attributional spotlight on performance impediments residing within the individual (i.e., are *internal*), and which may be fairly stable, but which are relatively less central (less important) to the individual's sense of personal well-being than are the attributes of competence and ability. As defined by Snyder and Smith (1982),

> Self-handicapping may be understood as a process wherein a person, in response to an anticipated loss of self-esteem resulting from the possibility of inadequate performance in a domain where performance clearly implicates ability or competence, adopts characteristics or behaviors that superficially constitute admission of a problem, weakness, or deficit, but assist the individual in (1) controlling attributions (made by oneself or others) concerning performance so as to discount the self-relevant implications of poor performance and augment the self-relevant implications of success, (2) avoiding the threatening evaluative situation entirely, or (3) maintain existing environmental conditions that maximize positive self-relevant feedback and minimize negative self-relevant feedback. (p. 107)

In addition to revising the definition of self-handicapping to emphasize the strategic use of internal factors, Snyder and Smith (1982) proposed two dimensions along which handicaps vary. The first was the handicap's *duration*. Although some handicaps (e.g., "test anxiety") might exist long before the advent of a specific evaluation arena, others (e.g., fatigue) might be more short lived and tailor-made. The second dimension was the extent to which handicaps are "self-evident versus requiring the self-handicapper's avowal" (p. 108). Some handicaps (e.g., acute alcohol intoxication) are so easily observed (self-evident) that the individual needs to make no mention of them. Others (e.g., premenstrual syndrome) are less overtly apparent and need to be explicitly avowed before they can serve to increase attributional ambiguity for external audiences (cf. M. L. Snyder & Wicklund, 1982).

Of the three benefits of self-handicaps described by Snyder and Smith (1982), only the first two are clearly paralleled in the discussions offered by Jones and Berglas (1978; Berglas & Jones, 1978). There is obvious agreement concerning the utility of handicaps for discounting inability attributions for failure and for augmenting ability attributions for success. Also, Snyder and Smith's notion that self-handicaps may serve to avoid threatening evaluations entirely can be viewed as an extreme instance of the use of self-handicaps to thwart *meaningful* evaluations. Their third proposition (i.e., that self-handicaps serve to maintain favorable existing environmental conditions), however, added an entirely new dimension to the self-handicapping concept.

It is clear from their discussion that Snyder and Smith conceived of self-handicapping as going well beyond an evaluatively threatened individual's embracing "any factor reducing personal responsibility for mediocrity and enhancing personal responsibility for success" (Jones & Berglas, 1978, p. 202). Their concept included, for example, strategic symptom presentations that are designed to secure an environment that affords esteem-enhancing opportunities and is benign in the sense that it minimizes challenges to the individual's sense of competence and mastery (cf. Braginsky *et al.*, 1969; Kaplan, 1980). By focusing on the use of self-handicaps to protect self-esteem via the securing of tangible benefits, Snyder and Smith, in this specific regard, relegated the self-protective benefits of self-handicaps to the status of secondary gains.

Smith, Snyder, and Handelsman (1982) reported the first study of their symptom-based model of self-handicapping. The subjects, who were selected to be either high or low test anxious, believed the research was designed to generate updated norms for an intelligence test that would be presented to them in two timed parts and that they would be given feedback about their ability. After working on part 1 of the test (difficult cognitive problems) for 10 minutes, the subjects were (1) told nothing about the effects of anxiety on performance (implicit handicapping condition), (2) told that anxiety had been shown to impair performance (explicit handicapping condition), or (3) told that anxiety had been shown to have no effect on performance (no-handicapping condition). The subjects then completed a retrospective measure of the amount of anxiety they experienced during part 1 of the test before beginning work on part 2.

Based on speculation that high trait levels of test anxiety would be associated with tendencies to use such symptoms as handicaps, Smith *et al.* (1982) predicted that high test-anxious (but not low test-anxious) subjects in the explicit and implicit handicapping conditions would inflate their reports of state anxiety prior to part 2 of the "intelligence test." The results confirmed their expectations for low test-anxious subjects, but only partially supported their predictions concerning high test-anxious subjects. Only those high test-anxious subjects in the implicit handicapping condition reliably increased their pre-part-2 reporting of anxiety (relative to those in the anxiety-has-no-effect condition). The authors concluded that high test-anxious subjects use their symptoms to self-handicap, but speculated that this may be suppressed when the excuse value of doing so is publicly salient. They also suggested that "for such strategies to be effective, they may have to include an element of self-deception . . . so as to prevent full awareness of the purposeful nature of the strategy" (pp. 319–320).

By 1985, Snyder and his colleagues had published three additional studies examining the strategic reporting of psychological or physical symptoms to derail inability attributions. Using procedures nearly identical to those of Smith *et al.* (1982), Smith, Snyder, and Perkins (1983) and Snyder, Smith, Augelli, and Ingram (1985), respectively, found high-hypochondriacal and high-shy subjects (but not subjects low on these dimensions) to strategically increase their symptom reporting. In a somewhat similar vein (no individual differences variables were examined), DeGree and Snyder (1985) found that subjects increased their reporting of traumatic life events when such experiences could plausibly account for poor performances.

When considered along with the findings described by Smith *et al.* (1982), the above studies provided solid backing for the view that people adopt "characteristics or behaviors that superficially constitute admission of a problem, weakness, or deficit" (Snyder & Smith, 1982, p. 107) in order to discount the ability implications of potentially substandard performances. But, did such behavior represent self-handicapping in the sense proposed by Jones and Berglas (1978; Berglas & Jones, 1978)? Berglas (1985, 1988a) weighed in with a dissenting opinion.

BERGLAS'S CRITIQUES

By 1985, Berglas had switched from having a primary professional identification with social psychology to having a primary identification with clinical psychology. Along with this switch came a greater involvement in treating clients and a heightened awareness of the importance of taxonomic clarity in the matters of conceptualizing etiology and planning treatment (Berglas, personal communication, July, 1988). Within this frame of reference, Berglas was concerned that the expanded view of self-handicapping espoused by Snyder and Smith (1982) threatened to limit rather than enhance the heuristic value of the concept. As he stated it,

> When a classification or diagnosis is used to amalgamate rather than differentiate persons or cases, there exists a danger of ignoring significant subtypes or species . . . while attending to the more easily recognized genus. . . In addition, the risk is run that such conceptual merging may invalidate the utility of the self-handicapping concept by exceeding its original "range of convenience"—that portion of the real world wherein a theory provides us with descriptive and predictive power. (Berglas, 1985, p. 238)

Berglas's (1985, 1988a) critiques of Snyder and Smith's (1982) Adlerian reformulation of the self-handicapping concept followed two major lines of reasoning. The first derived from an examination of Adler's writings concerning the motivations underlying the safeguarding function of symptoms and from an examination of the methodology used by Snyder and his colleagues in their "symptom"-reporting studies. The second, related, line of reasoning focused on the counterproductive attributional consequences of warding off dispositional ability attributions by encouraging attributions to other internal characteristics. Both of these arguments merit closer inspection.

The Issue of Motivation

Another Look at Adler. In their introductory discussions of self-handicapping, Jones and Berglas (1978; Berglas & Jones, 1978) emphasized that the strategy served to preserve a generally positive but uncertain sense of self. In response to Snyder and Smith's (1982; Smith *et al.*, 1982) assertion that Adler's view of symptoms as safeguarding devices was compatible with Jones and Berglas's view of self-handicapping, Berglas (1985, 1988a) argued that a careful consideration of the motivations underlying the two concepts reveals them to be quite distinct.

Specifically, Berglas contrasted his view of self-handicapping as being motivated by a desire to *preserve* a positive but shaky self-concept with Adler's view that neurotic safeguarding strategies are designed to *conceal* an underlying feeling of inferiority (e.g., Adler, 1930). According to Berglas (1985), the mechanism underlying Adler's safeguarding use of symptoms is, therefore, "*compensatory* in the sense that it is a cover-up for a deficit, as opposed to self-handicapping strategies . . . which are *defensive* in the sense of preventing the loss of a valued resource" (emphasis added; p. 248).

Although Berglas correctly identified feelings of inferiority as a central dynamic in Adler's psychology, his analysis of the issue fell short of presenting the complexity of Adler's thinking. It is important, for example, to avoid using Adler's term "inferiority" too narrowly. For Adler, feelings of inferiority are a universal human experience: "Thus it becomes clear that to be a human being means to possess a feeling of inferiority which constantly presses towards its own conquest" (in Ansbacher & Ansbacher, 1967, p. 116). As I attempted to show earlier in this chapter (see section entitled "The Clinical Tradition"), Adler came to regard the primary compensation for the individual's inevitable feelings of inferiority as the creation of a fictive life goal—superiority (i.e., self-actualization). Within this system, the individual's fictive goal provides him or her with a basis for self-esteem that exists apart from any current difficulties. So long as the individual can sustain at least the illusion of making progress toward achieving superiority, there is reason to regard safeguarding strategies as, to borrow Berglas's (1985) words, "defensive in the sense of preventing the loss of a valued resource" (p. 248).

The Clash of Research Paradigms. Berglas also used detailed examinations of the research methodology employed by Smith *et al.* (1982) to substantiate his assertion that their symptom-reporting findings implicated a different self-protective process from that involved in his (Berglas & Jones, 1978) and similar (Higgins & Harris, 1988; Kolditz & Arkin, 1982; Tucker *et al.*, 1981) drug–alcohol self-handicapping studies. His analysis focused largely on the contrasting experiences subjects in these studies had prior to their opportunity to self-handicap. As noted earlier, Berglas and Jones (1978) exposed subjects in their self-handicapping groups to a noncontingent success experience (i.e., success feedback following insolvable problems), and then gave them an opportunity to select either a performance-enhancing or a performance-inhibiting drug prior to an anticipated retest on similar materials. Smith *et al.* (1982; see also DeGree & Snyder, 1985; Smith *et al.*, 1983; Snyder *et al.*, 1985), however, merely exposed their subjects to a highly difficult set of cognitive problems prior to giving them an opportunity to self-handicap (symptom report) in anticipation of a second, similar test.

Berglas argued that, in contrast to the subjects in the alcohol–drug self-handicapping studies who had a positive, if illicit, image to protect following noncontingent success, subjects in the Smith *et al.* (1982) study had a very different self-protective motive: "Considering the nature of the Smith *et al.* pretest we must assume that many subjects who reported that they had been anxious . . . were attempting to excuse a failure which they anticipated hearing about following the posttest" (Berglas, 1985, p. 250). In effect, Berglas suggested that the Smith and Snyder subjects were employing a *retrospective* excuse for a past (probable) failure rather than proactively self-handicapping.

Berglas's point here is well taken, but there is a potential danger in assuming that subjects don't have a positive image to protect simply because an experimental protocol doesn't provide one. In their discussions of the conditions that might lead to a pattern of self-handicapping behavior, for example, Jones and Berglas (1978; Berglas & Jones, 1978) emphasize the formative consequences of early child-rearing and socialization experiences. Indeed, in introducing their own self-handicapping studies, Berglas and Jones (1978) explain their interest in giving subjects a noncontingent success pretest experience as follows: "The hope is that this will provide an *analogue* to comparable conditions in the *prior socialization environment* of the alcohol- or drug-prone adult" (p. 406; emphasis added).

Clarifying the Limits of Self-Handicapping. There is yet another observation to make concerning Berglas's (1985) arguments regarding the motivational differences underlying the findings of Smith *et al.* (1982) and those of the drug–alcohol self-handicapping studies. That is that, relative to the original formulation of Jones and Berglas (1978), Berglas (1985) introduced several restrictive clarifications concerning the range of applicability of the self-handicapping concept.

For example, Berglas (1985) took the position that the self-handicapping concept cannot be legitimately applied to cases of people using symptomatic presentations to avoid confirming negative self-images—it applies only to instances of avoiding *disconfirmation* of positive self-images. Although Jones and Berglas (1978) did emphasize that there must be "something in the person's history that has created a fragile and ambiguous, but not a wholly negative, self-concept" (p. 205), they also indicated that the self-handicapper "has an *abnormal* investment in the question of self-worth" (p. 205; emphasis added) and suffers from a "competence complex" (p. 204).

These observations reveal that Jones and Berglas recognized self-handicappers as having deep-seated suspicions that they are, *in fact*, incompetent or seriously flawed. Indeed, in discussing problem drinkers' strategic use of alcohol to avoid meaningful assessments of their ability, Jones and Berglas observed that "the *suspected truth* is too horrible to risk" (p. 203; emphasis added). Later, in discussing the etiology of the competence complex that they believed to underlie self-handicapping, they wrote that "one source . . . may be the *tentative discovery* that he or she is not unconditionally loved. The very unpleasantness of this experimental *outcome* may support the disinclination to conduct similar unconfounded experiments in the future" (p. 204; emphasis added).

The preceding illustrations are offered to make the point that, in the original formulation of self-handicapping theory, Jones and Berglas appeared to imply that self-handicapping may often serve to avoid confirming suspected, *unpleasant* truths as well as to preserve the positive foundations of self-regard. In the interests of maximizing the clarity, distinctiveness, and diagnostic utility of the self-handicapping concept, however, Berglas (1985) subsequently restricted the phenomenon to clear instances of people seeking to preserve esteem gains flowing from (frequently illicit) previous successes.

In the service of the same goals, Berglas also sharpened the boundaries of the self-handicapping concept as it applies to those individuals, the "mentally ill," who have bent under the burdens of an often-difficult and esteem-eroding existence. Jones and Berglas (1978) had acknowledged sick-role behavior to be "a form of self-handicapping where the body is seen as outside the system of personal responsibility" (p. 201), and appeared to embrace the strategic illness presentations of "neurotic" individuals and "mental" patients as exemplars of self-handicapping (see pp. 201–202). Berglas (1985) again, however, clarified a limiting distinction. He regarded such behaviors as self-handicapping only so long as "a self-handicapper is capable of *temporarily* claiming a controllable sick role" (p. 254). Only under such conditions, he wrote, can self-esteem be protected. The logic underlying this qualification is the topic of the following section.

The Issue of Counterproductive Consequences

In introducing this discussion of Berglas's (1985, 1988a) reviews of Snyder and Smith's (1982; Smith *et al.*, 1982) reformulation of the self-handicapping concept, I noted that his critique was based to two general lines of reasoning. The first of these, the matter of underlying motivations, was elaborated above. I take up the second argument next.

Symptoms and Dispositional Attributions. According to Berglas (1985), "should a self-handicapping strategy persist past the point of being *transient* and *controllable*, the strategy or symptom would assume the diagnosticity of a disposition at which point the strategist's competence image is judged anew" (p. 252). The attributional logic of this observation is inescapable (cf. Jones & Davis, 1965; Kelley 1971).

If an individual's mediocre work performance is consistently (across situations and times) preceded by evidence of alcohol intoxication, for example, Kelley's (1967, 1971) analysis of covariance theory of attribution predicts that the individual's performance will come to be attributed to his or her being a problem drinker (a dispositional attribution). Additionally, it is likely that this dispositional attribution would be used to predict subsequent behavior. In effect, the symptom-oriented or persistent single-strategy self-handicapper invites others to define him or her in terms of that strategy and risks experiencing a variety of related negative consequences (e.g., being labeled an "alcoholic," experiencing restricted freedom, having people assume that he or she also has related unsavory characteristics).

On the basis of the attributional consequences of enduring and consistent handicaps, Berglas (1985) argued that, "for a self-handicapping strategy to function effectively as a self-protective maneuver, the agent adopted by the self-handicapper must be like the weather: seen as external to the 'self' and something that will, by definition, be limited in duration" (p. 252). Under these ground rules, using "symptoms" as self-handicaps fails the test. Not only are such symptoms "internal," but they (e.g., shyness, somatic complaints) are also likely to persist over time, leading to supplementary dispositional attributions (e.g., "social phobic," "hypochondriac"). Once the shift to dispositional attributions has occurred, Berglas argued, the self-protective effect of the strategy is degraded from being one of "quit while you're ahead" (self-handicapping) to being one of "cutting one's losses" (p. 254). (See above discussion of the motivational bases for self-handicapping.)

The Problem of Secondary Gains. Berglas (1985, 1988a) was also concerned with another aspect of symptom-based self-protective maneuvers—their frequent association with important secondary gains (e.g., Braginsky *et al.*, 1969; Carson, 1969; Ullmann & Krasner, 1969). As noted above, Snyder and Smith (1982) included strategic efforts to secure and maintain environmental supports in their revision of self-handicapping theory. For Berglas, however, self-handicapping strategies (which are sustained by their ability to relieve evaluative anxiety and to preserve positive self-conceptions) must be clearly differentiated from self-presentations that are designed to secure a status of privilege or other rewards (e.g., relief from responsibility, access to nurturing relationships). The key distinction is that, in contrast to self-handicapping, which "is seen as *preserving* previously accrued psychological gains to an individual's self-esteem," secondary gains provide the individual "with supplements to his self-conception that did not exist prior to the manifestation of his symptoms" (1985, p. 256).

Berglas also argued that, unlike self-handicapping strategies which

serve "to *retain* the privileges associated with prior success," the secondary gains associated with sick roles involve a status shift "downward to
a position of dependence" (1985, p. 256). In effect, then, Berglas asserted
that self-handicapping strategies must be "pure plays." To the extent
that anticipatory self-protective strategies lead to secondary gains, the
motivational focus on the preservation of *prior* esteem gains is lost, and
the unique value of the self-handicapping concept is compromised.

Contrasting Perspectives. From the point of view of Snyder and
Smith's (1982) reformulation of the self-handicapping concept, Berglas's
dual requirements that the self-handicapper must get away scot-free
(i.e., must not invite other dispositional attributions) and must not be
motivated by secondary benefits are unrealistic (Snyder, personal communication, June, 1988). The idea that a self-handicapper should have to
emerge from his or her self-protective ploy without encumbering any
significant costs violates the life principle that there are no "free
lunches."

Snyder and Smith's version of self-handicapping theory is perspectivistic in the sense that the only truly competent judge of a strategy's
effectiveness (i.e., its relative costs and benefits) is the proffering individual. For example, a potential cost that deters one individual may be
quite acceptable for another person as a function of the intensity of his or
her need to avoid a diagnostic evaluation (cf. Smith *et al.*, 1982; Smith *et
al.*, 1983; Snyder *et al.*, 1985). Also, a cost that is excessive in one evaluational arena may be willingly paid in another as a function of the seri-
ousness of the threat it poses (cf. Higgins & Snyder, 1989; McCaghy,
1968).

The crucial theoretical issue for Snyder and Smith is that any personal characteristic that serves as a self-handicap must be *relatively superficial* (as compared to ability or competence) in terms of its importance
for the individual's continuing positive self-regard. Moreover, Snyder
and Smith "anticipated" Berglas's (1985, 1988a) concerns about the adverse attributional consequences of symptom-based handicaps by detailing what they believed to be some of the features that differentiate
"normal" from "pathological" self-handicapping. Implicit in this distinction is the existence of a *continuum of adaptiveness,* with those handicapping efforts occupying positions at the more "pathological" end of the
continuum being characterized by the types of counterproductive consequences (e.g., loss of behavioral freedom, social labeling, etc.) that led
Berglas to reject them as exemplars of handicapping. From this perspective, self-handicapping does not cease being self-handicapping once
these adverse consequences accrue—rather, it becomes a trap.

Concerning Berglas's (1985) assertion that self-protective strategies that result in secondary gains violate the definitional boundaries of self-handicapping, this issue may itself be best regarded as a matter for causal attributional analysis. It is explicitly assumed by theories of causal attribution (e.g., Jones & Davis, 1965; Kelley, 1967), for example, that individual acts often have more than one consequence or outcome. In such instances, the inferential task is to discern the actor's *intended* outcomes. Having said this, however, it must be acknowledged that Snyder and Smith's (1982) revision of the self-handicapping concept to include maintaining environmental supports as a handicapping goal involved a sweeping expansion of the concept beyond its original limits. Moreover, it is not clear that this expansion is grounded even in Adlerian theory. It is an innovation in need of theoretical clarification.

RECENT DEVELOPMENTS IN SELF-HANDICAPPING RESEARCH AND THEORY

Given that self-handicapping has been a topic of active empirical and theoretical inquiry for only a decade, a review of "recent" developments encompasses a period of time that just narrowly exceeds some publication lags. Realizing this only serves to make the fact that there is a substantial and diverse literature on the subject all the more remarkable. Without question, Jones and Berglas (re)discovered a phenomenon that captured the imaginations of many and that added impetus to the developing "interface" between clinical and social psychology as few other topics have.

In the pages that follow, I will briefly delineate the more noteworthy aspects of this rapidly evolving field. In so doing, however, I will not attempt to be exhaustively comprehensive in my review. Rather, the following sections will serve to orient the reader to more comprehensive discussions in subsequent chapters. Although I have attempted to survey the major stages in the development of the self-handicapping concept in the previous sections of this chapter, I have omitted discussing the research aimed at exploring some of the more specific theoretical issues. It is to this task that I now turn.

SELF-HANDICAPPING FOR SELF-ESTEEM OR SOCIAL ESTEEM?

Both the Jones and Berglas (1978) and Snyder and Smith (1982) formulations of self-handicapping proposed that self-handicapping behaviors are primarily motivated by private- rather than public-esteem concerns. As Jones and Berglas put it, self-handicapping "is probably augmented by the presence of an audience, but we emphasize that the public value of the strategy is not its original impetus" (p. 202). Berglas and Jones (1978, experiment 1) reported that they had empirically supported the hypothesized primacy of self-esteem motives by showing that self-handicapping drug selection occurred under conditions of total privacy and was not augmented by public performance conditions. Kolditz and Arkin (1982), however, soon argued that Berglas and Jones had failed to convincingly isolate public- from private-esteem motives. Kolditz and Arkin then proceeded to present the most thoroughgoing effort to date to differentiate them. Their results indicated that public-esteem (impression-management) motives were more potent motivators of self-handicapping than private-esteem motives.

Although there have been other isolated attempts to manipulate the privacy of self-handicapping behaviors (e.g., Slaughter, Shaver, & Arkin, 1988; Tice & Baumeister, 1984), most investigators have studied self-handicapping within conditions that are best regarded as "public." Accordingly, the relative importance of public- and private-esteem concerns in motivating self-handicapping remains obscure, although the available evidence suggests that handicapping tendencies are stronger under public than under private conditions (Arkin & Baumgardner, 1985; Shepperd & Arkin, 1987; Slaughter et al., 1988; see Chapter 2, this volume, for related discussion).

Does Self-Handicapping "Work?"

Theoretically, self-handicapping is designed to capitalize on Kelley's (1971) augmenting and discounting principles. In other words, handicaps should result in the discounting of ability attributions following performance failures, but should result in the augmentation of ability attributions following performance successes (Jones & Berglas, 1978; Snyder & Smith, 1982). In their review of the self-handicapping literature, however, Arkin and Baumgardner (1985) observed that there were *no* published studies examining the effects of self-handicaps. Despite the theoretical and pragmatic importance of the effectiveness issue, all of the available studies focused exclusively on how and under what conditions people engage in handicapping. More recent reviews of the effects of attributional excuse strategies (Chapter 4 in this volume; Snyder & Higgins, 1988), however, have identified a variety of *discounting*-related self-handicapping benefits in such diverse areas as affect/self-esteem, performance, and health. Even so, it may still be said that there is no direct research support for esteem-*augmenting* benefits flowing from handicapped performances that eventuate in success. (See Chapter 4 for extended treatment of the effectiveness issue.)

The Characteristics of Self-Handicappers

Despite the differences in their definitions of and methodological approaches to self-handicapping, Jones and Berglas (1978; Berglas, 1985, 1988a; Berglas & Jones, 1978) and Snyder and Smith (1982; Smith et al., 1982) are in basic agreement that those individuals who are most likely to self-handicap are characterized by uncertainty concerning their abilities and competence. Both groups of authors, for example, proposed that individuals who are confident either of their ability or of their lack of ability are unlikely to be routine self-handicappers. These speculations point to the probable existence of important individual differences in self-handicapping tendencies. Also, as I noted earlier in this chapter, Jones and Berglas implicated chaotic reinforcement histories and failures to develop feelings of being unconditionally loved and valued as probable developmental factors underlying self-handicappers' competency complexes. This suggests that self-handicapping may be associated with underlying character traits.

Individual Differences Research

The theoretical emphasis placed on individual differences in self-handicapping tendencies has spawned a body of literature aimed at more carefully delineating the critical person factors. At least two basic approaches to this issue can be identified. First, much of the work of Snyder and his colleagues (e.g., DeGree & Snyder, 1985; Smith et al., 1982; Smith et al., 1983; Snyder et al., 1985) has focused on the differential tendencies of individuals who are high and low on measures of particular types of "symptoms" (e.g., shyness, hypochondriasis, test anxiety) to use strategic reporting of those symptoms to self-handicap. These studies have uniformly indicated that individuals high on the symptom dimensions are more likely to use the symptoms as self-handicaps than are individuals low on the symptom dimensions. Also, in a closely related study, Higgins and Harris (1989) found that individuals who reported high frequencies of engaging in the particular *behavior* of alcohol consumption were more likely to use that behavior to self-handicap than were infrequent drinkers.

A second general line of research has examined the role of individual differences on such measures as self-esteem (e.g., Harris, Snyder, Higgins, & Schrag, 1986; Tice & Baumeister, 1984), self-esteem certainty

(Harris & Snyder, 1986), and Type A/B coronary-prone behavior pattern (Harris *et al.*, 1986; Weidner, 1980) on such handicapping behaviors as effort withdrawal and drug selection. Similarly, following the development of the Self-Handicapping Scale (Jones & Rhodewalt, 1982), scores on this scale have been examined as predictors of self-handicapping behavior (e.g., Baumeister & Kahn, 1982; Rhodewalt & Davison, 1986; Rhodewalt, Saltzman, & Wittmer, 1984; Strube, 1986; Strube & Roemmele, 1985). Although there have been some inconsistencies in the findings emerging from this body of research, especially with regard to the involvement of high versus low self-esteem (cf. Harris & Snyder, 1986), the findings clearly support the notion that there are important individual differences associated with self-handicapping behavior. (See Chapter 3, this volume, for a more detailed discussion of this issue.)

Self-Handicapping and Personality Disorder

Recently, Berglas (1985, 1988a, 1988b) has pursued the goal of conceptualizing self-handicapping as a type of self-protective behavior that is exhibited by individuals with the characteristics of personality disorders as defined in the Diagnostic and Statistical Manual of the American Psychiatric Association (DSM). In his original effort along these lines, Berglas (1985) pursued his interest in clearly delineating the boundaries of the self-handicapping concept (see above discussion) by developing specific criteria for identifying individuals with a "self-handicapping disorder" (p. 262). By 1986, Berglas (see Berglas, 1988a) had moved further toward conceptualizing self-handicapping behavior as a manifestation of underlying character structure, and likened self-handicappers to individuals who exhibited narcissistic personality disorder (American Psychiatric Association, 1980). Most recently, Berglas (1988b) has suggested that the self-protective aspects of the newly proposed self-defeating personality disorder (American Psychiatric Association, 1978) bear a striking resemblance to self-handicapping behaviors. (See Chapters 5 and 6, this volume, for further discussions of this issue.)

THE CHARACTERISTICS OF SELF-HANDICAPPING SITUATIONS

According to both the Jones and Berglas (1978) and Snyder and Smith (1982) formulations of self-handicapping, such behavior is stimulated by evaluative situations within which the individual experiences uncertainty regarding his or her likelihood of success and within which failure would represent a threat to self-esteem. In the years following the introduction of the self-handicapping concept, considerable attention has been given to further delineating those aspects of *evaluative contexts* (as opposed to person variables—see above) that either increase or decrease the probability of handicapping behavior.

Contextual factors that have been shown to *increase* the likelihood of self-handicapping include high importance of the evaluative task (Rhodewalt *et al.*, 1984; Shepperd & Arkin, 1989), noncontingent as opposed to contingent success experiences on previous exposures to the evaluative task (Berglas & Jones, 1978; Kolditz & Arkin, 1982; Slaughter *et al.*, 1988; Tucker *et al.*, 1981; Higgins & Harris, 1988), public as opposed to private performance situations (Kolditz & Arkin, 1982; Shepperd, Miller, & Arkin, 1986), and high attribute ambiguity concerning the motive underlying the self-handicapping behavior (Handelsman, Kraiger, & King, 1985).

On the other hand, contextual factors that have been related to a *decreased* likelihood of self-handicapping have included positive extrinsic incentives for good performance (Greenberg, Pyszczynski, & Paisley, 1985), the availability of familiar performance-enhancing options (Tucker *et al.*, 1981), the presence of preexisting environmental handicaps (Shepperd & Arkin, 1989), and high public salience of the excuse value of the handicapping behavior (Smith *et al.*, 1982). With regard to the inhibiting influence of high public salience of the excuse value of handicaps, it should be noted that this has been observed in only one symptom-reporting study, and relevant studies involving placebo alcohol consumption (i.e., Higgins & Harris, 1989) or drug selection (i.e., Berglas & Jones, 1978; Kolditz & Arkin, 1982) as handicaps have observed no such inhibiting effects. Higgins and Harris (1989) suggested that this difference between symptom-reporting and drug–alcohol handicapping studies may derive from there being less social stigma associated with ingesting a performance-inhibiting substance than with highlighting personal weaknesses when attention is focused on them. (See Chapter 2, this volume, for more extensive discussion of these issues.)

SUMMARY AND CONCLUSIONS

In the preceding pages, I have traced the early evolution of thinking about a peculiar and seemingly paradoxical approach to life's vicissitudes, and have sampled most of the major areas of subsequent empirical investigation. Despite the superficial absurdity of the notion that people sustain their competence images by flirting with defeat and gain control over their lives by being willing "victims" of circumstances, the evidence is mounting that self-handicapping is a rational, exceedingly common, and perhaps uniquely effective means of accomplishing those very goals.

Although the remainder of this book is devoted to telling the tale of self-handicapping in greater detail, the general outlines of the story line already may be discerned. It is a story of an idea born in heresy during the waking moments of dynamic psychology, rejected and long over-shadowed by an orthodoxy now in decline, and, finally, independently rediscovered and given new theoretical garb by the contemporary heirs of a legacy that can be traced back to Alfred Adler.

The story of self-handicapping is also one of conflict and schism. As we have seen, Adler's articulation of a theory that was rich in its appre-ciation for the subjective, self-creating powers of a forward-looking psyche led to his acrimonious split with Freud and the disciples of Freud's deterministic, backward-looking archaeology of the mind. Al-though the aforementioned current "debate" over the legitimate param-eters of the self-handicapping concept does not involve fundamental philosophical differences concerning "human nature," it does appear to involve strongly contrasting perspectives that are, in effect, conservative (Berglas, 1985, 1988a) and liberal (Smith *et al.*, 1982; Snyder & Smith, 1982) interpretations of the self-handicapping phenomenon. Happily, the discerning reader will detect the seeds of a reconciliation of these perspectives in the pages that follow. In the end, it seems likely that pragmatic efforts to provide encompassing frameworks that nonetheless maintain fundamental conceptual distinctions (e.g., Arkin & Baum-gardner, 1985; Chapter 7, this volume) will prevail.

Regardless of the ultimate outcome of the contemporary paradigm "clash," inquiry into the subject of self-handicapping promises to enrich our appreciation for the tenacious adaptability of the human animal as well as our knowledge of the coping processes that underlie our psycho-logical resilience. Like the hypnotherapist who encourages resistance in order to transform it into cooperation, or the judo artist who capitalizes on her opponent's aggression, the self-handicapper is emerging as a "naive" expert on the use of attributional principles to transform poten-tial defeat into an ally. Therein lies the solution to the paradox that isn't.

ACKNOWLEDGMENTS

I would like to express my gratitude to C. R. Snyder, Edward E. Jones, and Steven Berglas for their helpful comments on this chapter.

REFERENCES

Adler, A. (1926). *The neurotic constitution.* New York: Dodd, Mead.

Adler, A. (1929). *Problems of neurosis: A book of case histories.* London: Kegan, Paul, Trench, Truebner.

Adler, A. (1930). *Problems of neurosis.* New York: Cosmopolitan Book Corporation.

Allport, G. W. (1937). *Personality: A psychological interpretation.* New York: Holt.

American Psychiatric Association. (1980). *DSM-III: Diagnostic and statistical manual of mental disorders* (3rd ed.). Washington, DC: Author.

American Psychiatric Association. (1987). *DSM-III-R: Diagnostic and statistical manual of mental disorders* (3rd ed. revised). Washington, DC: Author.

Ansbacher, H. L., & Ansbacher, R. R. (1967). *The individual psychology of Alfred Adler.* New York: Harper & Row.

Arkin, R. M., & Baumgardner, A. H. (1985). Self-handicapping. In J. H. Harvey & G. W. Weary (Eds.), *Attribution: Basic issues and applications* (pp. 169–202). New York: Academic Press.

Artiss, K. (1959). *The symptom as communication in schizophrenia.* New York: Grune and Stratton.

Baumeister, R. F., & Kahn, J. (1982). *Obesity as a self-handicapping strategy: Don't blame me, blame my fat.* Unpublished manuscript, Case Western Reserve University, Cleveland.

Belknap, I. (1956). *Human problems of a state mental hospital.* New York: McGraw-Hill.

Berglas, S. (1976). *"I have some good news and some bad news: You're the 'greatest'."* Unpublished manuscript, Department of Psychology, Duke University.

Berglas, S. (1985). Self-handicapping and self-handicappers: A cognitive/attributional model of interpersonal self-protective behavior. In R. Hogan (Ed.), *Perspectives in personality* (Vol 1, pp. 235–270). Greenwich, CT: JAI Press.

Berglas, S. (1988a). The three faces of self-handicapping: Protective self-presentation, a strategy for self-esteem enhancement, and a character disorder. In S. L. Zelen (Ed.), *Self-representation: The second attribution-personality theory conference, CSPP-LA, 1986* (pp. 133–169). New York: Springer-Verlag.

Berglas, S. (1988b, March). The "self-protective" subtype of the self-defeating personality disorder. *The Psychiatric Times* (Vol V, No. 3).

Berglas, S., & Jones, E. E. (1978). Drug choice as a self-handicapping strategy in response to noncontingent success. *Journal of Personality and Social Psychology, 36,* 405–417.

Berne, E. (1964). *Games people play: The psychology of human relationships.* New York: Grove Press.

Bradley, G. W. (1978). Self-serving biases in the attribution process: A reexamination of the fact or fiction question. *Journal of Personality and Social Psychology, 36,* 56–71.

Braginsky, B. M., & Braginsky, D. D. (1967). Schizophrenic patients in the psychiatric interview: An experimental study of their effectiveness at manipulation. *Journal of Consulting Psychology, 31,* 546–551.

Braginsky, B. M. Braginsky, D. D., & Ring, K. (1969). *Methods of madness: The mental hospital as a last resort.* New York: Holt, Rinehart & Winston.

Braginsky, B. M., Grosse, M., & Ring, K. (1966). Controlling outcomes through impression-management: An experimental study of the manipulative tactics of mental patients. *Journal of Consulting Psychology, 30,* 295–300.

Braginsky, B. M., Holzberg, J., Ridley, D., & Braginsky, D. D. (1968). Patient styles of adaptation to a mental hospital. *Journal of Personality, 36,* 283–298.

Carson, R. C. (1969). *Interaction concepts of personality.* Chicago: Aldine.

Coyne, J. C. (1976). Toward an interactional description of depression. *Psychiatry, 39,* 28–40.

DeGree, C. E., & Snyder, C. R. (1985). Adler's psychology (of use) today: Personal history of traumatic life events as a self-handicapping strategy. *Journal of Personality and Social Psychology, 48,* 1512–1519.

Dunham, H. W., & Weinberg, S. K. (1960). *The culture of the state mental hospital.* Detroit: Wayne State University Press.

Fontana, A. F., & Gessner, T. (1969). Patient's goals and the manifestation of psychopathology. *Journal of Consulting and Clinical Psychology, 33,* 247–253.

Fontana, A. F., & Klein, E. B. (1968). Self-presentation and the schizophrenic "deficit." *Journal of Consulting and Clinical Psychology, 32,* 250–256.

Fontana, A. F., Klein, E. B., Lewis, E., & Levine, L. (1968). Presentation of self in mental illness. *Journal of Consulting and Clinical Psychology, 32,* 110–119.

Freud, A. (1948). *The ego and the mechanisms of defence.* London: Hogarth Press.

Freud, S. (1936). *Inhibitions, symptoms and anxiety* London: Hogarth Press.

Freud, S. (1943). *A general introduction to psychoanalysis.* New York: Garden City Publishing Company.

Freud, S. (1953). *Sigmund Freud: Collected Papers* (Vol. 1). London: Hogarth Press.

Goffman, E. (1959). *The presentation of self in everyday life.* New York: Doubleday.

Goffman, E. (1961). *Asylums.* Garden City, NY: Anchor Books.

Goldstein, K. (1939). *The organism; A holistic approach to biology derived from pathological data in man.* New York: American Book Company.

Greenberg, J., Pyszczynski, T., & Paisley, C. (1985). Effect of extrinsic incentives on the use of test anxiety as an anticipatory attributional defense: Playing it cool when the stakes are high. *Journal of Personality and Social Psychology, 47,* 1136–1145.

Haley, J. (1963). *Strategies of psychotherapy.* New York: Grune and Stratton.

Handelsman, M. M., Kraiger, K., & King, C. S. (1985, April). *Self-handicapping by task choice: An attribute ambiguity analysis.* Paper presented at the meeting of the Rocky Mountain Psychological Association, Tucson, AZ.

Harris, R. N., & Snyder, C. R. (1986). The role of uncertain self-esteem in self-handicapping. *Journal of Personality and Social Psychology, 51,* 451–458.

Harris, R. N., Snyder, C. R., Higgins, R. L., & Schrag, J. L. (1986). Enhancing the prediction of self-handicapping. *Journal of Personality and Social Psychology, 51,* 1191–1199.

Hastorf, A., Schneider, D., & Polefka, J. (1970). *Person perception.* Reading, MA: Addison-Wesley.

Heider, F. (1944). Social perception and phenomenal causality. *Psychological Review, 51,* 358–374.

Heider, F. (1958). *The psychology of interpersonal relations.* New York: Wiley.

Higgins, R. L., & Harris, R. N. (1988). Strategic "alcohol" use: Drinking to self-handicap. *Journal of Social and Clinical Psychology, 6,* 191–202.

Higgins, R. L., & Harris, R. N. (1989, April 14). *Self-handicapping social performance through "alcohol" use: The interaction of drinker history and expectancy.* Paper presented at the meeting of the Southwestern Psychological Association, Houston, TX.

Higgins, R. L., & Snyder, C. R. (1989). Excuses gone awry: An analysis of self-defeating excuses. In R. C. Curtis (Ed.), *Self-defeating behaviors: Experimental research, clinical impressions, and practical implications* (pp. 99–130). New York: Plenum.

Horney, K. (1950). *Neurosis and human growth.* New York: Norton.

James, W. (1890). *The principles of psychology* (Vols. 1 & 2). New York: Holt.

Jones, E. (1955). *The life and work of Sigmund Freud, Vol, 2.* New York: Basic Books.

Jones, E. E. (1964). *Ingratiation: A social-psychological analysis*. New York: Appleton-Century-Crofts.

Jones, E. E., & Berglas, S. (1975, April). *Strategies of externalization and the appeal of alcohol and drugs*. Paper presented at the UCLA Conference on the Social Psychology of Drug and Alcohol Abuse, Los Angeles.

Jones, E. E., & Berglas, S. (1978). Control of attributions about the self through self-handicapping strategies: The appeal of alcohol and the role of underachievement. *Personality and Social Psychology Bulletin, 4*, 200–206.

Jones, E. E., & Davis, K. E. (1965). From acts to dispositions: The attribution process in person perception. In L. Berkowitz (Ed.), *Advances in experimental social psychology*, (Vol. 2, pp. 219–266). New York: Academic Press.

Jones, E. E., & Rhodewalt, F. (1982). *Self-Handicapping Scale*. (Available from the authors at the Department of Psychology, Princeton University or the Department of Psychology, University of Utah.)

Jones, E. E., & Wortman, C. B. (1973). *Ingratiation: An attributional approach*. Morristown, NJ: General Learning Press.

Jones, S. C. (1973) Self- and interpersonal evaluations: Esteem theories versus consistency theories. *Psychological Bulletin, 79*, 185–199.

Kaplan, H. B. (1980). *Deviant behavior in defense of self*. New York: Academic Press.

Kelley, H. H. (1967). Attribution theory in social psychology. In D. Levine (Ed.), *Nebraska symposium on motivation, 1967* (pp. 192–238). Lincoln: University of Nebraska Press.

Kelley, H. H. (1971). *Attribution in social interaction*. New York: General Learning Press.

Kolditz, T. A., & Arkin, R. M. (1982). An impression management interpretation of the self-handicapping strategy. *Journal of Personality and Social Psychology, 43*, 492–502.

Ludwig, A. M., & Farrelly, F. (1966). The code of chronicity. *Archives of General Psychiatry, 15*, 562–568.

Ludwig, A. M., & Farrelly, F. (1967). The weapons of insanity. *American Journal of Psychotherapy, 21*, 737–749.

MacAndrew, E., & Edgerton, R. B. (1969). *Drunken comportment*. Chicago: Aldine.

Maslow, A. H. (1954). *Motivation and personality*. New York: Harper & Row.

McCaghy, C. H. (1968). Drinking and deviance disavowal: The case of child molesters. *Social Problems, 16*, 43–49.

Miller, D. T., & Ross, M. (1975). Self-serving bias in the attribution of causality: Fact or fiction? *Psychological Bulletin, 82*, 213–225.

Miller, D. T., Norman, S. A., & Wright, E. (1978). Distortion in person perception as a consequence of the need for effective control. *Journal of Personality and Social Psychology, 36*, 598–607.

Mozdzierz, G., Macchitelli, F., & Lisiecki, J. (1976). The paradox in psychotherapy: An Adlerian perspective. *Journal of Individual Psychology, 32*, 169–184.

Munroe, R. L. (1955). *Schools of psychoanalytic thought*. New York: Dryden Press.

Nunberg, H., & Federn, E. (1974). *Minutes of the Vienna Psychoanalytic Society, Vol III: 1910–1911* (Translated by M. Nunberg). New York: International Universities Press.

Peter, L. J., & Hull, R. (1969). *The Peter principle*. New York: Bantam Books.

Rhodewalt, F., & Davison, J. (1986). Self-handicapping and subsequent performance: Role of outcome valence and attributional ambiguity. *Basic and Applied Social Psychology, 7*, 307–323.

Rhodewalt, F., Saltzman, A. T., & Wittmer, J. (1984). Self-handicapping among competitive athletes: The role of practice in self-esteem protection. *Basic and Applied Social Psychology, 5*, 197–210.

Rogers, C. R. (1965). *Client-centered therapy.* Boston: Houghton Mifflin. (Originally published by the Riverside Press, Cambridge, MA, 1951.)

Sandler, J., & Freud, A. (1985). *The analysis of defense: The ego and the mechanisms of defense revisited.* New York: International Universities Press.

Sarbin, T. R., & Mancuso, J. C. (1980). *Schizophrenia: Medical diagnosis or moral verdict?* New York: Pergamon Press.

Scheff, T. J. (1971). *Being mentally ill: A sociological theory.* Chicago: Aldine.

Schlenker, B. R. (1980). *Impression management: The self-concept, social identity, and interpersonal relations.* Monterey, CA: Brooks/Cole.

Shaw, B. (1982). Stress and depression: A cognitive perspective. In R. W. J. Neufeld (Ed.), *Psychological stress and psychopathology* (pp. 125–146). New York: McGraw-Hill.

Shepperd, J. A., & Arkin, R. M. (1989). Determinants of self-handicapping: Task importance and the effects of pre-existing handicaps on self-generated handicaps. *Personality and Social Psychology Bulletin, 15,* 101–112.

Shepperd, J. A., Miller, P. J., & Arkin, R. M. (1986, May). *Self-handicapping and self-consciousness.* Paper presented at the meeting of the Midwestern Psychological Association, Chicago.

Slaughter, J. G., Shaver, K. G., & Arkin, R. M. (1988, May). *Self-assessment and self-protection: The roles of uncertainty and response context.* Paper presented at the meeting of the Midwestern Psychological Association, Chicago.

Smith, T. W., Snyder, C. R., & Handelsman, M. M. (1982). On the self-serving function of an academic wooden leg: Test anxiety as a self-handicapping strategy. *Journal of Personality and Social Psychology, 42,* 314–321.

Smith, T. W., Snyder, C. R., & Perkins, S. C. (1983). The self-serving function of hypochondriacal complaints: Physical symptoms as self-handicapping strategies. *Journal of Personality and Social Psychology, 44,* 787–797.

Snyder, C. R., & Higgins, R. L. (1988). Excuses: Their effective role in the negotiation of reality. *Psychological Bulletin, 104* (1), 23–35.

Snyder, C. R., & Smith, T. W. (1982). Symptoms as self-handicapping strategies: The virtues of old wine in a new bottle. In G. Weary & H. L. Mirels (Eds.), *Integrations of clinical and social psychology* (pp. 104–127). New York: Oxford University Press.

Snyder, C. R., Higgins, R. L., & Stucky, R. J. (1983). *Excuses: Masquerades in search of grace.* New York: Wiley Interscience.

Snyder, C. R., Smith, T. W., Augelli, R. W., & Ingram, R. E. (1983). On the self-serving function of social anxiety: Shyness as a self-handicapping strategy. *Journal of Personality and Social Psychology, 48,* 970–980.

Snyder, M. L., & Wicklund, R. A. (1981). Attribute ambiguity. In J. A. Harvey, W. J. Ickes, & R. F. Kidd (Eds.), *New directions in attribution research* (Vol. 3, pp. 197–221). Hillsdale, NJ: Erlbaum.

Steffenhagen, R. A. (1974). Drug abuse and related phenomena: An Adlerian approach. *Journal of Individual Psychology, 30,* 238–250.

Stepansky, P. E. (1983). *In Freud's shadow: Adler in context.* Hillsdale, NJ: The Analytic Press. Distributed by Erlbaum.

Strube, M. J. (1986). An analysis of the Self-Handicapping Scale. *Basic and Applied Social Psychology, 13,* 211–224.

Strube, M. J., & Roemmele, L. A. (1985). Self-enhancement, self-assessment, and self-evaluative task choice. *Journal of Personality and Social Psychology, 49,* 981–993.

Sullivan, H. S. (1953). *The interpersonal theory of psychiatry.* New York: Norton.

Szasz, T. (1961). *The myth of mental illness.* New York: Paul B. Hoeber.

Tice, D. M., & Baumeister, R. F. (1984, May). *Self-handicapping, self-esteem and self-presenta-*

tion. Paper presented at the meeting of the Midwestern Psychological Association, Chicago.

Tucker, J. A., Vuchinich, R. E., & Sobell, M. B. (1981). Alcohol consumption as a self-handicapping strategy. *Journal of Abnormal Psychology, 90*, 220–230.

Ullmann, L. F., & Krasner, L. (1969). *A psychological approach to abnormal behavior*. Englewood Cliffs, NJ: Prentice-Hall.

Vaihinger, H. (1925). *The philosophy of "as if"; A system of the theoretical, practical and religious fictions of mankind*. New York: Harcourt, Brace.

Weeks, G. R., & L'Abate, L. (1982). *Paradoxical psychotherapy: Theory, and practice with individuals, couples, and families*. New York: Brunner/Mazel.

Weidner, G. (1980). Self-handicapping following learned helplessness treatment and the Type A coronary-prone behavior pattern. *Journal of Psychosomatic Research, 24*, 319–325.

Weinstein, E. (1968). The development of interpersonal competence. In D. Goslin (Ed.), *Handbook of socialization theory and research* (pp. 753–775). Chicago: Rand McNally.

Wortman, C. B. (1976). Causal attributions and personal control. In J. H. Harvey, W. J. Ickes, & R. F. Kidd (Eds.), *New directions in attribution research* (Vol. 1, pp. 23–52). Hillsdale, NJ: Erlbaum.

Zimbardo, P. G., & Radl, S. (1981). *The shy child*. New York: McGraw-Hill.

Zuckerman, M. (1979). Attribution of success and failure revisited, or: The motivational bias is alive and well in attribution theory. *Journal of Personality, 47*, 245–287.

CHAPTER 2

SITUATIONAL INFLUENCES ON SELF-HANDICAPPING

ELIZABETH A. SELF

> *The notion of self-protecting strategies implies, after all, that the strategist has something to protect. There has to have been some experience of success, something in the person's history that has created a fragile and ambiguous, but not wholly negative, self-concept . . .*
> *(Jones & Berglas, 1978, p. 205)*

INTRODUCTION

Recently I went bowling for the first time in 10 years. There was a reason for my long absence from the alleys. The last time I had spent an evening trying to roll the ball toward the pins, it had perversely clung to the gutters, resulting in an abysmal score that amused by companions. Not finding this especially enjoyable, I abandoned bowling and spent the next decade developing other aspects of myself. On this particular evening, however, a new set of friends persuaded me to join them, and I found myself once again facing the long, polished wood alley surrounded by the sinister gutters and ending in the distant, glimmering pins. "Oh well," I thought. "What difference does it make? I have nothing to lose." And I dropped the ball as close to the center of the alley as I could, hoping it would at least roll for a while before coming to a stop. To

ELIZABETH A. SELF • Department of Psychology, University of Kansas, Lawrence, Kansas 66045.

my surprise it reached the end of the alley and knocked down several pins, delighting both me and my friends.

I cannot say that I was transformed that night into a three-digit scorer, but I did roll a strike or two, each time without doing more than shrugging my shoulders, aiming at the center of the floor, and dropping the ball. I came away thinking that bowling was rather fun, and that I might try it again in a few years. I ended the evening as I began it; bowling was irrelevant to my self-concept.

This example is intended to illustrate the fact that even when there is reason to believe that one will probably perform poorly, self-handicapping will not invariably occur. Since the initial theoretical formulation of self-handicapping (Jones & Berglas, 1978), researchers have clarified several situational factors that influence whether or not this strategy will be employed. Some factors appear to elicit self-handicapping, while others seem to inhibit it. The following chapter will report these situational influences and explore their implications for further refinement of the self-handicapping construct.

FACTORS THAT ELICIT SELF-HANDICAPPING

In accordance with the theoretical model of self-handicapping, empirical research has found that this strategy is only used when an important self-concept is going to be tested. Furthermore, there must be some uncertainty about the ability in question; noncontingent success and other methods have been used to create this uncertainty and increase the likelihood of self-handicapping.

In addition, self-handicapping needs to be viewed in its social context. It appears that the expected attributions of others are of major concern to the individual who self-handicaps. When others will be evaluating an individual's performance, when the evaluation standards depend on the performance of another, or when they are quite high, self-handicapping has been shown to increase.

Research documenting the situational factors that increase self-handicapping will be described in the following section, beginning with the creation of an important self-concept.

THE IMPORTANCE OF THE SELF-CONCEPT

Although several descriptions of self-handicapping (Berglas, 1989; Snyder, Chapter 4, this volume; Snyder & Smith, 1982) have been offered since that of Jones and Berglas (1978) quoted above, all explain self-handicapping as an attempt to protect the self-concept. Theoretically, before self-handicapping can occur, there must be a self-concept to protect, as Jones and Berglas (1978) pointed out.

In the first empirical demonstration of self-handicapping, Berglas and Jones (1978) gave male and female college students success feedback after they had worked on either solvable or unsolvable problems. Noncontingent success subjects were expected to be more likely to choose a performance-inhibiting drug before a second test of the same ability. This choice would preserve their image of competence by obscuring the diagnosticity of the second test.

This prediction was fulfilled in two experiments, but the results were significant only for male subjects: instead of self-handicapping, females in both experiments attributed their success to luck more often than did males. Berglas and Jones concluded that the females may have had "less reason to protect a success readily acknowledged to be based on luck" (p. 416). For females, then, it may have been that the noncontingent success manipulation did not create the intended competence image. That some individuals may be successful at a task without developing a self-concept including that task has been demonstrated in work by Cross and Markus (1989).

Not only must there be a self-concept to protect, but once created, this self-concept must be important (Snyder & Smith, 1982). In Chapter 4 of this volume, for example, Snyder specifies that handicapping occurs when there is uncertainty about success in an "important performance arena." Some arenas may be more important than others. Thus, self-handicapping does not occur whenever failure is a possibility; most people do not have an immoderate need to be competent regardless of what ability is being tested. Although one might regard the self-concept as an undifferentiated structure that is vulnerable to threats of any kind, it may be more productive to view the self-concept as "an amalgamation of images that one holds about oneself across a variety of situations" (Snyder, 1989, p. 133).

Some elements of these images may recur in several situations. Due to their frequency of activation, these elements might be viewed as more "central" to the self-concept, and more likely to be accessed when one is thinking about the self (cf. Gergen, 1968). Other images may occur only rarely and only in particular situations. This view of the self-concept as consisting of a pool of selves rather than a monolithic structure (Cantor, Markus, Niedenthal, & Nurius, 1986) calls for examination of self-handicapping in more specific ability arenas. Thus we need to distinguish tasks that reflect important, central components of the self-concept from tasks that do not.

It was argued above that females in the Berglas and Jones (1978) study may have failed to self-handicap because their success did not create success images that were central to their self-concepts. Pyszczynski and Greenberg (1983), however, did find self-handicapping among females. Subjects in their "high ego-relevance" condition were told that the test was "highly respected and a good predictor of academic and career success" (p. 415), and that their instructor was interested in their scores. In contrast, "low ego-relevance" subjects were told that the test problems were not standardized, their scores would not be meaningful, and that they should "have fun with the problems" (p. 415). Subjects were also given practice problems that were either easy or difficult as a crosscutting manipulation of their expected probability of success on the upcoming test.

In the high ego-relevance condition, subjects with a low probability of success reported intending to exert less effort than subjects with a high probability of success. This reduction in intended effort was interpreted by Pyszczynski and Greenberg as a strategy for protecting subjects' self-esteem. If they did not try to solve the difficult problems, their anticipated failure would not be due to their lack of ability, but to their lack of effort. As expected, probability of success did not affect level of anticipated effort in the low ego-relevance condition. Pyszczynski and Greenberg argued that when the task was not important, effort should be low in any case.

Further work varying task importance was reported by Shepperd and Arkin (1989a, 1989b). In their first study (1989a), subjects were told either that they would be taking a test that was "a reliable and valid predictor of college and career success," or that the test "had yet to be validated or shown useful for any predictive purposes" (p. 104). This manipulation is quite similar to that used by Pyszczynski and Greenberg (1983), reported above. However, the dependent measure in this case was choice of performance-enhancing or performance-inhibiting music. (Shepperd and Arkin also studied the effect of having a preexisting handicap available to explain potentially poor performance; this effect will be described later in this chapter.) Handicapping was found in the important but not in the unimportant test conditions. A second study (Shepperd & Arkin, 1989b) examined individual differences in public self-consciousness and also varied test importance using the same method. Again handicapping was found only among subjects expecting to take the important test.

Turning to a different performance arena, Rhodewalt, Saltzman, and Wittmer (1984) examined self-handicapping among competitive swimmers and golfers before important and less important athletic

events. In study 1, swimmers rated each upcoming meet for its importance to the team's seasonal standing; the consensus of ratings determined the importance of the meet. Before important meets, which could
be assumed to provide more competition and more challenge to perceived ability, those who had been defined as low self-handicappers
increased their level of practice, according to reports from their coach
(see Rhodewalt, Chapter 3, this volume, for a description of the method
of defining high and low self-handicappers). High self-handicappers,
on the other hand, did not increase their practice time before important meets. In fact, they exerted less effort when more effort was called
for, presumably in an attempt to provide a ready excuse should they do
poorly in the upcoming meet. This was true even though the meet was
clearly a test of an important ability, and in fact, high self-handicappers
rated these meets as even more important than did low self-
handicappers.

A similar effect was found in study 2. Here, golfers rated various
tournaments on importance. Those who were identified as low rather
than high self-handicappers increased their practice before important
tournaments.

Given that an upcoming performance is expected to test an ability
that is an important component of the self-concept, what else is necessary for self-handicapping to occur? Theoretically, there must be some
uncertainty about the ability in question. Various methods have been
used to create this uncertainty, beginning with Berglas and Jones's (1978)
use of noncontingent success feedback.

CREATION OF UNCERTAINTY

The assumption underlying the Berglas and Jones (1978) experiments was that noncontingent success feedback would create, in the
laboratory, a situation analogous to the reinforcement histories of individuals who are prone to self-handicapping. Such individuals were said
to have received unearned rewards; the lack of connection between their
actions and successful outcomes created uncertainty over whether they
could in fact reproduce the outcomes. Berglas and Jones argued that, to
the extent that being able to produce the outcomes was important to
these individuals, whether because it reflected a personally valued ability or because others appeared to value them for this ability, this uncertainty was preferable to finding out that they could not truly earn the
rewards. Maintaining the uncertainty would maintain the hope that
they would prove competent someday. Use of a handicap, then, would
maintain this uncertainty by putting off the crucial test until later.

As previously noted, male subjects in the Berglas and Jones (1978) experiments did respond to noncontingent success feedback by choosing a handicapping drug. Subsequent studies also have produced handicapping using noncontingent success (e.g., Higgins & Harris, 1988; Kolditz & Arkin, 1982; Mayerson & Rhodewalt, 1988; Tucker, Vuchinich, & Sobell, 1981).

Widening the focus of self-handicapping theory, Snyder and Smith (1982) were the first to present the argument that noncontingent success is not the only method of creating an uncertain self-image. (This point is made elsewhere in this volume as well: Berglas, Chapter 5; Higgins, Chapter 1; Snyder, Chapter 4.) Self-handicapping researchers now appear to agree that the important prerequisite to self-handicapping is the belief that the positive self-image *may* be accurate, without the certainty that this is so. Subjects may arrive in the experimental setting already holding an important, but tentative, positive self-image concerning the ability being tested. From this perspective, self-handicapping may result if the experimental situation merely arouses concern over the maintenance of the self-image.

In support of their argument, Snyder and Smith (1982) cited two studies that found self-handicapping without the direct experience of noncontingent success. In the first study, Smith, Snyder, and Handelsman (1982) presented high and low test-anxious subjects with a set of difficult test problems that they were unable to finish in the allotted time. Before continuing with a second set of problems, subjects were given the opportunity to self-handicap by reporting their level of state anxiety. They were also given various instructions about the effect of anxiety on performance; some were told that it would hurt performance, some that it had no effect on performance, and some were told nothing about anxiety's effects on performance. High test-anxious subjects claimed more state anxiety when they were told nothing about its effects than when they were told that anxiety had no effect on performance. This differential claiming of anxiety was interpreted by Smith *et al.* as a strategic use of symptom reporting in order to excuse potential poor performance. Because of the difficult nature of the problems on the first test, uncertainty about future success led to self-handicapping; a direct experience of noncontingent success was not required.

The second study cited by Snyder and Smith (1982) was reported by Smith, Snyder, and Perkins (1983). In another examination of symptom reporting, these investigators recruited females who scored high on a measure of hypochondriasis. Before participating in a role-play test of their social intelligence, the subjects were presented with difficult "social perception" problems in order to create uncertainty about future success. They were then given an opportunity to self-handicap by reporting physical symptoms, as well as instructions concerning the effects of such symptoms on tests of social intelligence (either that symptoms would hurt performance, that they would not affect performance, or no information was given about symptoms and performance). Again, subjects reported symptoms differentially, based on the instructions they had been given, causing Smith *et al.* to conclude that self-handicapping was resulting from uncertainty about success. The difficult social problems apparently created this uncertainty without the necessity for noncontingent success feedback. Other research has also produced self-handicapping when subjects are exposed to a difficult task that implies the potential for future failure (e.g., Pyszczynski & Greenberg, 1983; Snyder, Smith, Augelli, & Ingram, 1985).

In contrast, some studies have found that without noncontingent success feedback, handicapping does not occur. For example, Berglas and Jones (1978) included a no-feedback condition in their second experiment. Most subjects receiving unsolvable problems did not choose to inhibit their performance with Pandocrin under these circumstances. Tucker *et al.* (1981) found greater self-handicapping in the form of alcohol consumption when subjects had received noncontingent success feedback than when they had received no feedback on an intellectual test. In other work, no handicapping effects were found in the no-feedback conditions of Kolditz and Arkin (1982) and Higgins and Harris (1988).

It should be noted that the lack of self-handicapping under no-feedback conditions has been found exclusively in studies that required subjects to actively acquire an impediment to future performance, that is, to ingest alcohol or drugs. Conversely, all the studies that have found self-handicapping after exposure to difficult problems (without noncontingent success feedback) have involved claims of an internal handicap of some kind, such as anxiety, shyness, or lack of effort. The reason for the different findings may lie in the different types of self-handicapping they reflect. Claiming a symptom will not necessarily impede future performance, while ingesting drugs or alcohol is quite likely to do so. Among noncontingent success subjects, findings of self-handicapping by choosing to consume an inhibiting substance may reflect a greater willingness to risk immediate performance losses in the service of maintaining a positive self-concept. Noncontingent success may create a positive but tenuous public success image that an individual is willing to protect by sacrificing an upcoming performance. Without such a public image, however, the motivation to protect the self-concept may not be strong enough to justify actively sabotaging one's performance. Thus, simple uncertainty about future performance may be sufficient to result in claims of handicaps but not active acquisition of handicaps.

There is one exception to this distinction between the use of claimed and acquired handicaps when no feedback is given. Higgins and Harris (1989) gave male subjects a test of their "social competence" and, without telling them their scores, led them to believe that their social skills were going to be evaluated during an interaction with an attractive female assistant. Before this interaction, subjects were given an opportunity to self-handicap by consuming vodka (actually a placebo), and were given varying instructions about alcohol's effects on social performance, (alcohol helps, alcohol hurts, alcohol has no effect, or no instructions). Heavy (but not light) social drinkers increased their consumption of the placebo in the "alcohol hurts" condition, relative to a no-evaluation control group. In the "alcohol helps" condition, drinking was decreased.

Apparently, the heavy drinkers in this study used alcohol consumption as a self-handicapping strategy in response to uncertainty about their performance during the upcoming social interaction. Thus, they actively impeded their performance in spite of the absence of noncontingent success feedback designed to create a public success image. It may be that the anticipation of a prolonged public evaluation created enough self-protection concern that these drinkers were willing to sacrifice their performance, unlike no-feedback subjects in other substance consumption studies.

Creation of uncertainty, then, may result either from noncontingent success feedback or from threats to an already established, albeit tenuous, positive self-image. Such threats can take two forms: (1) exposure to a performance task that is difficult, so that a person is left without clear information about ability but with the suspicion that success on a future task may be out of reach, or (2) failure on an initial task, so that a person has some negative information about ability but is not totally convinced that the information is conclusive. Thus, failure feedback prior to additional testing may lead to self-handicapping if the failure threatens the self-image, but does not decisively settle the question of one's competence.

A few studies have directly examined the effects of failure feedback on use of self-handicapping. Rhodewalt and Davison (1986), for example, argued that failure should result in self-handicapping only when (1) there in uncertainty about the cause of the failure and (2) there is uncertainty about how to avoid another failure. This perspective is similar to that taken above. That is, failure must not definitely be attributed to lack of ability or there will be no positive image to protect. Subjects in Rhodewalt and Davison's study received either contingent or noncontingent success or failure feedback on analogy problems. Noncontingent failure was created by giving subjects problems that were either difficult or impossible to solve, telling them that they had solved 10 out of 20, and reporting earlier that the average student solved 15 out of 20.

Although it was expected that noncontingent failure subjects, like the noncontingent success subjects, would self-handicap by choosing performance-inhibiting music to listen to during a second test, the preference for handicapping music was significant only among male noncontingent success subjects. Nevertheless, some individual failure subjects did choose handicapping music, and internal analyses revealed these subjects to have had more belief in the potential controllability of their first failure and to have exerted more effort on the second test than did failure subjects who did not choose such music. Also, those failure subjects who did *not* handicap tended to attribute their failure to ability or to the difficulty of the problems. Thus, it could be argued that failure subjects who did choose inhibiting music were not giving up in the face of failure, that their competence image was uncertain but not destroyed, and that they therefore chose the music in an attempt to provide an excuse for a potential second failure. Nonetheless, Higgins and Harris (1988) included both contingent and noncontingent failure feedback conditions in their experimental design and found no evidence of handicapping by either group, casting doubt on the idea that failure feedback may produce handicapping. Again, this study involved use of an acquired impediment, alcohol, to self-handicap; it is possible that failure feedback subjects were motivated to self-handicap, but not to the extent that they would actively impede their performance.

A third study that used noncontingent failure feedback was reported by Weidner (1980). This research examined Type A coronary-prone subjects and Type B non-coronary-prone subjects. After completing an initial baseline measure of intelligence (on which they received noncontingent failure or contingent success feedback), subjects were offered a choice between varying dosages of a drug that was said to enhance performance or one that would decrease performance, just as in Berglas and Jones (1978). The results showed that individual differences in coronary-prone behavior patterns interacted with test feedback. Type A persons who received failure feedback chose a drug dosage that was described as resulting in a level of performance that was just below neutral, while Type A persons who received contingent success feedback, and Type B persons regardless of feedback, chose drug dosages that would enhance performance. Weidner argued that Type A persons are more threatened by failure than Type B persons; therefore, they provided themselves with an external excuse for future failure. The fact that, after failure, Type A persons chose a drug dosage that would have only a slightly negative effect on performance is not evidence of a strong motive to self-handicap; only in comparison to the performance enhancement choices of the other groups did the Type A persons appear to be strategically lowering their performance.

In contrast to these results with Type A individuals, Baumgardner, Lake, and Arkin (1985) argued that public failure should be less likely to produce self-handicapping because the handicapping would not excuse the earlier failure. Subjects' failure at an initial task was either clearly known to the experimenter, or supposedly unknown to the experimenter. All subjects were then given an opportunity to self-handicap by claiming depressive symptoms that ostensibly would interfere with their performance. Baumgardner *et al.* indeed found that subjects reported depressive symptoms only when they thought their prior failure was not publicly known. (The issue of the publicity of one's performance and one's handicap will be discussed further below.) Apparently, subjects who self-handicapped had a public competence image that was not destroyed by failure.

Although Baumgardner *et al.* argued that handicapping a future performance could not excuse prior failure, this may not always be the case. It is true that choosing a behavioral impediment will not explain an earlier failure. But reference to any of a number of long-term disabilities that can serve as justifications for poor performance should serve to excuse both prior and anticipated failures. Such handicaps can be used as a reason for lack of success in the past as well as in the future. (For more on such "incorporated" handicaps see Higgins & Berglas, Chapter 6, this volume; Snyder & Higgins, 1989.)

So far, the evidence that failure feedback produces self-handicapping is weak. It is difficult to assess when failure is seen as conclusive, and when it may threaten but not demolish a competence image. Without checks on the manipulation of failure, it is not clear whether subjects in failure conditions are unmotivated to self-handicap because they lack a positive self-concept to protect.

The crucial issue appears to be the existence of a positive self-image that one wants to uphold both in one's own eyes and in the eyes of others. While noncontingent success feedback may not be necessary to create this image for individuals who enter an experimental situation with an image already established, public congratulations by the experimenter may increase concern with protecting public attributions about the self, and thus especially increase the likelihood of self-handicapping through actively acquiring an impediment to performance. Similarly, while failure feedback may not destroy a previously created success image, it may discourage individuals from attempts to engineer public attributions about ability. The social context of self-handicapping will be discussed more fully below.

COMPETITIVE AND COOPERATIVE TASKS

On some tasks, success is defined not by reaching an absolute score or standard, but relative to the performance of others. Competitive tasks, for example, require that one surpass the performance of others. Success on cooperative tasks, on the other hand, implicitly demands that both the self and others should perform well, while the relative contributions of each performer are not always clear. Under either circumstance, the individual's proactive interference with performance outcomes may obscure the diagnosticity of the performance and preserve an uncertain competence image. For example, one might insure that competitors have advantages other than superior ability, or arrange things so that co-actors have inadequacies which can explain poor joint performance. Structuring the performance situation in these ways will serve to discount negative attributions about the self-handicapper's own ability.

To determine whether threatened individuals would indeed actively give their competitors an advantage, Shepperd, Arkin, Walker, and McSpadden (1989) gave subjects practice problems in the presence of a confederate subject who appeared to be solving the problems much more quickly or slowly than they. This was intended to create expectations of either success or failure among those subjects who believed their upcoming performance would be compared to the confederate's. Subjects were then given an opportunity to choose performance-enhancing or performance-inhibiting music for the confederate to listen to during the test. Those expecting a comparison of performances, and expecting to perform worse than their competitor, chose music that was significantly more performance-enhancing for the confederate. Thus, they obtained a ready excuse for anticipated failure relative to the confederate—it was not that he had more ability, but that the music helped him to do well.

Earlier work (Gould, Brounstein, & Sigall, 1977; Shepperd, 1988) had established that people will try to manage attributions about their performance in competitive situations by verbally citing the advantages of a competitor, but the Shepperd et al. (1989) study provided the first evidence that people will actively contribute to those advantages. Although such behavior does not directly impede one's own performance, it does provide a "handicap" when that performance is being evaluated relative to another. Resorting to this mode of self-handicapping should be especially probable in situations where the competitor appears likely to outperform the individual, and where recognizable aids to performance exist. Under such circumstances the individual may graciously donate these performance aids to the competitor, simultaneously preventing negative ability attributions and encouraging attributions of generosity and fair play.

Joint tasks are sometimes structured in such a way that individual contributions to the outcome cannot be clearly evaluated. This can occur in two ways. It may happen that both people are performing the same task and the quantity or quality of their individual contributions is not recorded. Or, they may be performing different components of a larger task, but an evaluating audience neglects to observe their individual performances and is unable to disentangle them merely from observing the overall outcome. In such cases there is again an opportunity to obscure ability attributions, which may be especially desirable when an individual believes that an evaluating audience is motivated to assign individual responsibility for the joint outcome.

Under the guise of studying the social functioning of volunteers who had taken performance-inhibiting or performance-enhancing drugs, Self (1989) gave male and female subjects contingent or noncontingent success feedback before a second, similar task that would be jointly performed. It was emphasized that individual contributions to the joint score would not be identifiable. Subjects were then allowed to choose a partner who had taken a performance-inhibiting or performance-enhancing drug. Comparison of the choices of females and contingent success males against the choices of the noncontingent success males revealed that the latter group chose an inadequate partner significantly more often, thus providing themselves with someone to blame for anticipated poor performance. The absence of this effect among females was not unexpected, given that the first test was essentially a replication of Berglas and Jones (1978), who also failed to find significant handicapping among females (see Rhodewalt, Chapter 3, this volume, for a further discussion of females and noncontingent success feedback).

Handicapping a joint performance by choosing an inadequate partner, or by arranging circumstances so that a partner's performance will be disrupted, should be most likely in situations where this behavior will not itself cause negative attributions about the individual. Thus, the handicapper should not appear to *desire* an inadequate partner, nor to deliberately inhibit a partner's performance. When the situation provides some other excuse for one's actions, however, this form of self-handicapping may be utilized. (The need to maintain ambiguity regarding the intent to self-handicap will be discussed further below.)

Competitive and cooperative tasks involve threats to a self-concept that is defined relative to others. In a larger sense, the self-concept is always defined with some consideration for what others believe is important, even if the standards for evaluation appear to be absolute. In the next section, I will consider the effects that others may have on the creation and protection of an important self-concept.

SOCIALLY CREATED STANDARDS

As noted above, the self-concept may be viewed as consisting of components that are more or less important or central rather than as a unified structure of equally fervently held beliefs about the self. This perspective on the self implies that the various components do not just reflect experience, but they also direct experience and change in response to experience (Markus & Wurf, 1987). Snyder (1989) proposed that people "negotiate" personal theories of themselves by responding to social experience in a way that accounts for this experience but also maintains a positive overall evaluation of the self. In other work, Snyder and Higgins (1988) described this "negotiated reality" as a reflection of a "biased compromise that the person considers 'valid' and that outside sources (e.g., observers) would not seriously question should the person verbalize it" (p. 32; see also Snyder, Chapter 4, this volume, for further discussion of self-handicapping as reality negotiation).

In situations that threaten important components of the self-concept, a renegotiation with "outside sources" may be in order, to satisfy the internal audience of the self as well as the external audience. One method of negotiation is to use a handicap to prevent negative attributions about an ability that has been socially defined as positive. Thus, whatever ability is in question can remain a part of the self-concept. In embracing a handicap, however, it is necessary to consider both the values and the beliefs of others, so that there will be no "serious questions" concerning one's ongoing self-theory.

The values of others are often responsible for the standards by which performance is judged, even if these values are internalized and no others are physically present at the time. Higgins and Berglas (Chapter 6, this volume) refer to the ongoing creation of the self-concept as ideally being a process of steadily increasing one's beliefs in efficacy as one moves toward mastering challenges. It is important to note that this cannot be accomplished all at once; one does not master any difficult

task on the first try. However, when socially defined standards of performance do not allow for progression toward mastery, but, rather, imply
that immediate mastery is expected, these standards may be internalized as part of the self-concept, creating justifiable uncertainty that
they can be met. This is a situation ripe for self-handicapping.

For an example of the idea that lower standards might remove the
need for self-handicapping, we can return to the bowling alley mentioned at the beginning of this chapter. My friends' delight at my knock-
ing down any pins at all indicated that their standards for success were
reachable; I did not have to be a "good bowler." This may have contributed to my lack of concern with appearing competent.

An empirical example of a similar phenomenon was provided by
Anderson (1983) in a study measuring motivation and performance on a
persuasion task. Subjects were told that they would be soliciting blood
donations over the telephone; one group was told that failure to persuade others to donate was probably due to a basic inability to persuade,
while another group was told that failure simply involved not trying
hard enough to find the right strategies. All subjects then made a practice call and failed to persuade a confederate to donate. Subsequently,
the strategy/effort group showed higher motivation than the ability
group. This group also was more successful in persuading people to
donate blood. Those in the strategy group may have believed that early
failures were allowable as they grew toward mastery of the task, while
those in the ability group may have thought that early failures indicated
that they might be unable to demonstrate mastery. This is suggested by
analysis of subjects' expectancies for success in future persuasive attempts; the strategy/effort group expected more future success. Because
this study did not directly provide subjects with an opportunity to self-
handicap, however, it is not known whether those in the ability group
would have self-handicapped under these circumstances. If individuals
believe that immediate mastery is expected, and that their initial efforts
will unequivocally reveal whether or not they have an important ability, theoretically they should be motivated to self-handicap to the degree that they feel uncertain about their competence. Further study is
needed, taking into account those factors described above in the section
on the creation of uncertainty.

PUBLIC KNOWLEDGE OF THE HANDICAP

That an individual's perception of the beliefs of others is important
in the creation and maintenance of the self-concept has been demonstrated in research investigating the public versus private nature of the

self-handicapping motive. Berglas and Jones (1978) theorized that the primary function of handicaps was to prevent an individual from having to confront information that would disconfirm a privately held positive competence image. To test this idea, they manipulated the publicity of their success feedback. In the public condition, the experimenter asked about the subjects' scores and congratulated them on their success, while in the private condition, the experimenter explicitly emphasized the necessity of his not knowing their score on the first test. Thus for some subjects there was a public competence image to protect, as well as a private one. Even in the condition where the competence image was supposedly totally private, subjects preferred the performance-inhibiting drug, supporting Berglas and Jones's argument that handicapping arises out of a need to protect private esteem.

Kolditz and Arkin (1982), however, argued that the experimental assistant had been aware of the success feedback in all conditions in the Berglas and Jones (1978) experiment, thus there had been a failure to create a truly private competence image. Furthermore, the act of self-handicapping itself was public in the Berglas and Jones study because the experimenter was present during subjects' drug choice. From the point of view of the subject, the experimenter would be able to explain potential failure on the second test as a function of the performance-inhibiting drug; even though the experimenter might not be aware of the subject's prior success, having a ready excuse might prove less embarrassing. For these reasons, Kolditz and Arkin replicated the contingency manipulations of Berglas and Jones, but made the handicapping act private by asking subjects to choose their drug while the experimenter was absent and to enclose all leftover drugs in an envelope. This envelope, along with the second test form, was to be directly mailed to a pharmaceutical company; thus the experimenter would have no awareness of any handicap, nor of the subject's performance on the second test.

Kolditz and Arkin found that, of the subjects who believed both that their score would remain private and that their choice of drug would be unknown, none chose a performance-inhibiting drug. However, they pointed out that "to characterize self-handicapping as a self-presentation strategy does not mean that it has no influence on attribution of self-competence" (p. 501). Success in convincing others that one is competent might lead to conviction that the competence indeed exists. From a reality negotiation perspective, the self-theory is constantly being defined with reference to others' beliefs about the self, so that the notion of purely private self-esteem in anomalous. But, without the presence of others to seriously question one's self-theory, it may be easier to provide oneself with any of a number of retrospective excuses, or alternative anticipatory excuses, than to actively handicap one's performance.

It would be useful to offer subjects a choice between actively handicapping their performance or merely claiming a symptom that should interfere with performance, while varying the publicity of the performance and the handicap. If the reasoning above is correct, under private conditions subjects should prefer to console themselves with the thought that ongoing symptoms might keep them from performing up to their true ability level. They should reject the option of actively behaving in a way that would handicap their performance, because this choice would seem to preclude the chance that they might still surmount the handicap and perform well. But, when there is an audience that requires convincing, it may appear safer to actively impede one's performance in order to insure that the audience will be convinced that one could not have done better. Merely claiming to have some symptom that might interfere with performance may not provide enough tangible evidence; the audience may suspect that the symptom does not exist.

Evidence directly contrasting these two modes of handicapping under public and private conditions is not available. But there is evidence that suggests a different interpretation of Kolditz and Arkin's (1982) results with subjects in a private handicapping condition. Although these subjects did not actively self-handicap by choosing a performance-inhibiting drug, this may not mean that they had no motive to self-handicap, but that they chose not to *actively* self-handicap.

The research supporting this interpretation was reported by Greenberg, Pyszczynski, and Paisley (1985). These investigators led subjects to believe that their responses throughout the entire testing session would be anonymous, exposed them to some difficult sample problems, and gave them the opportunity to claim test anxiety before taking the test itself. Some subjects did self-handicap under these circumstances. However, because the only handicapping strategy they had available was to claim that they were experiencing test anxiety, it is not known whether this strategy would have been chosen more often than some type of behavioral impediment, under such private conditions, nor whether an active impediment would have been preferred under public conditions. Greenberg *et al.* did find that making these claims of test anxiety did not impede performance; no performance differences were found between any of the experimental groups.

Other evidence on the relation between self-handicapping and a concern with audience attributions can be found in work examining individual differences in social anxiety (Leary, 1986) and public self-consciousness (Shepperd & Arkin, 1989b; see Rhodewalt, Chapter 3, for a discussion of individual difference variables in self-handicapping).

FACTORS THAT INHIBIT SELF-HANDICAPPING

Protecting the self-concept is often an important motive, but handicapping oneself in the service of this motive is not without cost. Certainly one risks losing the benefits associated with successful performance, such as unambiguously positive ability attributions and tangible rewards. Although Kelley's (1972) augmenting principle would predict that people who *do* succeed while handicapped will be given even more credit for ability (and although they will presumably reap the tangible rewards as well), such benefits are jeopardized to the extent that an individual actively creates impediments to performance. Furthermore, obscuring or avoiding diagnostic information about one's ability by impeding one's performance may be comforting in the short run, but also counterproductive when one needs to know how much one will be able to accomplish within a certain time, or whether a goal is attainable and thus worth striving for. Finally, continuing the reality negotiation perspective that one's self-concept continuously responds to the perceived values and standards of others, it becomes clear that self-handicapping to protect the self-concept may simultaneously make it vulnerable to the disapproval of others who detect the use of this strategy. The following section will explore situations that elicit motives that compete with the motive to self-handicap, and thus inhibit its expression.

EXPLICITLY OFFERING A HANDICAP

Negotiating an ongoing positive self-concept requires that the causal attributions constructed by an individual be acceptable to witnessing others, as well as the self. Thus a self-handicapper must believe that his or her handicap will be viewed by others as a legitimate reason for potential failure. Because the self-theory is a joint production, the self-handicapper must also be convinced that the handicap is legitimate. However, to the extent that self-handicapping appears to be an attempt to cover up the "real reason" (lack of ability) for potential failure, the handicap may lose legitimacy in the eyes of the audience (Springston & Chafe, 1987) and the self-handicapper (cf. Snyder, 1985).

Claiming a handicap that has recently been suggested by others may appear to be capitalizing on their suggestion rather than honestly suffering from an impediment to performance. This threat to the legitimacy of the handicap was suggested by Smith *et al.* (1982), whose work was described briefly above as it related to handicapping in response to the creation of uncertainty. Their study examined claims of test anxiety before a difficult test among subjects selected for high and low trait test anxiety. They reasoned that subjects characteristically high in test anxiety would be accustomed to using anxiety as an explanation for poor test performance, while subjects low in test anxiety would not have this experience. Therefore, after taking the first half of a difficult test, high (but not low) test-anxious individuals should refer to their test anxiety as an anticipatory means of structuring attributions about poor performance on the second half of the test.

Although subjects were asked to report how anxious they *had felt* during the first test period, rather than how anxious they felt *just prior to*, or *expected* to feel during the second test period (which would have been a more direct test of self-handicapping *per se*), the predicted effects were found. High test-anxious individuals reported more anxiety than those low in test anxiety, but this effect was qualified by the attributional context provided by the experimenters. When test anxiety was ruled out as a legitimate reason for failure, claims of anxiety among high test-anxious subjects were lessened relative to when anxiety was not mentioned at all. Furthermore, when anxiety was *explicitly* mentioned as a probable cause of poor performance, subjects did *not* claim to have been anxious significantly more often than when they were told it would not excuse poor performance.

This latter result was unexpected, but Smith *et al.* suggested that to claim anxiety after being clearly offered anxiety as an excuse might have seemed too obvious an attempt to manage attributions about potential failure. In other words, when the handicapping excuse was too salient, it would disrupt the illusion that it was indeed a legitimate reason for failure and would instead appear to be an intentional strategy to "cover up" the truth. Further evidence that situations increasing the salience of an excuse may ultimately reduce its use can be found in work by Arkin, Appelman, and Burger (1980), and by Arkin, Gabrenya, Appelman, and Cochran (1979).

There is, however, some evidence that contradicts the idea that potential self-handicappers hesitate to use salient excuses; this research was reported by Higgins and Harris (1989) and was also described briefly above in the section on the creation of uncertainty. As in the Smith *et al.* (1982) research, subjects were given various *a priori* attributional contexts with which to explain potential failure. Under the guise of studying the effects of alcohol on social skills, male subjects (who had been preselected on the basis of their drinking habits) were told that they would be evaluated during a 10-minute conversation with an attractive female. Before the conversation, subjects were given an opportunity to drink as much as they wanted of what purportedly was vodka and tonic. But before drinking, some subjects were told that research had shown that alcohol would probably help their social performance, while others were told that it would probably hurt their performance, or were told nothing about alcohol's effect on performance. Thus the legitimacy of alcohol as a handicap was manipulated, similar to the legitimacy of test anxiety as a handicap in the Smith *et al.* (1982) work.

Measures of "alcohol" consumption revealed that, prior to the social evaluation (but not when they did not expect to be evaluated), heavy social drinkers drank more in the "alcohol hurts" condition than when they were told that "alcohol helps" or were given no information about alcohol's effects on social performance. This effect was not found among light drinkers. Heavy drinkers, then, showed no restraint in their use of alcohol when it was explicitly acknowledged as a legitimate handicap to performance, unlike Smith *et al.*'s test anxious subjects, who claimed less test anxiety when anxiety was an explicit excuse.

It may be that heavy drinkers are less sensitive to the nuances of attributional contexts. Or, as suggested above, behavioral self-handicaps, which require actively impeding performance, may be seen by handicappers as unquestionably legitimate; self-reported handicaps, which require that the audience "take the handicapper's word" that there is indeed a handicap, may appear to be more vulnerable to audience suspicion (see Leary & Shepperd, 1986, for discussion of the distinction between behavioral and self-report modes of handicapping).

Higgins and Harris's own interpretation of their finding that explicitly offering an excuse did not reduce handicapping was that ingesting a substance made one's handicap externally caused, as opposed to being due to some internal trait such as test anxiety. Although test anxiety would be preferable to lack of ability as an explanation for poor performance, such a symptom still carries the potential to elicit negative dispositional attributions by others, whereas substance consumption may result in situational attributions unless the substance use becomes chronic (see Higgins & Snyder, 1989). In this vein, every study (i.e., Berglas & Jones, 1978; Kolditz & Arkin, 1982; Weidner, 1980) that has used the performance-enhancing or -inhibiting drug paradigm (as opposed to using alcohol—a drug with effects that are already widely recognized) has necessarily included specific instructions describing the effects of the drugs. These instructions have not prevented handicapping by choosing to ingest an external substance.

Furthermore, studies allowing subjects to choose music described

as performance-inhibiting (Rhodewalt & Davison, 1986) or telling them
that poor performance might be due to noise (Leary, 1986) have either
found self-handicapping, or indirectly inferred it, in spite of the salience
of these excuses. Again, it could be argued that these types of handicaps
are external, posing less threat of being linked to undesirable characterological qualities. More research is needed to clarify the phenomenological impact on potential self-handicappers of explicitly being offered an *a priori* excuse. The timing and wording of such an excuse, as
well as specific aspects of the excuse itself, such as its external or internal
nature, may be crucial.

LACK OF AN ALTERNATIVE EXPLANATION FOR HANDICAPPING

Explicitly offering an excuse to a potential self-handicapper may
make the excuse appear to be too obvious and paradoxically diminish its
use. To effectively maintain the self-concept, the handicap must seem
involuntary or incidental, not chosen or exploited strategically. Situations vary in the degree to which they contain elements which could
plausibly account for self-handicapping behavior. When self-handicapping appears to be chosen as an attempt to avoid revealing "the truth," it
defeats its own purpose. Situations that contain a legitimate reason for
self-handicapping behavior may be more likely to elicit such behavior
than situations that fail to offer such a reason. Without an alternative
explanation for their handicapping, individuals might be uncomfortably
aware of their attempts to engineer attributions about their ability.
Mehlman and Snyder (1985), for example, found increased negative
affect among subjects whose excuses might be revealed.

Situations that do offer an implicit reason for handicapping behavior contain "attribute ambiguity" (M. L. Snyder, Kleck, Strenta, & Mentzer, 1979). In other words, such situations include more than one possible cause that can be used as an explanation for an action. Under these
circumstances, Kelley's (1972) discounting principle applies: "the role of
a given cause in producing a given effect is discounted if other plausible
causes are also present" (p. 10). This discounting should be desirable to
self-handicappers to the extent that they wish to shield themselves and
others from the awareness that they are strategically embracing an anticipatory excuse. Some subjects in Berglas and Jones's (1978) study, for
example, implicitly recognized the importance of attribute ambiguity
when they explained that they had chosen the performance-inhibiting
drug in order to "help the experimenter." However, the Berglas and
Jones design did not vary the availability of this plausible motive; that
task remained for future researchers.

Handelsman, Kraiger, and King (1985) examined college students' use of a handicap when they were provided with a plausible reason to adopt the handicap. Subjects were offered a choice of two tests of social competence; one was quite accurate while the other was too difficult to accurately predict their social ability. Each test was supposedly available in two formats—multiple choice and true–false, but copies were limited. In the high-ambiguity condition, subjects were then told that they could choose between one test in a true–false format and another in multiple-choice format. This provided subjects in this condition with a plausible reason for choosing the difficult test, thereby avoiding any potential revelation that they were socially incompetent. Subjects in the low-ambiguity condition were given the choice between the two tests, but they were always in the same format, due to the "limited number of copies."

Handelsman *et al.* found that significantly fewer subjects chose the difficult, inaccurate test in the low-ambiguity condition, thus supporting the idea that, without an alternative explanation, people may refrain from choosing a handicap. Especially in public situations, where is a need to attend to the beliefs of the audience, it appears that the lack of a plausible alternative motive for self-handicapping may diminish the use of this strategy. However, just as the absence of an audience may allow an individual to choose retrospective excuses or anticipatory excuses that do not impede performance, once a self-handicap is chosen it may be much easier for an individual to justify this choice to himself or herself when there is no need to contend with an audience.

Preexisting Handicaps

While situations that lack plausible alternative explanations for self-handicapping may diminish the use of this strategy, situations that offer a ready-made handicap obviate the necessity to create or claim further impediments to performance. Here the advantage to the performer is not that the situation contains a built-in excuse for self-handicapping, but that it contains a built-in handicap. Thus, people may negotiate self-concept protection by relying on excuses inherent in the performance situation.

Effects of the presence of such an excuse were reported in a study by Leary (1986). Subjects in this study were given a test to determine their degree of social anxiousness (Leary, 1983) and told that the study would assess the effects of background noise on their interaction with a member of the opposite sex. All subjects heard the same background noise, but some were told by the experimenter that it probably would not interfere with their conversation, while others were told that it probably would interfere.

After the conversation, subjects rated themselves on the possession of several positive social attributes. Low socially anxious subjects rated themselves highly regardless of the experimenter's prediction about the effect of the noise; but high socially anxious subjects rated themselves highly only when the experimenter had described the noise as interfering. The availability of this handicap apparently allowed high-anxious subjects to attribute any poor social performance to the noise, thus protecting their self-concepts.

The above study demonstrated that individuals will benefit from the presence of a situation containing a ready-made handicap, but it did not directly address the issue of whether *other* handicaps are more or less likely to be used under these circumstances. One might argue that awareness of a handicap that is inherent in the situation would put subjects in a handicapping "frame of mind," and thus they would be more likely to self-handicap in other ways, if these were plausible, as extra insurance for their self-concepts.

In contrast to this argument, Shepperd and Arkin (1989a) reasoned that the presence of a preexisting handicap should eliminate the necessity for additional self-handicapping. Especially when the preexisting handicap is one that the audience will not seriously question, adopting an additional handicap may tip the balance of attributions against the self-handicapper. Although the presence of multiple causes diminishes the weight given to any one cause as an explanation for an outcome (Kelley, 1972), this can be a double-edged sword; a preexisting handicap may diminish attributions to lack of ability, but the presence of another potentially less plausible handicap may diminish attributions to the preexisting one. Therefore, those desiring to protect their competence images should play it safe by exploiting the existing handicap rather than adopting another. (See Leddo, Abelson, & Gross, 1984, for an alternative perspective. These researchers found that, rather than discounting the power of any one cause, multiple causes are more persuasive than single causes. Of course, it is what potential self-handicappers *believe* about how their excuses will be received, and not necessarily the actual attributional processes engaged in by an audience, that is crucial in the determination of self-handicapping.)

To test their prediction that a preexisting handicap would eliminate further self-handicapping, Shepperd and Arkin (1989a) gave subjects a choice of a range of performance-inhibiting and performance-enhancing music to listen to while performing a test of their intellectual abilities. In addition, some subjects were told that the experiment was investigating dichotic listening and that, therefore, they would hear a high-pitched ringing noise through their right earphone, while the left earphone would transmit whatever music they selected. These subjects were thus provided with a preexisting handicap in the form of the noise, which the experimenters claimed had been documented as disruptive in previous research. Those in the handicap-absent condition were merely to select music and were told nothing about noise.

When the intellectual task was described as valid (see the above section on task importance), subjects chose more debilitating music than when it was described as potentially invalid, but this effect occurred only when the preexisting handicap was absent. Apparently the presence of the noise made additional handicapping unnecessary.

Because the preexisting handicap in this study had been "demonstrated in previous research" to disrupt performance, while the effects of the performance-inhibiting music were still being tested, the noise should have appeared to subjects as an unquestionably legitimate excuse for any poor performance. Although Shepperd and Arkin cited research showing that symptom reporting is likely when an experimenter makes it clear that a symptom is "widely acknowledged as a handicap to performance," the fact remains that explicitly offering an excuse for potential poor performance did not lead to self-handicapping in the Smith *et al.* (1982) study reported above. It was argued there that self-handicappers may sometimes fear that use of an explicitly acknowledged handicap might be too obvious. From the above evidence it appears that in some cases acknowledgement is reassuring and increases reliance on a handicap.

The degree of certainty an individual has that an audience will accept a handicap as a legitimate cause of poor performance probably varies with the individual's familiarity with the audience and with the degree of consensual reality shared by the audience and the individual. Referring to "scientific research" as the basis for a claim that a handicap will indeed serve as a handicap should bolster confidence that it will not be questioned later, because science is the ultimate source of consensual reality for most individuals in our society. Similarly, subcultures may share consensually agreed-upon excuses that are more valid within the subculture than without.

For example, heavy drinkers may excuse their inability to go fishing on Sunday morning by referring to the presence of a hangover. This excuse may elicit sympathetic grimaces from fishing-and-drinking buddies but may not serve as well when explaining absence from church to one's minister. In this vein, Carducci and McNeely (1981) found that drinking husbands were generally given less blame for wife abuse than were sober husbands, except by recovering alcoholics, who attributed more blame to a drinking husband. Consumption of alcohol no longer served as a legitimate excuse within the subculture of recovering alcoholics. It would be interesting to see if drinking husbands would be granted even more immunity by still-practicing alcoholics.

The above perspective implies that some audiences may share a specific consensual reality; moreover, they may be motivated to maintain that reality just as much as a self-handicapper. Not only may audiences need to preserve a general sense of control, as Snyder (Chapter 4, this volume) argues, but they may also be motivated to preserve the legitimacy of some excuses in case they themselves need to resort to them in the future. When self-handicappers perceive audiences to share a specific consensual reality and to be motivated to maintain that reality, use of specific handicaps (in lieu of other less consensually agreed-upon handicaps) should increase. Further research is needed to investigate this "tailor-made" approach to self-handicapping, but related work by Tetlock (1981) has demonstrated that subjects alter their self-presentations depending upon the experimental situation.

EXTERNAL INCENTIVES

The practice of self-handicapping may not always succeed in protecting the self-concept, but rather, may damage it both in the eyes of others and in the individual's own eyes. When the risk of this damage is especially salient, the motive to self-handicap no longer serves the motive to protect the self-concept; instead these motives are in conflict. Conflicting motives may also arise when there are substantial external incentives for performing well.

Greenberg et al. (1985) examined claims of test anxiety as a self-handicap under conditions of varying incentives for good performance. Subjects were to take a difficult intellectual test on which the highest scorer would be awarded either $5 (low incentive) or $25 (high incentive). As in the Smith et al. (1982) study described above, some subjects were told that anxiety had no effect on performance, while others were given no instructions about anxiety. When anxiety was ruled out as a possible anticipatory explanation for poor performance, subjects did not claim as much anxiety as when they were given no information about anxiety. But this effect held only in the low-incentive condition; in the high-incentive condition, reports of anxiety did not depend on its legitimacy as an excuse for poor performance.

To explain this, Greenberg et al. argued that, in the high-incentive, no-information condition, subjects may have believed that anxiety would indeed handicap their performance, so they were motivated to perceive *less* anxiety in themselves, rather than to perceive *more* anxiety as an *a priori* excuse. From this perspective, use of behavioral modes of self-handicapping (e.g., partying the night before an important performance) should be even more unlikely than use of symptomatic modes of self-handicapping, when external incentives are high. This is because behavioral self-handicapping may actually create impediments to performance. The act of claiming a symptom may also harm performance, to the extent that it becomes a self-fulfilling prophecy, but apparently this was not the case in the Greenberg *et al.* research; despite what subjects may have believed, no performance differences were found among the experimental groups.

DESIRE FOR DIAGNOSTIC INFORMATION

In their initial research on the self-handicapping phenomenon, Berglas and Jones (1978) contrasted two opposing assumptions about people's desire to learn about their competence. The first, contained in the first hypothesis of Festinger's (1954) social comparison theory, simply posits that people want information about their abilities. In contrast, achievement motivation theory modifies this assumption: people may indeed want diagnostic information, but the strength of this desire may vary depending on their motivation to achieve. In support of this second assumption, Trope (1975) found that "subjects high in achievement motive can be said to be more interested in such information than subjects low in achievement motive" (p. 1012), but that there was an overall preference for high-diagnostic tasks as opposed to low.

Berglas and Jones argued that the fear of failure may come to predominate over the desire for achievement and over the consequent desire for diagnostic information about the presence of abilities necessary to that achievement. This was their proposed dynamic underlying use of the self-handicapping strategy: the motive to avoid unequivocal diagnostic information about a tenuous competence image.

Although the body of self-handicapping research supports the idea that people will act to protect an important self-concept by embracing a handicap that will serve as an alternative explanation for poor performance, and will thus make the performance nondiagnostic, there is also more specific work investigating people's preferences for nondiagnostic performance settings.

Sachs (1982) gave male subjects contingent or noncontingent success feedback on an analogy test and then asked them to create their own second test by choosing from four sets of problems. These problems were described as easy but nondiagnostic of ability, easy and diagnostic, difficult and nondiagnostic, and both difficult and diagnostic. A main effect of contingency and diagnosticity was found such that subjects receiving contingent feedback chose more diagnostic items, regardless of difficulty, than subjects receiving noncontingent feedback. Those receiving noncontingent feedback apparently were the ones who were most interested in protecting their competence image. Further analysis of subjects' preferences for the four types of tests revealed that, overall, diagnostic tests were preferred. Thus the desire for diagnostic information was present, but it was modified by the competing motive of self-concept protection.

In a similar study, Slaughter, Shaver, and Arkin (1988) also varied the contingency of success feedback on a first test and gave subjects an opportunity to design their own second test. Additionally, however, they manipulated the perceived privacy of the testing situation by giving and collecting all information via computer for half the subjects, while the others chose their test items in the presence of an experimenter. In the private (computer) condition, regardless of contingency, subjects preferred highly diagnostic, easy items. Interestingly, this preference was echoed by subjects in the public (experimenter present) condition only when they had received contingent feedback. In the public condition, noncontingent subjects showed no preference for high-diagnostic over low-diagnostic items; they merely preferred easy items regardless of diagnosticity. For these subjects, the desire for self-concept protection apparently predominated over the desire for diagnostic information.

Thus there is evidence that people are indeed motivated to assess their abilities, but that this motive may be modified or eclipsed by the desire to protect an important self-concept. When an important self-concept is threatened, specific situations that appear to be diagnostic of ability may be less strongly preferred. It is likely that the motive for diagnostic information gains strength when people anticipate continuing performance in a particular arena. As Festinger (1954) pointed out, "inaccurate appraisals of one's abilities can be punishing or even fatal in many situations" (p. 117). When one needs to know about ability level in order to act, diagnostic information should be preferred. In other circumstances, when instrumental action can be postponed and the task arena is merely symbolic of one's competence to perform such instrumental action *someday* (as many performance arenas are), self-concept protection should play a greater role.

SUMMARY AND CONCLUSIONS

The present chapter has explored several situational factors that appear to increase or decrease the likelihood of self-handicapping. Taking a components approach to the self-concept, it was found that upcoming performances that appear to threaten important aspects of the self-concept are more likely to elicit self-handicapping.

There must be a positive but uncertain competence image relative to these important components of the self-concept; however, the positive image and the uncertainty need not be created simultaneously. While noncontingent success both creates a positive image and renders it fragile, a subject may also arrive in an experimental situation with a positive image already created. If this positive image is then threatened with failure, either by a subject's attempting difficult problems or by receiving feedback that he or she has failed to solve such problems, self-handicapping may result. More work is needed to document the effects of failure feedback on various modes of self-handicapping; it was suggested that reference to incorporated, or dispositional handicaps may be preferred to actively adopting an impediment to a second performance when such an impediment would not explain the initial failure.

Sometimes performance is not evaluated in comparison to an absolute standard, but can only be inferred relative to the performance of others. In these circumstances, threats to the self-concept may result in behavior intended to enhance or inhibit the performance of others, thus obscuring the diagnosticity of the performance. Similarly, a reality-negotiation perspective on self-concept protection assumes that others are actively influential in the maintenance of the desired self-concept. Thus the communication of standards for performance that demand excellence may be especially likely to result in self-handicapping. However, the evidence for this idea is indirect; more research is needed examining self-handicapping under varying performance standards.

The presence of others who may make attributions about one's ability appears to influence the nature and degree of self-handicapping. It was found that self-handicapping is more common when both the expected performance and the self-handicapping act are public, and when there is reason to believe that the handicap will be accepted as a legitimate cause of potential failure. Paradoxically, some research shows that explicitly acknowledging the excuse value of a handicap may make it less likely to be used, presumably because of concern that it will appear to be too obvious and thus lose legitimacy. However, the evidence for this phenomenon is mixed; more work is needed to document its existence, again with reference to the types of handicaps most likely to be employed.

Situations that do not allow for ambiguity as to the reason a handicap is adopted appear to decrease the incidence of self-handicapping. Without the presence of a plausible alternative motive for the self-handcapping behavior, potential self-handicappers risk revealing the strategic nature of their anticipatory excuses, both to themselves and to an audience. To avoid this risk they may forgo use of self-handicaps. This further supports the idea that self-handicappers evaluate the legitimacy of their handicap in their own eyes and in the eyes of others. Similarly, when a situation contains a preexisting handicap that will clearly excuse poor performance, additional handicaps are not adopted. The legitimacy of handicaps may vary depending on the degree of consensual reality shared by the self-handicapper and his or her audience. It was suggested that members of specific subcultures may agree on the excuse value of certain handicaps and may in fact be motivated to maintain their legitimacy. This should result in preferences for certain consensually agreed-upon handicaps over others; this hypothesis has yet to be tested empirically.

Some situations may elicit motives that compete with the desire to self-handicap. The presence of substantial extrinsic incentives, for example, appears to reduce self-handicapping, presumably because the handicap would impede performance and reduce the probability of attaining the incentives. Here, too, attention to preferences for self-report over behavioral self-handicaps could clarify the effects of incentives on handicapping.

A second motive that might conflict with the motive to self-handicap is the desire for accurate information about one's ability. In performance situations, an uncertain competence image appears to decrease the preference for items from diagnostic as opposed to nondiagnostic tests. Nonetheless, the desire for diagnostic information does not appear to be entirely eliminated by concern for one's image.

Self-concept protection can be accomplished through several means. Self-handicapping seems to be most likely when an important component of the self-concept is threatened with public disconfirmation, when handicaps are readily available and clearly legitimate, and when the performance is largely symbolic, rather than instrumental, in gaining important tangible incentives. (The implication of results showing less self-handicapping when a performance involves tangible rewards is that people believe that a handicap would impede their performance and jeopardize attainment of the rewards. Ironically, it should be noted that the available literature does not show that handicaps actually impede performance. See Snyder, Chapter 4, this volume, for further discussion of this "paradox that isn't.")

Numerous questions remain regarding preferences for specific types of self-handicapping under various circumstances. Furthermore, there is a need for clarification of the circumstances affecting the perceived legitimacy of a handicap. As an example of this, one circumstance might be the fact of sharing subculture membership with an audience that is motivated to preserve the legitimacy of an excuse for future use. If these questions remain unanswered, perhaps we can agree to absolve ourselves from blame; after all, one cannot do *everything*, and becoming an excellent bowler demands a certain amount of time.

ACKNOWLEDGMENTS

The author wishes to acknowledge the encouragement, support, and helpful comments of Jack Brehm, Ray Higgins, and C. R. Snyder.

REFERENCES

Anderson, C. A. (1983). Motivational and performance deficits in interpersonal settings: The effect of attributional style. *Journal of Personality and Social Psychology, 45,* 1136–1147.

Arkin, R. M., Appelman, A. J., & Burger, J. M. (1980). Social anxiety, self-presentation, and the self-serving bias in causal attributions. *Journal of Personality and Social Psychology, 38,* 23–35.

Arkin, R. M., & Baumgardner, A. H. (1985). Self-handicapping. In J. H. Harvey & G. W. Weary (Eds.), *Attribution: Basic issues and applications* (pp. 169–202). Orlando, FL: Academic Press.

Arkin, R. M., Gabrenya, W. K., Jr., Appelman, A. S., & Cochran, S. T. (1979). Self-presentation, self-monitoring, and self-serving bias in causal attribution. *Personality and Social Psychology Bulletin, 5,* 73–76.

Baumgardner, A. H., Lake, E. A., & Arkin, R. M. (1985). Claiming mood as a self-handicap: The influence of spoiled and unspoiled public identities. *Personality and Social Psychology Bulletin, 11,* 349–357.

Berglas, S. (1989). Self-handicapping behavior and the self-defeating personality disorder: Toward a refined clinical perspective. In R. C. Curtis (Ed.), *Self-defeating behaviors: Experimental research and practical implications* (pp. 261–288). New York: Plenum.

Berglas, S., & Jones, E. E. (1978). Drug choice as a self-handicapping strategy in response to noncontingent success. *Journal of Personality and Social Psychology, 36,* 405–417.

Cantor, N., Markus, H., Niedenthal, P., & Nurius, P. (1986). On motivation and the self-concept. In R. M. Sorrentino & E. T. Higgins (Eds.), *Handbook of motivation and cognition: Foundations of social behavior* (pp. 96–127). New York: Guilford.

Carducci, B. J., & McNeely, J. A. (1981, August). *Alcohol and attributions don't mix: The effect of alcohol on alcoholics' and nonalcoholics' attributions of blame for wife abuse.* Paper presented at the meeting of the American Psychological Association, Los Angeles.

Cross, S. E., & Markus, H. (1989, May). *The role of self-schemas in effective performance.* Paper presented at the meeting of the Midwestern Psychological Association, Chicago.

Festinger, L. (1954). A theory of social comparison processes. *Human Relations, 7,* 117–140.

Gergen, K. J. (1968). Personal consistency and the presentation of the self. In C. Gordon & K. J. Gergen (Eds.), *The self in social interaction* (Vol, 1, pp. 299–308). New York: Wiley.

Gould, R., Brounstein, P. J., & Sigall, H. (1977). Attributing ability to an opponent: Public aggrandizement and private denigration. *Sociometry, 40,* 254–261.

Greenberg, J., Pyszczynski, T., & Paisley, C. (1985). Effect of extrinsic incentives on use of test anxiety as an anticipatory attributional defense: Playing it cool when the stakes are high. *Journal of Personality and Social Psychology, 47,* 1136–1145.

Handelsman, M. M., Kraiger, K., & King, C. S. (1985, April). *Self-handicapping by task choice: An attribute ambiguity analysis.* Paper presented at the meeting of the Rocky Mountain Psychological Association, Tucson, AZ.

Higgins, R. L., & Harris, R. N. (1988). Strategic "alcohol" use: Drinking to self-handicap. *Journal of Social and Clinical Psychology, 6,* 191–202.

Higgins, R. L., & Harris, R. N. (1989, April). *Self-handicapping social performance through "alcohol" use: The interaction of drinker history and expectancy.* Paper presented at the meeting of the Southwestern Psychological Association, Houston, TX.

Higgins, R. L., & Snyder, C. R. (1989). Excuses gone awry: An analysis of self-defeating excuses. In R. C. Curtis (Ed.), *Self-defeating behaviors: Experimental research and practical implications* (pp. 99–130). New York: Plenum.

Jones, E. E., & Berglas, S. (1978). Control of attributions about the self through self-handicapping strategies: The appeal of alcohol and the role of underachievement. *Personality and Social Psychology Bulletin, 4,* 200–206.

Kelley, H. H. (1972). Attribution in social interaction. In E. E. Jones, D. E. Kanouse, H. H. Kelley, R. E. Nisbett, S. Valins, & B. Weiner (Eds.), *Attribution: Perceiving the causes of behavior.* Morristown, NJ: General Learning Press.

Kolditz, T. A., & Arkin, R. M. (1982). An impression management interpretation of the self-handicapping strategy. *Journal of Personality and Social Psychology, 43,* 492–502.

Leary, M. R. (1983). Social anxiousness: The construct and its measurement. *Journal of Personality Assessment, 47,* 66–75.

Leary, M. R. (1986). The impact of interactional impediments on social anxiety and self-presentation. *Journal of Experimental Social Psychology, 22,* 122–135.

Leary, M. R., & Shepperd, J. A. (1986). Behavioral self-handicaps versus self-reported handicaps: A conceptual note. *Journal of Personality and Social Psychology, 51,* 1265–1268.

Leddo, J., Abelson, R. P., & Gross, P. H. (1984). Conjunctive explanations: When two reasons are better than one. *Journal of Personality and Social Psychology, 47,* 933–943.

Markus, H., & Wurf, E. (1987). The dynamic self-concept: A social psychological perspective. *Annual Review of Psychology, 38,* 299–337.

Mayerson, N. H., & Rhodewalt, F. (1988). The role of self-protective attributions in the experience of pain. *Journal of Social and Clinical Psychology, 6,* 203–218.

Mehlman, R. C., & Snyder, C. R. (1985). Excuse theory: A test of the self-protective role of attributions. *Journal of Personality and Social Psychology, 49,* 994–1001.

Pyszczynski, T., & Greenberg, J. (1983). Determinants of reduction in intended effort as a strategy for coping with anticipated failure. *Journal of Research in Personality, 17,* 412–422.

Rhodewalt, F., & Davison, J. (1986). Self-handicapping and subsequent performance: The role of outcome valence and attributional ambiguity. *Basic and Applied Social Psychology, 7,* 307–322.

Rhodewalt, F., Saltzman, A. T., & Wittmer, J. (1984). Self-handicapping among competitive athletes: The role of practice in self-esteem protection. *Basic and Applied Social Psychology, 5,* 197–210.

Sachs, P. R. (1982). Avoidance of diagnostic information in self-evaluation of ability. *Personality and Social Psychology Bulletin, 8,* 242–246.

Self, E. A. (1989, April). *Self-handicapping via a partner in a cooperative task.* Paper presented at the meeting of the Southwestern Psychological Association, Houston, TX.

Shepperd, J. A. (1988). *Cognitive other-enhancement: Protecting the self by perceiving advantages in a competitor.* Unpublished dissertation, University of Missouri, Columbia.

Shepperd, J. A., & Arkin, R. M. (1989a). Determinants of self-handicapping: Task importance and the effects of preexisting handicaps on self-generated handicaps. *Personality and Social Psychology Bulletin, 15,* 101–112.

Shepperd, J. A., & Arkin, R. M. (1989b). Self-handicapping: The moderating roles of public self-consciousness and task importance. *Personality and Social Psychology Bulletin, 15,* 252–265.

Shepperd, J. A., Arkin, R. M., Walker, M., & McSpadden, C. (1989, May). *Behavioral other-enhancement: An extension of self-handicapping.* Paper presented at the meeting of the Midwestern Psychological Association, Chicago.

Slaughter, J. G., Shaver, K. G., & Arkin, R. M. (1988). *Self-assessment and self-protection: The role of uncertainty and response context.* Paper presented at the annual meeting of the Midwestern Psychological Association, Chicago.

Smith, T. W., Snyder, C. R., & Handelsman, M. M. (1982). On the self-serving function of an academic wooden leg: Test anxiety as a self-handicapping strategy. *Journal of Personality and Social Psychology, 42,* 314–321.

Smith, T. W., Snyder, C. R., & Perkins, S. (1983). The self-serving function of hypochondriacal complaints: Physical symptoms as self-handicapping strategies. *Journal of Personality and Social Psychology, 44,* 787–797.

Snyder, C. R. (1985). Collaborative companions: The relationship of self-deception and excuse-making. In M. W. Martin (Ed.), *Self-deception and self-understanding* (pp. 35–51). Lawrence, KS: Regents Press of Kansas.

Snyder, C. R. (1989). Reality negotiation: From excuses to hope and beyond. *Journal of Social and Clinical Psychology, 8,* 130–157.

Snyder, C. R., & Higgins, R. L. (1988). Excuses: Their effective role in the negotiation of reality. *Psychological Bulletin, 104,* 23–35.

Snyder, C. R., & Higgins, R. L. (1989). Reality negotiation and excuse-making: President Reagan's 4 March 1987 Iran arms scandal speech and other literature. In M. J. Cody and M. L. McLaughlin (Eds.), *Psychology of tactical communication* (pp. 207–228). Clevedon, England: Multilingual Matters.

Snyder, C. R., & Smith, T. W. (1982). Symptoms as self-handicapping strategies: The virtues of old wine in a new bottle. In G. Weary and H. L. Mirels (Eds.), *Integrations of clinical and social psychology* (pp. 104–127). New York: Oxford University Press.

Snyder, C. R., Smith, T. W., Augelli, R. W., & Ingram, R. E. (1985). On the self-serving function of social anxiety: Shyness as a self-handicapping strategy. *Journal of Personality and Social Psychology, 48,* 970–980.

Snyder, M. L., Kleck, R. E., Strenta, A., & Mentzer, S. J. (1979). Avoidance of the handicapped: An attributional ambiguity analysis. *Journal of Personality and Social Psychology, 37,* 2297–2306.

Springston, F. J., & Chafe, P. M. (1987, June). *Impressions of fictional protagonists exhibiting self-handicapping behaviors.* Paper presented at the meeting of the Canadian Psychological Association, Vancouver, B.C.

Tetlock, P. E. (1981). The influence of self-presentation goals in attributional reports. *Social Psychology Quarterly, 44,* 300–311.

Tucker, J. A., Vuchinich, R. E., & Sobell, M. (1981). Alcohol consumption as a self-handicapping strategy. *Journal of Abnormal Psychology, 90,* 220–230.

Trope, Y. (1975). Seeking information about one's own ability as a determinant of choice among tasks. *Journal of Personality and Social Psychology, 32,* 1004–1013.

Weidner, G. (1980). Self-handicapping following learned helplessness treatment and the Type A coronary-prone behavior pattern. *Journal of Psychosomatic Research, 24,* 319–325.

CHAPTER 3

SELF-HANDICAPPERS
INDIVIDUAL DIFFERENCES IN THE PREFERENCE FOR ANTICIPATORY, SELF-PROTECTIVE ACTS

FREDERICK RHODEWALT

INTRODUCTION TO INDIVIDUAL DIFFERENCES IN SELF-HANDICAPPING

In 1984, at a point that many felt was the twilight of his golf career, Lee Trevino found himself leading the PGA Championship after the first round. Trevino had not won a tournament since 1981. At the age of 44, he was leading one of the premier events in his sport, a tournament that he would win three days later. When asked to explain his resurgence he replied that he had quit practicing, at his doctor's orders. Trevino, who had been suffering from chronic back problems, was instructed by his physician to give up his career-long habit of hitting 600 practice shots a day. Trevino cited an unanticipated benefit of his new regimen that was adding to the enjoyment he found in golf; "if I have a bad round, I say, 'What the hell, my doctor won't let me practice' " (Fowler, 1984, p. D1).

Jones and Berglas (1978) suggested that, "self-handicappers are legion in the sports world, from the tennis player who externalizes a bad

FREDERICK RHODEWALT • Department of Psychology, University of Utah, Salt Lake City, Utah 84112.

shot by adjusting his racket strings, to the avid golfer who systematically avoids taking lessons or even practicing on the driving range" (p. 201). Lee Trevino's comments provide vivid documentation of this observation. At his doctor's suggestion, Trevino forwent practice, when that very practice is usually thought to contribute to a good athletic performance. In so doing, Trevino reaped the benefits of the attributional principles of augmentation and discounting (Kelley, 1972). In the face of defeat, it was difficult to question Trevino's golf ability because of the equally plausible performance-inhibiting cause of lack of practice. We (and Trevino) are willing to *discount* the extent to which we infer that a lack of golf ability caused the poor play because of the presence of an inhibitory cause—lack of practice. Had we tuned in on the Sunday after Trevino won the tournament, it is possible that we could have witnessed the flip side of a process that is inherent in self-handicapping. That is, we (and possibly Trevino) would have *augmented* the attribution of the victory to Trevino's great golf ability, because it occurred in spite of the fact that he had neglected to practice. Win or lose, Lee Trevino's self-esteem was protected by the self-handicap.

Almost a decade of research now supports and elaborates upon Jones and Berglas's (1978) original self-handicapping formulation. Anticipated threats to self-esteem (Snyder & Smith, 1982) or, more specifically, uncertainty about one's ability (Berglas & Jones, 1978) appear to motivate the enactment of self-handicapping strategies. Self-handicapping can also occur in the service of self-presentational concerns (Kolditz & Arkin, 1982). Moreover, a wide range of self-handicapping strategies have been demonstrated. For example, the self-handicapping functions of drug and alcohol consumption (Berglas & Jones, 1978; Higgins & Harris, 1988a, 1988b; Tucker, Vuchinich, & Sobell, 1981), lack of practice (Rhodewalt, Saltzman, & Wittmer, 1984), reduced effort (Pyszczynski & Greenberg, 1983), unfavorable performance settings (Rhodewalt & Davison, 1986), test anxiety (Smith, Snyder, & Handelsman, 1982), and symptom reports (Smith, Snyder, & Perkins, 1983), among others, have been documented. In fact, the list of potential self-handicaps is so vast that Arkin and Baumgardner (1985) have proposed a self-handicapping taxonomy with which to organize this research. They suggest that self-handicaps may be acquired (e.g., consumption of alcohol) or claimed (e.g., reports of symptoms; see also Leary & Shepperd, 1986; Snyder & Smith, 1982). Furthermore, self-handicaps may also be internal (e.g., withdrawal of effort) or external (e.g., choice of nondiagnostic performance settings). Finally, there is evidence that self-handicaps are used attributionally by the self-handicapper in a self-protective fashion (Mayerson & Rhodewalt, 1988).

In sum, the conceptual underpinnings of self-handicapping appear to be fairly well documented, and demonstrations of the phenomenon are commonplace. It is with this background that I turn to the central issue of this chapter: Given that people in general employ self-handicapping strategies in order to protect self-esteem, are there individual differences in people's tendencies to choose this strategy? I will approach this question from several perspectives. First, I will examine individuals' proclivities to rely on what will be termed domain–strategy-specific self-handicaps. Next, I will describe attempts to assess more general and pervasive individual differences in self-handicapping tendencies. After surveying this work I will turn to an examination of other individual differences that are relevant to different self-handicapping motivations, such as self-esteem protection and self-presentational concerns. Consideration then will be given to the subject of sex differences in self-handicapping behavior. Finally, I will conclude by outlining future research directions and by drawing the implications of the individual difference findings for self-handicapping theory.

PREFERENCES FOR DOMAIN–STRATEGY-SPECIFIC SELF-HANDICAPPING

Lee Trevino's use of lack of practice as a self-handicapping strategy exemplifies one way in which individual differences in self-handicapping can be manifested. On his doctor's recommendation he dropped his extensive practice routine. One would assume that Trevino learned of the self-handicapping benefits of this prescription only after suspending practice to cure his aching back. There are many such circumstances in which people initially engage in a behavior for motives other than self-esteem protection. For example, one may consume alcohol to reduce stress, or delay in preparing for a task as a consequence of other, more pressing demands. However, by serendipity or otherwise, people may come to appreciate the self-handicapping function of a behavior or characteristic and continue to use it in a self-protective role in future settings. In this way, behaviors may be maintained or even expanded because of their self-handicapping utility.

Domain–strategy-specific handicaps may be limited to circumscribed evaluative situations or may be broader and reduce the diagnosticity of potential self-evaluative feedback across a range of performance and social settings. An example of the former would be continually foregoing practice prior to a skill-dependent performance, while an example of the latter would be continually acting out the "sick role" associated with a chronic but nondebilitating illness or injury. Jones and Berglas (1978; Berglas, 1986) suggest that alcoholism and underachievement are just such handicaps. The alcoholic and the chronic underachiever have grasped the notion that drinking or lack of effort spares them from confronting the more self-damaging implications of failure feedback.

Symptoms as Domain–Strategy-Specific Self-Handicaps

Claims of psychological distress or physical symptoms are good examples of domain–strategy-specific self-handicaps. In fact, Snyder and Smith (1982) argued for such a conclusion when they updated the self-handicapping concept by incorporating the Adlerian notion of the self-protective, strategic use of symptoms (see Chapter 1, this volume, for discussion of this perspective). In this formulation, individuals cite, and may well experience, physical and psychological afflictions in the service of self-esteem protection. The laborer who injures his back on the job may come to learn that the lingering back pain shields his fragile athletic ego when he plays third base on the company softball team. Indeed, in a recent investigation, Mayerson and Rhodewalt (1988) demonstrated that pain reports could be used in such a self-handicapping fashion. Under the guise of studying a measure of intelligence that was relatively unaffected by distraction, we administered two analogy tests to subjects. They took the first test while listening to distracting noise and the second while experiencing painful stimulation (one hand immersed in ice water). After the first test, subjects received either response-contingent or noncontingent success feedback. In other words, all subjects performed well under trying circumstances, but only half were uncertain about their ability to perform well again.

Prior to taking the second test, subjects provided baseline ratings of the painfulness of the ice water. They were informed that, although test performance was relatively unaffected by pain distraction, this was only true up to moderate levels of pain. If the individual found the ice water too painful it would, in fact, reduce the validity of the test results. Subjects were asked to provide the baseline pain ratings to help us interpret their performance on the upcoming test. Subjects then took the second test with their nondominant hand immersed in the ice water and learned that they were either successful or unsuccessful on this test. The findings clearly indicate that pain reports can be used as a self-handicap. Noncontingent success subjects were more likely to offer baseline pain ratings that would reduce the diagnosticity of feedback on the second test. This interpretation is corroborated by the self-attributions offered by self-handicappers and non-self-handicappers after they learned that they had succeeded or failed on the second test. Specifically, in the failure feedback condition, self-handicappers reported that their poor performance did not reflect low ability, and non-self-handicappers indicated that their poor performance was attributable to lack of ability. Failing self-handicappers also claimed that the pain interfered with their performance, while non-self-handicappers did not.

Thus, we have clear experimental evidence that individuals who anticipate a potential threat to self-esteem will use symptom reports in a strategic, self-protective fashion (see also Smith *et al.*, 1982; Smith *et al.*, 1983; Snyder, Smith, Augelli, & Ingram, 1985). Although as yet untested, an underlying interest in this research is the generalizability of our findings to chronic pain patients. Such patients suffer from the persistent and often debilitating experience of pain. Very often it is difficult to identify the organic cause of the symptoms. Moreover, although the pain is fairly constant, pain patients typically report wide variation in the intensity of symptoms. Although at present highly speculative, we suggest that one source of variation in the symptom reports of chronic pain patients is the level of potential self-esteem threat they encounter from day to day.

INDIVIDUAL DIFFERENCES IN THE STRATEGIC USE OF SYMPTOM REPORTS

The above conjectures about self-handicapping and chronic pain patients gain plausibility when considered in the context of a series of studies conducted by Smith, Snyder, and their colleagues (Smith *et al.*, 1982; Smith *et al.*, 1983; Snyder *et al.*, 1985). Overall, this work supports the proposition that individuals vary in their employment of "trait"- or "state"-specific self-handicaps. For example, individuals who are characteristically high in social shyness, test anxiety, or hypochondriasis appear to be more prone than individuals who are low on those characteristics to modulate their symptom reports as a function of self-esteem threat.

In the Smith and Snyder paradigm, subjects who are characteristically high or low in the propensity to report specific psychological or physical symptoms are told that the symptom is not a viable excuse for poor performance on an ego-relevant task. For example, Smith *et al.* (1982) preselected subjects on the basis of their responses to the Test Anxiety Questionnaire (Sarason, 1980). High and low test-anxious individuals were led to believe that they were taking a two-part test that was either to provide local norms for a standardized intelligence test (high evaluative threat) or to provide pilot data for experimental materials (low evaluative threat). Crosscutting the evaluative threat manipulation was information subjects were given about the effects of anxiety on test performance. Subjects were informed that the test either was or was not adversely influenced by anxiety, or they were provided no information. Measures of state anxiety obtained after subjects completed the first test indicated that test-anxious subjects reported elevated levels of anxiety only if they were confronted with a threat to self-esteem *and* if anxiety was a reasonable excuse for failure. The experimental manipulations had no effect on the anxiety reports of low test-anxious individuals. Interestingly, high test-anxious individuals who believed they were taking an important test that was unaffected by anxiety reported that they were expending reduced effort compared to other subjects. This finding suggests that high test-anxious individuals' appreciation for self-handicapping extends beyond their strategic use of anxiety reports—a point to which I will return in the next section.

SUMMARY

In sum, the research by Smith, Snyder, and colleagues provides consistent evidence that an individual difference variable (test anxiety, social shyness, or hypochondriasis) predicts the strategic use of self-handicapping in response to potential threats to self-esteem. Consistent with the analysis of symptom reports as self-handicaps, Baumeister and Kahn (1982) suggest that obesity might also serve a self-handicapping function in some overweight individuals.

Test anxiety, shyness, and hypochondriasis are similar in that they all rely on reports of debilitating physical or psychological conditions. However, they differ in terms of the ranges of situations they may affect. The subjective experience and public reports of test anxiety are limited to ability-relevant assessments. In the same way, shyness as a self-handicap is applicable to a limited number of socially evaluative situations. In contrast, the chronic health complaints of the hypochondriac or obese individual may serve self-protective functions across many different domains of self-esteem threat. A possible implication of this distinction is that attempts to treat or modify such "maladaptive behavior" will be more successful to the extent that the self-handicapping function is recognized and the range of contexts in which the handicap is employed is identified.

It is up to future research to elaborate the contribution of self-handicapping processes in the maintenance of a variety of seemingly self-limiting or self-defeating conditions. Of particular interest are the individual and situational preconditions that transform a transient condition into an enduring mode of self-handicapping (see Higgins & Snyder, 1989, for a related discussion of these issues).

GENERALIZED PREFERENCES FOR SELF-HANDICAPPING BEHAVIOR

The use of symptom reports as self-handicaps provides evidence that some individuals will chronically employ a circumscribed mode of self-handicapping. Another way of approaching the individual difference question is to ask if individuals reliably differ in their appreciation for and employment of a variety of self-handicapping strategies. That is, are there characteristic differences among people in the extent to which they enact a mixture of self-handicaps across a wide range of evaluative situations. Rather than being wedded to one handicapping strategy, perhaps deployed in a particular evaluative setting, it may be that certain individuals seek the opportunity to perform in nondiagnostic contexts whenever and wherever self-evaluative threat is anticipated. These individuals are flexible in that they will call upon any plausible claim or available impediment to performance. Again, Lee Trevino's comments at the 1984 PGA Tournament are illustrative. Recall that he reduced his practice time to cure a chronically aching back. Perhaps Trevino's readiness to appreciate the self-handicapping implications of lack of practice are related to his prior experience with the self-protective benefits of the back ailment.

Is there such a person as the chronic self-handicapper? In the late 1970s, Edward E. Jones and several of his students attempted to provide an answer to this question by devising a questionnaire that directly probed individuals about their self-handicapping behaviors and motivations. Our initial work with this scale indicated that it correlated substantially with low self-esteem (r's .30 to .50), a circumstance that appeared to be theoretically interesting but psychometrically problematic. We designed the Self-Handicapping Scale (SHS) to assess preferences for the use of self-handicapping behavior. Because we sought to demonstrate that the SHS was tapping more than a subject's willingness to confess unflattering or inappropriate behavior (i.e., low self-esteem), we attempted to reduce the overlap of the SHS with self-esteem. Over the next several years Jones and I modified the wording of items on the scale in order to reduce its negative correlation with self-esteem. In addition, we added items that we thought assessed domains of self-handicapping not previously tapped in earlier versions of the scale. The SHS employed in current research, and displayed in Figure 1, has remained unchanged since 1982.

This brief historical sketch of the early development of the SHS is provided as a backdrop against which to appreciate subsequent research with the scale. Our intent was to devise a face-valid "in house" instrument that assessed the extent to which people reported (admitted) engaging in self-handicapping behavior. Our training and interest are not in psychometric methodologies and concerns but rather in investigating theoretical issues that can often best be examined using the person-by-situation approach. Nonetheless, the SHS has demonstrated adequate validity and reliability. Admittedly, however, the SHS could benefit by refinement, an issue I will address momentarily. With this caveat stated, we can now turn to research using the SHS.

The SHS (Jones & Rhodewalt, 1982) is a questionnaire that asks respondents to indicate the extent to which they agree with the applicability of 25 self-descriptive statements. The scale probes respondents' tendencies to use such self-handicapping behaviors as lack of effort, illness, procrastination, or emotional upsettedness in conjunction with evaluative performances. The scale also includes items designed to assess concerns about achievement. Eight of the items, such as "I hate to be in any condition but my best," are worded in the direction of low self-handicapping. Respondents indicate their agreement with each statement on 6-point scales bounded by the endpoints, *agree very much* to *disagree very much*.

RELIABILITY AND VALIDITY OF THE SELF-HANDICAPPING SCALE

The SHS has been administered in large group-testing sessions and has exhibited acceptable internal consistency (Cronbach's alpha, $r(503) = .79$) and stability (test–retest reliability at one month, $r(90) = .74$). Data collected from several different samples provide a composite of the SHS's discriminant and convergent validity. As one can see in Table 1, high SHS scores are associated significantly with low self-esteem, as measured by the Janis and Field Feelings of Inadequacy Scale (see Robinson & Shaver, 1973). Also, as one might expect, high self-handicappers score low on the Marlowe–Crowne Social Desirability Scale (Crowne & Marlowe, 1964). In addition, high self-handicappers have a tendency to make situational attributions for their outcomes, as assessed by the Lowe and Medway (1976) Person–Environment Causal Attribution Scale. In contrast, the SHS appears to be unrelated to Mehrabian's (1968) measure of need for achievement. Finally, one can see that high self-handicappers also score high on the Profile of Limbic Lability, an instru-

Please indicate (by writing a number in the blank before each item) the degree to which you agree with each of the following statements as a description of the kind of person you think you are most of the time. Use the following scale:

0 = disagree very much
1 = disagree pretty much
2 = disagree a little
3 = agree a little
4 = agree pretty much
5 = agree very much

_____ 1. When I do something wrong, my first impulse is to blame the circumstances.
_____ 2. I tend to put things off to the last moment.
_____ 3. I tend to overprepare when I have any kind of exam or "performance."*
_____ 4. I suppose I feel "under the weather" more often than most people.
_____ 5. I always try to do my best, no matter what.*
_____ 6. Before I sign up for a course or engage in any important activity, I make sure I have the proper preparation or background.*
_____ 7. I tend to get very anxious before an exam or "performance."
_____ 8. I am easily distracted by noises or my own creative thoughts when I try to read.
_____ 9. I try not to get too intensely involved in competitive activities so it won't hurt too much if I lose or do poorly.
_____ 10. I would rather be respected for doing my best than admired for my potential.*
_____ 11. I would do a lot better if I tried harder.
_____ 12. I prefer the small pleasures in the present to the larger pleasures in the dim future.
_____ 13. I generally hate to be in any condition but "at my best."*
_____ 14. Someday I might "get it all together."
_____ 15. I sometimes enjoy being mildly ill for a day or two because it takes off the pressure.
_____ 16. I would do much better if I did not let my emotions get in the way.
_____ 17. When I do poorly at one kind of thing, I often console myself by remembering I am good at other things.
_____ 18. I admit that I am tempted to rationalize when I don't live up to others' expectations.
_____ 19. I often think I have more than my share of bad luck in sports, card games, and other measures of talent.
_____ 20. I would rather not take any drug that interfered with my ability to think clearly and do the right thing.*
_____ 21. I overindulge in food and drink more often than I should.
_____ 22. When something important is coming up, like an exam or a job interview, I try to get as much sleep as possible the night before.*
_____ 23. I never let emotional problems in one part of my life interfere with things in my life.*
_____ 24. Usually, when I get anxious about doing well, I end up doing better.
_____ 25. Sometimes I get so depressed that even easy tasks become difficult.

*Indicates the item is reverse scored.

FIGURE 1. Self-handicapping scale (Jones & Rhodewalt, 1982).

TABLE 1. Correlations between SHS and
Other Individual Difference Measures

Measure	Self-handicapping scale
Feelings of inadequacy[a]	−.43***
Social desirability[a]	−.43***
nachievement[a]	−.06
Person–environment[a] Causal attribution[a]	.20***
Profile of limbic lability[b]	.40***
Jenkins activity survey[b]	−.11
Beck depression inventory[c]	.43**
Feelings of inadequacy[c]	−.38** (−.37**)
Public self-consciousness[c]	.22* (.11)
Private self-consciousness[c]	.09 (.14)
Social anxiety[c]	.32** (.11)
Extraversion[c]	−.18 (−.17)
Other-directedness[c]	.36** (.26*)
Acting ability[c]	.00 (.05)

[a]Sample I, $n = 503$.
[b]Sample II, $n = 96$.
[c]Strube (1985) sample, $n = 168$; correlations for
females are in parentheses.
* = $p < .05$; ** = $p < .01$; *** = $p < .001$.

ment designed by Pennebaker (1982) to measure the extent to which people are aware of their somatic functioning. This correlation is consistent with the notion that self-handicappers are likely to attend to their physical status for self-handicapping purposes (Smith *et al.*, 1983; Snyder & Smith, 1982).

As one will note in Table 1, the SHS is unrelated to scores on the Jenkins Activity Survey (Krantz, Glass, & Snyder, 1974), a measure of Type A coronary-prone behavior. The absence of this association is important because several investigators have speculated that Type A's should be prone to self-handicapping (Harris & Snyder, 1986; Weidner, 1980). I will return to this issue later in this chapter.

I (Rhodewalt, 1984) have also examined the item structure of the SHS by subjecting the responses of 503 respondents to principal components factor analyses (Gorsuch, 1974). These analyses extracted seven factors, each with eigenvalues greater than 1.0; they accounted for 52.3% of the total item variance. However, closer examination of these eigenvalues via a scree test revealed that one major break occurred between

Factors 2 and 3. This suggests that the SHS has two major factors. The item factor loadings for the two-factor solution are presented in Table 2. An item was included in a factor if it had a loading of greater than .40 on that factor and less than .20 on the others.

Factor 1 accounts for 17.4% of the variance and comprises nine items. This factor appears to reflect a proclivity for excuse making and includes items such as "When I do something wrong, my first impulse is to blame the circumstances," "I suppose I feel 'under the weather' more often than most," and "I would do much better if I did not let my emotions get in the way." Factor 2 accounted for 10.9% of the item variance and included four items that appeared to reflect concern about effort or motivation. The items included, "I tend to put things off until the last minute" and "I would do a lot better if I tried harder." Table 2 displays the item factor loadings, the individual item–remainder correlations, and the item–self-esteem correlations. Finally, respondents scor-

TABLE 2. Self-Handicapping Scale Factor Loadings

Item	Factor 1	Factor 2	Item/remainder	Item/self-esteem
1	.43	.19	.47	−.20
2	.13	.71	.47	−.11
3			.04	−.00
4	.68	.00	.52	−.32
5	.08	.39	−.23	.13
6			.02	.01
7			.26	−.19
8	.18	.44	.44	−.25
9	.58	.11	.47	−.27
10			−.04	.08
11	.11	.63	.42	−.11
12			.37	−.12
13			.04	.06
14	.19	.42	.43	−.15
15	.59	.08	.51	−.16
16	.55	.06	.51	−.29
17			.22	.15
18	.43	.20	.50	−.11
19	.62	.14	.51	−.37
20			−.16	.05
21	.40	.16	.49	−.13
22			−.11	.04
23			.21	−.10
24			.13	.15
25	.66	.07	.58	−.36

ing in the upper and lower quartiles of the SHS were selected, and t tests were computed between the groups on each individual item score. This analysis mirrored the item–remainder correlational analysis in that six of the items (Items 3, 6, 10, 13, 20, and 22) failed to discriminate reliably between the extreme groups.

Further validity data are provided by Strube (1985), although caution needs to be exercised when interpreting these data because an earlier 20-item version of the SHS was used. Strube reasoned that the SHS might be useful in resolving the debate over whether self-handicapping is in the service of self-protective or self-presentational motives (Berglas & Jones, 1978; Kolditz & Arkin, 1982). Accordingly, he included the Self-Consciousness Scale (Fenigstien, Scheier, & Buss, 1975) in order to examine the relations among the SHS, Private Self-Consciousness, Public Self-Consciousness, and Social Anxiety. Additionally, he correlated the SHS with the Extraversion, Other-Directedness, and Acting subscales of the Self-Monitoring Scale (M. Snyder, 1974; Briggs, Cheek, & Buss, 1980). Finally, Strube included the Feelings of Inadequacy Scale (Robinson & Shaver, 1973) and the Beck Depression Inventory (Beck, Ward, Mendelson, Mock, & Erbaugh, 1961). As in our data, the SHS was modestly, negatively correlated with low self-esteem and positively related to depression. For both males and females, SHS scores were related to the Other-Directedness component of self-monitoring and, for males only, scores were related to Public Self-Consciousness.

Strube interpreted these findings to be consistent with the view that self-handicapping was primarily for self-presentational concerns. However, the data are not completely consistent with this conclusion. First, the correlations between SHS and Public Self-Consciousness and Social Anxiety are not significant when self-esteem is covaried. Second, there is the reliable negative association between the SHS and concerns for social desirability mentioned previously. Thus it may be that concerns about social approval accompany low self-esteem, but it is not necessarily the case that such concerns are the sole, or even prime, motivation to self-handicap.

Taken together, these analyses suggest that future research with the SHS should use an abridged form containing the 14 items loading on Factors 1 and 2 in order to increase its reliability. The coefficient alpha of .79 for the 14-item scale is comparable to that of the full 25-item SHS. Likewise, the short and long forms of the SHS evidence negative correlations with self-esteem that are similar in magnitude ($rs = -.41, -.43$, respectively).

It is also striking that Strube's (1985) factor analysis of an earlier version of the SHS led to essentially the same recommendation. Keep in mind, however, that the SHS described here and used in most of the research described in this chapter differs in several ways from the form used by Strube (1985). In addition to having more items tapping into more domains of self-handicapping behavior, carry-over items from earlier forms of the 25-item SHS have been reworded to load less in the direction of low self-esteem. These differences not withstanding, all 10 items included on the short form of the SHS recommended by Strube are included in slightly reworded form in the abridged SHS derived from our own analyses. Thus, the Strube data may be viewed as a cross validation of the factor analysis presented here. It is also noteworthy that Strube's short form of the SHS correlated somewhat higher with low self-esteem ($r = -.50$) than our abridged SHS, indicating that our attempt to reword items to be less self-esteem laden was somewhat successful.

Finally, it is of interest that the SHS's largest factor is one that appears to reflect a general proclivity for excuse making. This finding is noteworthy because it lends support to Snyder, Higgins, and Stucky's (1983) contention that self-handicapping belongs in the larger category of anticipatory excuse making. Thus, the SHS may be measuring a general tendency to employ self-protective strategies including self-handicaps, excuses, disclaimers (Hewitt & Stokes, 1975), and, possibly, rationalizations.

SELF-HANDICAPPING AND THE SELF-HANDICAPPING SCALE

Perhaps the most critical test in the validation of a measure of individual differences is its ability to predict the behavior or underlying characteristic in question. To what extent, then, is the SHS successful in predicting self-handicapping behavior? A handful of investigations now exist that document the predictive utility of the SHS for a variety of self-handicapping behaviors. Generally, this research finds that as the likelihood of threat to self-esteem increases, those scoring high on the SHS are more likely to acquire or claim a handicap than are those scoring low on the SHS.

For example, scores on the SHS should be inversely related to academic achievement. Jones and Berglas (1978) suggested that under-achievement is a particularly chronic manifestation of self-handicapping behavior. The underachiever, by being respected for his or her potential rather than actual accomplishment, is able to protect the illusion that his or her ability is quite high. As a subsidiary interest in our study of self-handicapping among competitive athletes (Rhodewalt, Saltzman, & Wittmer, 1984). Andy Saltzman and I attempted to construct an index of over–underachievement using subjects' SAT scores as the measure of aptitude and their grade point averages as the measure of achievement. In order to place this index on an interval scale, we employed the formula $1 + \log (GPA/SAT \times 1{,}000)$ and correlated the outcome with the subjects' SHS scores.

To illustrate, consider three students, all of whom have SATs of 1,200 but GPAs of 3.0, 2.0, and 1.0, respectively. Their corresponding over–underachievement scores would be 1.40, 1.22, and 0.92. In the Saltzman thesis (Rhodewalt et al., 1984), high SHS scores were associated with underachievement ($r = -.25$), but not reliably so. Suspecting that both the small sample size ($n = 27$) and restricted ranges of SATs and GPAs weakened the test, I (Rhodewalt, 1984) examined the same relationship in a larger sample of introductory psychology undergraduates (substituting ACT scores for the SAT) and found high SHS scores to be reliably correlated with underachievement ($r (90) = -.43, p < .01$).

Self-handicappers also seem to be quite willing to bear the label of "underachiever." Embedded among background information appended to the end of the SHS, respondents are typically asked to categorize themselves as either a "distinct underachiever," "normal achiever," or "distinct overachiever." This self-rating of achievement correlates negatively with SHS scores ($r(503) = -.26, p < .001$). Thus, consistent with Jones and Berglas's assertion, both "objective data" and self-reports indicate that high self-handicappers tend to be underachievers.

The major purpose of the Saltzman thesis (study 1, Rhodewalt et al., 1984) was to investigate differences between SHS-defined high and low self-handicappers in the strategic use of self-protective behavior. In particular, we were interested in the use of these strategies in the face of evaluative threat. We attempted to substantiate the Jones and Berglas (1978) contention that self-handicapping is prevalent in the world of athletics. In order to test this hypothesis, we collected SHS scores from all the members of the Princeton University men's swimming team in an unrelated context prior to the beginning of their season, and observed their behavior over the course of one season. Although a wide range of responses was collected, the focal dependent variables were the swimmers' strategic use of practice effort and claims of injury as self-handicaps. Evaluative threat was operationally defined as the team members' consensus rating of the importance of each swim meet to the success of the team's season. We then compared practice attendance and practice effort as rated by the coach prior to important and less important swim meets. In addition, on the day prior to each competition, the swimmers completed a questionnaire concerning their perceptions of their practice, health, visits to the trainer, eating and sleeping, and academic course load for the preceding week.

Our prediction was that high self-handicappers, as compared to low self-handicappers, would "take a dive" prior to important meets by withholding practice effort and by claiming health problems. The hypothesis was confirmed in a slightly altered fashion. For both practice attendance and coach's ratings of practice effort, low self-handicappers increased their training prior to important meets while high self-handicappers did not. In other words, high self-handicappers did not decrease training effort, they simply did not turn up their effort relative to their low self-handicapping counterparts. Interestingly, there were no high versus low self-handicapper differences on the coach's ratings of actual meet performance, nor were there differences in the swimmers' self-reported appraisals of their practice efforts. With regard to illness or injury reports, there was a marginally significant tendency for high self-handicappers to visit the team trainer more than low self-handicappers, regardless of meet importance.

Surprisingly, self-handicapping swimmers' self-reports of effort did not map on to their self-handicapping behavior as seen by their coach, nor did they engage in behavior that was obviously self-defeating. Our attempts to account for this paradox centered on the fact that participation in a team sport might inhibit one's more blatant attempts to self-handicap for fear of sanctions by teammates. Accordingly, Jerry Wittmer and I attempted to replicate our findings using athletes from an individual sport, golf (Study 2, Rhodewalt et al., 1984).

Professional golfers competing in state-level tournaments completed the SHS at the beginning of their competitive season and then completed questionnaires prior to each tournament. The questionnaires probed such issues as the number of hours the player practiced in the past week, nongolf hours worked, and personal or health problems encountered. Tournaments were grouped into high and low importance based on consensus estimates provided by the golfers. The findings indicated that higher as compared to lower self-handicappers claimed to spend less time practicing in general, and significantly less time practicing during the week prior to important tournaments. However, the pattern of data was similar to that for the Princeton swimmers in that the significant handicapping effect resulted from low self-handicappers increasing their practice time before important tournaments rather than from high self-handicappers decreasing their effort. Again, as with swimmers, there was a marginal tendency for high self-handicapping golfers to report being in poorer physical condition compared to low self-handicappers.

Despite their claims and protestations, high self-handicappers appeared to compete as well as, if not better than, low self-handicappers.

Golfers in the study were awarded Grand Prix points for their finishes in each tournament. An analysis of the total Grand Prix point rankings at the end of the season revealed a marginally significant tendency for high self-handicappers to accumulate more points than low self-handicappers. This finding supports C. R. Snyder's view (see Chapter 4) that self-handicapping frequently provides benefits to the individual.

In both of the above investigations, athletes identified as high self-handicappers by the SHS curbed their practice preparation prior to important athletic contests. Ironically, but consistent with self-handicapping theory, data available only in the swimmers study indicated that self-handicappers rated important meets as also being more personally important than did low self-handicappers. In neither study was there a clear preference for the athletes to use claims of injury as handicaps, although there were indications that self-handicappers might do so. Another theoretically consistent but unpredicted outcome observed in both studies was that self-handicappers rated the performance conditions of important competitions as less favorable for good performance than did low self-handicappers. This suggests that handicappers may use different self-protective attributional strategies simultaneously.

The findings from the above field studies demonstrate, at minimum, that Lee Trevino is not alone in his appreciation for the value of forgoing practice as means of protecting self-esteem.* However, the interpretive ambiguities inherent in field studies have led us to pursue the relations among self-handicapping, evaluative threat, and effort in the laboratory. To do so, Marita Fairfield and I (Rhodewalt & Fairfield, 1989) modified a paradigm developed by Pyzsczynski and Greenberg (1983). Participants who had completed the SHS in an earlier unrelated setting were led to

---

*Anecdotal evidence from the Rhodewalt, Saltzman, and Wittmer study provides testimonial to the temporal stability of the preference for this tactic. One of the golfers was experiencing a particularly difficult season during the summer of the study (1982). This followed a year in which he had been quite successful, winning several state tournaments. When approached by one of the research assistants just prior to the start of a tournament, he angrily claimed that neither his personal nor professional life had gone right since agreeing to participate in our study. With that announcement, he took the questionnaire offered by the research assistant and trampled it with his golf spikes. We viewed this as a request to withdraw his consent to participate but could not resist the temptation to look at his self-handicapping score. He had the highest score of any surveyed in the study. A sidebar to this incident is that the same golfer recently finished first in a qualifying tournament for the United States Open. His statement to the local press when asked to comment on his victory was that he was very pleased, especially because he had not had time to practice before the event.

believe that they would be participating in an evaluation study of a culture-fair test of general intelligence (high ego relevance) or helping to pilot materials for an upcoming study (low ego relevance). After completing a set of practice problems that was either somewhat easy or fairly difficult, the experimental session was interrupted by an individual purporting to represent the psychology department which, ostensibly, was surveying all psychology experiment volunteers. Subjects were given a questionnaire which queried them concerning their treatment and their perceptions of the experiment. It was stressed that their responses were anonymous (there was no obvious identifying information on the form), and that they were to be as candid as possible because their responses would help researchers better interpret information gathered in such studies. After the "department representative" collected the questionnaires and left the laboratory, subjects were administered 50 items from the Culture Fair Test of g (Cattell & Cattell, 1960).

As expected, subjects who encountered difficult practice problems anticipated doing more poorly on the test than did subjects who received easy practice problems; high ego-relevance subjects reported the test to be more important than did low ego-relevance subjects. In addition, high self-handicappers, as compared to low self-handicappers, stated that they felt the test was more important and that they would be more displeased with failure. With regard to reports of intended effort, high self-handicappers indicated that they intended to put forth less effort in general, but were particularly likely to do so if they expected the test to be difficult. This interaction between self-handicapping and expected difficulty held regardless of whether subjects believed the test to be an important assessment of their intelligence or an unimportant experimental exercise. Analyses of the number of problems correctly solved on the actual test indicated that self-handicappers' professions of low effort were born out in their performances. Pair-wise comparisons revealed that, although high and low self-handicappers did not differ in their performances when they expected the test to be easy, low self-handicappers performed significantly better than high self-handicappers when they expected the test to be difficult. Moreover, as the level of anticipated difficulty increased, so did the performance of low self-handicappers, while the performance of high self-handicappers decreased.

The overall picture that emerges from these findings is that, in the realms of athletic and intellectual performance, high self-handicappers, as defined by the SHS, both report expending less effort and actually withhold effort and practice in the face of potential self-damaging feedback.

Self-Handicapping and Self-Esteem

There is another explanation for the findings presented in the previous section. Because high scores on the SHS are associated with low self-esteem, it may be that it is low self-esteem that is the operative individual difference accounting for our findings. That is, all of the self-report and behavioral data may be attributable to individuals with low self-esteem giving up in the face of difficult or important events. There are several pieces of logical and empirical evidence that argue against this conclusion, however.

First, self-handicapping theoretically is enacted in the service of self-esteem protection (see Jones & Berglas, 1978; Snyder & Smith, 1982; and Chapters 1 and 2 in this volume for more extended discussions). People with completely negative self-concepts should have nothing to protect and, consequently, should have no need to self-handicap. In support of this reasoning, Tice and Baumeister (1984) found that high self-esteem (but not low self-esteem) individuals handicapped by not practicing for a test. Following from Jones and Berglas's (1978) theorizing it is *uncertainty* about one's positive self-conceptions and abilities that is the critical motive driving self-handicapping behavior. Theoretically, the propensity to self-handicap should be independent of level of self-esteem.

This latter speculation is supported by recent evidence provided by Harris and Snyder (1986). Subjects in the Harris and Snyder study filled out a self-esteem inventory and indicated how certain they were of their responses to each item. Subjects were then provided the opportunity to practice or "warm up" for an intelligence test on which they would subsequently receive feedback. Male subjects who were uncertain of their self-evaluations self-handicapped more (practiced less) than any other group of subjects. This effect was independent of their actual level of self-esteem and indicates that it is individuals who are uncertain about their wherewithal to generate positive feedback or to avoid negative feedback who are most likely to self-handicap.

The fact remains, however, that roughly 16 to 20% of the variance in the SHS is shared with self-esteem. Some of this relationship is probably accounted for by the content of the items on the SHS. The respondent is quizzed about his or her shortcomings, failures, and unpleasant experiences—events that are undoubtedly more likely to be included in the personal histories of low self-esteem individuals. It is also more likely that low self-esteem individuals are willing to admit committing acts that cast a publicly unflattering image of themselves. This raises the possibility that the SHS is providing a more accurate estimate of the self-handicapping tendencies of lower self-esteem individuals than of others.

On the Independence of Self-Handicapping and Self-Esteem

Self-handicapping and self-esteem are psychometrically intertwined, but, theoretically, they are independent constructs. Therefore, it should be possible to examine self-handicapping behavior independently of its association with self-esteem. A follow-up study by Rhodewalt and Fairfield (Study 2, 1989) indicates that this is the case. We replicated our earlier demonstration of self-handicapping and intended effort in anticipation of an easy or difficult test and added a measure of self-esteem in our pretest. As in our first study, high self-handicappers anticipating a difficult test indicated that they would put forth less effort than did low self-handicappers expecting a difficult test and both high and low self-handicappers expecting an easy test. More importantly, these findings emerged even when subjects' levels of self-esteem were controlled. With regard to actual performance or effort, the interaction between level of self-handicapping and expected difficulty was again obtained. However, the interaction was attributable both to low self-handicappers' performance increasing when they expected the test to be difficult and to high self-handicappers' performance declining slightly. We also included a thought-listing procedure designed to tap cognitive interferences experienced by the participant while taking the exam. High self-handicappers taking a test they expected to be difficult reported levels of cognitive interference that were significantly higher than levels reported by high self-handicappers in the expected easy test condition and low self-handicappers regardless of test difficulty condition. That is, self-handicappers who were performing in an evaluative setting they anticipated being difficult complained that, while working on the task, their minds wandered to thoughts such as, "I thought about my level of ability," "I thought about how much time I had left," and "I thought about things unrelated to the experiment." Again, these findings were independent of the subjects' levels of self-esteem.

In a study paralleling ours, Strube (Study 2, 1985) assessed students for levels of self-handicapping and self-esteem. Then, on two occasions (after a first exam and 2 days prior to a second exam), subjects completed a checklist of extenuating circumstances that could have prevented (or might prevent) them from exhibiting their true abilities on the tests. Self-esteem scores were covaried from these ratings, and SHS effects again remained reliable. Self-handicappers, particularly males, cited more extenuating factors being present both immediately after taking an exam (self-serving bias) and 2 days prior to taking an exam (claimed self-handicapping).

Strube and Roemmele (1985) have investigated the relation between SHS-defined self-handicapping and self-esteem from a different perspective than the one described above. Borrowing the self-evaluative task choice paradigm developed by Trope (1980), Strube and Roemmele (1985) asked SHS-defined high and low self-handicappers who were either above or below the median in self-esteem to select among tests of intelligence that varied in the diagnosticity of the success and failure feedback that they provided. Subjects were asked to indicate which test was most accurate and which they preferred. Although all subjects recognized that a highly diagnostic test is the most accurate, high self-handicappers who were low in self-esteem preferred (and actually opted to take) the test form that was high in diagnosticity for success but low in diagnosticity for failure. Interestingly, high self-esteem, high self-handicapping subjects evenly split in their test preferences. Some selected tests that were highly diagnostic of both success and failure, while others selected tests that were diagnostic of success only. Low self-handicappers, regardless of self-esteem level, preferred tests that were highly diagnostic of both success and failure.

On the Relation of Self-Handicapping to Self-Esteem

The findings discussed in the preceding section suggest that, although lower self-esteem is associated with high SHS scores, individual preferences for self-handicapping are fairly independent of self-esteem. Nonetheless, self-handicapping and self-esteem are intimately related in that the former is deployed in order to protect the latter. What, then, is the nature of the relationship between self-handicapping and self-esteem?

Among high self-handicappers, it is possible that level of self-esteem reflects a threshold for perceived threat to the self that triggers strategic self-protective behaviors. That is, low self-esteem, high self-handicapping individuals may engage in chronic self-handicapping, while high self-esteem, high self-handicapping individuals, may only self-handicap in the less frequent instances of perceived self-evaluative threat. An even more speculative hypothesis that we are presently exploring in our laboratory is that low self-esteem, high self-handicapping individuals exclusively engage in protective self-handicapping, but high self-esteem, high self-handicapping individuals enact self-handicapping for primarily acquisitive purposes. That is, whereas low self-esteem individuals may self-handicap to discount the negative implications of failure, high self-esteem individuals may self-handicap to position themselves to augment the positive self-attributions resulting from anticipated success. Of course, if something goes wrong, the high self-esteem self-handicapper is still protected.

In designing the SHS, Jones and I attempted to reduce its shared variance with measures of self-esteem. This attempt was based on the assumption that self-handicapping is in the service of protecting positive, but tenuously held, self-images. This line of reasoning implies that low self-esteem individuals should be less likely to self-handicap because they hold fewer positive self-conceptions. Thus, we viewed the correlations between the SHS and self-esteem as nothing more than an artifact of shared "method variance" (i.e., items on both scales asked subjects to admit something unflattering about themselves). Snyder and Higgins (1988a; see also Harris & Snyder, 1986), however, have suggested a way in which self-handicapping and self-esteem might be related. They contend that it is general uncertainty about the performance outcome which motivates self-handicapping. In this view, low self-esteem individuals are likely to self-handicap more frequently than are high self-esteem individuals because they encounter more situations were they are uncertain about their ability to *produce* an important or self-relevant, desired outcome. Low self-esteem individuals may also employ self-handicapping when they are uncertain about how to *avoid* a self-relevant, undesired outcome (see Rhodewalt & Davison, 1986).

Further research is needed to explicate the relationships between self-esteem and chronic self-handicapping, but the available evidence indicates that the two constructs should be treated as separate, but interactive, entities.

Self-Handicappers, Esteem Threats, and Self-Attributions

I wish to introduce one last data set before turning from the SHS to other individual differences in self-handicapping. The self-handicapping notion, as put forth by Jones and Berglas (1978), is stated in terms of self-attributional processes. In a laboratory setting we have shown that individuals will cite a handicap as a discounting cue in the event of failure but are hesitant to use it to augment success (Mayerson & Rhodewalt, 1988). We now have evidence that SHS scores are related to an attributional or explanatory style (Peterson & Seligman, 1984). For purposes unrelated to self-handicapping issues, we adapted the Attributional Style Questionnaire (Peterson, Semmel, Metalsky, Abramson, von Beyer, & Seligman,

1982), an inventory that requires respondents to make attributions for hypothetical desirable and undesirable events. In the adapted form (Rhodewalt, Strube, Hill, & Sansone, 1988), we included events or situations that varied somewhat orthogonally in their threat to personal control or their threat to self-esteem. Although these constructs are related to one another, it was possible through pilot testing to design events that were low in both self-esteem and control threat (i.e., "You miss a final exam which cannot be made up because the electricity goes off during the night and you oversleep"); low in self-esteem threat but high in control threat (i.e., "You have very little time to meet an important deadline and people keep interrupting you"); high in self-esteem threat but low in control threat (i.e., "You get the nerve to ask someone for a date and he or she says no because he or she does not like your type"); or high in both types of threat (i.e., "You are rejected by all the graduate schools to which you apply"). Four desirable events were included with the eight negative ones (two from each of the above categories). Respondents were then asked to imagine the events happening to them, to write open-ended responses describing the major causes, and to indicate on a series of scales the extent to which the causes were internal–external, stable–unstable, global–specific, and self-responsible–unresponsible. SHS scores and self-esteem scores (Janis and Field Feelings of Inadequacy Scale; Robinson & Shaver, 1973) were collected for all respondents, and subjects were divided into high and low self-handicappers based on a median split of SHS scores. Self-esteem was employed as a covariate. Judges then rated the open-ended major cause statements for the extent to which they were self- or situational attributions. Two sets of analyses were performed; one comparing positive to negative events and one comparing level of self-esteem threat to level of control threat. When high self-handicappers and low self-handicappers were explaining positive as compared to negative events, three effects emerged. First, everyone was somewhat self-serving, in that negative events were attributed to situational factors and positive events were attributed to the self. Second, high self-handicappers made greater situational attributions in general than did low self-handicappers. Third, and somewhat surprisingly, the tendency for high self-handicappers to make situational attributions was most pronounced when the events to be explained were positive.

Analyses of the subjects' scale responses were consistent with the portrait provided by their open-ended attributions. High self-handicappers rated positive outcomes as less internally caused but did not differ from low self-handicappers in their external attributions for negative events. Similarly, self-handicappers, relative to non-self-handicappers, viewed positive events as caused by less stable factors and negative events as caused by more stable factors. The two groups did not differ in their global–specific attributions or in how important they viewed the events to be.

Turning to negative events that varied in type and degree of threat, level of control threat did not lead to differing patterns of attributions between high and low self-handicappers. However, as level of threat to self-esteem increased, high self-handicappers were less likely to make internal self-attributions than were low self-handicappers. The pattern was slightly reversed for low esteem-threat events. The same interaction emerged for the internal–external ratings and for the stable–unstable ratings. The global–specific dimension was not used differentially by the two groups. High self-handicappers, however, viewed any self-esteem threat as more important than did low self-handicappers. Taken together, these findings indicate that self-handicappers tend not to use attributions in an acquisitive, self-enhancing fashion but do employ them in a self-protective manner in response to threats to self-esteem.

SUMMARY

The assumption guiding the line of research presented in this section is that individuals vary in their appreciation for and use of self-handicapping strategies. Accordingly, we have sought to develop a scale to probe individuals in a relatively straightforward way about these tendencies. To date, the SHS has demonstrated encouraging degrees of reliability and validity. Admittedly, more psychometric refinement is in order, and future researchers in the area might want to consider the recommendations for revision of the SHS made in this chapter. The SHS also has displayed impressive predictive validity. However, these demonstrations of validity largely have been limited to the domain of intellectual achievement and almost exclusively to claimed rather than acquired self-handicaps (cf. Arkin & Baumgardner, 1985). The next step is to demonstrate that the predictive utility of the SHS extends to other self-evaluative arenas such as social activities or interpersonal relationships and includes forms of self-handicapping other than anticipatory excuse making (e.g., the actual creation of impediments to performance).

It is noteworthy that available data suggest that high self-handicappers translate their claims into actions. When high self-handicappers avow not to expend effort on a task, their performance bears out their claim. Perhaps this conclusion is limited to the specific handicaps investigated by current research. It may be that other modes of self-handicapping, such as the choice of a nondiagnostic performance setting (see

Rhodewalt & Davison, 1986), free self-handicappers to expend greater effort than they would without the handicap.

There is one extremely paradoxical aspect of this individual difference approach to self-handicapping that has no doubt bothered the reader. We essentially identify high self-handicappers through their willingness to admit the use of self-handicaps. The paradox lies in the fact that the major theoretical perspectives on self-handicapping might argue that this approach should not work. One either employs self-handicaps for self-protective reasons (Jones & Berglas, 1978) or self-presentational reasons (or possibly both, Kolditz & Arkin, 1982; see also Chapter 2, this volume). Either motive should preclude an open admission of the use of such tactics.

Perhaps one can be aware of his or her general tendency to handicap but engage in it automatically in the face of self-evaluative threat—much like one can appreciate the process of dissonance reduction but yet get caught up in it. Or, one may be willing to confess to self-handicapping on a questionnaire and, yet, think of each enactment of self-handicapping as a discrete event in which the audience is not knowledgeable of his or her self-presentational modus operandi across other situations. In a related discussion, Snyder and Higgins (1988b) have placed excuse making on a continuum ranging from retrospective accounts to what they term incorporated excuses. It is incorporated excuses that are relevant here. The incorporated excuse maker has become, in a sense, the excuse. For example, test-anxious individuals always have the "handicap" of test anxiety available, and they are willing to confess to being anxious on self-report measures. Likewise, the chronic procrastinator and the "habitually ill" hypochondriac have "incorporated" those traits into their self-conceptions, and they will admit to them on the SHS while being "unaware" of their self-handicapping function.

It is also possible that the SHS is failing to identify the more discrete, selective, or self-deceptive self-handicapper. This suggests that other approaches to individual differences in self-handicapping might better enable us to triangulate the phenomenon. We turn next to these efforts.

ALTERNATIVE APPROACHES TO SELF-HANDICAPPING BEHAVIOR: DIFFERENCES IN SELF-HANDICAPPING MOTIVES

Rather than probing for individual differences in the admitted use of self-handicapping strategies, one might search for individual differences in the motives to self-handicap. If it is uncertainty about one's ability that motivates self-handicapping (Berglas & Jones, 1978; Snyder & Smith, 1982), then there may be consistent differences among people in their tendencies to question their abilities. Likewise, if it is self-presentational concerns that drive self-handicapping behavior (Kolditz & Arkin, 1982), then the question may become one of whether there are individual differences or self-presentational styles that predispose one toward self-handicapping.

PROTECTION OF DESIRED BUT UNCERTAIN SELF-CONCEPTIONS

In the Jones and Berglas (1978) formulation, uncertainty about one's skill or ability motivates self-handicapping. According to Jones and Berglas, desired but tenuously held self-conceptions are the ones that require protection. Several experiments have provided support for this view (Berglas & Jones, 1978; Higgins & Harris, 1988a; Kolditz & Arkin, 1982; Mayerson & Rhodewalt, 1988; Rhodewalt & Davison, 1986; Tucker *et al.*, 1981). Subjects provided with noncontingent success feedback, as compared to contingent success feedback, are more uncertain of their ability and more likely to self-handicap. Pursuing this line of reasoning, it follows that individuals who are characteristically uncertain of their self-conceptions or who are deficient in self-confidence would be tempted to self-handicap when entering situations that provide evaluative feedback. Harris and Snyder (1986), in a study mentioned previously, provided initial support for this proposition.

Subjects in the Harris and Snyder study were assessed for both their levels of self-esteem and the certainty with which they held these self-conceptions, and then were confronted with a test of intellectual performance. The amount of time they practiced was the measure of self-handicapping. As reported earlier, uncertain males, regardless of their actual level of self-esteem, practiced less than subjects in all other conditions. Compared to self-certain subjects, uncertain males also reported trying less.

Findings that can be interpreted as compatible with the Harris and Snyder data come from a study by Harris, Snyder, Higgins, & Schrag (1986). These researchers measured a variety of variables they thought to be pertinent to self-handicapping. They found that female subjects who were either high in test anxiety or high in covert self-esteem (a measure of how subjects inwardly felt about themselves) offered self-protective attributions prior to taking an important test. Although the authors did not report the interactions in their analyses, it appears from the stepwise multiple regression analyses that the effects of self-esteem on self-handicapping were mediated by test anxiety. Thus, self-handicappers might have been those individuals who wanted to maintain a desired self-image (high covert self-esteem) but were uncertain about their ability to do it (high test anxiety).

PROTECTION OF DESIRED PUBLIC IMAGES

A contrasting analysis of self-handicapping motives is that the self-handicapper wishes to maintain a positive public image (Kolditz & Arkin, 1982; see also Baumgardner, Lake, & Arkin, 1985). This view still implicates the role of self-certainty. It is the individual who has attained a positive public image on the basis of past performance, but is uncertain about his or her ability to replicate this performance, who is most likely to self-handicap. Kolditz and Arkin demonstrated that when subjects performed in private (no one else knew their test scores), the frequency of self-handicapping decreased. Are there individual differences, then, that might predispose people to be unduly concerned about their public images and, thus, to be drawn to self-handicapping?

Findings reported by Tice and Baumeister (1984) indicate that self-esteem is a reasonable candidate. As mentioned previously, they recruited high and low self-esteem subjects and permitted them to practice for an upcoming test of their abilities. Amount of practice was the measure of self-handicapping behavior. Half of the subjects practiced alone (private condition) and half practiced in front of the experimenter (public condition). High self-esteem subjects practiced less (handicapped more) in the presence of the experimenter than when alone, but low self-esteem subjects tended to practice more in public. Thus, we have some evidence that high self-esteem individuals are concerned about their public image and will engage in self-handicapping to protect it.

Unfortunately, other attempts to take an individual differences approach to self-presentational concerns and public self-handicapping have failed to provide consistent findings. Shepperd and Arkin (1989) have speculated that public self-consciousness (Fenigstein *et al.*, 1975) might be associated with the self-presentational motive to handicap. Subjects who scored high and low on the Public Self-Consciousness subscale of the Self-Consciousness Scale were placed in the Rhodewalt and Davison (1986) paradigm in which they were permitted to chose to perform in a diagnostic or nondiagnostic setting. The task was represented as either important or unimportant. High Public Self-Consciousness males who anticipated an ego-relevant test selected the nondiagnostic performance setting more than others, although the percentage doing so raises doubts that subjects were self-handicapping to a reliable degree.

Even more problematic is the fact that Arkin and Shepperd (1988) failed to replicate the high versus low Public Self-Consciousness effect in a study that essentially was identical to that of Shepperd and Arkin (1989). They did, however, find that subjects low in Social Anxiety (another subscale of the Self-Consciousness Scale) self-handicapped in public conditions. The picture is further clouded by the fact that Kolditz and Arkin (1982) reported that separate analyses of their data using median splits on each of the Self-Consciousness Scale subscales (Public Self-Consciousness, Private Self-Consciousness, and Social Anxiety) failed to account for variance in self-handicapping behavior. Findings reported by Gibbons and Gaeddert (1984) are also inconsistent with a self-presentational perspective on self-handicapping. In their investigation self-consciousness was experimentally manipulated, and they found that *non*-self-conscious subjects reported pill side effects that were consistent with strategic self-handicapping.

Even if the data consistently supported the predictive utility of one or the other subscales of the Self-Consciousness Scale, clear understanding of the meaning of these results would be difficult, because Public Self-Consciousness, Private Self-Consciousness, and Social Anxiety are correlated. Moreover, Strube (1985) found, for males but not females, that both Public Self-Consciousness and Social Anxiety are correlated with the SHS. Thus, the operating individual difference and, therefore, the motive are somewhat in question. Additional research is needed to clarify the relations among individual difference variables, self-presentational concerns, and self-handicapping behavior. Just as self-esteem and self-handicapping are intertwined, self- and social-esteem may be inseparable and mutually operative in self-protective behavior (Snyder, Higgins, & Stucky, 1983).

PROTECTION OF SELF-EFFICACY

Arkin and Baumgardner (1985) raised the intriguing possibility that self-handicapping may, at times, be in the service of maintaining one's sense of personal control (see also Rhodewalt & Davison, 1986; Snyder & Higgins, 1988a; Chapter 4, this volume, for similar discussions). In essence, the self-handicapper who is caught in a hopeless situation may entertain the belief that he or she could be effective if it were not for the handicap. This line of speculation leads to the nomination of control-related individual differences as candidates for the prediction of self-handicapping. Arkin and Baumgardner suggest that expectations or fears of no control are the antecedent to this form of self-handicapping and speculate that low self-esteem people or those high on the SHS might be prone to this tactic.

I am aware of no research to date that directly addresses these hypotheses. However, Weidner (1980) reports research that, on the surface, appears to provide findings pertinent to this discussion. She predicted that Type A individuals, because of their concerns about achievement and control, would be more likely to self-handicap than Type B's. In a modification of the Berglas and Jones (1978) paradigm, Weidner instructed Type A and B subjects to perform a pretest in which they received either contingent success feedback or noncontingent failure feedback. They did this in anticipation of taking the actual test. Prior to taking the test, subjects chose to take a performance-facilitating, -hindering, or -neutral drug. The results indicated that noncontingent failure Type A's avoided taking the performance-enhancing drug to a greater extent than subjects in all other conditions. There was no clear evidence, however, that Type A's preferred to self-handicap. Even if they had done so, inferring the underlying motive would have been difficult because achievement motives (failure) were confounded with control motives (noncontingent feedback). Moreover, Harris *et al.* (1986) found Type A or B to be unrelated to self-handicapping attributions.

Finally, because we found the Weidner finding curious, James Davison included a measure of Type A in his dissertation study (Davison, 1985), which was an extension of Rhodewalt and Davison (1986). Among his measures were questions probing subjects about their choice of distracting, facilitating, or neutral music. Type A's, regardless of manipulated condition, opted to perform while listening to distracting music. The reason they provided for this choice was that it made the task more challenging. This finding should raise concern among researchers about the confidence with which they interpret their operationalizations of self-handicapping behavior. It also argues that Type A behavior is not a useful person variable in the study of self-protective behavior and perceptions of self-efficacy. The Type A self-handicapping findings notwithstanding, the Arkin and Baumgardner (1985) hypothesis is interesting and, I believe, merits further investigation.

SELF-HANDICAPPING AND SEX DIFFERENCES

The phenomenon of self-handicapping is provocative and has sparked a full decade of research. One of the most consistent findings in this effort has been that men and women differ in their self-handicapping behaviors. Unfortunately, no systematic investigation of these differences has been undertaken. Thus, one can only speculate, as have others (e.g., Snyder, Ford, & Hunt, 1985), about the nature of these sex effects.

There are only a handful of studies that have directly compared males' and females' self-handicapping behavior. In practically all such cases, males have been found to self-handicap, while females have not. The post hoc conjecturing about these findings has been as varied as the studies in which the differences were observed.

For example, Berglas and Jones (1978) found that males, but not females, who experienced noncontingent success selected a performance-inhibiting drug. Their explanation for this finding centered on differences in the attributions males and females offer for success. It appeared in their data that noncontingent success males were more willing to make ability attributions than were females. Males also appeared to be less confident of their attributions. Although the Berglas and Jones speculation is quite reasonable, the data across the two studies they reported are not completely consistent with this explanation.

In a conceptual replication of Berglas and Jones (1978), Rhodewalt and Davison (1986) used an external acquired handicap (choice of nondiagnostic performance setting) and found that only noncontingent success males handicapped. Unfortunately, we failed to find an interpretable pattern of attributional differences between males and females. Because subjects preferred either distracting music (the handicap) or pleasant music over neutral music, Rhodewalt and Davison speculated that there may be several pathways available to defend against potential threats to self-esteem. Individuals might focus on self-esteem threats (and thus handicap), or they might focus on negative affective states presumed to be associated with such self-esteem threats (and thus attempt to blunt or reduce the affect by listening to pleasant music).

Other sex differences in self-handicapping have been reported. For example, Snyder et al. (1985) found that shy males scored higher on a measure of social avoidance in anticipation of taking a test of social intelligence than did shy females. Their account of these findings centered on differences between males and females in the ways shyness is displayed: Shy males tend to be more socially avoidant, while shy females are more passively pleasing (cf. Pilkonis, 1977). Snyder et al. thus argued that the dependent measure in their study was a more appropriate handicapping vehicle for males than for females. Finally, Harris and Snyder (1986) reported that males who were uncertain of their self-esteem self-handicapped by withholding practice effort to a greater degree than did self-uncertain females and self-certain males and females. In brief, although there are demonstrations of self-handicapping among females, self-handicapping behavior is more prevalent in males.

There are probably several reasons for the preference for self-handicapping among males. Only additional research directed specifically at the sex difference issue will be able to unravel the cause(s) of these effects. Nonetheless, existing data might provide some clues concerning which variables might be critical. In order to facilitate the examination of sex differences in self-handicapping, Table 3 presents the available studies organized by subject population (male, female, or both), the mode of self-handicapping (acquired and claimed), the nature of the threat to self-esteem (intellectual ability or social skill), and whether or not certainty of positive performance was manipulated.

At first glance, the findings summarized in Table 3 appear highly inconsistent and not very informative. On closer inspection, however, several themes emerge that might be useful in guiding future research. In addition to the tendency of males to self-handicap more frequently than females, there is very little evidence that females will engage in acquired or behavioral self-handicapping (Leary & Shepperd, 1986). Six studies using only males found behavioral self-handicapping. Of the four studies comparing males and females on behavioral self-handicapping, only Strube and Roemmele (1985) found no gender differences in that both male and female low self-esteem, SHS-defined self-handicappers selected tests nondiagnostic of failure. One other study, that of Tice and Baumeister (1984), apparently did not analyze for sex of subject and is not informative.

In a study designed to test issues other than self-handicapping, Gibbons and Gaeddert (1984) had female subjects ingest a placebo that was represented as being arousing (in one condition it was stated to inhibit performance and in another it was stated to facilitate performance). Attentional self-focus was experimentally manipulated while subjects worked on a mathematics task portrayed to be a correlate of general intelligence. In contrast to self-aware females, non-self-aware females reported experiencing more pill-induced arousal when the arousal could be an excuse for poor performance than when it could not. This finding is consistent with a self-handicapping, self-protective attribution prediction. However, it is probably better categorized as an example of claimed handicapping because subjects did not choose to handicap. Overall, there is fairly consistent evidence that women will claim a handicap, but will not actively erect an impediment to performance.

Two other features of Table 3 are informative. First, evaluative threat has been manipulated in two ways in studies of self-handicapping. Many studies simply manipulate the evaluative feedback and assume it is ego relevant. For example, subjects anticipate an exam that is either a valid measure of some desired ability like intelligence or a test that is unimportant. In contrast, other studies lead subjects to anticipate engaging in an ego-important performance, and they are made uncer-

tain about their ability to perform well. This uncertainty is either manipulated through noncontingent success feedback on practice items or is
measured as an individual difference variable such as low self-esteem,
high self-uncertainty, test anxiety, or social anxiety. In almost every
study in which concerns about ability to perform have been directly
manipulated or assessed as an individual difference, males have self-
handicapped.

It appears that, for males, it is being called upon to display desired
but weakly held self-conceptions that motivates self-handicapping. For
females, in contrast, noncontingent success feedback (Berglas & Jones,
1978; Rhodewalt & Davison, 1986) or uncertainty about the self (Harris &
Snyder, 1986) does not appear to motivate self-handicapping. Only dispositional test anxiety, which in all likelihood reflects a chronic level of
uncertainty about one's ability, has been found to promote self-handicapping in women. And, when females do handicap, it is through the
claimed mode of appeals to test anxiety, lack of effort, or traumatic recent
experiences rather than through the behavioral mode. As Berglas and
Jones (1978) suggested, it may be that differing patterns of performance
attributions underlie the differences in self-handicapping behavior between males and females. This contention appears to be well supported
empirically (see Ickes & Layden, 1978). For example, Deaux and
Emsmiller (1974) examined male and female performance attributions
for outcomes on masculine and feminine tasks. Males were more likely
than females to attribute success to skill regardless of the nature of the
task.

It is also noteworthy that, when women do self-handicap it is in the
form that was earlier labeled domain–strategy-specific self-handicapping. That is, test-anxious women will claim test anxiety, and hypochondriacal women will claim symptoms. These data may be taken as further
evidence that self-handicapping, as a general strategy, is not normally
preferred by women. Perhaps when women do self-handicap, they do
so because they have come to learn of the self-handicapping benefits of a
behavior initially performed for other reasons.

SUMMARY AND CONCLUSIONS

Do certain individuals have a tendency to engage in self-handicapping behavior more than others? In this chapter this question has been
approached from several perspectives and the answer from each appears to be "yes." Research indicates that an aspect of many limiting or
apparently defeating behaviors is their potential use as a self-handicap.
Individual differences in test anxiety, social shyness, and symptom re-

TABLE 3. Gender Differences in Self-Handicapping

	Handicap	Attribute	Certainty manipulated	Results
I. *Males only*				
Greenberg, Pyszczynski, & Paisley (1985)	Claimed (test anxiety)	I.Q.	Test anxiety	Test-anxious subjects (S's) handicapped
Higgins & Harris (1988a)	Acquired (alcohol)	I.Q.	Yes	Uncertain S's handicapped
Higgins & Harris (1988b)	Acquired (alcohol)	Social competence	No	Heavy drinkers handicapped
Kolditz & Arkin (1982)	Acquired (drug choice)	I.Q.	Yes	Uncertain S's handicapped
Mayerson & Rhodewalt (1988)	Claimed (reported pain)	I.Q.	Yes	Uncertain S's handicapped
Rhodewalt, Saltzman, & Wittmer (1984)	Claimed & acquired (practice effort)	Athletic ability	???	S's both claimed and acquired when threatened
Tucker, Vuchinich, & Sobell (1981)	Acquired (alcohol)	I.Q.	Yes	Uncertain S's handicapped
Weidner (1980)	Acquired (drug choice)	I.Q.	Yes, but confounded	Uncertain S's handicapped
II. *Females only*				
Baumgardner, Lake, & Arkin (1985)	Claimed (mood)	Social I.Q.	No	S's used mood as a handicap when it was suggested by the exp.
DeGree & Snyder (1985)	Claimed (high life change)	Social I.Q.	No	High threat S's handicapped
Gibbons & Gaeddert (1984)	Claimed (pill side effects)	I.Q.	No	Non-self-aware S's reported arousal if it served as a handicap

Study	Type	Domain	Gender difference	Result
Harris, Snyder, Higgins, & Schrag (1986)	Claimed (effort)	I.Q.	Test anxiety	Test-anxious and high self-esteem S's handicapped
Pyszczynski & Greenberg (1983)	Claimed (effort)	I.Q.	Yes, expected difference	Anxious S's handicapped
Smith, Snyder, & Handelsman (1982)	Claimed (test anxiety)	I.Q.	Test anxiety	Test-anxious S's handicapped
Smith, Snyder, & Perkins (1983)	Claimed (physical symptom reports)	Social I.Q.	No	Hypochondriacal S's handicapped
III. Males and females				
Berglas & Jones (1978)	Acquired (drug choice)	I.Q.	Yes	Uncertain males handicapped
Harris & Snyder (1986)	Acquired (practice effort)	I.Q.	Yes	Uncertain males handicapped
Snyder, Smith, Augelli, & Ingram (1984)	Claimed (shyness)	Social I.Q.	No	Shy males handicapped
Rhodewalt & Davison (1986)	Acquired (performance setting)	I.Q.	Yes	Uncertain males handicapped
Rhodewalt & Fairfield (1989)	Claimed (effort)	I.Q.	Yes, expected difference	Females who expected hard test handicapped most
Strube (1985)	Claimed (excuses)	Academic performance	No	Only males handicapped
Strube & Roemmele (1985)	Acquired (task choice)	I.Q.	No	No gender differences found. High SHS low self-esteem S's handicapped
Tice & Baumeister (1984, May)	Acquired (practice)	Game performance	No	Sex differences not analyzed

porting, among others, also identify those who frequently self-handicap. These differences were discussed in terms of domain–strategy-specific self-handicaps. That is, individuals are thought to differ in their propensities to use one mode of handicapping or handicap (i.e., symptom reports) in circumscribed domains (i.e., scholastic evaluations).

From a different research perspective, a growing body of evidence shows that one can identify individuals who possess a general inclination to self-handicap across a variety of domains, employing a wide range of handicapping strategies. Although additional validation work is necessary, research with the Self-Handicapping Scale shows promise in this direction.

While the SHS measures preferences for the use of self-protective coping strategies, other research indicates that it is also fruitful to investigate individual differences in the motivational concerns that predispose certain individuals to self-handicap. Individual differences in certainty about desired self-conceptions, in concerns about public images, and perhaps in cares about self-efficacy all tend to promote the use of self-handicapping strategies. Finally, studies consistently reveal differences between males and females in the employment of self-handicapping, although the precise form of and explanation for these differences is not clear.

Taken together these literatures support the merit of an individual differences approach to the study of self-handicapping behavior. At the same time, they highlight the need for additional programmatic and integrative research. In particular, the developmental antecedents of self-handicapping tendencies have received little attention (see, however, Chapter 5 in this volume for further discussion of this issue).

The basic question that needs to be addressed concerns the preconditions that will simultaneously cause people to be uncertain of their traits and abilities and to choose self-handicapping as the coping response over other strategies. Stated differently, one might ask if there is a group of core dispositions or developmental experiences that set the stage for chronic self-handicapping. Jones and Berglas (1978) have proposed that inconsistent (noncontingent) positive reinforcement histories promote self-handicapping. Although there is laboratory evidence to support this contention (Berglas & Jones, 1978, among others), noncontingent positive reinforcements alone do not necessarily, inevitably lead to self-handicapping. The same experiences could just as well lead individuals to overprepare, perseverate, and overachieve (see Jones & Berglas, 1978). Research on individual differences in self-handicapping, then, should focus on the identification of the necessary antecedent conditions that result specifically in chronic self-handicapping.

The findings surveyed in this chapter lead me to propose that individual differences in explanatory style (Peterson & Seligman, 1984) is a likely candidate for future research. It may be that an external explanatory style combines with uncertainty about the self, perhaps stemming from a capricious reinforcement history, to produce the chronic self-handicapper. That is, a person who characteristically construes negative self-relevant outcomes as externally caused and who is uncertain about how to produce a self-flattering outcome or avoid a self-damaging outcome might be the person most drawn to self-handicapping.

The above speculation implicitly suggests a second direction research with the SHS should go. Both the factor structure of the SHS and differences between high and low self-handicappers in the self-attributions they offer for negative events suggest that the SHS may be measuring a general individual difference in the tendency to externalize potential self-damaging outcomes. In other words, the SHS is assessing individual differences in excuse making. If this observation is accurate, then research is needed to demonstrate the relation between SHS-defined high self-handicappers and their use of other self-protective "defenses" such as rationalization and externalization.

Finally, it appears that many of the issues concerning the development and maintenance of individual tendencies to self-handicap would be better understood if a life span approach was employed in research. In order to illustrate this suggestion I return one last time to Lee Trevino.

Trevino may not have been inclined to self-handicap earlier in his career but, perhaps as he aged and his physical skills declined, he became more likely to engage in self-handicapping behavior. Research strategies such as those employed by Cantor and her colleagues would be useful in exploring issues such as how self-handicapping becomes incorporated into the "social intelligence" of the person (Cantor, Norem, Niedenthal, Langston, & Brower, 1987). Investigations of this type would view self-handicapping as a cognitive–behavioral strategy for coping with life tasks such as age-related decline. Such a research strategy would also permit the identification of the individual and situational antecedents, the chronicity, and the short- and long-term benefits and costs associated with strategic self-handicapping.

REFERENCES

Arkin, R. M., & Baumgardner, A. H. (1985). Self-handicapping. In J. H. Harvey & G. Weary (Eds.), *Attribution: Basic issues and applications* (pp. 169–202). New York: Academic Press.

104   FREDERICK RHODEWALT

Arkin, R. M., & Shepperd, J. (1988). *The role of social anxiety in self-presentational self-handicapping.* Unpublished manuscript, University of Missouri, Columbia.

Baumeister, R. F., & Kahn, J. (1982). *Obesity as a self-handicapping strategy: Don't blame me, blame my fat.* Unpublished manuscript, Case Western Reserve University, Cleveland. Cleveland.

Baumgardner, A. H., Lake, E. A., & Arkin, R. M. (1985). Claiming mood as a self-handicap: The influence of spoiled and unspoiled public identities. *Personality and Social Psychology Bulletin, 11,* 349–357.

Beck, A. T., Ward, C. H., Mendelson, M., Mock, J., & Erbaugh, J. (1961). An inventory for measuring depression. *Archives of General Psychiatry, 4,* 561–571.

Berglas, S. (1986). A typology of self-handicapping alcohol abusers. In M. J. Saks & L. Saxe (Eds.), *Advances in applied social psychology, Vol. 2* (pp. 29–56). Hillsdale, NJ: Erlbaum.

Berglas, S., & Jones, E. E. (1978). Drug choice as a self-handicapping strategy in response to noncontingent success. *Journal of Personality and Social Psychology, 36,* 405–417.

Briggs, S. R., Cheek, J. M., & Buss, A. H. (1980). An analysis of the Self-Monitoring Scale. *Journal of Personality and Social Psychology, 38,* 679–686.

Cantor, N., Norem, J. K., Niedenthal, P. M., Langston, C. A., & Brower, A. M. (1987). Life tasks, self-concept ideals, and cognitive strategies in a life transition. *Journal of Personality and Social Psychology, 53,* 1178–1191.

Cattell, R. B., & Cattell, A. K. S. (1960). *Test of "g": Culture Fair.* Champaign, IL: The Institute for Personality and Ability Testing.

Crowne, D. P., & Marlowe, D. (1964). *The approval motive.* New York: Wiley.

Davison, J. (1985). *Self-handicapping and failure: The role of contingency and attributions for failure.* Unpublished doctoral dissertation, University of Utah, Salt Lake City.

Deaux, K., & Emsmiller, T. (1974). Explanations of successful performance on sex-linked tasks: What is skill for the male is luck for the female. *Journal of Personality and Social Psychology, 29,* 80–85.

DeGree, C. E., & Snyder, C. R. (1985). Adler's psychology (of use) today: Personal history of traumatic life events as a self-handicapping strategy. *Journal of Personality and Social Psychology, 48,* 1512–1519.

Fenigstien, A., Scheier, M. F., & Buss, A. H. (1975). Public and private self-consciousness: Assessment and theory. *Journal of Consulting and Clinical Psychology, 43,* 522–527.

Fowler, B. (1984, August 17). Trevino finds new life with putter. *The Salt Lake Tribune,* p. 10B.

Gibbons, F. X., & Gaeddert, W. P. (1984). Focus of attention and placebo utility. *Journal of Experimental Social Psychology, 20,* 159–176.

Gorsuch, R. L. (1974). *Factor analysis.* Philadelphia: Saunders.

Greenberg, J., Pyszczynski, T. & Paisley, C. (1985). Effects of extrinsic incentives on use of test anxiety as an anticipatory attributional defense: Playing it cool when the stakes are high. *Journal of Personality and Social Psychology, 47,* 1136–1145.

Harris, R. N., & Snyder, C. R. (1986). The role of uncertain self-esteem in self-handicapping. *Journal of Personality and Social Psychology, 51,* 451–458.

Harris, R. N., Snyder, C. R., Higgins, R. L., & Schrag, J. L. (1986). Enhancing the prediction of self-handicapping. *Journal of Personality and Social Psychology, 51,* 1191–1199.

Hewitt, J. P., & Stokes, R. (1975). Disclaimers. *American Sociological Review, 40,* 1–11.

Higgins, R. L., & Harris, R. N. (1988a). Strategic "alcohol" use: Drinking to self-handicap. *Journal of Social and Clinical Psychology, 6,* 191–202.

Higgins, R. L., & Harris, R. N. (1988b). *Self-handicapping social performance through "alcohol" use: The interaction of drinker history and expectancy.* Manuscript submitted for publication.

Higgins, R. L., & Snyder, C. R. (1989). Excuses gone awry: An analysis of self-defeating excuses. In R. Curtis (Ed.), *Self-defeating behaviors: Experimental research and practical implications* (pp. 99–130). New York: Plenum.

Ickes, W. J., & Layden, M. A. (1978). Attributional styles. In J. H. Harvey, W. Ickes, & W. F. Kidd (Eds.), *New Directions in Attribution Research* (Vol. 2, pp. 119–152. Hillsdale, NJ: Erlbaum.

Jones, E. E., & Berglas, S. (1978). Control of attributions about the self through self-handicapping strategies: The appeal of alcohol and the role of underachievement. *Personality and Social Psychology Bulletin, 4*, 200–206.

Jones, E. E., & Rhodewalt, F. (1982). The Self-Handicapping Scale. (Available from the authors at the Department of Psychology, Princeton University, or the Department of Psychology, University of Utah.)

Kelley, H. H. (1972). *Causal schemats and the attribution process.* Morristown, NJ: General Learning Press.

Kolditz, T. A., & Arkin, R. M. (1982). An impression managment interpretation of the self-handicapping strategy. *Journal of Personality and Social Psychology, 43*, 492–502.

Krantz, D., Glass, D., & Snyder, M. L. (1974). Helplessness, stress level, and the coronary-prone behavior pattern. *Journal or Experimental Social Psychology, 10*, 284–300.

Leary, M. R., & Shepperd, J. A. (1986). Behavioral self-handicaps versus self-reported handicaps: A conceptual note. *Journal of Personality and Social Psychology, 51*, 1265–1268.

Lowe, C., & Medway, F. (1976). Effects of valance, severity, and relevance on responsibility and dispositional attributions. *Journal of Personality, 44*, 518–538.

Mayerson, N. H., & Rhodewalt, F. (1988). The role of self-protective attributions in the experience of pain. *Journal of Social and Clinical Psychology, 6*, 203–218.

Mehrabian, A. (1968). Male and female scales of the tendency to achieve. *Educational and Psychological Measurement, 28*, 493–502.

Pennebaker, J. W. (1982). *The psychology of physical symptoms.* New York: Springer-Verlag.

Peterson, C., & Seligman, M. E. P. (1984). Causal explanations as a risk factor for depression: Theory and evidence. *Psychological Review, 91*, 347–374.

Peterson, C., Semmel, A., Metalsky, G., Abramson, L., von Beyer, C., & Seligman, M. E. P. (1982). The Attributional Style Questionnaire. *Cognitive Therapy and Research, 6*, 287–289.

Pilkonis, P. A. (1977). The behavioral consequences of shyness. *Journal of Personality. 45*, 596–611.

Pyszczynski, T., & Greenberg, J. (1983). Determinants of reductions in intended effort as a strategy for coping with anticipated failure. *Journal of Research in Personality, 17*, 412–422.

Rhodewalt, F. (1984). [Self-handicapping scale: Convergent and discriminant validity]. Unpublished data. (Available from the author at the Department of Psychology, University of Utah, Salt Lake City.)

Rhodewalt, F., & Davison, J. (1986). Self-handicapping and subsequent performance: Role of outcome valence and attributional certainty. *Basic and Applied Social Psychology, 7*, 307–323.

Rhodewalt, F., & Fairfield, M. L. (1989). *Claimed self-handicaps and the self-handicapper: The effects of reduction in intended effort on performance.* Manuscript submitted for publication. University of Utah, Salt Lake City.

Rhodewalt, F., Saltzman, A. T., & Wittmer, J. (1984). Self-handicapping among competitive athletes: The role of practice in self-esteem protection. *Basic and Applied Social Psychology, 5*, 197–209.

Rhodewalt, F., Strube, M. J., Hill, C. A., & Sansone, C., (1988). Strategic self-attribution and Type A behavior. *Journal of Research in Personality, 22,* 60–74.

Robinson, J. P., & Shaver, P. R. (1973). *Measures of psychological attitudes.* Ann Arbor: University of Michigan Press, Institute for Social Research.

Sarason, I. G. (1980). Introduction to the study of test anxiety. In I. G. Sarason (Ed.), *Test anxiety: Theory, research, and application* (pp. 3–15). Hillsdale, NJ: Erlbaum.

Shepperd, J., & Arkin, R. M. (1989). Self-handicapping: The mediating roles of public self-consciousness and task importance. *Personality and Social Psychology Bulletin, 15,* 252–265.

Smith, T. W., Snyder, C. R., & Handelsman, M. M. (1982). On the self-serving function of an academic wooden leg: Test anxiety as a self-handicapping strategy. *Journal of Personality and Social Psychology, 42,* 314–321.

Smith, T. W., Snyder, C. R., & Perkins, S. C. (1983). The self-serving function of hypochondriacal complaints: Physical symptoms as self-handicapping strategies. *Journal of Personality and Social Psychology, 44,* 787–797.

Snyder, C. R., & Higgins, R. L. (1988a). Excuses: Their effective role in the negotiation of reality. *Psychological Bulletin, 104,* 23–35.

Snyder, C. R., & Higgins, R. L. (1988b). From making to being the excuse: An analysis of deception and verbal/nonverbal issues. *Journal of Nonverbal Behavior, 12,* 237–252.

Snyder, C. R., & Smith, T. W. (1982). Symptoms as self-handicapping strategies: The virtues of old wine in a new bottle. In G. Weary & H. L. Mirels (Eds.), *Integrations of clinical and social psychology* (pp. 104–127). New York: Oxford University Press.

Snyder, C. R., & Higgins, R. L., & Stucky, R. J. (1983). *Excuses: Masquerades in search of grace.* New York: Wiley-Interscience.

Snyder, C. R., Ford, C. E., & Hunt, H. A. (1985, August). *Excuse-making: A look at sex differences.* Paper presented at the American Psychological Association Convention, Los Angeles.

Snyder, C. R., Smith, T. W., Augelli, R. W., & Ingram, R. E. (1985). On the self-serving function of social anxiety: Shyness as a self-handicapping strategy. *Journal of Personality and Social Psychology, 48,* 970–980.

Snyder, M. (1974). Self-monitoring of expressive behavior. *Journal of Personality and Social Psychology, 30,* 256–237.

Strube, M. J. (1985). An analysis of the Self-Handicapping Scale. *Basic and Applied Social Psychology, 7,* 211–224.

Strube, M. J., & Roemmele, L. A. (1985). Self-enhancement, self-assessment, and self-evaluative task choice. *Journal of Personality and Social Psychology, 49,* 981, 993.

Tice, D. M., & Baumeister, R. F., (1984, May). *Self-handicapping, self-esteem, and self-presentation.* Paper presented at the meeting of the Midwestern Psychological Association, Chicago.

Trope, Y. (1980). Self-assessment, self-enhancement, and task preference. *Journal of Experimental Social Psychology, 16,* 116–129.

Tucker, J. A., Vuchinich, R. E., & Sobell, M. (1981). Alcohol consumption as a self-handicapping strategy. *Journal of Abnormal Psychology, 90,* 220–230.

Weidner, G. (1980). Self-handicapping following learned helplessness treatment and the Type A coronary-prone behavior pattern. *Journal of Psychosomatic Research, 24,* 319–325.

CHAPTER 4

SELF-HANDICAPPING PROCESSES AND SEQUELAE
ON THE TAKING OF A PSYCHOLOGICAL DIVE

C. R. SNYDER

INTRODUCTION

One of my most vivid childhood memories centers around a playground ritual that I repeatedly faced. Because my family moved frequently, I found myself having to meet a new group of peers at the beginning of each school year. Being a grade-school male, a typical ceremony involved taking the new kid (me) to the local vacant lot and having him fight a string of other males until a place in the pecking order was established. After a few of these "educational" squirmishes in which I fought my way up through several bouts until I had settled somewhere in the middle of the "male hierarchy," I struck upon a new strategy. Instead of beginning at the bottom of the fighting hierarchy, I somehow saw that there might be advantages in starting right at the top. In other words, I expressly asked to fight the biggest, meanest kid in the entire schoolyard. And, of course, he pounded on me until he tired of this

C. R. SNYDER • Department of Psychology, University of Kansas, Lawrence, Kansas 66045.

activity. But, much to my delight, I found that I did not have to fight any more. So, as I had vaguely hoped would be the case, there were some advantages to my psychological dive. Indeed, by picking the toughest kid on the playground, I not only shortened the entire sequence into one fight, but I also found that I was able to preserve some semblance of esteem and control in this very difficult situation. After all, who could be expected to succeed against such a gorilla? And, however long I did last in such a fight seemed like such a valiant effort against insurmountable odds.

The purpose of my opening story is not to recount the macho memories of a childhood past, but rather to suggest (like the subtitle of this book) that seemingly paradoxical behaviors may be understandable when we examine them from the perspective of their protagonists. Such is the case for the phenomenon of self-handicapping, which is the scholarly name for the process of taking a psychological dive.

Why would any sane person make things harder for himself or herself by purposely adopting an impediment of some sort? Is this the behavior of a deviant or severely disturbed individual? As my story and the preceding chapters attest, it simply is not the case that taking a psychological dive is that out of the ordinary. On the contrary, such self-handicaps consistently have been demonstrated in empirical research over the last decade. And such behaviors appear in different "kinds" of people. Indeed, although some persons are especially prone to self-handicapping, there are certain circumstances that may lead the perfectly "normal" person to engage in self-handicapping. So, if some of the people tend to self-handicap most of the time, and most of the people tend to self-handicap some of the time, a reasonable conclusion is that people must be getting something out of such maneuvers. What is that something (or somethings)? And, how can we conceptualize self-handicapping in order to better understand this phenomenon and its effects? This chapter is an attempt to answer these latter questions.

In the following pages I will first detail the prerequisite components of self-handicapping, and thereafter will provide a brief overview of some of the paradigmatic issues that have marked the theory and research on this topic. Based on an analysis of these prerequisite and paradigmatic issues, an overarching definition of self-handicapping will be formulated. I will then examine the sequelae of self-handicapping, including effects involving causal linkage to the act, self-esteem and affective responses, competence and control, performance, and health. Finally, I will place the self-handicapping effects in the context of a larger process by which individuals and society more generally attempt to negotiate conceptualizations of "reality."

PERSPECTIVES ON SELF-HANDICAPPING

COMPONENTS

The prerequisite components of self-handicapping are illustrated in Model #1 of Figure 1. Obviously, there must be a protagonist, and that person must anticipate an upcoming "performance" arena in which there is the possibility of an outcome that does not meet personal or societal standards. The time arrow at the top of Model #1 indicates that in the temporal progression of events, the actor is the "author" of the subsequent bad act. Thus, there is an important causal link reflecting any information that ties the actor to a potential bad act. In regard to the bad act and the causal link, the phenomenology of the person should be highlighted in order to understand self-handicapping behaviors. That is to say, although external sources (e.g., powerful other people) certainly serve to influence judgments of the negativeness of the act, as well as the degree of linkage to that act, it is the perception of the actor that is the central, driving force in the initiation and maintenance of the self-handicapping behaviors. Furthermore, some persons are undoubtedly more predisposed to perceive the negativeness of potential acts, and are also prone to overemphasize the linkage to such acts. As such, these persons should be especially prone to engage in self-handicapping because they are literally "live wires" when it comes to their sensitivity and perceived linkage to negative actions (see Rhodewalt, Chapter 3 in this volume; Snyder, Higgins, & Stucky, 1983).

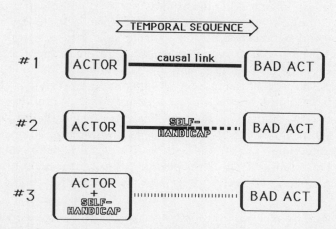

FIGURE 1. Components of self-handicapping (Model #1), anticipatory self-handicapping (Model #2), and incorporated self-handicapping (Model #3).

THE ANTICIPATORY SET

In regard to the actor–linkage–bad act components in the aforementioned model, it should be emphasized that there have been two guiding notions about the nature of this relationship. In the original presentation of the self-handicapping concept, Berglas and Jones (1978; Jones & Berglas, 1978) hypothesized that the necessary antecedent conditions involved a phenomenological state in which the individual has a tenuous positive image in a performance arena and also anticipates the necessity of performing in that arena again. The dilemma for the individual in such a situation is that he or she is uncertain that the previous high level of performance can be sustained in the subsequent, similar performance arena. It is the uncertainty of such circumstances, wherein the person may be linked with a bad outcome that could invalidate his or her usual sense of esteem and competency, that elicits the need to self-handicap. As Berglas and Jones (1978) put it, "We speculate that self-handicapping tendencies reflect a basic uncertainty concerning how competent one is" (p. 406).

What is noteworthy about the aforementioned perspective on self-handicapping antecedents is that the anticipation of being linked to a potential bad outcome has been operationalized only by a previous sense of noncontingent success in that particular performance arena. That is, noncontingent success was employed in the original empirical article by Berglas and Jones (1978), and its importance has been re-emphasized in subsequent papers by Berglas (1985, 1988). The emphasis that Berglas places on noncontingent success appears to derive both from its role in engendering uncertainty and from its role in producing a positive, though tenuous, image to protect from debasement.

A second perspective on the actor–linkage–bad act sequence as it pertains to self-handicapping is exemplified in the work of Snyder and his colleagues (e.g., Snyder & Smith, 1982). The crux of this theoretical position is simply that the individual experiences uncertainty about success in an upcoming important performance arena. Within this perspective, how one attains this sense of uncertainty is not the key issue. Rather, the driving force behind any self-handicapping behaviors is the sense of uncertainty about one's successful performance in an impending arena (assuming also that the performance arena is an important one for the individual's identity).* This latter viewpoint thus suggests that a

*When the person is either absolutely certain of succeeding or not succeeding, the sense of anticipatory uncertainty obviously is not operative. However, I would argue that such extreme circumstances are very rare, and that the overwhelming majority of instances involving anticipatory sets do involve some degree of uncertainty.

history of noncontingent success is one powerful determinant of the necessary uncertain anticipatory set, but that there are other histories that also may engender uncertain anticipation. (Interestingly, Jones and Berglas espoused a similar sentiment in their 1978 theoretical piece, but Berglas [1985, 1988] subsequently has emphasized the role of noncontingent success.) The impending situation itself, for a variety of reasons, may make us feel uncertain about our performance. Situational factors that may engender such uncertainty include, to name a few, new or somewhat different tasks or environments, rising or ambiguous expectations on the part of others, erratic previous performances, novel time constraints, and the like. There are also individual differences in the level of uncertainty that people feel in regard to their likelihood of success in a given performance arena; moreover, these individual differences in sense of uncertainty of success may hold across a variety of performance arenas.

A second distinction between the original Jones and Berglas and the Snyder perspective is that this latter approach has not insisted that there be *prima facie* evidence that the individual has a tenuous, positive image. By employing the noncontingent success manipulation, as Berglas has emphasized, one can be certain that the potential self-handicapper has a tenuous, positive sense of self to protect. In the perspective espoused by Snyder, however, it is argued that most people may implicitly experience such a tenuous, positive sense of self under a variety of circumstances, and that there are individual differences variables that should predispose some persons to such a tenuous state.

For the purpose of the present chapter, I have adopted a version of the actor–linkage–bad act chain that emphasizes the importance of the uncertain anticipatory set itself, however it is derived, rather than the involvement of noncontingent success in achieving this uncertain anticipatory set. That is, however the individual attains the sense of uncertainty that portends the possibility of a subsequent bad act, it is the uncertainty of subsequent success that is the key to understanding the self-handicapping phenomenon and its effects. I maintain this working assumptions for two reasons. First, it is untenable to constrain the antecedents for the uncertainty expectation to a noncontingent success background: There are many other plausible precursors to the uncertainty set. Second, the practical implications of the self-handicapping construct are much greater when the uncertainty set is not constrained. If one were to enforce the restriction of noncontingent success as the only history that elicits uncertainty concerning future success, then the study of self-handicapping could be reviewed in a relatively small number of experiments, most of which do not test for the subsequent effects of the handicapping. Because one of the foci of the present chapter is upon the sequelae of self-handicapping, it is important to cast a wider net in regard to the uncertain anticipatory set. Further, it is my belief that much of the richness of the evolving empirical literature on self-handicapping owes to the fact that the sense of uncertainty in regard to future success has been generated by manipulations in addition to the noncontingent success one. Finally, the unrestricted uncertainty viewpoint fosters a tie between the recent empirical work and the preexisting wealth of clinical writings and lore (see introductory chapter in this volume).

THE BEHAVIORAL VERSUS SELF-REPORT MODE OF THE HANDICAP

The self-handicapping literature has evolved with two major ways of measuring the "handicap" (see Arkin & Baumgardner, 1985a; Leary & Shepperd, 1986; Snyder *et al.*, 1983). The gist of this issue involves whether the handicap is a behavior that is observable, or whether it simply is self-reported. In an early statement of this distinction, Snyder *et al.* (1983) noted that excuses in general, and self-handicaps in particular, can take a verbalized form, or they may be manifested in a physical form that is observable. They labeled these two versions as avowed and self-evident, respectively. Addressing themselves solely to the self-handicapping concept, Arkin and Baumgardner (1985a) suggested a similar distinction, which they characterized as claimed versus acquired self-handicaps.

The most thorough explication of this distinction has been provided by Leary and Shepperd (1986), who have argued that the terms *behavioral* and *self-reported self-handicapping* may provide useful descriptors for two differing classes of handicaps. In this conceptualization, behavioral self-handicaps "refer to the actions of people who construct handicaps that augment nonability attributions for possible failure" (Leary & Shepperd, 1986, p. 1267); moreover, self-reported handicaps are defined as "the use of verbal claims that one possesses handicaps that interfere with one's performance . . ." (p. 1267). Thus, within this distinction, Leary and Shepperd include in behavioral self-handicaps such variables as drug ingestion (Berglas & Jones, 1978; Gibbons & Gaeddert, 1984; Tucker, Vuchinich, & Sobell, 1981), lack of effort (Baumeister, Hamilton, & Tice, 1985; Pyszczynski & Greenberg, 1983; Rhodewalt, Saltzman, & Wittmer, 1984; Shepperd & Arkin, 1989a), and evaluation under difficult circumstances (Frankel & Snyder, 1978; Greenberg, 1985; Snyder, Smoller, Strenta, & Frankel, 1981). Conversely, self-reported handicaps are characterized by Leary and Shepperd as instances where, in anticipation of an ego-involving and yet uncertain outcome performance arena, people verbally claim to be ill (Smith, Snyder, & Perkins, 1983), socially anxious (Snyder & Smith, 1986; Snyder, Smith, Augelli, & Ingram, 1985), test anxious (Smith, Snyder, & Handelsman, 1982), in a bad mood (Baumgardner, Lake, & Arkin, 1985), or a victim of traumatic life events (De-Gree & Snyder, 1985).

This distinction between behavioral and self-reported handicaps is useful in dissecting the various types of handicaps, but care should be taken not to draw hard and fast differentiations between the two types. For example, in those studies where people have self-reported handicaps (often in the form of symptoms), one presumption (e.g., Leary & Shepperd, 1986, p. 1266) is that the verbal "claim" may or may not be true and that the individual does not necessarily have any behavioral manifestations that are actually an impediment. In point of fact, there are no empirical demonstrations of whether actual behavior impediments accompany the self-report of a handicapping state. The closest finding in this vein is that persons who strategically employ the report of test anxiety as a self-handicap do not also evidence the predicted cognitive, interfering thoughts (Greenberg, Pyszczynski, & Paisley, 1985). For some types of self-reported handicaps, however, it may well be the case that there are associated behavioral manifestations that are impediments. This follows because most psychological symptoms are accompanied by impediment-laden behavioral manifestations. Also, in the progression of the handicapping tendencies over a person's life, it may be necessary to "document" a verbalized handicap with actual behavioral impediments (Higgins & Snyder, 1989; Snyder & Higgins, 1988b). With these caveats in mind in regard to the potential blurring of the behavioral–self-report distinction, however, it should be acknowledged that this distinction is useful in providing an understanding of the self-handicapping phenomenon.

Originating Source of the "Self"-Handicap

One important, and yet rarely discussed, dimension of self-handicapping relates to the originating source. Although the literature has clearly evolved with two originating sources for the handicap, to date this distinction has been touched upon in only one paper related to self-handicapping (i.e., Snyder & Higgins, 1986). The most common viewpoint on self-handicapping is that the person is the primary source of the handicap. In such person-initiated handicaps, the individual introduces his or her own impediment. Whether it is through the behavioral mode of manifesting a handicap, such as lowered effort (e.g., Harris & Snyder, 1986), a behavioral–self-report mode such as choice of debilitating drug (e.g., Berglas & Jones, 1978), or a self-report mode such as symptom reporting (Snyder & Smith, 1982), the research participant responds to the particular situational context with the handicap. In other words, the self-handicapping behavior is a dependent variable that the research subject generates in response to the independent variables of the particular experiments. This is the framework from which Berglas and Jones (1978) originally operationalized self-handicapping.

As the interest in the concept of self-handicapping has grown, however, so too have the ways of studying handicaps changed. For example, researchers have expanded their methodologies in order to study the effects of handicapping situations on people. Within this latter conceptualization, handicapping circumstances have been employed as independent variables, the effects of which are then examined in relation to a range of other dependent variables measures exhibited by research participants. This latter viewpoint, in contrast to the aforementioned person-initiated handicaps, may be conceptualized as situation-imposed handicaps. Such imposed handicaps can be examined in terms of their effects on the person undergoing the handicap. Included in these independent variable, imposed handicaps have been such impediments as loud background noise (Arkin & Baumgardner, 1985b; Leary, 1986), alcohol (Isleib, Vuchinich, & Tucker, 1988), and drugs (Weiner & Sierad, 1975). Additionally, outside observers' reactions to persons who are undergoing the effects of such situation-imposed handicaps have received considerable attention (e.g., Arkin & Baumgardner, 1985b; Carducci & McNeely, 1981; Critchlow, 1985; Richardson & Campbell, 1980, 1982; Schouten & Handelsman, 1987; Springston & Chafe, 1987).

Although the "pure" self-handicapping notion obviously springs from the person-initiated (dependent variable) perspective, researchers have increasingly examined the effects of situation-imposed (independent variable) handicaps. In this latter sense, the "self" in self-handicapping is a bit of a misnomer in that the protagonist is not initiating the handicapping process. However, in many (if not most) real-life situations, it is the case that there may be some hint of an inherent impediment in the situation, and the protagonist thus takes advantage of this in the subsequent "use" of the handicap (see Sheppard & Arkin, 1989a). That is to say, what may be a situationally imposed handicap at one point in time, may become a learned, strategically employed, person-initiated self-handicap at a subsequent point in time. Because both the person-initiated and situation-imposed self-handicaps may contribute to a greater understanding of this overall phenomenon, and because the sequelae of both types have been investigated, I will include both bodies of research in the subsequent pages.

Locus of Self-Handicap

In contrast to the distinction drawn in the previous section about the instigating source of the handicap, a distinction also can be drawn in regard to the locus of the handicap itself. The basis for this latter distinction has been articulated by Arkin and Baumgardner (1985a) when they characterize two general loci—internal and external—for the handicap. By internal, they refer to handicaps that actually represent something that is located inside of the person. For example, they cite such handicaps as drug ingestion, alcohol consumption, reduced effort, test anxiety, social anxiety, physical complaints, and depression as being internal. Conversely, by external, they refer to those impediments that have a location outside of the person. In this vein, they cite the choosing of performance-impeding conditions or the citing of the difficulty of a task as exemplifying the external handicaps (see Shepperd, Strathman, & Arkin, 1987, for an interesting extension of this logic). In addition to introducing this distinction, Arkin and Baumgardner (1985a, p. 176) also theorize that internal handicaps may be more persuasive than external ones. Although they do not elaborate on the reasons for the greater impact of internal as compared to external handicaps, I would posit that the internal handicaps are more "convincing" and therefore serve more effectively to weaken the linkage to subsequent bad acts.

Before leaving this section on the locus of the handicap, I would like to comment on the somewhat misleading classification by Arkin and Baumgardner (1985a) of drug ingestion and alcohol consumption as representing internal handicaps. While alcohol or the drug eventually may reside inside the person, they are external agents that must be ingested by the individual. Thus, such drug and alcohol handicaps may represent an external–internal mixture.

Timing of Self-Handicap

Self-handicaps operate to obfuscate and weaken the causal link between the actor's core sense of self and an impending bad act (see again Model #1 of Figure 1). As such, these handicaps may appear anywhere from shortly before to a long time prior to the performance itself. Wherever the handicap appears relative to the performance, however, it must diminish the causal linkage in order to operate effectively.

In the original exposition of the self-handicapping notion in the experimental setting, Berglas and Jones (1978) presented a methodology and a viewpoint that emphasized the acquisition and manifestation of the handicap just prior to an uncertain performance retest arena. Further, the focus of these investigators was on the situational factors that influence most people to manifest an impediment, without regard to any individual differences in disposition to engage in such handicaps. The general temporal schematic for this perspective is shown in Model #2 of Figure 1. As shown in that schematic, once the self-handicap is presented, it subsequently should serve to obscure and weaken the causal linkage to any poor performance. In this conceptualization of self-handicapping, given that the person is uncertain of performing well in a subsequent important performance arena, the handicap may be manifested for the first time; moreover, in a temporal sense, that handicap should be evidenced shortly before the performance. This is the typical temporal perspective on self-handicapping, and, as shown in Model #2, I have called this *anticipatory* self-handicapping.

The aforementioned temporal perspective on self-handicapping arose from a situationalistic, social psychological tradition (Berglas, 1988; Handelsman, Fox, & Kraiger, 1987). However, there has been another perspective that acknowledges the role of dispositional factors in the manifestation of self-handicaps. This latter viewpoint has roots in an individual differences tradition, as well as in personality theory (i.e., "an original or recurrent disorder" as articulated by Berglas, 1985), and the clinical literature more generally (see introductory chapter for more detailed discussion). With the development of an individual differences measure of self-handicapping by Jones and Rhodewalt (1982; see also Rhodewalt, Chapter 3 in this volume; Strube, 1986), the viewpoint that some persons may be especially predisposed to handicapping has gained additional support. Likewise, as symptom-reporting studies (see Snyder & Smith, 1982) began to suggest that persons with high levels of particular psychological symptoms (e.g., anxiety, hypochondriasis, etc.) may strategically report these symptoms in a self-handicapping manner, the role of dispositional factors gained further support.

What is especially noteworthy about these disposition-based conceptions of self-handicapping is that they implicitly assume that handicapping tendencies are incorporated into the person's self-view. In other words, some people "carry" their handicaps around with them most of the time; as can be seen in Model #3 of Figure 1, I have labeled this temporal type of handicapping as *incorporated* (see Snyder & Higgins, 1988b, for further discussion of the anticipatory–incorporated distinction). With an incorporated self-handicap, therefore, the person does not expressly have to accentuate the handicap just prior to the performance arena that portends failure; rather, such a person is implicitly not strongly linked to subsequent bad acts (note the dotted line reflecting such a broken line in Model #3). And, for purposes of the present subsection, it should be noted that such incorporated self-handicaps begin to weaken clear causal linkages at a potentially long period of time prior to any particular threatening performance arena. Also, when self-handicaps tend to be given at earlier points in time relative to specific threatening performance arenas (i.e., more incorporated rather than simply anticipatory), the greater should be the probability that dispositional factors are operative.

Audiences for Handicap

In the initial presentations of the self-handicapping concept, Berglas and Jones (1978; Jones & Berglas, 1978) acknowledged the importance of self-esteem motives and emphasized the internal audience of the self as being more salient than external audiences in driving the handicapping process. Although these authors did note that self-handicaps also could be influenced by potentially relevant external audiences, the theoretical focus of the concept was obviously on the self. This latter conclusion is supported by the authors' statements that self-handicapping should occur "under conditions of total privacy" (Berglas & Jones, 1978, p. 407) or "even in the absence of others" (Jones & Berglas, 1978, p. 202). This emphasis on the role of private self-esteem motives was buttressed by an experimental manipulation of a public–private variable to ascertain whether handicapping abated under the private set. When differences did not appear in the public and private conditions, Berglas and Jones (1978) concluded that, at minimum, self-handicapping is addressed to the private audience of the self.

In a subsequent and more stringent test of the relative propensity of persons to self-handicap in private versus public conditions, Kolditz and Arkin (1982) tried to make certain that the private conditions were established as effectively as is possible in an experimental setting. Under such constraints, although some trends for self-handicapping emerged in the private condition, the effect was largely eliminated in comparison to the strong effect in the public condition. An analysis of the subsequent self-handicapping literature suggests a similar conclusion: The strength of the self-handicapping phenomenon appears to be stronger in more public as compared to private conditions (see Arkin & Baumgardner, 1985a, p. 191; Arkin & Shepperd, 1988; Baumgardner et al., 1985; Shepperd & Arkin, 1989b).

In actuality, the experiments performed to date have not attained a truly private condition in that the research participants always have known that they were in a psychology experiment, and even in these "private" conditions, there usually have been experimenters present. In fact, a pure empirical test of the private–public audience factors as they relate to self-handicapping may never be possible. This audience issue is clouded further when one considers that the internal audience represents an inculcation of the norms, viewpoints, and values of external audiences (e.g., parents, teachers, authorities, etc.). Lacking such pure experimental sets, however, it is probably accurate to conclude that self-handicapping has important implications for both the self and external audiences. In future studies involving self-handicapping and audiences issues, one way to tease apart the influences of the internal and external audiences would be to employ longer-term methodologies in which the protagonist and external audiences have to "negotiate" about the validity of the handicap. Such studies would enable one to better understand the relative contributions of the internal and external audiences to the self-handicapping process.

Although one can not easily conclude, based on the presently available literature, when the internal or external audience concerns are prepotent (see Shepperd & Arkin, 1989b, for a notable exception), the evolving literature does allow for an examination of the effects of self-handicapping on the internal audience of the self, as well as the effects of such self-handicapping on the external audiences who may observe it. Therefore, the major heuristic of the internal–external audience debate for the present chapter is that it yields a means of categorizing the effects of self-handicapping that may eventually lead us to a better understanding of this phenomenon. Indeed, in the subsequent portions of this chapter on the sequelae of self-handicapping, I will review the effects from the perspective of both the person giving the handicap and the external audiences who are the witnesses to these handicaps.

UNDERLYING MOTIVES

In the Jones and Berglas (1978) introductory article on self-handicapping, the authors hypothesized that this phenomenon rests upon the maintenance and protection of self-esteem needs. A point that is not widely acknowledged about this original article, however, is that these authors also noted that the self-handicapping phenomenon was fueled by competency and control motives. In their own words, ". . . we propose that the basic purpose behind such strategic choices is the control of the actor's *self*-attributions of competence and control" (p. 407). Likewise, in a subsequent elaboration of the definition of self-handicapping, Snyder and Smith (1982, p. 107) also accentuated the esteem and competency motives as they wrote, "the individual may gain tangible rewards (e.g., money, privileges), but these are viewed in the present formulation only insofar as they serve to foster an underlying sense of self-esteem and competence."

After reviewing the growing self-handicapping literature of the early 1980s, Arkin and Baumgardner (1985a) concluded that self-handicapping is undergirded by a motivation to maintain social esteem, as well as self-esteem and a sense of control. They wrote,

> self-handicapping can be viewed as a strategy for maintaining one's sense of personal control. It is not the sort of personal control that is ordinarily discussed in the literature of social psychology; instead, self-handicapping would be viewed as a sort of "enabling tactic," a strategy that would permit the individual to maintain public esteem and the "illusion of control," but would not contribute directly to any genuine sense of control. The self-handicapper would be able to maintain face in social relations, because self-doubts are prevented from becoming certain disabilities. But the individual does not enjoy any increase in genuine control. (p. 185)

This thinking obviously raises serious questions about the real effectiveness of self-handicaps in fulfilling the very needs that the protagonists are motivated to sustain. Later, in this same review, however, Arkin and Baumgardner (1985a) noted that the literature available at that time in regard to the actual effects of self-handicapping was virtually nonexistent, and as such they advised that further speculation about the underlying motives should await the evidence. Although there have not been a great number of studies bearing on the topic of the effects of self-handicapping, there is a sufficient number now accumulated so that we can more seriously address this effectiveness issue. I will turn to these effects in a subsequent section of this chapter.

AN ELABORATED DEFINITION

Based on my analysis of the aforementioned issues related to self-handicapping, I would like to offer a definition that is an elaborated, more liberal one than most previous definitions. I advocate this elaborated definition because it not only accommodates the previous theoretical perspectives, but it also facilitates my subsequent analysis of a wide range of studies in regard to the effects of self-handicapping. Thus, for purposes of this chapter, my working definition is the following: Self-handicapping is a process of preserving the personal theory of self, wherein the person, experiencing uncertainty about success in an anticipated important performance arena, utilizes seeming impediments in order to (1) decrease the linkage to that impending performance should it prove to be poor (i.e., discounting), and (2) increase the linkage should the performance prove to be good (augmentation).

A first point in regard to this definition is that it builds upon the actor–linkage–bad act model that I presented earlier, and it emphasizes the role of the uncertain anticipatory set about an important, ego-involving performance. It is this uncertain anticipatory set regarding the success of a future performance that theoretically ignites the self-handicapping process.

A second point of elaboration in regard to this definition is that it expressly emphasizes the linkage dimension as a essential vehicle by which the handicapping operates. That is, self-handicapping works by weakening the linkage of the potential negative outcome to the person's core sense of self. By introducing the impediment (handicap) in the causal chain, the self-handicapper establishes a state of attribute ambiguity (see M. L. Snyder & Wicklund, 1981) wherein the direct, inferential causal linkage from the bad act to the person's overall positive sense of self is obscured. (See Higgins and Harris, 1989, for empirical support of the role of placebo alcohol consumption in producing attributional ambiguity for potential poor performance in a social interaction arena.) Although this analysis suggests that the concealing properties of the handicaps play an important role in the process, it should be emphasized that the underlying motive is to lessen the linkage between the bad act and the person's positive sense of self.

This weakening of the attributional link is a *discounting process* (see Berglas & Jones, 1978; Jones & Berglas, 1978; Kelley, 1971) when the outcome does eventuate in the poor quality that the self-handicapper prognosticated. Additionally, however, should the performance outcome be better than expected, there is a theorized *augmentation process* in which the linkage is actually accentuated (Berglas & Jones, 1978; Jones & Berglas, 1978; Kelley, 1971). In other words, the valence of the actual performance outcome should reverse the "linkage" such that (1) self-handicaps preceding poor outcomes decrease the protagonist's linkage and (2) self-handicaps preceding good outcomes increase the linkage. Given that self-handicapping was introduced as a strategy whereby people deal with potential negative personal feedback, it is not surprising that the literature has focused on the role of self-handicapping in decreasing the linkage prior to poor performance outcomes.

By engaging in this self-handicapping process of linkage diminishment in the case of an actual subsequent poor performance, and linkage enhancement in the case of the rarely examined positive subsequent performance, the person seeks to preserve the personal theory of who he or she is. Previous thinking in regard to self-handicapping has advocated the motivational role of self-esteem and control, and in the present definition, these interactive motives can be inserted as the two major premises upon which many personal theories of self are built. Thus, being a "good/in control" person may be the cornerstone of personal theories of self (see Snyder & Higgins, 1988a; Taylor & Brown, 1988, for related discussions).

This definition provides the latitude to include under the self-handicapping rubric both the person-initiated and situation-imposed handicaps, as well as both the behavioral and self-report modes with loci that may be internal or external (note the definitional clause "utilizes seeming impediments"). Likewise, in regard to the timing of the self-handicap, this definition allows for anticipatory and incorporated types of handicaps. Finally, given the present ambiguity in the literature regarding the audience focus of self-handicapping, this definition implicitly opens the possibility of both audiences being explored. In this latter vein, I will subsequently explore the effects of self-handicaps for the internal audience of the self, as well as for the observing external audiences. Further, all of the theoretical and empirical issues that I have discussed in this section will, at various points, be touched upon in the next major section on the effects of self-handicapping.

Before turning to the discussion of the effects of self-handicapping, I would like to briefly note one body of research that I will not discuss subsequently as exemplifying self-handicapping. In particular, there is an accumulating body of evidence suggesting that people, in anticipation of an uncertain, impending performance, will engage in a variety of behaviors to reframe *the performance itself* as not being a failure (see Snyder *et al.*, 1983, pp. 125–129). For example, given the chance, people will select tasks wherein it is difficult to label the performance itself as a "failure." In other words, in anticipation of uncertain upcoming performances, people will purposefully avoid tasks that are diagnostic of failure (e.g., Handelsman, Kraiger, & King, 1985; Sachs, 1982); moreover, selected subpopulations, such as low self-esteem persons (Meyer & Starke, 1982), test-anxious persons (Arkin & Haugtvedt, 1984), and low self-esteem, high self-handicapping persons (Strube & Roemmele, 1985), especially seek out nondiagnostic situations. Unlike the self-handicapping construct in which the focus is on the weakening of the linkage to a potential bad act by means of an impediment, however, the aforementioned anticipatory, image-protection strategies are expressly aimed at lessening the certainty of a negative evaluation of the performance itself. Although this latter tactic may be a first approach that people take prior to employing handicapping impediments, and self-handicapping may be accompanied by, or may implicitly use, maneuvers that also serve to cloud the diagnosticity of failure (e.g., Phares & Lamiell, 1974), the two phenomena are distinguishable. By definition, the self-handicap must contain an impediment (or a seeming impediment), whereas the behaviors aimed at clouding the diagnosticity of failure may or may not contain such an impediment. The selection of a very difficult task is an example of a strategy that involves both an impediment and diagnostic blurring; conversely, the selection of a very easy task would not contain an impediment but would involve a clouding of diagnosticity. Thus, the example involving the selection of a difficult task would reflect self-handicapping, while the selection of an easy task would not.

SELF-HANDICAPPING SEQUELAE

The questions posed by the earliest research on the self-handicapping concept tended to be theoretical ones such as those outlined in the previous section of this chapter. This emphasis in the early self-handicapping research flowed out of the fact that it was a theory-based construct from its inception. Similar to the evolution of most new constructs, self-handicapping first yielded a variety of studies that basically demonstrated that it existed. In the next phase of the development of the self-handicapping concept, the key questions should revolve around whether self-handicapping really "works," and, in the degree to which it does work, do the results support the underlying premises of the theory. In the present section I will address these latter questions by reviewing the accumulated evidence. In order, I will address the questions of how self-handicaps influence the (1) perceived causal link to the bad act, (2) self-esteem and affective responses, (3) the sense of competence and control, (4) performance in various arenas, and (5) health.

THE CAUSAL LINKAGE

The underlying process by which self-handicaps are theorized to operate is through an attributional distancing of the actor from the particular negative act (see again Model #1 of Figure 1). Given this fundamental assumption, it is critical to ascertain whether self-handicaps actually serve to weaken the actor's perceived linkage to the bad act. Interestingly, there are no studies that address this central theoretical issue from the perspective of the person who is the purveyor of the handicap. However, there are several studies that have implicitly studied this question from the perspective of outside audiences who are asked to evaluate handicapped individuals. Given the fact that the following studies do not test the lessening of the linkage from the perspective of the self-handicapper, the results should be taken as suggestive of the implicit notions that people may have about the linkage-weakening properties of handicaps.

Schouten and Handelsman (1987) explored theoretical speculations that depressive symptoms may enable the person to lessen or avoid attributions of responsibility. Students reacted to hypothetical case studies in which the protagonists were either presented as engaging in spousal abuse or being confronted with job loss because of poor performance. Additionally, the protagonists in these scenarios were portrayed in one of the three following ways: (1) as having ongoing depressive symptoms; (2) as having ongoing depressive symptoms and a history of psychiatric involvement; or (3) as having no depressive symptoms or history. Results showed that the protagonists in both depression conditions were perceived as being less the cause of their behavior, less responsible for the consequences of their actions, and less blameworthy than the protagonist with no depressive problems.

Another body of research has addressed how alcohol consumption may influence the degree to which persons are held responsible for their bad acts. In one such study, Richardson and Campbell (1980) asked college students to give their reactions to a description of an incident of wife abuse. The involvement of alcohol was varied by describing the wife, the husband, and both or neither as being intoxicated at the time of the incident. The abusing husband was rated as being less responsible for his actions when he was intoxicated. (Interestingly, however, the wife was seen as been more responsible for the beating when she was intoxicated.) These results have been replicated and extended in a subsequent study by Carducci and McNeely (1981). In this latter study, college students again found the intoxicated husband to be less responsible for his actions, while a sample of recovering alcoholics judged the intoxicated husband as being most accountable.

Richardson and Campbell (1982) examined the effects of alcohol intoxication on responsibility attributions in an instance of acquaintance rape. As was the case in the aforementioned studies, the intoxication of the victim and offender were varied. The college student judges regarded the offender as being less blameworthy and less responsible when he was intoxicated as compared to when he was sober. However, the victim was rated as being more responsible for the rape when she was drunk.

In another study with college students serving as evaluators, Critchlow (1985) presented scenarios from each of four categories that varied in terms of their negativeness (i.e., crimes, mild indiscretions, neutral actions, and socially desirable acts); moreover, the protagonists in these scenarios were described as being either drunk or sober, and as either chronic alcoholics or social drinkers. The results revealed that the drunken protagonists were rated as being less responsible, less blameworthy, and less the cause of their actions in comparison to their sober counterparts. Furthermore, the alcoholics, in comparison to the social drinkers, were judged to be less responsible and to have played less of a causal role in regard to the particular outcomes.

There is at least one other audience reaction study that bears on the topic of alcohol. Gorney (1985) recruited a sample of mental health professionals (social workers and psychologists) in order to ascertain their reactions to a case of spousal abuse in which the involvement of alcohol was varied in a factorial design (i.e., the wife, the husband, both, or neither were intoxicated). In terms of rated responsibility for their actions, there were no clear effects for alcohol intoxication, although the raters in the alcohol-involved conditions did report that the alcohol played a causal role in the incident.

The aforementioned studies on observer ratings of a transgressor's responsibility for his or her bad acts have an obvious limitation in terms of their applicability for the linkage-weakening process that is inherent in self-handicapping. Namely, we do not know that the protagonists in these hypothetical scenarios actually employed their handicap strategically in any anticipatory sense. Although clinical literature suggests that therapists believe that abusive alcohol drinkers "drink in order to provide an excuse for becoming violent" (Gelles, 1972, p. 116; see also Snell, Rosenwald, & Robey, 1964), it would be informative to ascertain whether observers lessen the causal responsibility when the protagonist is portrayed as engaging in the anticipatory handicapping in a purposeful fashion.

SELF-ESTEEM AND AFFECTIVE RESPONSES

One of the basic motives that self-handicapping has been theorized to fulfill is the preservation of self-esteem. The definition of self-esteem is captured nicely in the words of Coopersmith (1967, pp. 4–5): "By self-esteem we refer to the evaluation the individual makes and customarily maintains with regard to himself: it expresses an attitude of approval or disapproval." Consistent with this general definition, measures of self-esteem typically have involved an evaluative report that the individual makes about himself or herself (e.g., the Janis–Field Feelings of Inadequacy Scale, Robinson & Shaver, 1973; the Rosenberg Self-Esteem Scale, Rosenberg, 1965).

There is only one reported study that examines the effects of "self"-handicapping on the protagonist's subsequent self-esteem; this study employs a situation-induced handicap. Isleib *et al.* (1988) exposed male college social drinkers to a noncontingent success experience on an unsolvable intellectual performance task, varied whether or not they received (and believed they had received) an alcoholic beverage, and then gave them either success or failure feedback regarding their performance on a subsequent retest on (largely) unsolvable cognitive problems. Contrary to prediction, on a single-item rating of self-concept, subjects who believed they had consumed alcohol reported lower self-esteem than did subjects who believed they had not consumed alcohol. However, an analysis of subjects' scores on the Rosenberg Self-Esteem Scale did reveal a tendency for subjects who believed they had consumed alcohol to report higher self-esteem than those subjects who believed that they had not consumed alcohol (regardless of whether they were in the success or failure condition).

For purposes of the present section, the affective responses exhibited by, or toward, the self-handicapping person will be grouped along with esteem findings. The logic here is that there are emotional states that often accompany potential losses or gains in esteem, and as such these affective reactions serve to provide valuable additional information about the effects of self-handicapping. Simply put, how one feels in general and how one feels about oneself are closely related.

An example of a study involving the affective repercussions of a self-handicapping strategy is provided by Harris and Snyder (1986). In this study, the self-handicapping dependent variable was the level of practice effort exhibited by college males in advance of the second part of an ambiguous intellectual task. Additionally, however, these investigators took self-report anxiety measures before and after the practice effort measure. For those males who were most prone to engage in the self-handicapping strategy of lowering effort in terms of less time spent practicing (i.e., males with a dispositionally low sense of certainty about their self-esteem, whether that esteem was high or low), decreases in practice effort were reliably associated with lowered anxiety from before to after the practice period. In other words, for this subset of males with dispositionally uncertain self-esteem who were especially prone to the self-handicapping strategy of not practicing, their lowered effort strategy appeared to be related also to a diminishment of their reported level of anxiety.

In a study involving a social interaction task with opposite-sex pairs, Arkin and Baumgardner (1985b) had all subjects listen to a background of white noise. Half of the subjects were told that the noise interfered with performance (the imposed handicap condition), while the other half were given no such instructions. Differential effects were obtained for the high as compared with low socially anxious subjects. In particular, the low socially anxious subjects reported less comfort and happiness in the handicapping as compared to the nonhandicapping condition; conversely, the high socially anxious subjects reported more comfort and happiness in the handicapping as compared to nonhandicapping condition. In a conceptually similar study, Leary (1986) engaged high and low socially anxious college students in a social interaction task in the presence of a background noise. For half of the subjects the background noise was described as "loud and distracting" (the handicapping condition), while for the other half of the subjects the noise was described as "moderately loud, but not particularly distracting" (the nonhandicapping condition). On self-presentational, self-report adjectives, more positive ratings were obtained for the low as compared to the high socially anxious subjects under the nonhandicapping condition (this is a typical finding). Interestingly, however, in the handicapping condition the high socially anxious subjects evidenced positive self-adjectives that were comparable to those reported by the low socially anxious subjects. That is to say, the handicapping condition appeared to have beneficial affective effects for the high socially anxious subjects.

In contrast to the aforementioned studies in which the protagonists' affective responses to the person- and situation-induced handicaps are measured, there is one reported study in which an affect-related response of observers to the self-handicapping protagonist is surveyed. In this study by Springston and Chafe (1987), subjects read three stories involving three different protagonists, each of whom was experiencing an impending test of competence. One scenario involved a protagonist with no interfering factors; a second scenario involved a protagonist with a handicap that was accidental; a third scenario portrayed a protagonist who voluntarily engaged in the handicapping. For example, in the scenario in which the protagonists were to take an important test of intellectual functioning the next morning, the nonhandicapping person gets a good night's sleep, the accidental handicapper has out-of-town guests arrive unexpectedly and stays up late entertaining them, and the purposeful handicapper invites friends over and parties late. Although observers were asked to make evaluations of each of the three protagonists on several dimensions, others of which I will discuss at later points in this chapter, the measure involving perceived liking of the protagonist is germane for the present topic of emotional reactions to self-handicapping. Results showed that the raters liked the nonhandicapping and accidental handicapping protagonists equally highly, but evidenced significantly less liking for the purposefully self-handicapping protagonist.

COMPETENCE AND CONTROL

In addition to the motives related to self-esteem, the theorization undergirding the self-handicapping construct has posited that such behaviors serve to preserve the individual's sense of competence and control. In this section, I will review first those studies that have addressed competence-related sequelae of self-handicapping, and thereafter I will examine the available results pertaining to control sequelae. Obviously, although I have separated competence and control for purposes of exposition, these two concepts are similar and interrelated.

Competence

The closest measure to the concept of competence that researchers have explored involves ratings of the self-handicapper's ability. That is, the focus has been on whether the protagonist's perceived ability in the particular performance arena is preserved because of the self-handicapping behavior. For example, Mayerson and Rhodewalt (1988) examined the use of pain as a situation-induced handicap, as well as the attributional effects of these pain reports. After receiving contingent or noncontingent success feedback on a first anagram task, subjects were asked to complete a second anagram task with their nondominant hand submerged in cold water. Next, subjects were given success or failure feedback on the second task. Results showed that the failure subjects who reported high levels of pain prior to the second test also especially claimed the elevated pain of the cold water after the second test, and, most importantly for the present discussion, these same subjects emphasized the fact that their poor performance was not due to ability. In other words, the handicapping behavior appeared to maintain the protagonist's evaluation of an underlying intellectual ability to succeed at the anagram task should the handicap be removed.

The aforementioned Mayerson and Rhodewalt (1988) study obviously examines the ability inferences that a situationally handicapped protagonist generates because of the handicapped behavior. There are two additional studies that look at the question of ability inferences from the perspective of external audiences who observe the handicapping. In a first study, Arkin and Baumgardner (1985c) had subjects read written descriptions of an individual who, prior to an important examination, either willfully self-handicapped, was involuntarily handicapped by circumstances, or was handicap-free. Also, the person's actual examination performance was characterized as either poor, average, or good. Regardless of whether the handicap was described as willfully or involuntarily adopted, subjects tended to make ability attributions for successful examination performance (i.e., some support for augmentation) and nonability attributions for poor performance (i.e., some support for discounting). However, the subjects rated the person as being less competent *in general* when he voluntarily self-handicapped as opposed to when he was handicapped by circumstances. Thus, there appeared to be performance-specific ability benefits that the raters associated with both the person-initiated and situation-imposed types of handicaps; moreover, these same raters appeared to form more negative general competence impressions only of the person-initiated (willful) handicapper.

A second study provides further information about observers' reactions to the underlying ability of handicapping persons. In this study by Springston and Chafe (1987), which has been previously discussed in this chapter, raters were asked to respond to several questions that pertained to the underlying ability of a protagonist in a story. In one condition, the protagonist was described as a nonhandicapper; in a second condition the protagonist was depicted as an accidental handicapper; and, in a third condition the individual was described as a willful self-handicapper. When subjects were asked "To what extent was pure ability reflected in each girl's performance?" ability was rated as being significantly less relevant for the two handicapping persons as compared to the nonhandicapping person (there were no differences for the two handicapping persons). This finding expands upon the previously described studies showing that self-handicaps tend to weaken the causal linkage, and suggests that the handicap can lessen the linkage to such a degree that the protagonist's underlying ability is not perceived as being clearly evaluated. Additionally, Springston and Chafe pursued this question even further when they asked their subjects to "Rate the true ability (e.g., intelligence) of each girl taking all factors into account." On this measure, the two handicapping persons were rated as being significantly more intelligent than the nonhandicapping person (there were no differences in the two handicapping persons). Thus, both the accidental and voluntary handicaps preserved the protagonists' perceived ability in the eyes of the external raters.

Control

Unlike the "competence" studies in which the measures all tapped ability, the available studies pertaining to "control" are more varied in the nature of their measures. There is one study by Rhodewalt and Davison (1986) that directly tapped the subjects' sense of control. In this study, subjects were instructed that they were to take two analogies tests. After taking the first test, half received either success or failure feedback that was response contingent or noncontingent. Next, subjects could select a level of music that supposedly was either debilitating or facilitating on the second analogies task. Only the noncontingent success males (but not females) exhibited a clear preference for the debilitating music; moreover, these handicapping subjects performed more poorly on the second part of the analogies test. Additional results, however, showed that the failure subjects who did select the debilitating music actually performed better on the second test than did the failure subjects who selected the facilitating music or the success subjects choosing either debilitating or facilitating music. These latter results are more pertinent for the subsequent section of this chapter on the effects of self-handicapping on performance, but what is noteworthy for the present section is that the authors also took self-report measures of the subjects' sense of control and effort. Internal analyses revealed that the failure subjects who selected the debilitating music perceived the outcome (i.e., the failure) on the first test as being under their control and being due to not trying hard enough. Interestingly, these same subjects thereafter tended to exert more effort and do better on the second analogies task.

There is one other person-initiated handicapping study that warrants a description for the present purposes of unraveling control-related effects. In a study described previously in this chapter, Greenberg *et al.* (1985) demonstrated that high test-anxious persons strategically self-reported their anxiety as a self-handicap in anticipation of an uncertain performance arena. The authors also had their subjects complete the Cognitive Interference Questionnaire (Sarason, 1980), which is a measure of task-interfering cognitions while taking exams (e.g., "I thought about how much time I had left," "I thought about how poorly I was doing," and "I thought about my level of ability"). To the extent which persons undergoing testing situations experience such cognitions, they are not "in control" in that they are not attending to the relevant task cues. Greenberg *et al.* found that the high test-anxious persons who strategically reported an elevated level of anxiety in a self-handicapping fashion did not evidence any parallel elevation in their interfering cognitions as measured by the Cognitive Interference Questionnaire. Although these findings have been interpreted by some writers (e.g., Berglas, 1985) as indicating that the self-report of symptoms such as test anxiety is not "genuine" self-handicapping, there is another plausible interpretation that relates to the present section. Namely, if self-handicapping is at all effective in preserving some sense of control, then the lack of task-interfering cognitions is a theoretically predicted derivative of the handicapping phenomenon.

Turning to the studies that approach the control-related effects of handicaps from the perspective of the external observers of such handicaps, there are at least three relevant studies. Two of these studies focus on alcohol, and the other one focuses on psychological symptoms. In addition to the measures involving the responsibility of an acquaintance rape perpetrator that were described previously in regard to the Richardson and Campbell (1982) study, raters were also asked to estimate whether the protagonist would be found guilty. The male raters felt that the offender was most likely to be found guilty when neither he nor the victim was drunk. Female raters, on the other hand, felt that conviction was most likely when the offender was drunk and the victim was sober. Sobell and Sobell (1975) conducted a telephone survey in which persons were asked to make judgments about the appropriate sentencing for an intoxicated person who performed a violent crime. If the protagonist was described as a first offender or a social drinker, then the "judges" tended to recommend a reduced level of punishment; conversely, if the offender was described as an alcoholic, the level of punishment was more severe. The relative degree of punishment received for a bad action should impact upon the person's sense of control, and it is for this reason that these latter two studies involving observer reactions to the protagonists' "intoxication" were included here.

In the Schouten and Handelsman (1987) study that was outlined in the previous section on causal linkage effects, the authors also asked their respondents to complete questions that are related, albeit inferentially, to control. For example, in this study raters were less likely to recommend that the protagonist in a work scenario be fired if he or she was depressed (with or without a psychiatric history). Further, the depressed protagonist in the work scenario was expected by the raters to assume fewer job-related duties only if he or she had a history of psychiatric involvement.

PERFORMANCE

Beyond the previously discussed issues pertaining to the effects of self-handicapping on esteem, affect, competence, and control, other interesting sequelae pertain to whether there are any actual repercussions for the performance itself. That is to say, does the self-handicapping protagonist actually experience any decrements in performance because of the impediments? Most of the research to date that is relevant to this question has explored the effects of handicaps on cognitive-intellectual performance. I will address this literature first in this section, and thereafter will briefly review, in turn, the sparse literatures on performances in social interaction and sports arenas.

Cognitive-Intellectual Performances

In the same year that Berglas and Jones introduced the self-handicapping concept, Frankel and M. L. Snyder (1978) were also introducing a study that had provocative results. Although these latter authors originally construed their research as providing an attribution-based explanation of the then evolving learned helplessness theory (see Abramson, Seligman, & Teasdale, 1978, for revised theory; and Seligman, 1975, for earlier version), their methodology nicely fits the handicapping definition and paradigms described in this chapter. Their research procedure involved a two-part anagram task, in which subjects completed either solvable or unsolvable anagrams on the first part, and thereafter were told that they would be taking a second part that comprised either moderately or highly difficult anagrams. This latter manipulation is similar to a situation-imposed handicap. For the subjects who had taken the unsolvable anagrams in the first part, and thus were in an uncertain anticipatory set regarding the second part, those subjects who were told that the anagrams on the second task were highly difficult performed better on this task than did the subjects who were told that the anagrams were moderately difficult. Furthermore, internal analyses indicated that this superior performance was related to greater effort on the second part of the task.

Weiner and Sierad (1975) performed another study that may be categorized as utilizing a situation-imposed handicap. High and low achievement-motivation subjects were apprised that they would be taking a cognitive task, and prior to the beginning of that four-trial digit-symbol task, half were given a pill that purportedly "interfered with" performance and the other half were given no such pill. The pill ingestion resulted in poorer performance for the high achievement-motivation subjects, and better performance for the low achievement-motivation subjects.

In contrast to the two above-reviewed studies employing situation-imposed handicaps, there are at least four reported studies that explore the performance effects of person-initiated handicaps. For example, Smith et al. (1982) found that high test-anxious college students strategically reported an elevated level of anxiety as a handicap in anticipation of a cognitive laboratory task. However, these same subjects did not show any actual performance decrements relative to the subjects in the other conditions of this study. These results have been replicated by Greenberg et al. (1985). Also, I have provided an earlier discussion of the Harris and Snyder (1986) study in which uncertain self-esteem males were shown to practice less for an impending cognitive task than certain self-esteem males. What can be appropriately added in the present context is that these uncertain self-esteem males did not perform any more poorly than their certain self-esteem counterparts. The last person-initiated handicapping study is by Rhodewalt and Davison (1986), and it has been reviewed thoroughly in the previous section on competence and control effects. The Rhodewalt and Davison results represent a mixed bag in terms of the performance effects, in that the noncontingent success males were the ones who especially preferred the handicapping option (debilitating music), and they performed more poorly on the subsequent analogies test. However, additional analyses of the failure condition subjects who selected the debilitating music suggested that these persons performed better on the subsequent analogies test than did the subjects who chose less debilitating music.

A remaining survey study involving a cognitive-intellectual task focused on the observers' reactions to handicaps, rather than examining the performance effects on the handicapping protagonists themselves (as has been the case in the previously described studies in this subsection). In this observer-rating study by Springston and Chafe (1987), which I have described in some detail in the section on competence and control effects, the raters also were asked to respond to an additional question that has interesting implications. For this question, "To what degree could each girl *succeed* in her field as a permanent career?" the raters concluded that the nonhandicapping person and accidentally handicapping person were more likely to succeed than the voluntarily handicapping individual (no statistics are reported on the comparison of nonhandicapping vs. accidentally handicapping conditions).

Sports

Rhodewalt and his colleagues have provided some data on the intriguing question of self-handicapping sequelae in the sports arena. The basic methodology involves the administration of the self-report Self-Handicapping Scale (Jones & Rhodewalt, 1982; see also Rhodewalt, Chapter 3 in this volume), and thereafter tracing the actual behaviors of the persons with differing self-handicapping scores (Rhodewalt *et al.*, 1984). In a first study by Rhodewalt *et al.* (1984), the Princeton University varsity swimming team members' Self-Handicapping Scale scores were correlated with several other indices. Although the coach's ratings indicated that the high self-handicappers did not increase their practice for important meets, while their low self-handicapping counterparts did (thus providing construct validational support for the scale), there were no differences in the actual meet performances of the high and low self-handicappers. In a second study by Rhodewalt *et al.* (1984), a sample of professional golfers was recruited. As predicted, the low as compared to high self-handicappers (as measured by the scale) practiced less for important events (again providing validational support for the scale). However, there was a trend for the high as compared to low self-handicappers to accumulate more Grand Prix points over the entire season.

Social Interaction

In the Arkin and Baumgardner (1985b) study discussed previously in the esteem and affective response effects section, it may be recalled that the high, but not the low, socially anxious subjects rated their conversations in the dyadic interactions as being more enjoyable when there was an imposed handicap of interfering background noise as compared to no information about the interference of the background noise. What should be added for the present section is that the dyadic partners also rated the interaction performance of these same high socially anxious subjects as being better in the handicap (noise interferes) as compared to no-handicap condition.

Health

There are only three reported studies that bear on the topic of the health-related effects of self-handicapping. In a first study by Leary (1986), high and low socially anxious subjects undertook a social interaction task in which there was a background noise that was described as either being likely or unlikely to influence their performance. Results showed that when the noise was described as being impairing, as compared to when it was not so described, there were lower pulse rates, and this effect was especially marked for the high socially anxious subjects.

The other two studies related to health effects utilized the Self-Handicapping Scale. In the previously discussed Rhodewalt et al. (1984) study of the Princeton University swimming team members, no differences emerged in the high and low handicappers' reported physical problems, or in their eating and sleeping behaviors. In a second study of professional golfers, Rhodewalt et al. (1984) reported that there was a trend for the high self-handicappers to have more doctor visits and to report being in poorer physical condition than their low handicapping counterparts. However, no differences in actual injuries appeared between the high and low self-handicappers. These latter findings raise the interesting possibility that persons who are dispositionally high in self-handicapping may phenomenologically accentuate their physical problems.

Overview and Critique of Sequelae Research

In order to review the self-handicapping process and the associated effects, I refer the reader to the schematic depicted in Figure 2. Going from the top to the bottom of this sequence, I have illustrated a hypothesized temporal progression of events for a particular handicapping-effects episode. In depicting this schematic as representing one episode of self-handicapping and its associated sequelae, however, I am mirroring the bias of the experimental literature in looking at handicapping and its effects in a very short temporal envelope. In part, this may have reflected the ease with which it is possible to study the short-term effects of handicapping in laboratory settings. Additionally, it may be assumed that many of the effects of self-handicapping are relatively temporally delimited (viz., esteem–affect, competence–control). In the extent to which self-handicapping may involve a give-and-take interaction be-

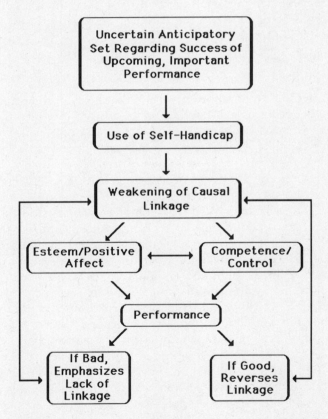

FIGURE 2. Temporal sequencing and sequelae of self-handicapping.

tween the protagonists and external audiences, however, there is a need to expand the present "snapshot" experimental mentality in order to examine a more protracted handicapping sequence and the corresponding effects at the various points in this sequence. Interestingly, in the early and more recent work on the related topic of excuse making, researchers have also advocated a longer-term analysis of that protective strategy as a series of negotiations (e.g., Scheff, 1968, Schönbach, 1985; Scott & Lyman, 1968; Snyder & Higgins, 1990).

The previous pages have described the effects of handicaps that have varied in terms of whether the handicap is behaviorally manifested or self-reported, is instigated by the protagonist or is imposed by the situation, is located inside or outside of the person, and so on. It is evident that the study of self-handicapping has grown to include a large number of potential handicaps that protagonists may "use" in order to lessen the linkage to the impending, potential poor performance. Future research will undoubtedly further expand this list of handicaps. For now, however, what do we know about the role of self-handicaps in lessening the causal linkage (see "Weakening of Causal Linkage" box in Figure 2)? Taken together, the reviewed studies involving observers' ratings of the handicapping conditions of depression and alcohol intoxication provide tentative support for the theoretical proposition that handicaps should weaken the causal linkage between the actor and the bad act. These observer studies are noteworthy because previous empirical laboratory studies have indicated that persons do employ depressive mood (e.g., Baumgardner *et al.*, 1985) and alcohol consumption (e.g., Higgins & Harris, 1988, 1989; Tucker *et al.*, 1981) as self-handicaps. What is needed in regard to such observer studies, additionally, is an examination of the potential causal weakening that may occur in association with such other handicaps as lowered effort, selection of difficult performance arenas, and the like. Likewise, there are no reported studies that address this weakening of the causal linkage from the perspective of the person who is employing a handicap. It logically would follow that self-handicappers should believe that such handicaps obscure and weaken the causal linkage to a potentially bad action, but this critical point awaits empirical documentation.

I would propose that the believability of the handicap, for the protagonist and especially for the external audiences, is a key issue that should determine whether the handicap serves to diminish the causal linkage to bad acts. Therefore, in order to expand the utility of the various paradigmatic issues regarding self-handicapping (e.g., behavioral vs. self-report mode, person- vs. situation-initiated, internal vs. external locus, anticipatory vs. incorporated), I would recommend that the effects of each of these dimensions on the believability of the handicap would provide important information in regard to the workings of the overall handicapping phenomenon.

Another issue that is relevant to believability relates to the role of audiences in the deception process. In the extent to which there are not readily apparent external audiences who are involved in some way in the evaluation of the self-handicap, then the self-handicapper's propensity for self-deception about the believability of the handicap should be maximized. When external audiences become more salient in this process, then the self- and other-deception about believability should be a more tenuous proposition. However, as I will argue later in this chapter, even in this latter scenario, the protagonist and handicapper can often arrive at a collaborative illusion about the believability of the handicap.

One of the hypothesized repercussions of the lessening of the causal linkage to the potential bad act is a preservation of the handicapping person's esteem and positive affective state (see "Esteem/Positive Affect" box in Figure 2). Because of the central role that self-esteem preservation has been hypothesized to play in the self-handicapping process, it is surprising that only one reported study (Isleib *et al.*, 1988, described above) directly has tested for the effects of handicapping (situation-induced) on the protagonist's self-esteem. Other studies examining the effects of self-handicapping on self-esteem are obviously needed. However, the one available study does suggest that there are self-esteem benefits for the handicapped protagonist. Additionally, the reviewed studies related to the protagonists' affective responses to the self-handicapping also indicate that there are emotional payoffs to such strategies. Taken together, these studies provide support for the theoretical notion that the purveyors of self-handicaps should experience some esteem (and affective) protection. The one available study that taps the observers' reactions to various types of handicaps (i.e., Springston & Chafe, 1987) may provide a caveat to the aforementioned positive affect-related responses. Namely, if the handicap is perceived as being purposeful, the observing audience appears to like such a handicapper less than an accidental and nonhandicapping person. This latter inference is derived on the basis of only one study, and as such warrants further research. Nevertheless, this does raise the possibility that self-handicapping may be seductive from the protagonist's point of view, but from the viewpoint of observing audiences it may have counterproductive effects under certain circumstances (see Higgins & Snyder, 1989). Indeed, the aforementioned counterproductive effects may result because the external audiences do not believe in the genuineness of the purposeful handicapper's impediment.

Another postulation in regard to the weakening of the causal linkage to a potential bad act is that there should be salutary effects on the handicapper's sense of competence and control (see "Competence/Control" box of Figure 2). The strands taken from the studies reviewed in the previous section on competence and control effects, when woven together, indicate that self-handicapping may yield a seductive cloak of competence and control. This overarching conclusion needs to be tempered, however, by those studies (i.e., Arkin & Baumgardner, 1985c; Schouten & Handelsman, 1987) that indicate that very obvious or chronic handicapping may have backfiring, external audience-generated effects on the protagonist's sense of competence and control. It may be that such obvious handicaps have costs associated with their benefits. It also should be cautioned that there are certain external audiences who may eliminate or reverse the "normal" competence–control benefits. This may be a believability-driven effect in that certain audiences may be especially critical of the veracity of the "impediment." Having stated these provisos, however, it should be highlighted that the presently reviewed results do provide some support for the competence–control theoretical underpinnings of self-handicapping. And, contrary to earlier speculation that handicapping may not result in any "increase in genuine control" (Arkin & Baumgardner, 1985a), the presently reviewed competence–control findings, especially when taken in conjunction with the esteem–affect results, suggest some very real cognitive–emotional benefits for the handicapper.

As can be seen by examining the arrow that unites the "Esteem/Affect" and "Competence/Control" boxes depicted in Figure 2, I have posited that these two states interact with each other. That is to say, handicapping effects that serve to protect a person's sense of esteem–affective state also should serve to foster a sense of competence–control. On this point, related research indicates that an elevated mood results in greater self-reward, perceived likelihood of success, and task persistence (Brown, 1984; Wright & Mischel, 1982). Conversely, factors that increase a sense of control–competency also elicit increases in positive affects (see for review, Langer, 1983).

Moving downward in the schematic shown in Figure 2, the esteem–affect and competence–control states should influence the handicapper's actual performance (see "Performance" box). What do the reviewed studies tell us about performance effects? The relevant studies reveal a complex pattern in which there are sometimes benefits, sometimes liabilities, and sometimes no apparent performance sequelae of self-handicapping. First, in regard to those studies in which the handicap is situationally imposed, it appears that there are performance benefits that accrue to most protagonists (i.e., Frankel & Snyder, 1978; Springston & Chafe, 1987), and to particular subgroups of people such those who are highly socially anxious (Arkin & Baumgardner, 1985b) and low in need for achievement (Weiner & Sierad, 1975). Second, in regard to person-initiated handicaps, the effects are more varied in that two studies suggest performance benefits (i.e., Rhodewalt & Davison, 1986; Rhodewalt *et al.*, 1984, study #2), four reveal no differential performance effects (i.e., Harris & Snyder, 1986; Greenberg *et al.*, 1985; Rhodewalt *et al.*, 1984, study #1; Smith *et al.*, 1982), and two show performance liabilities (i.e., Higgins & Snyder, 1989; Springston & Chafe, 1987). In fact, taking a simple scorecard approach to the reviewed studies, an overriding conclusion is that handicaps definitely are not always true impediments to performance. Also, the performance effects must be weighed in conjunction with the total set of effects that accrue to the handicapper.

Before leaving the topic of the performance-related effects of self-handicapping, I would direct the reader's attention to the two arrows that depict the ensuing effects should the performance turn out to be bad or good. If the poor performance does eventuate (the lower left box in Figure 2), then the discounting process should theoretically continue in that the implications can continue to be drawn in regard to weakening the causal linkage. As can be seen in the lower right hand box of the schematic, if a good performance should eventuate, then the augmenting process should theoretically reverse the linkage and result in even more beneficial effects (e.g., "Why, I succeeded in spite of that big obstacle!"). Whether self-handicapping persons actually have such augmentation-based thoughts, however, has not been explored empirically. Therefore, one key issue in this area will be to ascertain whether augmentation-based cognitions even occur to self-handicappers when they actually succeed. It may be that the self-handicapper has focused to such a degree on the weakening of the linkage to the potential bad act so as to *protect* the personal theory of self, that it is difficult to "switch gears" and *enhance* the self theory by emphasizing a sense of linkage to the outcome should it be positive. Although there is some literature attesting to the fact that the persons who engage in protective processes also engage in enhancing processes (see Snyder, 1989, for review), this issue awaits further investigation in the self-handicapping research area.

If the self-handicapping person actually experiences success, one would expect that he or she should expressly emphasize the linkage to the available audiences if the hypothesized augmentation process is operative. Empirically, therefore, we would expect such persons to highlight the handicap after success. These discounting and augmenting processes also could be empirically investigated by having the handicap-ping protagonist, and observers, rate the causal linkage and the other effects after receiving feedback that the performance is a failure or a success (e.g., see Arkin & Baumgardner, 1985c). There are two reported studies that indirectly address this augmentation issue (Arkin & Baumgardner, 1985c; Springston & Chafe, 1987), but they provide only suggestive evidence for its viability.

The health effects are not shown on Figure 2 because the literature to date is very limited. Although it is extremely tenuous to speculate about these effects given the small number of studies, a conservative conclusion is that the available evidence does not suggest any consistent health liabilities associated with the handicapping.

In the degree to which a self-handicap, through the lessening of the linkage to the impending, possible negative performance, enables the protagonist to focus on the upcoming task and not upon himself or herself, then one would expect the aforementioned esteem–affect, com-petence–control, and performance benefits (and perhaps even health benefits). Simply put, the successful handicap may enable the pro-tagonist to focus on the relevant task cues and not the potentially inter-fering self-relevant emotions and cognitions. Indeed, recent literature has consistently shown that there are psychological benefits associated with the avoidance as compared with the accentuation of self-focus (Pyszczynski & Greenberg, 1987). For example, self-focused attention appears to lower self-esteem (Duval & Wicklund, 1972; Pyszczynski & Greenberg, 1987), increase depressive affect (Gibbons, Smith, Brehm, & Schroeder, 1981), and reduce persistence (Carver, Blaney, & Scheier, 1979). Furthermore, the benefits of this nonintrospective stance appear to be especially marked following failure experiences (e.g., Carver & Scheier, 1981; Duval & Wicklund, 1972). Given the emergence of this literature on focus of attention, measures tapping this variable may provide an excellent mediational indicator of the processes by which self-handicapping works to provide benefits or liabilities.

SELF-HANDICAPPING AND THE NEGOTIATION OF CAUSAL REALITY

Having discussed the specific experimental processes and effects of self-handicapping in the two previous major sections of this chapter, I would like to place the phenomenon of self-handicapping in a larger theoretical context in this final section. In order to more fully address the topic of the processes and sequelae of self-handicapping, in this section I will first describe how people employ the notions of causality and reality in order to make sense of their world. Thereafter, I will propose that people employ reality-negotiation maneuvers in an attempt to preserve their theories of causality–reality, both at a personal level and at a larger societal level. Self-handicapping will be highlighted as one type of reality negotiation. Finally, I will conclude with a brief examination of the fundamental ambivalence that people have about "handicaps" as a means of negotiating with reality.

THE CAUSALITY CONNECTION AND REALITY

The notion of causality is one of the cornerstones of the human species' attempt to bring order and understanding to its existence. In the words of Snyder, Ford, and Harris (1987, p. 3),

> Human beings are constantly trying to make sense out of the events in their lives. This search for understanding makes *Homo sapiens* the most sophisticated theory or model generator among the multitude of living organisms. Although living organisms, for survival reasons, are intimately involved in unraveling the cause and effect relationships in their life arena, humankind not only appears to generate the more intricate set of behaviors, but also develops the most complex explanations for the cause–effect sequences. Most people have a multitude of theories to explain the events in their lives and the lives of other people. A theory is a viewpoint or perspective, a way of looking at causality or the relationship between things.

The personal theories of "causation" may not follow the strict scientific definitions of causality, but in the minds of people there are simple linear chains of events in which one event logically follows another. Such correlations or associations begin to take on the status of cause–effect in the phenomenology of people. And, more importantly, these causal models of one's world are carefully nurtured and sustained because they bring some order to the potential chaos of events that occur in one's life spheres. In fact, it could be argued that one major developmental task is the refinement of a good, working set of causal explanations for one's world.

Moving beyond the aforementioned exposition of the importance of causality in explaining one's world, it is obvious that it is necessary to add antecedent and consequent conditions to this mental equation. That is to say, the causal linkage serves to tie antecedent conditions to subsequent consequences. In this vein, reality reflects the person's conceptualization of such causally determined strings of events. This analysis of action-linkage-consequences sequences also emphasizes the phenomenology of each person in determining the veracity of such perceptions. As such, one person's theory of reality may or may not correspond to another person's theory. In the extent to which these personal theories are explicitly articulated, they naturally may have to be revised in order to accommodate the prevailing "realities" of other people. This latter assertion is most apparent for the operation of science, where "reality," or the "facts," reflect the prevailing and accepted point of view about a particular action-linkage-consequence sequence.

SMALL POCKETS OF REALITY: REALITY NEGOTIATION AND THE INDIVIDUAL

Just as we may hold theories about the action-linkage-consequence sequences associated with external events in our world, so too do we hold personal theories about ourselves. These personal theories may apply to our behavior in particular situations, or they may portray our self-views across a multitude of situations. In these personal theories, or self-schemata, the typical sequence of events involves the actor (oneself) behaving in a particular fashion (the causal linkage) so as to elicit a particular outcome (the consequence). Such personal theories are employed by people in order to guide their responses to particular situations. This exposition of personal theories borrows heavily from the work of previous writers (e.g., world models, Bowlby, 1969; personal theories, Epstein, 1984; structures of meaning, Marris, 1975; assumptive worlds, Parkes, 1975; identity theories of self, Schlenker, 1985). The idea of personal theories also has a distinctly Adlerian flavor (see introductory chapter in this volume).

Personal theories of "self" are more than cold, dispassionate guides for understanding who we are and how we are to react to our world. Rather, these underlying personal theories are driven by basic human motives (see, for related discussion, Epstein, 1980). As I have postulated elsewhere (Snyder & Higgins, 1988a), two such fundamental motives are the maintenance of esteem and the maintenance of a sense of control. That is, the personal theories of most people are based on the motivational premise that they are "good/in control" people, and there is a propensity to preserve these personal theories in the face of contradictory information. One instance that portends contradictory input relevant to the "good/in control" personal theory is when the individual anticipates a possible poor performance in an upcoming, important life arena. The process of responding to such discrepant (as well as non-discrepant), self-relevant feedback so as to preserve the personal theory of self is *reality negotiation* (Snyder & Higgins, 1988a).

There are at least two points of elaboration that are worthy of mention in regard to the reality-negotiation concept. First, because this hypothesized process is aimed at preserving the "good/in control" personal theory of self, it should be emphasized that the protagonist biases information so as to preserve the underlying motives upon which the self-theory is built. Interestingly, a recent review suggests that such esteem- and control-related illusions about oneself are associated with adaptive consequences such as greater happiness, caring for others, motivation, persistence, and task performance (Taylor & Brown, 1988).

A second point of elaboration in regard to reality negotiation is that this process must also attend to relevant external audiences (Schlenker, 1985, 1987). The reality of an event sequence, as I have discussed previously in this section, rests upon consensus among the external audiences. Therefore, in order to negotiate reality,

> We acknowledge the external audience's rules, opinions, and so forth, but we weigh more heavily our personal interpretation of events as they pertain to us. A negotiated reality thus reflects a biased compromise that the person considers "valid" and that outside sources (e.g., observers) would not seriously question should the person verbalize it (Snyder & Higgins, 1988a, p. 10).

LARGE POCKETS OF REALITY: REALITY NEGOTIATION AND SOCIETY

Just as there are personal theories that the individual applies to himself or herself, there are also theories formed about the nature of actor–causal–linkage–outcome sequences that the individual applies to people in general. In this vein, I propose that the members of society have an investment in such theories because they provide a framework for understanding one's environment. Furthermore, such theories, like the ones that are applied by the individual to the self, have motivational determinants. A principal motivation that underlies larger societal theories is the need to preserve the perception of control. That is, in the extent to which we have, at a societal level, shared theories about the nature of causality in regard to human behavior, then we can expect a certain degree of order and predictability.

At the societal level, the prevailing view is that people are basically the authors of their own existence. This conclusion is derived from an analysis of the practical solution to an age-old philosophical debate involving determinism and choice in human behavior (see Ryle, 1980). The doctrine of determinism is rarely applied in everyday life (Kemeny, 1959), and as such the accepted viewpoint is that people have free will (choice). And, having choice, the next logical inference is that people are "responsible" for the events in their lives (e.g., Berofsky, 1966; Franklin, 1968; Sartre, 1956).

This philosophical tradition of responsibility implicitly emphasizes a norm of personal, internal causation relating actors to subsequent consequences. This latter proposition is similar to the "norm of internality" (Jellison & Green, 1981), which is a research-derived, social-psychological principle. Another way of stating this latter principle is that there is a natural tendency for people to be seen as the causal agents in given sequences of events.

If there is a tendency to perceive people as being causally linked to outcomes, then it should not be surprising that society establishes agreed upon, codified rules for evaluating appropriate actor–linkage–outcome sequences. What is especially noteworthy for the present chapter, however, is that these same codified laws also deal extensively with the circumstances wherein the actor is *not* held as being causally responsible for an outcome. In other words, there are instances in which an outcome is negative, and society has formal procedures (i.e., the legal system) for assessing whether the normally applied principle of internal causality (linking an actor to an outcome) should be lessened or undone.

By implementing a set of laws that "explain" why, under certain prescribed circumstances, actors are not causally responsible for bad outcomes, the society as a whole can preserve its theory about how people are causal agents. On a larger scale, therefore, this is a reality negotiation process whereby society maintains its sense of control. By finding a particular defendant innocent, for example, the society "congratulates itself for having a rule structure for effectively determining its citizens' linkage to actions" (Snyder, 1989, p. 148). Conversely, should the defendant be found guilty, that person is "punished and perhaps even incarcerated; in turn, the act of incarceration reifies the societal need to preserve the theory that there is a sense of control and order among its nonincarcerated citizens" (Snyder, 1989, p. 148).

SELF-HANDICAPPING AS REALITY NEGOTIATION

Just as there are formalized, legal means of lessening the linkage to bad acts should we ever commit bad acts of sufficient magnitude, in the day-to-day toils of life there are ways of dealing with anticipated psychological jams. In the attempt to cope with the uncertainty of success in an impending performance arena, for example, self-handicaps (as documented in this chapter) are aimed at protecting the protagonist's "good/in control" personal theories of self. As such, self-handicapping is one strategy that exemplifies the overarching reality-negotiation process that I have described in this last section.

Given the similarity in the underlying reality-negotiation motives for both the individual and society, as I have argued in the previous two subsections, the self-handicapping protagonist and society may be primed to form a collaborative illusion regarding the efficacy of the handicap. In further support of this speculation, research shows that external audiences appear to be positively biased toward others (e.g., Schneider, Hastorf, & Ellsworth, 1979; Sears, 1983). And, if external audiences are asked to deliver negative feedback, they tend to bias this feedback toward the positive (Tesser & Rosen, 1975), or they do not deliver the feedback at all (Darley & Fazio, 1980). These collaborative processes, which have been explored with "normal" populations, are also operative should the person progress from anticipatory to incorporated handicaps. In this vein, prevailing medical models of "mental illness" reinforce the handicap in terms of a particular "diagnostic label" (Higgins & Snyder, 1989; Snyder & Smith, 1982). Indeed, the society may encourage the handicap label such that it "spreads" to encapsulate the protagonist (Wright, 1983), and, in turn, that protagonist may be expected to demonstrate behaviors consistent with the self-report manifestations of the handicap.

Against the backdrop of factors that facilitate the operation of the self-handicap, however, there remains a fundamental ambivalence for the protagonists and the observers of self-handicapping. This ambivalence may be related to the prevailing norm that people "should" be causal agents. It also may relate to the fact that, at some level, we do not like the fact that the self-handicapping person has an impediment. Indeed, the literature on disabilities suggests that people in general, including helping professionals, have subtle, negative attitudes about a "disability" (Altman, 1981; Antonak & Livneh, 1988; Roessler & Bolton, 1978; Wright, 1983). As Wright (1983, p. 280) put it,

> Attitudes toward a person with a disability not infrequently reflect both positive and negative feelings, either simultaneously or at least in rapid succession. Thus people with a disability may be admired for their accomplishments and yet pitied because they are "cripples."

Although research to date on self-handicapping hints at this ambivalence, especially the audience reaction studies that show costs associated with the benefits (e.g., Arkin & Baumgardner, 1985c; Schouten & Handelsman, 1987; Springston & Chafe, 1987), the clarification of the nature of this ambivalence awaits further empirical exploration.

Whatever the degree of ambivalence about this phenomenon, however, it appears that self-handicapping is the tactic of choice by many a person who has, or will face, the uncertainty of future success. As such, self-handicapping is but one tactic, among several in the reality-negotiation armamentarium, for coping with the larger existential fight with our inevitable fallability. In this latter, ultimate sense, the paradox of "taking a psychological dive" is solved.

ACKNOWLEDGMENTS

Gratitude is expressed to Raymond L. Higgins, Mark R. Leary, James A. Shepperd, and Elizabeth A. Self for comments on this chapter.

REFERENCES

Abramson, L. Y., Seligman, M. E. P., & Teasdale, J. D. (1978). Learned helplessness in humans: Critique and reformulation. *Journal of Abnormal Psychology, 87*, 49–74.

Altman, B. M. (1981). Studies of attitudes toward the handicapped: The need for a new direction. *Social Problems, 28*, 321–337.

Antonak, R. F., & Livneh, H. (1988). *The measurement of attitudes toward people with disabilities.* Springfield, IL: Charles C Thomas.

Arkin, R. M., & Baumgardner, A. H. (1985a). Self-handicapping. In J. H. Harvey & G. W. Weary (Eds.), *Attribution: Basic issues and applications* (pp. 169–202). New York: Academic Press.

Arkin, R. M., & Baumgardner, A. H. (1985b). *The facilitative effects of providing a handicap.* Unpublished manuscript, University of Missouri, Columbia.

Arkin, R. M., & Baumgardner, A. H. (1985c). *When self-handicapping fails to serve a purpose: Impressions of the strategic procrastinator.* Unpublished manuscript, University of Missouri, Columbia. Reported in Baumgardner, A. H., & Arkin, R. M. (1987). Coping with the prospect of disapproval: Strategies and sequelae. In C. R. Snyder & C. E. Ford (Eds.), *Coping with negative life events: Clinical and social psychological perspectives* (pp. 323–346). New York: Plenum.

Arkin, R. M., & Haugtvedt, C. (1984). Test-anxiety, task difficulty and diagnosticity: The roles of cognitive interference and fear of failure as determinants of choice of task. In H. van der Ploeg, R. Schwarzer, & C. D. Spielberger (Eds.), *Advances in test anxiety research* (Vol. 3, pp. 147–162). Hillsdale, NJ: Erlbaum.

Arkin, R. M., & Shepperd, J. M. (1988). *The role of social anxiety in self-presentational self-handicapping.* Unpublished manuscript, University of Missouri, Columbia.

Baumeister, R. F., Hamilton, J. C., & Tice, D. M. (1985). Public versus private expectancy of success: Confidence booster or performance pressure. *Journal of Personality and Social Psychology, 48*, 1447–1457.

Baumgardner, A. H., Lake, E. A., & Arkin, R. M. (1985). Claiming mood as a self-handicap: The influence of spoiled and unspoiled public identities. *Personality and Social Psychology Bulletin, 11*, 349–357.

Berglas, S. (1985). Self-handicapping and self-handicappers: A cognitive/attributional model of interpersonal self-protective behavior. In R. Hogan (Ed.), *Perspectives in personality* (Vol. 1, pp. 235–270). Greenwich, CT: JAI.

Berglas, S. (1988). The three faces of self-handicapping: Protective self-presentation, a strategy for self-esteem enhancement, and a character disorder. In S. L. Zelen (Ed.), *Self-representation: Clinical and theoretical applications of attributions* (pp. 133–169). New York: Springer-Verlag.

Berglas, S., & Jones, E. E. (1978). Drug choice as a self-handicapping strategy in response to noncontingent success. *Journal of Personality and Social Psychology, 36*, 405–417.

Berofsky, B. (1966). *Freewill and determinism.* New York: Harper & Row.

Bowlby, J. (1969). *Attachment and loss. Vol. 1: Attachment.* London: Hogarth.

Brown, J. D. (1984). Effects of induced mood on causal attributions for success and failure. *Motivation and Emotion, 8,* 343–353.

Carducci, B. J., & McNeely, J. A. (1981). *Alcohol and attributions don't mix: The effect of alcohol on alcoholics' and nonalcoholics' attributions of blame for wife abuse.* Paper presented at the meeting of the American Psychological Association, Los Angeles, CA.

Carver, C. S., Blaney, P. H., & Scheier, M. F. (1979). Reassertion and giving up: The interactive role of self-directed attention and outcome expectancy. *Journal of Personality and Social Psychology, 37,* 1859–1870.

Carver, C. S., & Scheier, M. F. (1981). *Attention and self-regulation: A control-theory approach to human behavior.* New York: Springer.

Coopersmith, S. (1967). *The antecedents of self-esteem.* San Francisco: Freeman.

Critchlow, B. (1985). The blame in the bottle: Attributions about drunken behavior. *Personality and Social Psychology Bulletin, 11,* 258–274.

Darley, J. M., & Fazio, R. H. (1980). Expectancy confirmation processes arising in the social interaction sequence. *American Psychologist, 35,* 867–881.

DeGree, C. E., & Snyder, C. R. (1985). Adler's psychology (of use) today: Personal history of traumatic life events as a self-handicapping strategy. *Journal of Personality and Social Psychology, 48,* 1512–1519.

Duval, S., & Wicklund, R. (1972). *A theory of objective self-awareness.* New York: Academic Press.

Epstein, S. (1980). The self-concept: A review and the proposal of an integrated theory of personality. In E. Staub (Ed.), *Personality: Basic issues and current research* (pp. 82–132). Englewood Clifts, NJ: Prentice-Hall.

Epstein, S. (1984). Controversial issues in emotion theory. In P. Shaver (Ed.), *Review of personality and social psychology: Emotions, relationships, and health* (pp. 64–88). Beverly Hills, CA: Sage.

Frankel, A., & Snyder, M. L. (1978). Poor performance following unsolvable problems: Learned helplessness or egotism? *Journal of Personality and Social Psychology, 36,* 1415–1423.

Franklin, R. L. (1968). *Freewill and determinism: A study of rival conceptions of man.* London: Routledge & Kegan Paul.

Gelles, R. J. (1972). *The violent home.* Beverly Hills, CA: Sage.

Gibbons, F. X., & Gaeddert, W. P. (1984). Focus of attention and placebo utility. *Journal of Experimental Social Psychology, 20,* 159–176.

Gibbons, F. X., Smith, T. W., Brehm, S. S., & Schroeder, D. (1981). *Self-awareness and self-confrontation: The role of focus of attention in the process of psychotherapy.* Unpublished manuscript, University of Kansas, Lawrence.

Gorney, B. (1985). *Therapists' attitudes and treatment recommendations for domestic violence as a function of alcohol involvement.* Unpublished dissertation, University of Kansas, Lawrence.

Greenberg, J. (1985). Unobtainable goal choice as a self-handicapping strategy. *Journal of Applied Social Psychology, 15,* 140–152.

Greenberg, J., Pyszczynski, T., & Paisley, C. (1985). Effect of extrinsic incentives on the use of test anxiety as an anticipatory attributional defense: Playing it cool when the stakes are high. *Journal of Personality and Social Psychology, 47,* 1136–1145.

Handelsman, M. M., Fox, J. E., & Kraiger, K. (1987). *Construct validity evidence for the original Self-Handicapping Scale and a revised short form.* Paper presented at the Rocky Mountain Psychological Association Convention, Albuquerque, NM.

Handelsman, M. M., Kraiger, K., & King, C. S. (1985). *Self-handicapping by task choice: An attribute ambiguity analysis.* Paper presented at the meeting of the Rocky Mountain Psychological Association, Tucson, AZ.

Harris, R. N., & Snyder, C. R. (1986). The role of uncertain self-esteem in self-handicapping. *Journal of Personality and Social Psychology, 51,* 451–458.

Higgins, R. L., & Harris, R. N. (1988). Strategic "alcohol" use: Drinking to self-handicap. *Journal of Social and Clinical Psychology, 6,* 191–202.

Higgins, R. L., & Harris, R. N. (1989, April). *Self-handicapping social performance through "alcohol" consumption: The interaction of drinker history and expectancy.* Paper presented at the meeting of the Southwestern Psychological Association, Houston, TX.

Higgins, R. L., & Snyder, C. R. (1989). Excuses gone awry: An analysis of self-defeating excuses. In R. L. Curtis (Ed.), *Self-defeating behaviors: Experimental research, clinical impressions, and practical implications* (pp. 99–130). New York: Plenum.

Isleib, R. A., Vuchinich, R. E., & Tucker, J. A. (1988). Performance attributions and changes in self-esteem following self-handicapping with alcohol consumption. *Journal of Social and Clinical Psychology, 6,* 88–103.

Jellison, J. M., & Green, J. (1981). A self-presentational approach to the fundamental attributional error. *Journal of Personality and Social Psychology, 40,* 643–649.

Jones, E. E., & Berglas, S. (1978). Control of attributions about the self through self-handicapping strategies: The appeal of alcohol and the role of underachievement. *Personality and Social Psychology Bulletin, 4,* 200–206.

Jones, E. E., & Rhodewalt, F. (1982). Self-Handicapping Scale. Unpublished scale, Department of Psychology, Princeton University & University of Utah.

Kelley, H. H. (1971). *Attribution in social interaction.* New York: General Learning Press.

Kemeny, J. G. (1959). *A philosopher looks at science.* Princeton, NJ: Van Nostrand.

Kolditz, T. A., & Arkin, R. M. (1982). An impression management interpretation of the self-handicapping strategy. *Journal of Personality and Social Psychology, 43,* 492–502.

Langer, E. J. (1983). *The psychology of control.* Beverly Hills, CA: Sage.

Leary, M. R. (1986). The impact of interactional impediments on social anxiety and self-presentation. *Journal of Experimental Social Psychology, 22,* 122–135.

Leary, M. R., & Shepperd, J. A. (1986). Behavioral self-handicaps vs. self-reported handicaps: A conceptual note. *Journal of Personality and Social Psychology, 51,* 1265–1268.

Marris, P. (1975). *Loss and change.* Garden City, NY: Anchor/Doubleday.

Mayerson, N. H., & Rhodewalt, F. (1988). The role of self-protective attributions in the experience of pain. *Journal of Social and Clinical Psychology, 6,* 203–218.

Meyer, W. U., & Starke, E. (1982). Own ability in relation to self-concept of ability: A field study of information-seeking. *Personality and Social Psychology Bulletin, 8,* 501–507.

Parkes, C. M. (1975). What becomes of redundant world models? A contribution to the study of adaption to change. *British Journal of Medical Psychology, 48,* 131–137.

Phares, E. J., & Lamiell, J. T. (1974). Relationship of internal–external control to defensive preferences. *Journal of Consulting and Clinical Psychology, 42,* 872–878.

Pyszczynski, T., & Greenberg, J. (1983). Determinants of reduction in intended effort as a strategy for coping with anticipated failure. *Journal of Research in Personality, 17,* 412–422.

Pyszczynski, T., & Greenberg, J. (1987). Depression, self-focused attention, and self-regulatory preservation. In C. R. Snyder & C. E. Ford (Eds.), *Coping with negative life events: Clinical and social psychological perspectives* (pp. 105–130). New York: Plenum.

Rhodewalt, F., & Davison, J. (1986). Self-handicapping and subsequent performance: Role of outcome valence and attributional ambiguity. *Basic and Applied Social Psychology, 7,* 307–323.

Rhodewalt, F., Saltzman, A. T., & Wittmer, J. (1984). Self-handicapping among competitive athletes: The role of practice in self-esteem protection. *Basic and Applied Social Psychology, 5,* 197–210.

Richardson, D., & Campbell, J. (1980). Alcohol and wife abuse: The effect of alcohol on attributions of blame for wife abuse. *Personality and Social Psychology Bulletin, 6,* 51–56.

Richardson, D., & Campbell, J. (1982). Alcohol and rape: The effect of alcohol on attributions of blame for rape. *Personality and Social Psychology Bulletin, 8,* 468–476.

Robinson, J. P., & Shaver, P. R. (1973). *Measures of social psychological attitudes.* Ann Arbor: Institute for Social Research, University of Michigan.

Roessler, R., & Bolton, B. (1978). *Psychological adjustment to disability.* Baltimore, MD: University Park Press.

Rosenberg, M. (1965). *Society and adolescent self-image.* Princeton: Princeton University Press.

Ryle, G. (1980). *Dilemmas.* Cambridge: Cambridge University Press. (First published in 1954)

Sachs, P. R. (1982). Avoidance of diagnostic information in self-evaluation of ability. *Personality and Social Psychology Bulletin, 8,* 242–246.

Sarason, I. G. (1980). Introduction to the study of test anxiety. In I. G. Sarason (Ed.), *Test Anxiety: Theory, research, and applications* (pp. 3–14). Hillsdale, NJ: Erlbaum.

Sartre, J. (1956). *Being and nothingness* (Translated by Hazel Barres). New York: Philosophical Library.

Scheff, T. J. (1968). Negotiating reality: Notes on power in the assessment of responsibility. *Social Relations, 16,* 3–16.

Schlenker, B. R. (1985). Identity and self-identification. In B. R. Schlenker (Ed.), *The self and social life* (pp. 65–99). New York: McGraw-Hill.

Schlenker, B. R. (1987). Threats to identity: Self-identification and social stress. In C. R. Snyder & C. E. Ford (Eds.), *Coping with negative life events: Clinical and social psychological perspectives* (pp. 323–346). New York: Plenum.

Schneider, D. J., Hastorf, A. H., & Ellsworth, P. C. (1979). *Person perception.* Reading, MA: Addison-Wesley.

Schönbach, P. (1985). *A taxonomy for account phases: Revised, explained, and applied.* Unpublished manuscript, Fakutat für Psychologie, Ruhr Universitat, Bochum, West Germany.

Schouten, P. G. W., & Handelsman, M. M. (1987). Social basis of self-handicapping: The case of depression. *Personality and Social Psychology Bulletin, 13,* 103–110.

Scott, M. B., & Lyman, S. M. (1968). Accounts. *American Sociological Review, 33,* 46–62.

Sears, D. O. (1983). The person-positivity bias. *Journal of Personality and Social Psychology, 44,* 233–250.

Seligman, M. E. P. (1975). *Helplessness: On depression, development, and death.* San Francisco: Freeman.

Shepperd, J. A., & Arkin, R. M. (1989a). Determinants of self-handicapping: Task importance and the effects of preexisting handicaps on self-generated handicaps. *Personality and Social Psychology Bulletin, 15,* 101–112.

Shepperd, J. A., & Arkin, R. M. (1989b). Self-handicapping: The moderating roles of public self-consciousness and task importance. *Personality and Social Psychology Bulletin, 15,* 252–265.

Shepperd, J. A., Strathman, A. J., & Arkin, R. M. (1987). *Other enhancement: Self-handicapping through enhancing the performance of another.* Paper presented at the meeting of the American Psychological Association, New York.

Smith, T. W., Snyder, C. R., & Handelsman, M. M. (1982). On the self-serving function of an academic wooden leg: Test anxiety as a self-handicapping strategy. *Journal of Personality and Social Psychology, 42,* 314–321.

Smith, T. W., Snyder, C. R., & Perkins, S. C. (1983). The self-serving function of hypochondriacal complaints: Physical symptoms as self-handicapping strategies. *Journal of Personality and Social Psychology, 44,* 787–797.

Snell, J. E., Rosenwald, R. J., & Robey, A. (1964). The wifebeater's wife: A study of family interaction. *Archives of General Psychiatry, 11,* 107–113.

Snyder, C. R. (1989). Reality negotiation: From excuses to hope and beyond. *Journal of Social and Clinical Psychology, 8,* 130–157.

Snyder, C. R., & Higgins, R. L. (1986). *Excuses: Do they work?* Paper presented at the Second Attribution-Personality Theory Conference, September, Los Angeles, CA.

Snyder, C. R., & Higgins, R. L. (1988a). Excuses: Their effective role in the negotiation of reality. *Psychological Bulletin, 104,* 23–35.

Snyder, C. R., & Higgins, R. L. (1988b). From making to being the excuse: An analysis of deception and verbal/nonverbal issues. *Journal of Nonverbal Behavior, 12,* 237–252.

Snyder, C. R., & Higgins, R. L. (1990). Reality negotiation and excuse-making: President Reagan's March 4, 1987 Iran arms scandal speech and other literature. In M. J. Cody & M. L. McLaughlin (Eds.), *The Psychology of tactical communication* (pp. 207–228). Clevedon, England: Multilingual Matters.

Snyder, C. R., & Smith, T. W. (1982). Symptoms as self-handicapping strategies: The virtues of old wine in a new bottle. In G. Weary & H. L. Mirels (Eds.), *Integrations of clinical and social psychology* (pp. 104–127). New York: Oxford University Press.

Snyder, C. R., & Smith, T. W. (1986). On being "shy like a fox": A self-handicapping analysis. In W. E. Jones, J. M. Cheek, & S. R. Briggs (Eds.), *Shyness: Perspectives on research and treatment* (pp. 161–172). New York: Plenum.

Snyder, C. R., Higgins, R. L., & Stucky, R. J. (1983). *Excuses: Masquerades in search of grace.* New York: Wiley-Interscience.

Snyder, C. R., Smith, T. W., Augelli, R. W., & Ingram, R. E. (1985). On the self-serving function of social anxiety. *Journal of Personality and Social Psychology, 48,* 970–980.

Snyder, C. R., Ford, C. E., & Harris, R. N. (1987). The effects of theoretical perspective on the analysis of coping with negative life events. In C. R. Snyder & C. E. Ford (Eds.), *Coping with negative life events: Clinical and social psychological perspectives* (pp. 3–13). New York: Plenum.

Snyder, M. L., & Wicklund, R. A. (1981). Attribute ambiguity. In J. A. Harvey, W. J. Ickes, & R. F. Kidd (Eds.), *New directions in attribution research* (Vol. 3, pp. 197–221). Hillsdale, NJ: Erlbaum.

Snyder, M. L., Smoller, B., Strenta, A., & Frankel, A. (1981). A comparison of egotism, negativity, and learned helplessness as explanations for poor performance after unsolvable problems. *Journal of Personality and Social Psychology, 40,* 24–30.

Sobell, L. C., & Sobell, M. B. (1975). Drunkenness, a "special circumstance" in crimes of violence: Sometimes. *International Journal of Addictions, 10,* 869–882.

Springston, F. J., & Chafe, P. M. (1987, June). *Impressions of fictional protagonists exhibiting self-handicapping behaviors.* Paper presented at the Canadian Psychological Association Convention, Vancouver, B. C.

Strube, M. J. (1986). An analysis of the Self-Handicapping Scale. *Basic and Applied Social Psychology, 13,* 211–224.

Strube, M. J., & Roemmele, L. A. (1985). Self-enhancement, self-assessment, and self-evaluative task choice. *Journal of Personality and Social Psychology, 49,* 981–993.

Taylor, S. E., & Brown, J. D. (1988). Illusion and well-being: A social psychological perspective on mental health. *Psychological Bulletin, 103,* 193–210.

Tesser, A., & Rosen, S. (1975). The reluctance to transmit bad news. In L. Berkowitz (Ed.), *Advances in experimental social psychology* (Vol. 8, pp. 193–232). New York: Academic Press.

Tucker, J. A., Vuchinich, R. E., & Sobell, M. B. (1981). Alcohol consumption as a self-handicapping strategy. *Journal of Abnormal Psychology, 90,* 220–230.

Weiner, B., & Sierad, J. (1975). Misattribution of failure and enhancement of achievement strivings. *Journal of Personality and Social Psychology, 31,* 415–421.

Wright, B. A. (1983). *Physical disability—A psychosocial approach.* New York: Harper & Row.

Wright, J., & Mischel, W. (1982). Influence of effect on cognitive social learning person variables. *Journal of Personality and Social Psychology, 43,* 901.

CHAPTER 5

SELF-HANDICAPPING
ETIOLOGICAL AND DIAGNOSTIC CONSIDERATIONS

STEVEN BERGLAS

*A man who has been the indisputable favorite of his mother keeps for life the
feeling of a conqueror, that confidence of success that often induces real success.
(Sigmund Freud—cited in Jones, 1953, Vol. 1, p. 5)*

*I treated a case of drunkenness in a man thirty-two years of age, very intelligent,
well-educated and perfectly healthy, who had regular bouts of drinking. . . . He
lived extravagantly at the expense of his parents, paying the highest prices for
more or less useless things whenever he chose to do so. . . . Such a way of living
usually originates in the prototypic attitude of a pampered child, who feels
obliged to keep out of the firing-line of life because he is not prepared for it. This
man made his escape, by being a drunkard.*

*The usual tensions of every day were not severe enough to drive him to drink, and
he was able to use his sober intervals to display good intentions. . . . [His]
drunkenness would begin . . . when he was expected to go into society
[or] . . . when there was a demand of duty. . . . His evident aim was to be relieved
of every duty and to be supported for his own sake alone. Self-centered and wholly
lacking social adjustment, he had nevertheless attained a goal of superiority by the
elimination of defeat. He had no defeat in society for he did not enter it; no defeat
in work, for he had no occupation. . . . Subjectively, he triumphed over life, lived
it upon his own terms entirely; but objectively, of course, the terms he obtained
were almost the worst possible. . . . He proved to have been a spoiled child. . .
(Alfred Adler, 1930, pp. 126–129)*

STEVEN BERGLAS • McLean Hospital/Harvard Medical School, Belmont, Massachusetts
02178.

INTRODUCTION

The goal of this chapter is to understand why Freud's and Adler's insights into the consequences of being a child singled-out for special attention by his parents were both accurate and, apparently, contradictory. The answer to this question should account for why certain people with overtly favorable—or even lofty—competence images often feel threatened by evaluative interactions and seek to protect their fragile sense of self-esteem by self-handicapping.

Without engaging in a rigorous semantic analysis of "favorite" and "pampered," consider how similar in meaning the two concepts are. Each connotes a higher than average indulgence of physical needs as well as inordinate displays of affection. In addition, it is assumed that both "indisputable favorites" and "pampered children" are the products of similar, abundantly nurturing, parenting styles. Oddly, however, two of the world's preeminent psychoanalysts claimed that the sequelae of achieving these ostensibly similar statuses were entirely *dissimilar*. The fine line between being a mother's "indisputable favorite" and a "pampered (spoiled) child" is thought to mark the difference between a destiny of "true success" and a false sense of entitlement that provokes disorders such as alcohol abuse.

One major impetus behind the Jones and Berglas (1978; Berglas & Jones, 1978) original self-handicapping formulation was a concern over the consequences of the parenting style presumed to account for a "pampered child" like the one described above by Adler (1930). In fact, the first formal discussion of self-handicapping theory (Berglas, 1976) focused more on the potentially disruptive effects of "positive evaluative feedback"—praise, kudos, rewards—than on the manner in which self-handicapping behavior (then called "strategies of externalization") could protect the favorable but fragile competence images they create.

The present chapter will return to self-handicapping's original focus on the disruptive effects of positive evaluative feedback in an attempt to account for the etiology of self-handicapping behavior and self-handicapping disorders (Berglas, 1985, 1988a; see also, Chapter 6, this volume). The primary concern of the discussion that follows will be to examine how ostensibly nurturant parenting styles can "spoil" children instead of making them feel like a "conqueror." In doing so, consideration will also be given to the role that these parenting styles play in the etiologies of two psychiatric disorders related to self-handicapping.

I have previously reasoned (e.g., Berglas, 1985, 1986a, 1988a, 1988b) that chronic self-handicapping is one of many disorders that fall along a continuum of psychological disturbance caused by inappropriate or illegitimate positive evaluative feedback. Specifically, I have assumed that, as children, self-handicappers were provided with an *image* of being favored but were deprived of the inner *experience* of self-worth or competency needed to function in a manner commensurate with their ascribed social or familial status. I will examine this hypothesized continuum by identifying the patterns of praise or reward that cause ego-defensive disorders such as self-handicapping and will contrast the type of nurturance thought to evoke self-handicapping behavior with the parenting styles thought to cause more severe psychological disturbances such as Narcissistic or Self-Defeating Personality Disorders (American Psychiatric Association, 1987).

Before beginning this analysis, one conceptual clarification is in order. At first glance, the concepts discussed below may be deemed appropriate only to Jones and Berglas's (1978; Berglas & Jones, 1978) self-handicapping formulation and not to the one popularized by C. R. Snyder and colleagues (e.g., Snyder & Smith, 1982). Both Leary and Shepperd (1986) and I (Berglas, 1985, 1988a) have addressed the fact that the self-handicapping literature has become bifurcated since the first empirical study of this phenomenon by Berglas and Jones (1978). According to Leary and Shepperd, "self-handicapping now refers to two different phenomena" (1986, p. 1265). As a consequence of conceptualizing and operationalizing self-handicapping in different ways, studies spawned by the respective formulations often appear to be addressing distinct phenomena with unique etiologies (see also, Chapter 1, this volume).

Researchers who have patterned their investigations after Berglas and Jones's (1978) studies appear to regard self-handicapping as a behavioral strategy designed to make success on an ego-threatening task more difficult, thereby providing a justification for potential failure. Alternatively, studies in the "Snyder tradition" (e.g., Smith, Snyder, & Handelsman, 1982) typically treat self-handicapping as a verbal self-report that personal liabilities have debilitated one's performance on esteem-relevant tasks. Only those researchers who view self-handicapping as a behavioral strategy assume that a history of noncontingent success is a precursor to its emergence. The "verbal report" school postulates only that a threat of prospective esteem-threatening failure—not necessarily the threatened loss of an *inflated* competence image—must be felt prior to the initiation of self-handicapping (see Chapter 1, this volume, for a review).

Surprisingly, there is more concordance among adherents of the Berglas and Jones (1978) paradigm and the C. R. Snyder and colleagues model than is apparent from an examination of the contrasting way in which each group operationalized self-handicapping. It now seems clear that both perspectives see a vulnerable competence image or uncertain sense of self-esteem as the *sine qua non* of all forms of self-handicapping behavior (Berglas, 1985; see also Harris & Snyder, 1986). Thus, although the discussion that follows will focus on the failure of positive evaluative feedback to induce feelings of "favoriteness," a working assumption of this analysis will be that an experience of noncontingent success or exalted self-esteem is not common to all self-handicappers. Instead, it is assumed that the etiology of self-handicapping behaviors can be traced to parenting styles that blocked or inhibited the development of a sound, *experience*-based competence image.

In several ways, Adler's report of his "pampered" patient (1930, pp. 126–129) encapsulates the essential concerns of this chapter. To begin, this spoiled man, living extravagantly at the expense of his parents, would have been diagnosed a self-handicapping alcohol abuser (Berglas, 1986a, 1986b, 1987a) were he alive today. He had all of the earmarks of the disorder: binging "when there was a demand of duty"; no craving to suggest primary alcoholism; and an inflated sense of self-esteem that he protected with the handicap of inebriation. Moreover, in addition to this Axis I diagnosis of self-handicapping alcohol abuse, Adler's comments indicate that this patient's Axis II diagnosis would have been Narcissistic Personality Disorder (American Psychiatric Association, 1987).* Presumably, when Adler said that this man "lived extravagantly at the expense of his parents" and was "self-centered and wholly lacking social adjustment," he observed the interpersonal exploitativeness, entitlement, and grandiosity that typify individuals suffering from that disorder (see, American Psychiatric Association, 1987, p. 351). Previous discussions of the commonalities between self-handicapping and Narcissistic Personality Disorders (e.g., Berglas, 1985, 1988a) have noted similarities in both their symptom complexes and presumed etiologies.

It is important to underscore the importance that Adler placed on the process of *achieving* statuses in life as opposed to *attaining* them—a

---

*The most recent edition of the American Psychiatric Association's *Diagnostic and Statistical Manual of Mental Disorders* (DSM-III-R; APA, 1987) employs a multiaxial system for evaluating patients and planning treatment strategies. In this system, Axes I and II comprise the mental disorders, while Axes III–V present information concerning physical disorders, psychosocial stressors, and global assessment of functioning.

Axis I identifies clinical syndromes that are often the patient's chief or presenting complaint. Axis II identifies developmental disorders and personality disorders as well as specific personality traits or the habitual use of particular defense mechanisms when no personality disorder exists. In many instances patients will have a disorder on both axes, and it is often the case that an Axis I diagnosis is symptomatic of an Axis II personality disorder.

distinction central to the notion of "noncontingent success" described by Berglas and Jones (1978). From Adler's perspective, a pampered child is destined to suffer debilitating feelings of inadequacy because "confidence in his own strength" is lost as a consequence of pampering (Adler, 1969). Stated in behavioral terms, pampering deprives a child of an opportunity to act in a manner reflective of competence. Thus, the most devastating consequence of this type of upbringing is not necessarily the anger or rage that can result from being manipulated by narcissistic parents (e.g., Kernberg, 1975). Instead, it is often far more disruptive to chronically fear disconfirmation of a favorable competence image for wont of the opportunity—and ultimately the ability—to test it (Bandura, 1977; Berglas, 1985).

In addition to causing competence-image distortions, pampering undoubtedly instigates a number of self-handicapping disorders by preventing children from becoming desensitized to failure. The parent who chronically "runs interference" for a child against life's obstacles and hardships deprives him or her of an opportunity to learn important coping skills. In addition to diminishing the child's sense of self-efficacy, this type of parenting further blocks the child from developing an awareness that failure need not prove devastating and may, in fact, afford valuable lessons that can serve an adaptive function in the future. By generating inordinate fears of the *imagined* consequences of failure, pampering motivates many children to self-handicap as a means of averting "disaster."

Missing from Adler's assessment of the consequences of pampering is an analysis of the manner in which this process takes place. Although he did remark, "when we speak of a pampered child we . . . mean a child . . . whose parents are always hovering over it, who assume all responsibilities for it, [who] take away from the child the burden of fulfilling any of the tasks and functions it could fulfil" (Adler, 1964, p. 89), the linkage between this disruptive parenting style and a tendency to self-handicap when confronted by esteem-threatening interactions is left unaddressed.

This chapter will proceed from the assumption that the pampered lifestyle, one of the dominant factors responsible for self-handicapping and related disorders, is shaped, in large measure, by a parent's inappropriate use of positive evaluative feedback—praise, kudos, rewards, compliments, and the like.† While receipt of positive evaluative feedback is typically an emotionally uplifting and reinforcing experience

---

†It should be noted that another disruptive consequence of pampering children involves denying them the "privilege" to try various challenging tasks and, on occasion, fail. Most pampered children never have the opportunity to discover that failure can be a learning/growth experience rather than something to be feared.

capable of instilling "the feeling of a conqueror," it can also arouse a number of aversive reactions. Under the "right"—actually, from the perspective of building a healthy competence image, "wrong"—circumstances, positive evaluative feedback can be threatening, coercive, demeaning, and generally disruptive to an individual's sense of emotional equanimity.

After examining the factors that cause positive evaluative feedback to be experienced as stressful or aversive, consideration will be given to the continuum of ego-defensive disorders it causes. Finally, the specific determinants of self-handicapping behavior will be discussed along with a method for discriminating pathological forms of self-handicapping from related Axis II (personality) disorders.

THE MULTIPLE MEANINGS OF POSITIVE EVALUATIVE FEEDBACK

Positive evaluative feedback (hereafter called "praise") is generally understood to convey pleasure or satisfaction with individuals or their behavior (ideally, some skilled performance). Moreover, praise is thought to be gratifying and reinforcing. That is, it is intended to strengthen an actor's tendency to repeat a particular performance (Hill, 1963), in addition to making the actor feel good about himself or herself (Hill, 1968). The individual who accepts or "incorporates" the reinforcing aspects of praise will experience a range of positive consequences including: a boost in self-esteem and an increased sense of self-efficacy (Bandura, 1977); a raised level of aspiration along task-relevant dimensions (Festinger, 1954); the development of self-attributions of ability (Weiner, Frieze, Kukla, Reed, Rest, & Rosenbaum, 1972); expectations of more praise or comparable indicators of success in the future (Feather, 1966, 1968); and an enhanced attraction to the evaluator who conveyed the feedback (Backman & Secord, 1959).

The core attribute of communications considered to be instances of praise is the capacity to *favorably* compare target persons or their performance to some recognized standard of quality (cf. Festinger, 1954). This comparison may be direct, as in the case of certain compliments ("it's the best lecture ever delivered to our department"), or indirect, as in the case of material expressions of positive evaluative feedback (e.g., awards, trophies). This *evaluative* component of praise (Berglas, 1976) also informs a person how his or her skills or performance(s) compare to those of others (Deci, 1975; Thorndike, 1938).

Behaviors involving skill acquisition, competition(s), or creative tasks are the appropriate targets of the evaluative components of praise because they represent activities that can be judged "superior" or "inferior" according to discernible performance criteria. When praise is expressed for learning, winning, or creating, it may convey an evaluator's judgment that the performance in question was of a quality that differentiates it from the norm.

When authentic, the evaluative component of praise is *reactive;* an outcome-contingent consequence of behavior(s). One can only judge an outcome as being praise*worthy* after the fact. Yet, when administered without regard to a target person's immediate or ongoing behaviors, praise can convey metamessages unrelated to judgments of praiseworthiness. Specifically, rewards, accolades, kudos, and the like, can be used to express the wants, desires, and expectations of an evaluator when conveyed in advance of performances.

Praise obtained without regard to ongoing performance levels typically serves as a *cause* rather than as a consequence of behavior and may, in fact, be used to exert *control* over an individual (Deci, 1975; Thorndike, 1938). As Skinner noted, "we applaud a performer precisely to induce him to repeat a performance" (1971, p. 42). In the business world it is common knowledge that lucrative employment contracts can be mechanisms to "trap" valued employees in "golden handcuffs"—pressuring them to either remain with a particular organization or suffer precipitous declines in compensation. When praise is dispensed in order to provide information that is not evaluative—typically, to exert control over an individual—it is said to convey the *directive* component of positive evaluative feedback (Berglas, 1976). Whereas the evaluative component of praise informs an individual, "you did well," the directive component conveys the message, "you *should* do well."

Under most circumstances, the praise we receive contains a "healthy balance" of evaluative and directive feedback. The child who is praised for mastering a task (e.g., eating with a fork) receives simultaneous messages that she is meritorious for acquiring a complex skill (evaluative component) and that she is expected to employ this skill as part of her ongoing socialization (directive component). In this instance, both messages are equally important and impactful.

Unfortunately, this is not always the case. A number of factors affecting the context within which praise is transmitted, or biasing the manner in which it is received, can cause either component of praise to become distorted or exaggerated. It is a well-established fact that praise that conveys an excessively positive or flattering evaluation can have a disruptive effect upon skilled performances (Berglas, 1986a, 1987b), just as praise with an overemphasized directive component can have an adverse affect on a person's mood or self-concept (deCharms, 1968). In addition to causing transient disturbances, praise that conveys over-emphasized messages can induce psychological disorders.

UNBALANCED MESSAGES CONVEYED BY PRAISE

THE STRESS OF BEING TOLD, "YOU'RE A SUCCESS"

As noted above, people who incorporate the reinforcing aspects of praise will typically feel good about themselves for having executed the reinforced performance (Hill, 1968) in addition to experiencing a boost to their self-esteem, feelings of self-efficacy (Bandura, 1977), and an enhanced sense of competence (Weiner *et al.*, 1972). These beneficial effects are more likely to accrue when the praised outcome is difficult to attain and the individual works diligently to achieve it (cf. Aronson & Mills, 1959).

There is an interesting, reciprocal aspect of the feeling of self-efficacy and ability derived from earning praise: Those who receive praise, regardless of why, are expected to manifest the talent and tenacity needed to earn similar levels of rewarding outcomes on future occasions (cf. Lerner, 1975). The problem, as discussed in detail below, is that there are a number of reasons why people receive praise in excess of their manifest level of competency. At a minimum, exposure to "excessive" or noncontingent praise (Berglas, 1985, 1986a, 1987b) is typically quite stressful.

Praise becomes a stressor when it imposes performance demands or expectations that exceed an individual's perceived competency (Lazarus, 1981). Surprisingly, praise is often far more threatening than other performance demands because it imposes dispositional attributions upon those who receive it (see, Berglas, 1985; Jones & Davis, 1965). In accordance with the "law of reciprocity" (Lerner, 1975), people who receive applause, kudos, awards, or rewards are judged capable of *producing* praiseworthy performances on the basis of their stable dispositions or traits such as competence, talent, or drive, not transient, situational variables such as good fortune. This is reflected in the labels we use for those who achieve success: praise*worthy* people are referred to as being "talented" or "competent," not "having a good day" or "born under a lucky star." Consequently, people who receive praise feel that we expect them to continue to perform in a competent, successful manner (Baumeister, Hamilton, & Tice, 1985) over time and in a number of diverse contexts (cf. Kelley, 1967), thereby increasing the demand characteristics—or threats— imposed by such praise.

In a lay analysis of praise prepared for business executives, Farson (1963) captured the essence of the attributional process that turns praise from a rewarding experience to a potential stressor:

> . . . the most threatening aspect of praise is the obligation it puts on us to be praiseworthy people. If we accept praise, if we really believe the best about ourselves, then we are under an obligation to behave accordingly . . . if we really believe it when we are told that we are competent, or intelligent, or beautiful, then we are continually on the spot to *be* competent, or intelligent, or beautiful, not only in the eyes of the person who praised us but, even worse, in our own eyes. The responsibility to be continually at our best, to live up to our talents and abilities, is perhaps our most difficult problem in living—and we naturally defend against it. (p. 63)

Farson's (1963) description of the attributional process that accounts for praise becoming a potent stressor is somewhat exaggerated in that he is commenting on all forms of praise. Nevertheless, it is true that people do "defend against" praise in a variety of contexts, particularly when their self-esteem is either fragile or unstable. Under those circumstances, people are reluctant to accept praise that they must "live up to" in the future (cf. Eagly & Acksen, 1971; S. C. Jones & Pines, 1968).

S. C. Jones (1973) studied the stressful aspects of praise from the perspective that it would be salubrious only if it "fit" or was consistent with an individual's existing level of self-esteem. After analyzing research which consistently demonstrated that people will reject success feedback—as though it had negative implications or consequences—when it was *unexpected* (e.g., Mettee, 1971), Jones developed what might be called a "pragmatic self-esteem theory" (Berglas, 1976). Basically, his conclusion was that there is a tendency to exercise caution when accepting the esteem-enhancing implications of excessive praise because there is always a performance demand contained within it:

> . . . people [tend] to react to evaluative information in terms not only of its present but also its future implications. In general, people prefer to accept approval from others and reject disapproval. However, there are numerous occasions on which a person's accepting [excessively favorable] and inaccurate evaluations for himself has important and potentially hazardous consequences . . . [including] social embarrassment from misrepresenting himself or from the exposed discrepancy between other's expectancies and his actual effectiveness (S. C. Jones, 1973, pp. 193–194).

One important qualification to the notion that people defend against praise by refusing to accept it (Jones, 1973) comes from the laboratory of R. F. Baumeister. In a series of studies designed to assess how expectations of success affect ongoing performance (e.g., Baumeister, 1984; Baumeister *et al.*, 1985), it was shown that personally held expectancies of success typically led to improved performance, while an audience's expectancies of success were often disruptive. According to this research, even if a performer privately rejects audience feedback suggesting that he or she should succeed at a particular task, the mere knowledge that an audience will be disappointed by his or her failure is sufficient to generate a high level of stress for the performer.

One crucial implication of this research is that there are times when recipients of praise may have no choice but to accept its implications and prepare for inevitable performance pressure. The odd, counterintuitive prejudice that follows individuals who receive excessive, unwanted praise is that they are "marked" either to behave in a particular—successful— manner or to be judged "failures." One major exception to this rule, however, occurs when an individual is willing to forgo the label "mentally healthy" and to manifest psychological symptoms. As discussed in detail below, self-handicapping, self-defeating (Baumeister & Scher, 1988; Berglas, 1988b, 1989) and other symptomatic behaviors are often the best option available to an individual forced to cope with intolerable performance expectations imposed by excessive praise.

Overjustification Effects

In addition to creating stress-provoking performance demands, certain types of praise can undermine feelings of self-efficacy, control, and self-determination once derived from rewarding activities. A number of studies have demonstrated that praise following completion of an activity can dampen subsequent interest and involvement if the praise is deemed "inappropriate" (e.g., Deci, 1971, 1975; Kruglanski, Alon, & Lewis, 1972; Lepper, Greene, & Nisbett, 1973). Although virtually any form of praise can be "task-inappropriate" as a result of variations in the content or context of an activity, the type of praise most likely to disrupt sustained, self-generated interest in an activity is money or other forms of material reward.

Material rewards may diminish the psychological gratification derived from accomplishments by shifting the perceived control of the activity from *intrinsic* to *extrinsic* factors (Berglas, 1976, 1986a; deCharms, 1968; Deci, 1975). Self-generated activities enacted because of the joys derived from *doing* the task are said to be *intrinsically* motivated. Inherently rewarding pastimes, or avocations such as hobbies or activities thought of as "play," fall into this category. Behaviors that are under the control of external factors or situational forces, engaged in because of what one can *get from* the activity, are said to be *extrinsically* motivated.

Extrinsic rewards are not inherently disruptive. Few problems arise, for example, when onerous tasks initiated solely as a means of earning a salary do, in fact, secure one. If you can make a game of whitewashing the fence or, better yet, turn it into a benign scam, so much the better. Problems do arise, however, when money is paid to people engaged in intrinsically motivating tasks.

A person who is "paid to play"—getting two types of reward for one activity—is said to be "overjustified" (Lepper *et al.*, 1973; Notz, 1975) and forced to confront an ostensibly simple yet psychologically crucial question: "Why am I being given money for something I was doing, and would do, for free?" Should the answer to this question be some variant of "the person paying me is *governing* my actions," the consequences can include: a loss of interest in the activity (Deci, 1971, 1975); a poorer-quality work product (Amabile, Hennessey, & Grossman, 1986); loss of self-esteem gains that would otherwise derive from successfully completing the activity (Nisbett & Valins, 1971); and, in extreme instances, self-defeating behaviors (Baumeister & Scher, 1988; Berglas, 1988a, 1989).

The disruptive consequences of overjustification occur because rewards can make a person feel like a "pawn" as opposed to the "origin" of important activities in his or her life (deCharms, 1968). For people to derive satisfaction from producing a behavioral outcome, they must believe themselves to be the primary causal factor in the chain of events leading to that outcome. As Bandura noted, the impact of a performance outcome on existing competence images is solely a function of

> how people perceive the determinants of their behavior. They take pride in their accomplishments when they ascribe successes to their own abilities and efforts. They do not derive much self-satisfaction, however, when they view their performance as heavily dependent on external factors. (Bandura, 1978, p. 349)

The discussion thus far has been limited to the way in which material rewards can thwart the self-esteem gains that are ordinarily expected from the successful completion of a task. There are a number of other ways in which praise can fail to have its intended, salutary effect. Although there is no simple way to determine if once-gratifying rewards will become disruptive, it is possible to examine the social exchange processes involved in "praise transmission" (Carson, 1969; Foa & Foa, 1974) to understand how this transformation occurs.

SOCIAL FACTORS AFFECTING THE IMPACT OF PRAISE

Praise cannot be dispensed or received in a social vacuum; one person (the evaluator) with authority and/or power is needed to dispense praise, and another (target) person must receive it for the exchange process to occur. Because praise occurs in social interactions, attributes of both concerned parties will affect its impact. In functional terms, three aspects of the praise transmission process—who said it, what was said, and how it was said—determine whether the praise will have a salutary or a disruptive effect on the target person. Unfortunately, of these three factors, what was said typically proves to be the *least* significant determinant of the impact of praise (Berglas, 1986a).

TASK-BASED VERSUS PERSON-BASED PRAISE

The distinction between task- and person-based praise is linguistic; it is a *"how* he said it" variable. Praise that refers to the qualities of a performance with no explicit reference to its source is designated task-based. Praise that references either the source of the performance (the target person) or the attributes of the source is designated person-based (Berglas, 1976). Since praise is rarely 100% person- or task-based, it is important to recognize how emphasizing one type of praise over the other can affect a target person's mood and/or self-esteem.

Task-based praise appears to emerge as a direct consequence of a performance, as though it were linked directly to the outcome. High scores on a test and objectively assessed performance criteria (e.g., a fast time in a race measured by a stopwatch) are examples of task-based praise. When administered as intended, task-based praise conveys a purely comparative judgment from an independent observer. Regrettably, most of the praise we receive is neither objective nor measured mechanically.

Person-based praise is identifiable by the presence of subjective qualifying factors within the evaluation. "I can see the influence of your late, Pulitzer Prize-winning father in your incredibly interesting story" is an example of person-based praise. Regardless of how praiseworthy a story may be, the impact of the praise it garners from a reader who knows the author's background is less favorable than it would have been were the evaluator a disinterested party who referenced only the written product. Person-based praise is less an assessment of a target person's standing along some evaluative continuum than a personal message that conveys sentiments in conjunction with an evaluation.

There are times when person-based feedback can enhance the gratification derived from praise. Hearing, "the reason why we're number one is because you played like a pro out there today" (from one team member to another) goes well beyond conveying laudatory feedback; it also serves to strengthen in-group ties, thereby facilitating group locomotion toward a variety of shared goals. Yet person-based praise often expresses interests related to the directive component of praise that are typically not addressed by task-based feedback. When this occurs, the reinforcing potential of person-based praise may be severely compromised.

CRITERION OF THE FEEDBACK

The distinction between task- and person-based praise is reminiscent of Allport's (1940) idiographic–nomothetic distinction. In discussions of research techniques, Allport noted that investigators may choose to study behavior in terms of general principles applied to the largest possible number of cases (*nomothetic* analysis), or they may choose to focus on an individual case (*idiographic*) analysis (see Hall & Lindzey, 1957, p. 277). Person-based praise is idiographic. It is derived from the study of an individual case without reference to general standards. Consequently, such praise may appear qualified if it is thought to reflect the evaluator's assessment of the target person's performance relative to his or her *personal capabilities,* as opposed to universal standards. The slow-of-foot student who hears his gym teacher exclaim, "that was the best mile you've run all year," is receiving person-based praise of limited value. Granted, the praise has no negative effects—it actually tells the child that his teacher values his efforts at improving his speed—but it is not a useful indicator of his chances to be selected for a varsity team.

Praise in the form of "you're the hardest-working kid in the class" would be far more impactful on this slow-running student and would, simultaneously, provide him with more useful information. Task-based nomothetic praise like this—a comparative appraisal of his diligence relative to all appropriate comparison persons—can enhance the slow student's self-esteem because diligence is a trait that has value in a variety of contexts. More fundamentally, it can convey a true "superior" ranking relative to appropriate comparison objects. Although the feedback, "that was the best mile you've run all year," *implies* diligence and the child may *infer* that he possesses this desirable attribute, the person-based quality of the feedback could possibly obscure much of its intended positive regard.

THE PERSPECTIVE OF THE EVALUATOR

Until now, the focus of this discussion has been on the "form" of praise: verbal versus material; intrinsic versus extrinsic; task-based versus person-based. It has been argued that in order for praise to have a salutary impact on a target person, it must be appropriate in type, form, and intensity to the behavior and/or outcome it addresses (Kruglansky *et al.*, 1975).

An element of the praise transmission process as yet unexamined is the question of why an evaluator would convey praise to a target person—the *"who* said it" variable. Few evaluators are pure evaluators capable of functioning like meters, scales, or timers. Even professional evaluators (e.g., judges, teachers) are known to have biases that play a crucial role in determining the impact of praise on a target person. Targets of praise are legitimately concerned with "who said it." Unless it can be established that an evaluator is responding to a performance and its characteristics (not his or her own needs, wants, or desires), the evaluative implications of praise cannot be incorporated with any degree of confidence.

Nurturing Evaluators

Certain relationships preclude individuals from serving as effective evaluators of others. Role requirements, status differentials, expectations, and the like, make the praise that some people convey appear to be a function of external constraints. Paradoxically, those dyads most likely to suffer breakdowns in the praise transmission process are the ones involving "nurturing" evaluators—parents, spouses, friends—and target persons.

Nurturing evaluators are often in no-win positions vis-à-vis the target person they care for, precisely because they do care. Because their unique, favorable status is derived from a history of gratifying the needs of the target person in a variety of settings, nurturing evaluators are expected to be the source of praise in evaluative contexts (Kelley, 1971). The problem with being expected to serve as a source of praise is that when an evaluator acts in a role-governed manner his or her behaviors may be perceived as failing to reflect his or her true feelings (Jones & Davis, 1965; Jones, Davis, & Gergen, 1961).

Praise from nurturing evaluators to the target persons they care for regularly fails to deliver its intended impact precisely because of this attributional dilemma. "Good job, my son" from a parent to his child may be far less impactful than "good job, my son" from the parish priest serving the boy's community. Conversely, when nurturing others fail to deliver expected praise—owing to any number of factors *unrelated* to their assessment of the target person's behavior—the impact of providing no comment can be as damaging as stating "you blew it" (cf. Kelley,

1971). Because many nurturing evaluators believe that failing to praise dependent target persons would be disruptive to their developing egos, they habitually—and inappropriately—praise the very people who would benefit most by being weaned from *continuous* reinforcement and put on intermittent, task-contingent reward schedules (Berglas, 1976, 1986a; see also Ginott, 1965).

Elliot Aronson (1969) examined the manner in which praise can lose its significance within intimate relationships when dispensed too regularly or on a rule-governed basis. In a commentary (dubbed "Aronson's law of marital infidelity") that can help explain why many marriages fail, Aronson captured the problem that confronts nurturing evaluators who attempt to enhance the self-esteem of loved ones by praising them:

> Once we have grown certain of the good will (rewarding behavior) of a person (e.g., a mother, a spouse, a close friend), that person may become less potent as a source of reward than a stranger. Since . . . a gain in esteem is a more potent reward than the absolute level of the esteem, then it follows that a close friend (by definition) is operating near ceiling level and, therefore, cannot provide us with a gain. To put it another way, since we have learned to expect love, favors, and praise from a friend, such behavior is not likely to represent a gain in his esteem for us. (Aronson, 1969, p. 168)

Developmental psychologists have also observed consequences similar to Aronson's (1969) law of marital infidelity when "teaching" relationships are established between parents and their children. A number of studies (e.g., Gewirtz & Baer, 1958; Stevenson, Keen, & Knights, 1963; see also Ginott, 1965) have demonstrated a "satiation effect" (i.e., children showing less responsivity to rewards dispensed by parents than by teachers) attributable to the *continuous* support provided by nurturant parents. The paradox illuminated by findings such as these is that nurturance can be as disruptive to the development of self-esteem as punitive behavior. The section that follows will examine research which suggests a more dire conclusion: Certain patterns of nurturant—praising—behavior that overemphasize directive feedback and impose excessive performance expectations can be linked to the etiology of psychological disorders ranging from chronic self-handicapping to self-defeating personality disorders (Berglas, 1988a, 1988b, 1989).

THE CONTINUUM OF PRAISE-INDUCED DISORDERED BEHAVIOR

The discussion that follows will attempt to demonstrate the causal role played by disruptive patterns of praise in the etiology of narcissistic personality disorders (e.g., Millon, 1981), success depression (e.g., Seligman, 1975), and a range of related Axis I disorders. More importantly, it will be shown that the developmental influences common to people who develop these disorders can also be found in individuals prone to cope with ego-threatening circumstances by self-handicapping or by developing self-handicapping disorders (Berglas, 1985, 1988a; Chapter 6, this volume). The intention of this analysis is not to suggest that there is a 1:1 causal correspondence between disruptive praise and the development of a psychiatric disorder but, rather, to demonstrate how certain symptom complexes can be traced to parenting styles or reinforcement histories that use praise in a manner that disrupts the development of feelings of self-efficacy and a self-sufficient competence image.

NARCISSISTIC PERSONALITY DISORDERS

· Narcissistic personality disorders are not generally thought to derive from disordered patterns of praise. In fact, the two dominant perspectives on the etiology of narcissistic disturbances in general, and the narcissistic personality disorder (NPD) in particular (Kernberg, 1975; Kohut, 1971, 1977), trace the origin of these pathological conditions to negative occurrences ranging from parental rejection to trauma.

Kernberg (1975) attributes the development of narcissistic disturbances to the consequences of parental rejection, abandonment, or indifference. He claims that the experiential backgrounds of individuals destined to develop NPDs are dominated by chronically cold parents who often spitefully reject the child, forcing him or her to defend against the rage engendered by his or her parents' behaviors. Chief among these defensive strategies, according to Kernberg, is a haughty grandiosity and self-centeredness derived from the belief that the child must rely on himself or herself for love because he or she was never able to obtain it from "internalized good objects."

Kohut's (1971, 1977) views on pathological narcissism are difficult to summarize, but the distinction between his perspective and Kernberg's is apparent. Kohut's perspective is actually a developmental theory of the self (a separate and distinct "narcissistic libido") wherein narcissistic disturbances or NPDs typically result from failing to accomplish at least one of two goals of self-maturation: integration of either the "grandiose self" or the "idealized parental imago."

Simply stated, children are regularly confronted by elements of the real world that undermine naturally occurring infantile feelings of grandiosity or omnipotence. If children do not find a way to overcome these "disappointments," Kohut (1981) maintains that they will develop severe narcissistic disturbances, failing to develop feelings of self-worth. In the extreme, if these "disappointed" children are met with rejection or cold and unempathic parenting, borderline or psychotic reactions may ensue (Kohut, 1971).

Kohut also contends that children must be able to idealize their parents in order for a healthy sense of narcissism to develop. If this idealization is thwarted by a parent's indifference or rejection, the child feels devastated and, deprived of an appropriate "introject," chronically empty. It has been asserted that individuals who fail to integrate an idealized parental imago seek idealized parental surrogates "greater" than themselves throughout adulthood (Millon, 1981). Presumably, in an attempt to afford others an opportunity to overshadow them, these individuals often behave in a self-effacing manner or manifest interpersonal styles dominated by overtly low self-esteem or hypochondriacal behavior (Forman, 1975).

In contrast to the prevailing "bad-mothering" theories of narcissism stands Millon's (1981) social-learning theory. This perspective traces the origin of narcissistic disturbances "to the unrealistic overvaluation by parents of the child's worth" (Millon, 1981, p. 165), rather than to the devaluation presumed operative by Kernberg and others (e.g., G. Adler, 1970, 1981). According to Millon, because narcissists' parents have burdened them with "an enhanced self-image that cannot be sustained in the 'outer' world" (1981, p. 165), they must engage in a variety of symptomatic behaviors designed to address the consequences of failing to live up to internalized parental illusions of their self-worth. Millon does not suggest that individuals suffering NPDs engage in self-handicapping behavior. He does, however, maintain that their intolerance of criticism, their grandiosity, their sense of entitlement, and their preoccupation with fantasies of unlimited power, success, and brilliance (cf. American Psychiatric Association, 1987) represent a "proactive" attempt to comfort themselves in anticipation of failing to fulfill the expectations imposed upon them by unrealistic parental praise.

To my knowledge, there is only one published report documenting the comparability of symptoms manifested by individuals suffering NPDs and self-handicapping disorders. In a discussion of narcissistic factors in underachieving students, Baker (1979) maintained:

> Narcissistically vulnerable students feel damaged by their first encounter with . . . problems. . . . They [often] retreat to endless bull sessions, smoking marijuana [or other activities that avoid studying]. *Not studying offers two possibilities to maintain the grandiose self intact.* If an exam is flunked, it is only due to lack of study, not due to the lack of ability; if, however, it is passed without study, it is doubly delicious, providing a good grade and "confirming" magical powers of brilliance. (p. 422, emphasis added)

Thus we see that some narcissists use physical "aids" to accomplish the "retreat into fantasies of grandiosity" that Millon (1981) and others see as the hallmark of the narcissist's symptomatic armamentarium. Baker's comments are particularly interesting in light of my (Berglas, 1985) contention that the self-handicapper's attempts to structure no-lose situations by engaging in symptomatic behavior is designed to protect what psychoanalysts would call a grandiose sense of self.

Millon (1981) is not wholly alone in his advocacy of the social-learning theory of narcissistic disorders. Even Kernberg (1976) has asserted that future narcissists are often found to possess some special talent or status within the family such as intellectual "genius" or the "only child." Yet Kernberg is less committed to the notion that the child's special status plays a causal role in creating narcissistic disturbances. Instead, he sees the child's quality of specialness serving solely as a refuge that can protect him or her from hurt feelings brought about by the actions of devaluing parents (Millon, 1981).

Nemiah's (1961) description of what he calls "narcissistic character disorders" is virtually identical to Millon's social-learning perspective. Nemiah saw narcissists as displaying great ambition, setting highly unrealistic goals, and suffering grave intolerance of failures and/or imperfections in themselves, along with an almost insatiable craving for admiration (Akhtar & Thomson, 1982). Moreover, Nemiah assumed that people suffering from this disorder rarely behave in accordance with intrinsic needs. Instead, he saw their behaviors as governed by their perceptions of what would make others like them.

According to Akhtar and Thomson (1982), Nemiah conceived of an individual with a narcissistic character disorder as "a prisoner of aspirations," a condition created by parents who set unrealistically high performance standards. Anticipating Kernberg's (1975) arguments, Nemiah (1961) maintained that future narcissists who failed to live up to these lofty performance standards would receive harsh criticism. He concluded that narcissistic character disorders derived from children internalizing unrealistic attitudes toward performance and, in adult life, demanding too much of themselves.

In an attempt to summarize current opinion regarding the etiology of NPDs, Vaillant and Perry (1985) asserted:

> In the early familial environment of narcissistic individuals, a lack of parental empathy, warmth, and support or presence of frank abuse or neglect is supplemented by parental idealization of some positive characteristics attributed in the child. . . . These children derive a superficial sense of omnipotence and grandiosity from the parent's unrealistic attribution of such traits as uncanny power, beauty, intellect, talent to them. Furthermore, the

powerfully positive, if unrealistic, experience of this shared parent–child fantasy also encourages those children to disavow feelings of weakness, helplessness, and inferiority in themselves. (p. 974)

A literal interpretation of Vaillant and Perry's remark that "the parent's unrealistic attribution" of certain traits "encourages . . . children to disavow feelings of weakness, helplessness, and inferiority" (1985, p. 974) is obviously at variance with Millon's (1981) social-learning theory of narcissistic disorders and the data discussed above documenting the disruptive effects of noncontingent, person-based praise. In order to accept the contention that parental idealization can create a "superficial sense of omnipotence and grandiosity," we must assume that Vaillant and Perry (1985) intended to emphasize the word "superficial" and were referring to a highly vulnerable competence image.

If a parent imposes expectations of greatness on a child in order to fulfill his or her narcissistic fantasies, to compensate for prior devaluing acts, or for any other reason, this feedback could not enable the child to disavow feelings of weakness, helplessness, and inferiority (see, Miller, 1981), despite whatever transient salutary effects it produced. As Erikson (1963) noted:

In (developing a sense of self-esteem) children cannot be fooled by empty praise and condescending encouragement. They may have to accept artificial bolstering of the self-esteem in lieu of something better, but their ego identity gains real strength only from wholehearted and consistent recognition of real accomplishments. (p. 235)

The notion of "empty praise" leading to "artificial bolstering of the self-esteem" would appear to operationally define the type of parenting that Vaillant and Perry (1985) saw as responsible for the development of narcissistic disorders. The section that follows argues that mild variations in the type of "empty praise" an individual receives can account for the etiology of a number of Axis I psychiatric disorders ranging from "success depression" to self-handicapping disorders.

SUCCESS DEPRESSION

Learned helplessness research (e.g., Seligman, 1975) holds that exposure to uncontrollable events can produce a wide range of negative consequences, most notably depression. The "reformulated" learned helplessness model of depression (e.g., Abramson, Seligman, & Teasdale, 1978) demonstrated that helplessness effects do not obtain directly from noncontingent, uncontrollable outcomes. Instead, an individual's attributional style—how he construes the cause(s) of events—determines the emotional valence of uncontrollable outcomes (Seligman, Abramson, Semmel, & von Beyer, 1979; see also Peterson & Seligman, 1984, for a review).

Researchers typically investigate three aspects of attributional style: internality versus externality, stability versus instability, and globality versus specificity (Peterson & Barrett, 1987). Internal explanations attribute causality for outcomes to the self ("I got an A because I studied hard"), whereas external causal explanations implicate other people or circumstances ("I got an A because the judge liked my style"). Global causal explanations implicate a wide range of activities ("I'm a poor student"), whereas specific causal explanations are restrictive ("I just can't grasp calculus"). Stable versus unstable causal explanations deal with the distinction between enduring versus transient events or attributes such as intelligence (stable) versus fear-generated activity (unstable). According to Peterson and Seligman (1984), an individual who explains negative outcomes by attributing them to internal, stable, and global causes is more prone to experience depression than the individual who makes external, unstable, and specific causal explanations for the same outcome(s).

In arguments advanced well before the reformulated learned helplessness model of depression appeared, Seligman (1975) noted that learned helplessness effects can derive from exposure to *rewarding* stimuli including indicators of success (see Berglas, 1985, 1986a, for similar reasoning based on clinical observations). According to Seligman, *any* uncontrollable event, even noncontingent success, can prove to be noxious if it induces a sense of not *deserving* rewards. In cases such as this, an individual may ultimately experience a reactive depression:

> Not infrequently, when a person finally achieves a goal toward which he has been striving for years, depression ensues. . . . These depressions are paradoxical, since successful individuals continue to receive most of their old reinforcers, plus more new reinforcers than ever before.
>
> This phenomenon is not a paradox for the theory of helplessness. Depressed people tell you that they are now rewarded *not for what they're doing, but for who they are or what they have done.* Having achieved the goal that they strove for, their rewards now come independently of any ongoing instrumental activity. (Seligman, 1975, pp. 98–99, emphasis added)

In the language of the reformulated model of learned helplessness, success depression is derived from attributing positive outcomes to external, variable, and specific causes. For example, "I'm being asked to endorse products because I'm Johnny Carson's wife," suggests that the rewarded person believes that the attribute responsible for her success in advertising was *acquired*, not *achieved* on the basis of *her* abilities or instrumental behaviors. As "merely" the spouse of a media star, it is hard to attribute her "advertiser" status to attributes of the self if she does not clearly possess skills of her own. Moreover, her role as a product endorser is unstable because it is yoked to one external attribute (being a wife), not a variety of internal factors. Similarly, the attribution must be judged specific unless Mrs. Carson spends her entire workday living the role of a spouse. Success depressives suffer emotional distress because they are forced to acknowledge that the rewarding outcomes they receive are attributable to acquired or extraneous characteristics or former statuses, not current capabilities or self-generated conduct.

Because success depression is thought to develop after an individual has attained a status capable of securing praise and is independent of ongoing instrumental behaviors, it seems inappropriate to speculate on the parenting style that would create a success depressive. Nevertheless, research by Dweck and her colleagues (Dweck, Davidson, Nelson, & Enna, 1978; Dweck & Goetz, 1978) suggesting why women are roughly twice as likely as men to develop symptoms of depression (e.g., Weissman & Klerman, 1977) may shed some light on the factors that render an individual vulnerable to success depression.

Dweck and Goetz (1978) found that women manifest the attributional style correlated with depression—attributing failure to internal, stable, global factors such as lack of ability—far more frequently than males. Interestingly, this sex difference was thought to result from the patterns of performance feedback that children receive in school. According to these researchers, the feedback grade school girls received from teachers attributed their academic failures to intellectual inadequacy, whereas boys did not receive such feedback. Instead of blaming dispositional attributes, failure feedback delivered to boys implicated their conduct—an unstable behavioral dimension more readily subjected to volitional control. It is significant to note that when these patterns of feedback were subjected to experimental control and reversed, the previously observed sex difference was not obtained (Dweck et al., 1978), strongly suggesting that attributional style is a direct function of the type of feedback an individual receives.

Dweck et al.'s (1978) findings suggest that individuals raised in settings where person-based feedback ("that happened because you are a good/bad child") is the rule rather than the exception may be led to develop an attributional style that holds their character responsible for all outcomes. Consequently, these individuals would be expected to have more vulnerable competence images and weaker senses of self-efficacy than children exposed to task-based feedback that explicitly references behavior(s).

Because character is presumed to be stable and virtually immutable, children chronically exposed to person-based feedback are likely to conclude that they cannot adapt to situational demands or influence the nature of the outcomes they receive. Thus, when an ostensibly desirable outcome such as praise is attributed to *who* someone is (one's character) as opposed to controllable or *modifiable* behavioral attributes, it can lead recipients to fear that they will be unable to adapt to or control the performance expectations it imposes (Farson, 1963; S. C. Jones, 1973).

SELF-HANDICAPPING

It is widely recognized that people with no overt suggestion of psychological dysfunction often respond to situationally induced threats to self-esteem by self-handicapping. They may report psychological symptoms (e.g., Smith *et al.*, 1982), elect to receive performance-inhibiting drugs prior to a test (Berglas & Jones, 1978), or actually consume alcohol prior to tests of skilled performance (e.g., Tucker, Vuchinich, & Sobell, 1981), if such actions appear capable of providing a self-serving explanation for potential failure. Yet many people exhibit identical self-handicapping symptoms as an enduring pattern of relating to the environment, not merely in response to situational threats (Berglas, 1985, 1987b, 1988a). Although "strategic" (situation-specific) self-handicappers may, on occasion, exhibit the same symptoms as individuals suffering from a self-handicapping disorder (e.g., binge drinking), only chronic self-handicappers suffer from a psychological disturbance. I view chronic self-handicappers as being comparable to individuals suffering a personality disorder, particularly in view of their adaptive inflexibility and impaired interpersonal relationships (cf. American Psychiatric Association, 1987; Millon, 1981).

In turning attention to the etiology of self-handicapping and its relationship to other praise-induced disorders, it is important to underscore the fact that it will be considered a psychological *disorder* (Berglas, 1985, 1987b, 1988a; see also Chapter 6, this volume), not a situation-specific ego-defensive tactical behavior. Interestingly, self-handicapping behavior was initially thought to be a dispositional defensive style (see Chapter 1, this volume). When Jones and I (Berglas & Jones, 1978; Jones & Berglas, 1978) first described this so-called defensive dynamic, we maintained that self-handicappers behaved in a manner which suggested that they valued an inner sense or appearance of *possessing* competence more than the capacity to manifest competence on any given occassion. Even more suggestive of a dispositional disorder was Jones and Berglas's (1978) assertion that this preoccupation with competency—a "competence complex"—evolved from either of two distinct, developmental histories that affected the self-handicapper throughout his life. Before examining the conclusions drawn from the preceding review of praise-induced disordered behavior, it seems instructive to review what Jones and Berglas (1978) had to say about the etiology of self-handicapping over a decade ago.

One source of the competence complex underlying self-handicapping behavior was thought to be a parenting style that confounded the *exchange* and *signifying* aspects of praise (cf. Jones, 1964). In essence, Jones and Berglas argued that people destined to become self-handicappers have difficulty determining whether the praise they receive from significant others is attributable to their performances (the *exchange* value of rewards) or to unconditional love and caring (*signification*). Jones and Berglas argued that, as children, future self-handicappers typically feel pressure to separate the dual meanings of rewards, but decide to forgo behavioral analysis of the feedback they receive owing to the problems that would arise if they were to discover that they are not loved unconditionally. Fear of this discovery was thought to motivate an array of self-handicapping behaviors that *create* failures, thereby permitting the threatened child to maintain "a precarious hold on the illusion of love and admiration" (Jones & Berglas, 1978, p. 204).

The second major source of the competence complex was thought to be a history of noncontingent positive reinforcement. Jones and Berglas saw future self-handicappers as individuals who have been amply rewarded throughout life, but "they have not been able to determine consistently what the reward was for, or they suspect that they have been rewarded for extraneous reasons such as beauty or the ascribed status of simply being a family member" (1978, p. 205). Because future self-handicappers have difficulty discerning what they have *done* to merit the praise they receive, all subsequent tests of the abilities deemed necessary to retain the rewards or status they possess threaten to expose them to embarrassment for failing to fulfill expectations (cf. S. C. Jones, 1973). In addition, a history of noncontingent success was thought to increase the threat of performance evaluations because it obligates an individual to perform at ever-increasing levels of proficiency over time.

Assumptions concerning the role played by noncontingent success in the etiology of self-handicapping have been refined since Jones and Berglas (1978) first discussed them. I now assume that self-handicapping can emerge in response to either of *two* varieties of noncontingent success experiences (Berglas, 1986a, 1987b). Both forms deprive an individual of an experiential base from which to develop a sense of self-efficacy or self-esteem (Bandura, 1977; Erikson, 1963), and each imposes unique performance demands.

The type of noncontingent success discussed by Jones and Berglas (1978) is *externally based*. In other words, it is awarded on the basis of factors that have nothing to do with the development of a stable competence image. Although attributes responsible for externally based non-contingent success may be desirable—for example, beauty, charm—they have nothing to do with *achieving* success. Praise attributable to these factors leaves recipients wondering, "was I successful for what I *did*, or for what I *am*?"

A second type of noncontingent success is that which is *excessive*. In other words, the rewards far exceed normative expectations of deser-vingness for the behavioral outcome (Berglas, 1986a, 1987b). Similar to praise that leads to overjustification effects (e.g., Deci, 1975), excessive forms of noncontingent success are administered on the basis of skilled or successful behaviors, but they are of a quality or intensity inappropriate to the activity that secured them. The problem derived from receipt of large material rewards—for example, salaries or bonuses—is that they obligate an individual to act in accordance with the performance expectations they convey, thereby imposing performance demands that cause stress and its symptomatic sequelae (Lazarus, 1981; see also, Farson, 1963).

Apart from neglecting to consider alternative forms of noncontingent success, the only "problem" with Jones and Berglas's (1978) theory of the etiology of self-handicapping is that it failed to account for how the competence complex developed. In other words, why was the evaluative feedback provided to future self-handicappers confounded, confused, or contaminated to the point that it left them wondering whether they were loved as persons or as products? Stated another way, since it was assumed that the parents of self-handicappers informed them that they were favored or the "favorites" in the family (they *were* "amply rewarded"), why did they fail to develop the self-image of Freud's conqueror and, instead, behave like Adler's spoiled drunkard?

HYPOTHESES REGARDING THE ORIGIN
OF PRAISE-INDUCED DISORDERS

In order to address this question, the preceding analysis of NPDs and success depression will be used to formulate hypotheses regarding the parenting styles and types of praise thought to give rise to self-handicapping disorders:

HYPOTHESIS I

Hypothesis I states that an individual destined to develop a self-handicapping disorder will be singled out or praised excessively by his or her family because of one salient attribute or a complex of closely related attributes.

The characteristic shared by every individual suffering a praise-induced disorder is that they possess one quality or trait that was thought responsible for the status or level of praise they received in childhood or, in the case of success depressives, later in life. Regardless of whether the attribute was an actual talent (e.g., the etiology of NPDs according to Millon, 1981) or an attribute "imposed" on the children because their parents needed or wanted them to be "special" (Miller, 1981), these children were made to feel that their self-worth was derived from only one source.

Holding aside for one moment the emotional consequences of this parenting style (see Hypothesis II, below), it is assumed that the competence image derived from praise based solely upon the manifestation of one attribute would be highly vulnerable to disconfirmatory feedback. Even if all the praise an individual received for one attribute was contingent and task-based, his or her self-esteem would still be "resting" on a shaky foundation (analogous to a monopod) as opposed to a stable competence-image "base" established by receipt of praise for more than one attribute or accomplishment (analogous to a tripod). Particularly in those instances when there is "an overvaluation of the child's worth" because of one attribute (e.g., Millon's, 1981, theory of NPDs), individuals subjected to this type of parenting inevitably develop precarious, often inflated, senses of self-worth, that they are loath to risk for fear that the one "basket" holding all of their self-esteem "eggs" can easily shatter.

The few case studies of self-handicappers reported in the literature thus far (e.g., Berglas, 1986a, Chapter 11; Chapter 6, this volume) support the contention that praise linked to either the possession or manifestation of one attribute figures prominently in the etiology of this disorder. When asked to discuss their understanding of the consequences of failure on important tasks, self-handicappers uniformly report a feeling of "losing everything" or being a "complete failure" should one significant performance go poorly (Berglas, 1986a). This failure to compartmentalize ego-dystonic feedback, a characteristic of many depressed patients who engage in faulty information-processing patterns known as "absolutistic or dichotomous thinking" (Beck, Rush, Shaw, & Emery, 1979), is thought to derive, in large measure, from a reinforcement history that affords either of two polar outcomes—dramatic success or abysmal failure—for valued performance tasks.

The contention that self-handicappers have been praised for a single attribute receives further support from the fact that they resist skills-training psychotherapies (Kelly, 1955) and opportunities to learn to behave more proficiently in significant performance arenas (Berglas, 1985; Chapter 6, this volume). Rather than responding positively to behavioral interventions designed to reduce performance anxiety through skill acquisition, self-handicappers are made anxious by suggestions that they can learn to perform "as expected." In much the same manner that Nemiah's (1961) "prisoners of aspirations" suffered NPDs subsequent to internalizing parental demands for unreachable performance standards, self-handicappers appear to believe that they can never meet the inexorably upward-spiraling criteria for success that they are expected to attain in a particular realm. Thus, rather than attempting to perform as expected, self-handicappers adopt a permanently impaired self-image to prevent being exposed as deficient and "losing it all."

One of the few hypotheses advanced in Jones & Berglas's (1978) original self-handicapping formulation that has been repeatedly challenged in follow-up research is the notion that self-handicapping strategies are designed to protect both public *and* private competence images (e.g., Kolditz & Arkin, 1982). The consensus of opinion in the literature today is that self-handicapping strategies are designed primarily to protect an individual's public competence image. Thus, we can assume that the self-handicapper will be more concerned with pleasing those who dispense praise or sustaining a favorable image in their eyes (cf. Baumeister, 1984; Baumeister *et al.*, 1985) than with gratifying internally held needs.

This external orientation, common to virtually all praise-induced disorders, has been linked directly to an unempathic parenting style that rewards manifestations of a desired attribute and fails to reinforce other expressions of competence that are pleasing to the child (cf. Kernberg, 1975; Miller, 1981). This suggests that self-handicappers' symptoms afford them a mechanism for regulating emotionally charged relationships with highly conflictual people by permitting them to not perform as desired (as an expression of hostility) while preserving the belief that desired attributes will be manifest in the future (Jones & Berglas, 1978; see also, Chapter 6, this volume).

A corollary to Hypothesis I is that individuals destined to develop self-handicapping disorders have suffered from a paucity of task-based praise. Instead, it is highly likely that self-handicappers received the "empty praise and condescending encouragement" thought by Erikson (1963) to deny an individual the opportunity to develop a healthy sense of self-esteem. More specifically, because it is assumed that the parents of future self-handicappers are concerned only with whether or not their child will manifest a particular attribute, they ignore nomothetic performance criteria, opting instead to praise their child on the basis of idiographic criteria (cf. Allport, 1940).

The consensus of opinion regarding the etiology of praise-induced disorders supports the contention that self-handicapping arises in response to parenting behaviors that induce the feeling that praise is attributable to who or what someone *is* as opposed to what they did or can *do*. It is important to note, however, that the dynamic established by receiving person-based praise appears to be less a function of the magnitude of the praise (e.g., excessive noncontingent success feedback) than the directiveness of the praise. Person-based praise (and externally based noncontingent success feedback) leaves recipients frustrated by their inability to incorporate the feedback for fear that inflating their competence image will expose them to future embarrassment or loss. Furthermore, this type of praise leaves self-handicappers unable to abandon a relationship with an evaluator while they attempt to discern their motives.

This latter contention is supported by a further analysis of self-handicappers' reluctance to acquire the skills that may enable them to fulfill the performance expectations of significant others. It is possible to understand self-handicapping symptoms (self-imposed impediments to success or self-reported disabilities) as being the result of an unwillingness to continue to behave like a pawn (deCharms, 1968) operating in conjunction with an unwillingness to risk the consequences that would derive from actively refusing to do so. Stated another way, self-handicappers are ambivalently cathected to the evaluative interactions that cause them distress and elicit symptomatic behavior. This phenomenon is indicative of the fact that one of their goals is to structure a more tolerable relationship with those in control of significant reinforcers. Such intense attachments are reinforced by the parents of self-handicappers who permit them to retain their special status in the absence of achieved successes *provided* they are overtly impaired and promise to continually perform as desired.

HYPOTHESIS II

Hypothesis II states that the praise received by an individual destined to develop a self-handicapping disorder fails to address or fulfill his or her emotional needs.

This hypothesis is more than a corollary to the conclusion that self-handicappers have been victimized by a history of highly directive, person-based feedback and responded to primarily in terms of one attribute. It implies, specifically, that the parents of self-handicappers are unresponsive to the future self-handicapper's needs owing to a preoccupation with their own narcissistic concerns. Miller's (1981) discussions of the parenting styles that she sees as responsible for the etiology of NPDs captures the essence of this issue:

> . . . if the mother . . . is unable to take over the narcissistic functions for the child . . . as very often happens . . . [she] then tries to assuage her own narcissistic needs through her child, that is, she cathects him narcissistically. This does not rule out strong affection. On the contrary, the mother often loves her child as her self-object, passionately, but not in the way he needs to be loved . . . what is missing above all is the framework within which the child could experience his feelings and emotions. Instead, he develops something the mother needs, and this . . . may prevent him, throughout his life, from being himself. (pp. 34–35)

According to Miller (1981) the child's intellectual capacities can become fully developed at the hands of narcissistic parents because this is the attribute, or set of attributes, that they value and use for the fulfillment of their own needs. By trying to use the intellect (or favored attribute) to bolster an undervalued sense of self-worth, individuals raised by narcissistic parents are forced to derive love from attributes that should be securing respect or admiration. As a consequence, they ultimately develop the self-love and grandiosity that are the hallmarks of individuals suffering NPDs (cf. Kernberg, 1971). According to Miller, it is

> impossible for the grandiose (narcissistically disturbed) person to cut the tragic link between admiration and love. In his compulsion to repeat he seeks insatiably for admiration, of which he never gets enough because admiration is not the same thing as love. It is only a substitute gratification of the primary needs for respect, understanding, and being taken seriously (Miller, 1981, p. 40).

The preceding arguments sound remarkably similar to Jones and Berglas's (1978) musings on the origin of self-handicapping behavior.

Jones and I assumed that self-handicappers developed their disorder by being forced to solve the vitally important conundrum, "Do they love me for who I am or for what I do?" while fearing that the answer was, "for what I do." While distorted feedback can, in and of itself, disrupt an individual's ongoing level of behavioral functioning (e.g., Nisbett & Valins, 1971), nothing seems to affect a person's dispositional capacity to interact with the world as much as a parenting style that makes a child feel that he or she is a vehicle fueled by praise solely to fulfill a parent's needs.

This phenomenon may, in fact, account for the drastic difference between Freud's child, who was the "indisputable favorite" of his mother, and Adler's spoiled/pampered child. In essence, regardless of the level of verbal praise or material rewards children receive from their parents, the factor that determines their resultant self-esteem will be the respect shown for their independent feelings and need to manifest an autonomous sense of self (Kohut, 1971; Miller, 1981). As Adler (1930) noted, pampered children are regularly provided with money and creature comforts while being denied an opportunity to perform tasks that would lead them to develop feelings of self-efficacy—Freud's feeling of a conqueror (cf. Bandura, 1977; Erikson, 1963). When spoiling of this sort takes place, the dual message that gets delivered to the child is that he or she must behave in a particular way in order to receive love, and that self-initiated or intrinsically motivating behaviors are not only frowned upon, they may even incur parental displeasure.

Hypothesis III

Hypothesis III states that an individual's position along the continuum of praise-induced disorders is determined by the degree of anger aroused by the parenting they received and/or the degree of anger their self-initiated behaviors engendered in their parents.

Most perspectives on the etiology of praise-induced disorders maintain that being loved solely on the basis of manifesting one attribute causes more than detriments in feelings of self-worth: it is thought to provoke intense feelings of anger. Worse yet, many "special" children are brutally punished—often through covert mechanisms such as the withdrawal of love—if and when they fail to fulfill the wishes of narcissistic parents. This type of rejection, and the "bad mothering" received by children who later develop NPDs (Kernberg, 1975), is thought to evoke rageful counterresponses. In fact, the symptom patterns exhibited by individuals suffering NPDs are seen, in large measure, as devices designed to quell or suppress retaliatory reactions toward sadistic parents (Kernberg, 1975; Stolorow, 1975). While self-handicappers resent the controlling and directive praise they have received from narcissistic parents, their reactions to the burdensome expectations imposed by such feedback—from claims of incapacitation to self-imposed impediments to success—rarely result in the severe impairment experienced by individuals suffering NPDs.

It is instructive to consider how one disorder—at the moment a provisional diagnosis in DSM-III-R (American Psychiatric Association, 1987)—bears such a strong similarity to self-handicapping disorders, save for the intensity of its symptoms, which are often thought to serve a rage-repressing function (e.g., Stolorow, 1975). I am referring to the Self-Defeating Personality Disorder (SPD) (American Psychiatric Association, 1987) that has, according to a recent analysis (Berglas, 1989), three (out of eight) diagnostic criteria that are identical to self-handicapping symptoms. In fact, these criteria, the so-called self-protective subtype of the SPD, are virtually identical to the "diagnostic criteria" that I proposed (Berglas, 1985) when first advancing the notion that there was a self-handicapping *disorder* distinct from self-handicapping *strategies*.

Stolorow (1975) has claimed that people who behave masochistically—in opposition to the fundamental "law" that human behavior is directed at attaining pleasure or pursuing self-interests—often do so in order to support or repair a defective or damaged sense of self-esteem (see also Kaplan, 1980). Borrowing freely from Kohut's (1971) theories on the etiology of NPDs, Stolorow (1975) argues:

> masochistic activities may, in certain instances, represent abortive . . . efforts to restore and maintain the structural cohesiveness, temporal stability and positive affective colouring of a precarious or crumbling self-representation . . . such efforts in the service of maintaining the self-representation would constitute the "narcissistic function" of masochistic manifestations. (pp. 441–442)

A number of psychodynamically oriented theories on the origins of self-defeating behavior patterns trace them to disruptions in early mother–child relationships when damage to the self-representation—sense of self-worth—is likely to occur (Berglas, 1989). The consensus among these theories is that many individuals who engage in self-defeating behaviors do so in order to solidify a sense of self-identity and self-esteem by forming intimate, interdependent relationships ("merging") with aggrandized people ("idealized parent imago") (Stolorow, 1975). This end can be accomplished by actively debasing oneself in relationship to significant others so as to establish a dominant–submissive symbiosis in which the dependent partner is nurtured and provided with a structure to bolster a fragile sense of self-esteem. It can also be achieved indirectly by failing to attain the goals that would secure independence and autonomy from parenting relationships.

As noted above, self-handicappers often "fail" to accomplish tasks or behave autonomously in the context of intimate interpersonal relationships. Adler's (1930) patient described at the outset of this chapter appeared to be heavily involved with doting parents throughout the course of his disorder. They supported him in a luxurious lifestyle while he continued to binge prior to each opportunity to manifest competence in the real world and free himself from an involvement with ambivalently valued parents. Similarly, in the case report presented in Chapter 6 (this volume), we see how a self-handicapper's "mental block" for mechanical tasks keeps her ambivalently cathected to significant others who at once preserve her competence image while permitting her to vent angry feelings derived from a childhood that denied her the opportunity to become autonomous and develop a healthy sense of self-efficacy.

The symptoms of self-handicapping disorders that involve "self-defeatism" in relationship to significant others, and closely resemble symptoms of the proposed SPD (American Psychiatric Association, 1987), are thought to have a small but noticeable anger-repressing or anger-controlling function. By stunting one's personal development or sacrificing one's competence, an individual can achieve two important developmental goals: the preservation of a "special" childhood status and a denial of hostility toward manipulative parents who might punish such behaviors (Berglas, 1989). If we return to the essential feature of all praise-induced disorders—the attempt to discern if love is dependent upon what one does or is—we can see, as Jones and Berglas (1978) noted, it is often better to avoid discovery of the truth. Symptoms that preserve one's status as a dependent of individuals who lavish you with praise—regardless of its worth or authenticity—permit the perpetuation of the fantasy that you really are all that you are cracked up to be. The problem with this compromise is that it involves the infliction of self-imposed suffering and prohibits the actualization of one's potential.

Finally, clinicians may ask whether it is possible to infer the severity of a self-handicapping disorder on the basis of an individual's use of self-reported versus behavioral symptoms (cf. Leary & Shepperd, 1986). On the surface, an individual who attempts to control attributions of competence by claiming that she has a mental block for mechanical tasks (Chapter 6, this volume) appears better adapted than an individual who attempts to achieve the same goal by engaging in easily detectable extra-marital affairs that ruin his career (Berglas, 1988b). Yet, like all psychological syndromes, the severity of self-handicapping disorders can only be determined by assessing the amount of social and vocational impairment brought about by the sufferer's symptoms. The defensive aspects of *claiming* impairment may be just as effective and disruptive as *causing* impairment, in that they both exert control over significant aspects of the environment and regulate an individual's performance anxiety (Meissner, 1980). If self-handicapping symptoms adversely affect an individual's capacity to establish healthy relationships with significant people, regardless of how they are expressed, they represent serious manifestations of a psychological disorder.

CONCLUSION

In conclusion, it is interesting to consider how self-handicapping strategies, originally conceived to be actions that structured environments to achieve desired attributions (Schlenker, 1980), are actually quite distinct from the symptoms of self-handicapping disorders. Although chronic self-handicappers do manipulate the contexts within which evaluations take place in order to establish self-serving explanations for potential failures or to justify their failure to report for meaningful assessments of their abilities, the functional goal of their symptoms is the restructuring of relationships with significant others. All manifestations of self-handicapping can protect an individual's competence image, but the needs of an individual suffering a self-handicapping disorder go much deeper. As a result of being manipulated by condescending praise and denied the opportunity to develop a sense of self-efficacy, these individuals, like everyone who suffers a praise-induced disorder, strive to preserve in fantasy the belief that they are cared for and valued as persons, not merely for what they do as producers.

REFERENCES

Abramson, L. Y., Seligman, M. E. P., & Teasdale, J. D. (1978). Learned helplessness in humans: Critique and reformulation. *Journal of Abnormal Psychology, 87*, 49–74.

Adler, A. (1930). *Problems of neurosis.* New York: Cosmopolitan Book Corporation.

Adler, A. (1964). *Superiority and social interest: A collection of later writings.* Edited by H. L. Ansbacher & R. R. Ansbacher. Evanston, IL: Northwestern University Press.

Adler, A. (1969). *The science of living.* New York: Doubleday & Company.

Adler, G. (1970). Valuing and devaluing in the psychotherapeutic process. *Archives of General Psychiatry, 22*, 454–461.

Adler, G. (1981). The borderline-narcissistic personality disorder continuum. *American Journal of Psychiatry, 138*, 46–50.

Akhtar, S., & Thomson, J. A., Jr. (1982). Overview: Narcissistic personality disorder. *American Journal of Psychiatry, 139,* 12–20.

Allport, G. W. (1940). The psychologist's frame of reference. *Psychological Bulletin, 37,* 1–28.

Amabile, T. M., Hennessey, B. A., & Grossman, B. S. (1986). Social influences on creativity: The effects of contracted-for reward. *Journal of Personality and Social Psychology, 50,* 14–23.

American Psychiatric Association. (1987). *Diagnostic and statistical manual of mental disorders* (3rd ed., revised). Washington, DC: Author.

Aronson, E. (1969). Some antecedents of interpersonal attraction. In W. J. Arnold & D. Levine (Eds.), *Nebraska symposium on motivation* (Vol. 17, pp. 143–173). Lincoln: University of Nebraska Press.

Aronson, E., & Mills, J. (1959). The effects of severity of initiation on liking for a group. *Journal of Abnormal and Social Psychology, 59,* 177–181.

Backman, C. W., & Secord, P. F. (1959). The effect of perceived liking on interpersonal attraction. *Human Relations, 12,* 379–384.

Baker, H. S. (1979). The conquering hero quits: Narcissistic factors in underachievement and failure. *American Journal of Psychotherapy, 33,* 418–427.

Bandura, A. (1977). Self-efficacy: Toward a unifying theory of behavioral change. *Psychological Review, 84,* 191–215.

Bandura, A. (1978). The self system in reciprocal determinism. *American Psychologist, 33,* 344–358.

Baumeister, R. F. (1984). Choking under pressure: Self-consciousness and paradoxical effects of incentives on skillful performance. *Journal of Personality and Social Psychology, 46,* 610–620.

Baumeister, R. F., & Scher, S. J. (1988). Self-defeating behavior patterns among normal individuals: Review and analysis of common self-destructive tendencies. *Psychological Bulletin, 104,* 3–22.

Baumeister, R. F., Hamilton, J. C., & Tice, D. M. (1985). Public versus private expectancy of success: Confidence booster or performance pressure? *Journal of Personality and Social Psychology, 48,* 1447–1457.

Beck, A. T., Rush, A. J., Shaw, B. F., & Emery, G. (1979). *Cognitive therapy of depression.* New York: Guilford.

Berglas, S. (1976). *"I have some good news and some bad news: You're the 'greatest.'"* Unpublished manuscript, Department of Psychology, Duke University.

Berglas, S. (1975). Self-handicapping and self-handicappers: A cognitive/attributional model of interpersonal self-protective behavior. In R. Hogan & W. H. Jones (Eds.), *Perspectives in personality* (Vol. 1, pp. 235–270). Greenwich, CT: JAI Press.

Berglas, S. (1986a). *The success syndrome: Hitting bottom when you reach the top.* New York: Plenum.

Berglas, S. (1986b). A typology of self-handicapping alcohol abusers. In M. J. Saks & L. Saxe (Eds.), *Advances in applied social psychology* (Vol. 3, pp. 29–56). Hillsdale, NJ: Lawrence Erlbaum.

Berglas, S. (1987a). Self-handicapping model. In H. T. Blane & K. E. Leonard (Eds.), *Psychological theories of drinking and alcoholism* (pp. 305–341). New York: Guilford Press.

Berglas, S. (1987b). Self-handicapping and psychopathology: An integration of social and clinical perspectives. In J. E. Maddux, C. D. Stoltenberg, and R. Rosenwein (Eds.), *Social processes in clinical and counseling psychology* (pp. 113–125). New York: Springer-Verlag.

Berglas, S. (1988a). The three faces of self-handicapping: Protective self-presentation, a strategy for self-esteem enhancement, and a character disorder. In S. L. Zelen (Ed.),

Self-representation: The second attribution-personality theory conference, CSPP-LA, 1986 (pp. 133–169). New York: Springer-Verlag.

Berglas, S. (1988b, March). The "self-protective" subtype of the self-defeating personality disorder. *The Psychiatric Times* (Vol V, No. 3).

Berglas, S. (1989). Self-handicapping behavior and the Self-Defeating Personality Disorder: Toward a refined clinical perspective. In R. C. Curtis (Ed.), *Self-defeating behaviors: Experimental research, clinical impressions, and practical implications* (pp. 261–288). New York: Plenum.

Berglas, S., & Jones, E. E. (1978). Drug choice as a self-handicapping strategy in response to noncontingent success. *Journal of Personality and Social Psychology, 36,* 405–417.

Carson, R. C. (1969). *Interaction concepts of personality.* Chicago: Aldine.

deCharms, R. (1968). *Personal causation.* New York: Academic Press.

Deci, E. L. (1971). Effects of externally mediated rewards on intrinsic motivation. *Journal of Personality and Social Psychology, 18,* 105–115.

Deci, E. L. (1975). *Intrinsic motivation.* New York: Plenum.

Dweck, C. S., & Goetz, T. E. (1978). Attribution and learned helplessness. In J. H. Harvey, W. Ickes, & R. F. Kidd (Eds.), *New directions in attributional research* (Vol. 2, pp. 157–179). Hillsdale, NJ: Lawrence Erlbaum.

Dweck, C. S., Davidson, W., Nelson, S., & Enna, B. (1978). Sex differences in learned helplessness: II. The contingencies of evaluative feedback in the classroom and III. An experimental analysis. *Developmental Psychology, 14,* 268–276.

Eagly, A. H., & Acksen, B. A. (1971). The effect of expecting to be evaluated on change toward favorable and unfavorable information about oneself. *Sociometry, 34,* 411–422.

Erikson, E. H. (1963). *Childhood and society* (2nd ed.). New York: W. W. Norton.

Farson, R. E. (1963). Praise reappraised. *Harvard Business Review, 41,* 61–66.

Feather, N. T. (1966). Effects of prior success and failure on expectation of success and subsequent performance. *Journal of Personality and Social Psychology, 3,* 287–298.

Feather, N. T. (1968). Change in confidence following success or failure as a predictor of subsequent performance. *Journal of Personality and Social Psychology, 13,* 129–144.

Festinger, L. (1954). A theory of social comparison processes. *Human Relations, 7,* 117–140.

Foa, U. G., & Foa, E. B. (1974). *Societal structures of the mind.* Springfield, IL: Charles C Thomas.

Forman, M. (1975). Narcissistic personality disorders and the oedipal fixations. *Annual of Psychoanalysis* (Vol. 3, pp. 65–92). New York: International Universities Press.

Gewirtz, J. L., & Baer, D. M. (1958). Deprivation and satiation of social reinforcers as drive conditions. *Journal of Abnormal and Social Psychology, 57,* 165–172.

Ginott, H. (1965). *Between parent and child: New solutions to old problems.* New York: The Macmillan Company.

Hall, C. S., Lindzey, G. (1957). *Theories of personality.* New York: John Wiley & Sons.

Harris, R. N., & Snyder, C. R. (1986). The role of uncertain self-esteem in self-handicapping. *Journal of Personality and Social Psychology, 51,* 451–458.

Hill, W. F. (1963). *Learning.* San Francisco: Chandler.

Hill, W. F. (1968). Sources of evaluative reinforcement. *Psychological Bulletin, 69,* 132–146.

Jones, E. E. (1953). *The life and work of Sigmund Freud. Volume 1.* New York: Basic Books.

Jones, E. E. (1964). *Ingratiation: A social-psychological analysis.* New York: Appleton-Century-Crofts.

Jones, E. E., & Berglas, S. (1978). Control of attributions about the self through self-handicapping strategies: The appeal of alcohol and the role of underachievement. *Personality and Social Psychology Bulletin, 4,* 200–206.

Jones, E. E., & Davis, K. E. (1965). From acts to dispositions: The attribution process in person perception. In L. Berkowitz (Ed.), *Advances in experimental social psychology* (Vol. 2, pp. 219–266). New York: Academic Press.

Jones, E. E., Davis, K. E., & Gergen, K. J. (1961). Role playing variations and their informational value for person perception. *Journal of Abnormal and Social Psychology, 63,* 302–310.

Jones, S. C. (1973). Self- and interpersonal evaluations: Esteem theories versus consistency theories. *Psychological Bulletin, 8,* 185–199.

Jones, S. C., & Pines, H. A. (1968). Self-revealing events and interpersonal evaluations. *Journal of Personality and Social Psychology, 8,* 277–281.

Kaplan, H. B. (1980). *Deviant behavior in defense of self.* New York: Academic Press.

Kelley, H. H. (1967). Attribution theory in social psychology. In D. Levine (Ed.), *Nebraska symposium on motivation* (pp. 192–238). Lincoln: University of Nebraska Press.

Kelley, H. H. (1971). *Attribution in social interaction.* Morristown, NJ: General Learning Press.

Kelly, G. A. (1955). *The psychology of personal constructs* (Vol. 2). New York: W. W. Norton.

Kernberg, O. (1975). *Borderline conditions and pathological narcissism.* New York: Jason Aronson.

Kernberg, O. (1976). *Object relations theory and clinical psychoanalysis.* New York: Jason Aronson.

Kohut, H. (1971). *The analysis of the self.* New York: International Universities Press.

Kohut, H. (1977). *The restoration of the self.* New York: International Universities Press.

Kolditz, T. A., & Arkin, R. M. (1982). An impression management interpretation of the self-handicapping strategy. *Journal of Personality and Social Psychology, 43,* 492–502.

Kruglanski, A.W., Alon, S., & Lewis, T. (1972). Retrospective misattribution and task enjoyment. *Journal of Experimental Social Psychology, 8,* 493–501.

Kruglanski, A. W., Ritter, A., Asher, A., Margolin, B., Shabtai, L., & Zaksh, D. (1975). Can money enhance intrinsic motivation? A test of the content-consequence hypothesis. *Journal of Personality and Social Psychology, 31,* 744–750.

Lazarus, R. S. (1981). The stress and coping paradigm. In E. Eisdorfer, D. Cohen, A. Kleinman, & P. Maxim (Eds.), *Models for clinical psychopathology* (pp. 177–214). New York: Spectrum.

Leary, M. R., & Shepperd, J. A. (1986). Behavioral self-handicaps versus self-reported handicaps: A conceptual note. *Journal of Personality and Social Psychology, 51,* 1265–1268.

Lepper, M. R., Greene, D., & Nisbett, R. E. (1973). Undermining children's interest with extrinsic rewards: A test of the "overjustification" hypothesis. *Journal of Personality and Social Psychology, 28,* 129–137.

Lerner, M. J. (1975). The justice motive in social behavior: Introduction. *Journal of Social Issues, 31,* 1–19.

Meissner, W. W. (1980). Theories of personality and psychopathology: Classical psychoanalysis. In H. I. Kaplan, A. M. Freedmand, & B. J. Saddock (Eds.), *Comprehensive textbook of psychiatry* (Vol. 3, pp. 631–728). Baltimore: Williams & Wilkins.

Mettee, D. R. (1971). Rejection of unexpected success as a function of the negative consequences of accepting success. *Journal of Personality and Social Psychology, 17,* 332–341.

Miller, A. (1981). *The drama of the gifted child.* New York: Basic Books.

Millon, T. (1981). *Disorders of personality: DSM-III: Axis II.* New York: John Wiley & Sons.

Nemiah, J. C. (1961). *Foundations of psychopathology.* New York: Oxford University Press.

Nisbett, R. E., & Valins, S. (1971). *Perceiving the causes of one's own behavior.* Morristown, NJ: General Learning Press.

Notz, W. W. (1975). Work motivation and the negative effect of extrinsic rewards: A review with implications for theory and practice. *American Psychologist, 30,* 884–891.

Peterson, C., & Barrett, L. C. (1987). Explanatory style and academic performance among university freshmen. *Journal of Personality and Social Psychology, 53,* 603–607.

Peterson, C., & Seligman, M. E. P. (1984). Causal explanations as a risk factor for depression: Theory and evidence. *Psychological Review, 91,* 347–374.

Schlenker, B. R. (1980). *Impression management.* Monterey, CA: Brooks/Cole.

Seligman, M. E. P. (1975). *Helplessness: On depression, development, and death.* San Francisco: Freeman.

Seligman, M. E. P., Abramson, L. Y., Semmel, A., & von Beyer, C. (1979). Depressive attributional style. *Journal of Abnormal Psychology, 88,* 242–247.

Skinner, B. F. (1971). *Beyond freedom and dignity.* New York: Bantam/Vantage.

Smith, T. W., Snyder, C. R., & Handelsman, M. M. (1982). On the self-serving function of an academic wooden leg: Test anxiety as a self-handicapping strategy. *Journal of Personality and Social Psychology, 42,* 314–321.

Snyder, C. R., & Smith, T. W. (1982). Symptoms as self-handicapping strategies: The virtues of old wine in a new bottle. In G. Weary & H. L. Mirels (Eds.), *Integrations of clinical and social psychology* (pp. 104–127). New York: Oxford University Press.

Stevenson, H. W., Keen, R., & Knights, R. M. (1963). Parents and strangers as reinforcing agents for children's performance. *Journal of Abnormal and Social Psychology, 67,* 183–186.

Stolorow, R. D. (1975). Toward a functional definition of narcissism. *International Journal of Psycho-Analysis, 56,* 179–185.

Thorndike, E. L. (1938). The law of effect: A round table discussion, III. *Psychological Review, 45,* 204–205.

Tucker, J. A., Vuchinich, R. E., & Sobell, M. (1981). Alcohol consumption as a self-handicapping strategy. *Journal of Abnormal Psychology, 90,* 220–230.

Vaillant, G. E., & Perry, J. C. (1985). Personality disorders. In H. I. Kaplan and B. J. Sadock (Eds.), *Comprehensive Textbook of Psychiatry* (4th ed., pp. 958–986). Baltimore: Williams & Wilkins.

Weiner, B., Frieze, I., Kukla, A., Reed, L., Rest, S., & Rosenbaum, R. M. (1972). Perceiving the causes of success and failure. In E. E. Jones, D. Kanouse, H. H. Kelley, R. Nisbett, S. Valins, & B. Weiner (Eds.), *Attribution: Perceiving the causes of behavior* (pp. 95–120). Morristown, NJ: General Learning Press.

Weissman, N. M., & Klerman, G. L. (1977). Sex differences and the epidemiology of depression. *Archives of General Psychiatry, 34,* 98–111.

CHAPTER 6

THE MAINTENANCE AND TREATMENT OF SELF-HANDICAPPING
FROM RISK-TAKING TO FACE-SAVING— AND BACK

RAYMOND L. HIGGINS AND STEVEN BERGLAS

We look upon symptoms as creations, as works of art. Thus when we try to prove something from any particular symptom we can do so only if we look upon the symptom as a single part of a complete whole, that is, we must find in every symptom something that lies deeper than the outward and visible signs, something that underlies the actual manifestation and the form of the complaint itself. We must look behind the headache, the anxiety symptom, the obsession idea, behind the fact of an individual being a thief or a loafer in school. For behind lies something more, something personal and entirely individual. . . . But there is one assumption we can make in all cases: a symptom is connected with the individual's struggle to reach a chosen goal.

(Adler in Ansbacher & Ansbacher, 1967, p. 330)

INTRODUCTION

A CLINICAL CASE OF SELF-HANDICAPPING

Arms akimbo and legs crossed, Mary sat on the floor staring blankly at the instructions spread before her. Just how the hell was she supposed to

RAYMOND L. HIGGINS • Department of Psychology, University of Kansas, Lawrence, Kansas 66045.   STEVEN BERGLAS • McLean Hospital/Harvard Medical School, Belmont, Massachusetts 02178.

make sense of such gibberish, anyway! Barely attending to the directions for assembling her new bookcase, Mary was preoccupied with thoughts about her "damned mental block" for mechanical tasks. Finally, in mounting frustration, and without even unpacking the individual parts, she fled down the hall to the apartment of a male acquaintance for help.

As her friend worked to rescue her, Mary hardly took notice of what he was doing. She was absorbed in nursing her anger at her parents and at society for their "sexist" failure to adequately prepare her for independent living. The irony of her own inattentiveness to her friend's potentially instructive activities never occurred to her: When the bookcase was finally finished, Mary was just as helpless as ever.

This brief vignette from the life of a psychotherapy client illustrates several issues that will be elaborated in this chapter. Superficially, Mary's failure to apply herself to a task that threatened her sense of competence simply represents an obvious instance of self-handicapping through withholding effort. Closer inspection of the episode, however, exposes a subtle array of complexities. Consider, for example, the fact that her "tactic" was amply rewarded—she not only wound up with a functional bookcase, but she also enjoyed the ensuing social exchanges with her helpful friend (whose male ego, not coincidentally, was thoroughly massaged).

In considering this case study, the discerning reader may object "But these are secondary gains. What about the theoretically relevant outcome?" The answer to this question was forthcoming in a subsequent therapy session where Mary "had to admit" that she probably could have done the job herself if she hadn't given up so easily. This simple statement cuts to the theoretical heart of self-handicapping as an excuse strategy. By giving up without "really" trying, Mary *discounted* (in)ability explanations for her failure to assemble the bookcase by herself (Kelley, 1971), and preserved her image of being a person who was potentially capable of doing so (cf. Berglas & Jones, 1978; Jones and Berglas, 1978; Snyder & Smith, 1982).

It is likely that the combination of rewards accruing to Mary would have been sufficient to maintain similar self-handicapping behaviors in the future. There were, however, other sustaining factors at work. It is important to note, for instance, that Mary thought of herself as having a "mental block" when it came to mechanical tasks in general. This label-based self-conception virtually insured that future activities involving mechanical skills would challenge her sense of competence and control.

Also, in this as well as in previous instances, Mary had engaged in a form of social "contracting" by claiming to have a mental block as her reason for seeking assistance. In doing so, she essentially agreed to be

ineffectual in certain performance arenas (and to acknowledge the superiority of others in those arenas) *if*, in return, they would (1) assume
some of her responsibilities and (2) attribute her limitations to her mental block rather than to her fundamental capabilities. In this way, she
managed to safeguard her core sense of competence. In order to keep
her "image insurance" policy in effect, of course, she had to keep paying
the premiums. In other words, the ongoing viability of her social contract depended upon her continuing to suffer from her mental block.
Perhaps this accounted for Mary's disinterest in learning how her friend
approached the problem of assembling her bookcase.

This saga of Mary and her bookcase is almost finished. It remains,
however, to be explained why Mary found asserting her mental block to
be preferable to making efforts to master her environment. An impartial
observer might presume that adopting a disordered self-conception
(i.e., one of being a person with a mental block) would be more esteem-
eroding than occasionally failing to succeed in completing a mechanical
task. Such a presumption, however, neglects the intensely personal
consequences of growing up as the child of erratically accepting and
rejecting parents (cf. Berglas, 1985; Jones & Berglas, 1978; Chapter 5 in
this volume). It also fails to recognize that, in Mary's mind, she would be
more personally responsible for performance failures than for having a
mental block.

This latter "fault" was angrily laid at the feet of her parents and
society for encouraging her to grow up to be a stereotypical helpless
female. From her viewpoint, she was the unwilling victim of external
forces beyond her control. Moreover, there was enough "truth" in her
perspective that she had little difficulty in convincing herself *or others* of
its veracity. Although Mary was acutely aware that her mental block
represented an obstacle to her future happiness, she was only vaguely
aware of the "benefits" that she derived from it, and she seemed to have
no sense that she occasionally used it to her advantage.

LOOKING AHEAD

In the remainder of this chapter, we will examine the "clinical" side
of self-handicapping. As Mary's case illustrates, self-handicapping may
become an impediment to adaptive coping and a threat to positive self-
regard rather than the safeguard for self-esteem and sense of control
that it is intended to be. To the extent that self-handicapping becomes an
exercise in self-defeatism, it rightfully becomes a focus for therapeutic
interventions aimed at enabling the individual to reconnect with his or
her capacity for growth.

In the pages that follow, we will examine some of the influences that underlie the transition from adaptive to maladaptive self-handicapping. We will begin by focusing on those factors that support our self-handicapping efforts. Next, we will turn to an exploration of the sometimes insidious forces that may seduce us into betraying our unrealized potential in return for a false "security." Finally, we will discuss treatment strategies and techniques that may assist the clinician in helping the chronic self-handicapper to reclaim his or her birthright—the freedom, and the courage, to try and fail.

THE MAINTENANCE OF SELF-HANDICAPPING BEHAVIORS

In Chapter 5, Berglas reviewed many of the developmental considerations that may underly the acquisition of self-handicapping as a coping strategy. Here, we will proceed upon the assumption that, once initiated, self-handicapping behaviors fall under the sway of influences that further shape and either promote or inhibit their continuing expression. As the opening epigraph from Adler suggests, the most significant of these influences is the extent to which self-handicapping behaviors assist the individual in reaching his or her goals.

REALITY NEGOTIATION AS A FUNDAMENTAL COPING PROCESS

Theoretically, the motives underlying self-handicapping are the preservation of self-esteem and the maintenance of a sense of personal control in evaluative arenas wherein the individual experiences uncertainty concerning his or her ability to "measure up" to acceptable standards (Berglas, 1985; Jones & Berglas, 1978; Snyder & Smith, 1982). By capitalizing on the attributional principle of discounting (Kelley, 1971), for example, self-handicaps attenuate ability attributions following poor performances. In doing so, they assuage threats to the individual's positive self-conceptions and illustrate the operation of a broader coping process that has come to be known as "reality negotiation" (Snyder, 1989; Snyder & Higgins, 1988a, 1990; see Chapters 4 and 7, this volume, for further discussion).

As individuals, we not only have theories about the world in which we live, but we also have theories about ourselves and the kind of people we are (Epstein, 1980; Janoff-Bulman & Timko, 1987; Schlenker, 1985, 1987). As conceptualized by Snyder and Higgins (1988a), these personal theories reflect underlying motivations to secure positive self-images and a sense of control. The process of reality negotiation involves efforts to further these motives and to sustain the core features of our self-theories in the face of contradictory evidence. In the case of self-handicapping prior to potentially negative outcomes, for example, the individual may be regarded as attempting to negotiate a view of causal reality that forestalls ability attributions for failure, but that augments ability attributions for success (Kelley, 1971).

The self-concept or self-theory is a dynamic force in shaping our personalities. Rather than merely being a reactive reflection of the cumulative consequences of our behaviors and experiences, our self-theories direct our behavior and shape our perceptions of personally relevant outcomes. In the words of Markus and Wurf (1987), the self-concept "interprets and organizes self-relevant actions and experiences; it has motivational consequences, providing the incentives, standards, plans, rules, and scripts for behavior; and it adjusts in response to challenges from the social environment" (pp. 299–300). As a part of our ongoing reality-negotiation efforts, events (including our own behaviors) that threaten our self-theories tend to be perceived in a distorted and self-serving fashion. Reality negotiation, moreover, involves attempts to shape external audiences' interpretations of the events that concern us.

In contrast to post hoc efforts to cast negative outcomes in an ego-syntonic light, self-handicapping represents a more proactive approach to constraining the meaning that is attached to the products of our behavior. Consequently, the skillful use of self-handicapping can be a particularly effective means of coping with threats to our psychological integrity (see Chapter 4, this volume). Within the context of negotiating a palatable reality for ourselves, preemptively assuming a posture of impairment may enable us, paradoxically, to negotiate from a position of strength. This ability to shape the causal inferences that are drawn from performance outcomes affords us an important outlet for our need to exercise control. As we will discuss in later sections of this chapter, however, the power of self-handicaps to avoid disconfirmations of our positive self-theories may lead people who have adopted a defensive posture toward life to rely on such strategies excessively, in lieu of seeking more personally and socially useful outlets for their energies.

PERSONAL ILLUSIONS AND THE ROLE OF SELF- AND OTHER-DECEPTION

Despite growing evidence that excuse making is an important and adaptive process in attempting to cope with human limitations (e.g., Chapter 4 in this volume; Snyder & Higgins, 1988a; Snyder, Higgins, &

Stucky, 1983), it is typically regarded as a negative behavior by both professionals (e.g., Wahlroos, 1981) and lay people. Most negative behaviors are viewed more harshly when seen as intentionally enacted (e.g., Darley & Zanna, 1982; Shaw, 1968; Shaw & Reitan, 1969; Weiner, Amirkhan, Folkes, & Verette, 1987), and excuse making is no exception (Arkin & Baumgardner, 1985; Springston & Chafe, 1987). Indeed, it has been argued that knowingly making excuses threatens our positive self-conceptions and that, consequently, we are motivated to remain unaware of our excuse efforts (Higgins & Snyder, 1989; Snyder, 1985; Snyder & Higgins, 1988a; Snyder et al., 1983). Supporting this speculation is evidence that people are less willing to make excuses when such behaviors are likely to be salient to themselves or others (Handelsman, Kraiger, & King, 1985; Smith, Snyder, & Handelsman, 1982), and that making excuses that are likely to be detected results in heightened negative affect (Mehlman & Snyder, 1985).

We believe that the maintenance of self-handicapping is facilitated by our motivated self-deception (i.e., our lack of awareness) in regard to its enactment. This self-deception is associated with our capacity to distort information that conflicts with our positive self-theories (see above discussion of reality negotiation). Relatedly, Taylor and Brown (1988) have argued that mentally healthy individuals are characterized by *unrealistically* positive views of themselves. Such illusory specialness supports (and is supported by) a number of self-serving biases in people, one of which is our tendency to benignly regard *personal* excuse-making activities as "reasons" and "explanations," or even the "truth" (cf. Higgins & Snyder, 1989; Snyder, 1985; Snyder & Higgins, 1988a; Snyder & Higgins, 1990). In other words, ordinary people think of themselves as good and in control, and reflexively "honor" the excuses that distance them from outcomes that are inconsistent with those positive self-conceptions.

In the case of self-handicapping, our ability to deceive ourselves *and others* is abetted by the fact that many handicaps (e.g., obvious alcohol intoxication before an exam, limping prior to a big race) function effectively without our needing to explicitly acknowledge them—either to ourselves or to others (Snyder & Higgins, 1988b). Also, in terms of their role in weakening our causal linkage to negative outcomes, self-handicaps are temporally located to be maximally effective (i.e., they come *before* the outcome) and, therefore, are less likely to be challenged. This before-the-fact timing is also somewhat unexpected relative to our usual way of thinking about excuses as after-the-fact rationalizations, and as such they may be less likely to arouse skepticism (Berglas, 1985). As a simple example of the deceptive power of timing, imagine how we might react differently to two runners, one who complains about a strained calf muscle *after losing*, and another who says nothing, but spends inordinate time and energy massaging and "shaking out" his calf muscle *prior to* losing.

Although the timing of self-handicaps may render them particularly effective *and deceptive* from the perspective of external audiences, it is counterintuitive that people can strategically employ *anticipatory* excuses while deceiving themselves about doing so (Snyder & Higgins, 1988b). How can anything so apparently premeditated go unrecognized? There is no firm answer to this perplexing question, but there are possible explanations. Earlier, for example, we discussed people's naturally biased perceptions of personally relevant outcomes. In this vein, consider that anticipated esteem-threatening experiences are likely to stimulate emotional arousal. In some instances, people may construe their self-handicapping behaviors as efforts to directly mitigate such arousal. The person who is worried about an impending exam, for example, might consciously regard drinking alcohol or smoking a joint as an effort to calm down. If such behavior subsequently renders the exam less diagnostic of his or her ability, so be it. From the biased vantage point of the actor, the drug ingestion was for *other purposes*.

Anticipatory arousal, in other instances, may be "misattributed." According to Schachter's (Schachter, 1964; Schachter & Singer, 1962) two-factor theory of emotion, for example, the phenomenological meaning of arousal is determined by the label that is attached to it, rather than by its inherent characteristics. In this sense, the arousal associated with anticipating a threatening evaluation places the self-handicapper in a position to negotiate a creative solution to his or her dilemma. In other words, the individual's need to avoid disconfirmation of his or her self-image of being a competent, in-control person may subtly encourage self-serving explanations for the evaluative anxiety. The butterflies in the pit of the stomach and the clammy palms *could* signify a developing flu. Once initiated, such somatic self-monitoring has a good chance of eventuating in the individual's "not feeling at all well" by the time the evaluation rolls around. It should be noted that such misattribution of arousal does not require that the individual lose all awareness of evaluational apprehension—it may merely be confounded by an awareness of more self-serving possibilities (cf. Smith, Snyder, & Perkins, 1983).

Finally, self-deception in self-handicapping may often be promoted by "inattention" to detail. In two different studies of self-handicapping through alcohol (actually placebo) consumption, for example, reliable differences in actual beverage consumption were observed between handicapping and nonhandicapping subjects (Higgins & Harris, 1988,

1989). In neither study, however, were there reliable differences between handicapping and nonhandicapping subjects' *self-ratings* of the amount of beverage consumed. To the extent that such inattentiveness is involved in maintaining self-deception, however, it may primarily play a role in situations where the handicapping is public (i.e., is potentially observable), or where impression-management concerns are minimal relative to self-esteem concerns. In situations where impression-management motives are paramount, or where important external audiences may not have direct knowledge of the handicap, the individual's need to report (or even overreport) the handicapping activity may override self-deceptive concerns (cf. Harris & Snyder, 1986).

INTERFACING THE INTERNAL AND EXTERNAL AUDIENCES

Snyder and Higgins (1988a) defined excuse making as ". . . the motivated process of shifting causal attributions for negative personal outcomes from sources that are relatively more central to the person's sense of self to sources that are relatively less central, thereby resulting in perceived benefits to the person's image and sense of control" (p. 23). Self-handicapping is an anticipatory excuse strategy that is specifically designed to shift causal attributions away from the handicapper's ability. Although Jones & Berglas (1978; Berglas & Jones, 1978) emphasized the use of self-handicaps to shift attributions to *external* (environmental) or *temporary* internal factors (e.g., effort), subsequent authors have recognized that ability attributions may also be circumvented by implicating relatively stable, *internal* factors (Higgins & Snyder, 1989; Snyder & Smith, 1982).

Within this latter perspective, an ability-discounting excuse may simply serve to shift causal attributions to another, *less esteem-threatening* source within the person (e.g., shyness). This is significant because, by locating the handicapping condition *within* himself or herself, the individual largely negates any external audience's capacity to debunk the validity of the excuse and enhances the excuse's deceptive power. It is also significant because, even though ability may be effectively discounted, the *person* is still "responsible" for the negative acts and is, therefore, vulnerable to adverse repercussions resulting from them. For example, the college student who claims to be test anxious in order to discount negative ability attributions stemming from potentially poor test performances still has the grades on his or her record.

In order to understand why self-handicapping may persist despite adverse consequences, a second key concept within the definition of excuse making is that the success of the enterprise is determined *by the phenomenology of the excuse maker.* In other words, if the self-handicapper *perceives* benefits, the strategy has worked, regardless of what external audiences may think. The self-handicapper's perception of benefits is facilitated by the facts that people are likely to be more attuned to short-term benefits than to long-term costs (cf. Milburn, 1978; Platt, 1973), and that they are highly motivated to escape states of negative self-awareness (Duval & Wicklund, 1972; Wicklund, 1975). Also to be considered are findings that social audiences are often positively biased in their perceptions of others (Schneider, Hastorf, & Ellsworth, 1979; Sears, 1983), that audiences are unlikely to deliver unambiguously negative feedback (Darley & Fazio, 1980; Goffman, 1955; Tesser & Rosen, 1975), and that people tend to interpret ambiguous personal feedback as positive feedback (Jacobs, Berscheid, & Walster, 1971).

We have argued above, and will not elaborate again here, that the individual excuse maker is reflexively predisposed toward a (self-servingly) biased perception of information that is discrepant with his or her self-theory of being a good/in-control person. We have also cited evidence that external audiences are poor communicators (i.e., they pull their punches) when it comes to delivering negative or critical feedback. The net effect of these considerations is that, in the process of reality negotiation, the self-handicapper is unlikely to receive unlaundered feedback about the negative interpersonal consequences of his or her behavior (cf. Strack & Coyne, 1983). The self-handicapper, therefore, is likely to perceive that the costs of his or her behavior are less than they actually are. In effect, we are suggesting that audiences passively "collude" with the self-handicapper's motivated need to remain unaware of the darker side of his or her behavior, a state of affairs that has been called a "collaborative illusion" (Snyder, 1985). The result may be a face-saving deal that is too good to be true.

COUNTERPRODUCTIVE SELF-HANDICAPPING

In their review of the literature pertaining to self-defeating behavior, Baumeister and Scher (1988) categorized self-handicapping as a type of trade-off in which two desirable goals are in opposition. On one hand, there is a desire to succeed; on the other hand, there is a desire to maximize the positive (and minimize the negative) attributional inferences drawn from personal performances. In their words, the self-defeating aspect of self-handicapping "is evident in the deliberate acquisition of obstacles to success. There are both costs and benefits . . . in the short run, but in the long run, self-handicapping is likely

to lead to a performance record that falls far short of one's true capabilities . . ." (p. 9).

Does the fact that people take actions that jeopardize their potential
for accomplishment represent *prima facie* evidence that such behavior is
self-defeating? Based on the definition of self-defeating behavior advanced by Baumeister and Scher, the likely answer to this question is
"yes." According to them, self-defeating behavior is "any deliberate or
intentional behavior that has . . . negative effects on the self or on the
self's projects" (p. 3).* We, however, prefer the somewhat more "liberal"
definition of self-defeating *excuses* proposed by Higgins and Snyder
(1989):

> . . . self-defeating excuses are characterized by one or more of the following:
> (1) They undermine the maintenance of or interfere with the attainment of
> important external rewards (e.g., jobs, social approval), (2) they undermine
> or interfere with the actualization of the individual's potential (i.e., his or her
> attainment of "telic" goals), and/or (3) they result in the *long-range* undermin-
> ing of the individual's self-esteem or personal control. (p. 101)

Using this definition, self-handicapping—even to the extent that particular performances are adversely affected—is not necessarily self-defeating. The key issue is whether the costs of such behavior outweigh the
benefits.

Patterns of self-sabotage that meet the diagnostic criteria advanced
by the American Psychiatric Association (APA, 1987) for its provisional
Self-Defeating Personality Disorder have a complex similarity to self-
handicapping that is not captured by the Baumeister and Scher (1988)
analysis. Berglas (1988a) has argued that dispositional self-handicapping
is one distinct subtype of the "self-defeating personality" that has the
capacity to preserve a favorable competence image while avoiding
conflict-laden people or circumstances. The self-handicapper's uniquely
self-protective style has been shown to stand in contrast to other styles
that seem destined to endure chronic psychological discomfort and/or a
failed social status. Thus, while there is no doubt that self-handicapping

---

*Baumeister and Scher (1988) regard *deliberateness* and *intentionality* as central to their
definition of self-defeating behavior. We, however, have argued above that people are
often self-deceptively *unaware* of their self-handicapping, despite the fact that people's
self-handicapping is intentional in the sense that it is motivated by desires to maintain a
positive image and sense of control. It should be noted here that, although Baumeister
and Scher do not recognize self-deception about self-handicapping in discussing their
trade-off conceptualization of the phenomenon, they do acknowledge that there may be
factors (e.g., desires to escape aversive self-awareness, the temporal remoteness of potential adverse consequences) that operate to decrease the individual's awareness of potential negative consequences.

behaviors prevent an individual from realizing his or her maximum potential, their short-term costs are often relatively subtle. They are, therefore, frequently more difficult to treat than overtly self-defeating acts.

CHARACTERISTICS OF COUNTERPRODUCTIVE SELF-HANDICAPS

As we have indicated above, there are several aspects of self-hand-icapping excuses that potentiate their use despite adverse consequences. In the present section, we will examine some of the specific features of self-handicaps that may be self-defeating.

Obvious Self-Handicapping

In discussing the maintenance of self-handicapping, we noted the importance of self- and other-deception in the reality-negotiation process, and cited studies by Springston and Chafe (1987) and Arkin and Baumgardner (1985) as indicating that self-handicapping that is viewed as intentional is judged somewhat harshly. These studies reveal that, when audiences perceive handicapping to be deliberate, they may "honor" the handicap in the sense that specific ability attributions are discounted, but they may also form other, less savory impressions of the handicapper. Specifically, Arkin and Baumgardner (1985) found that subjects rated the *general* intelligence of a deliberate self-handicapper to be lower than that of an involuntary handicapper. Along similar lines, Springston and Chafe (1987) found that audiences expressed less liking for a willful than for an involuntary self-handicapper.

Even though self-handicapping is theoretically designed to avoid dispositional attributions, self-handicapping that is viewed as intentional appears to produce them (e.g., reduced general intelligence, unlikability). Deliberate self-handicapping justifiably calls the believability of the handicap into question and generates doubts about the handicapping individual's own confidence in his or her ability (see Chapter 4, this volume, for further discussion of the believability issue). Within an attributional framework (e.g., Jones & Davis, 1965; Kelley, 1967, 1971), moreover, intentions (motives) and dispositions are intimately interconnected. Both are seen as causes of behavior (cf. Heider, 1958; Peters, 1960) and serve to predict future behavior (Heider, 1958; Jones & Davis, 1965). In principle, dispositional attributions are formed only from behaviors that are perceived to be intentional (Jones & Davis, 1965).

Returning to our definition of self-defeating excuses, obviously intentional self-handicapping would appear to satisfy at least two of the three criteria. First, there is direct evidence that it interferes with the attainment of such external rewards as social approval (Springston & Chafe, 1987) and other social rewards such as jobs (Arkin and Baumgardner, 1985). Second, although direct evidence is lacking, transparent self-handicapping may contribute to the erosion of the individual's self-esteem and sense of control. This speculation derives from two considerations: (1) social-esteem and self-esteem are interrelated (Snyder *et al.*, 1983; Tetlock & Manstead, 1985) and, (2) to the extent that self-handicapping is obvious, the individual is unlikely to succeed in self-deceiving regarding its enactment.

Faustian Bargains

Popeye, the cartoon character, had a corpulent friend named Wimpy who was often heard to say, "I'd gladly pay you tomorrow for a hamburger today." Like Wimpy, some self-handicappers have eschewed a "pay-as-you-go" approach to life and adopted a "fly now, pay later" attitude. One such orientation, substance abuse, has received particular attention in the self-handicapping literature. Such behavior is unique among the various handicapping strategies that have been studied because drug intoxication involves more than simply putting a performance "at risk"—it involves altering one's ability to function. Although there may be other conceivable self-handicaps that are equally powerful performance impediments (e.g., soldiers who shoot themselves in the foot to avoid combat), to date there are none that have been experimentally examined. Accordingly, our present discussion of alcohol–drug self-handicapping will serve as an exemplar for the class of potential handicapping strategies that directly impairs functional capacity.

As an attribution-shifting excuse strategy, alcohol–drug intoxication is nearly perfect: it is widely acknowledged to impair performance (Critchlow, 1985; MacAndrew & Edgerton, 1969), it is not an inherent part of the individual, it is temporary, and it operates beyond the individual's voluntary control once the substance is ingested. When used excessively, however, it may also become a "Faustian bargain" (Snyder, 1984). In other words, although intoxication may serve as a remarkably effective self-handicapping strategy in the short run (cf. Berglas, 1986a, 1987a; Carducci & McNeely, 1981; Isleib, Vuchinich, & Tucker, 1988; Richardson & Campbell, 1980, 1982; Sharp, 1987), the effects of this strategy may backfire if its use becomes so pervasive that the individual is labeled an "alcoholic" or a "drug addict" (Berglas, 1985). In this sense, excessive drug use invites the same adverse attributional consequences associated with obvious self-handicapping (see above discussion). Moreover, Higgins and Snyder (1989) have suggested that people who come to be labeled as alcoholics may be regarded as having some voluntary control over their pathological behavior. This may account for findings that intoxication has less excuse value for alcoholics than for non-alcoholics (e.g., Schlosberg, 1985; Sobell & Sobell, 1975).

The instrumental potential of drug–alcohol self-handicapping has often been cited as one etiological factor that may underlie the development of abusive drug-use patterns (e.g., Berglas, 1986a; Berglas, 1987a; Berglas & Jones, 1978; Jones & Berglas, 1978; Snyder & Smith, 1982). Moreover, support for this possibility has been obtained in studies demonstrating that male college student research participants self-handicap with both drugs (i.e., Berglas & Jones, 1978; Kolditz & Arkin, 1982) and alcohol (i.e., Higgins & Harris, 1988, 1989; Tucker *et al.*, 1981) prior to esteem-threatening evaluations. Although there are no studies demonstrating that "alcoholics" self-handicap with alcohol or that alcohol self-handicapping leads to alcohol abuse, one of the above studies demonstrated that alcohol self-handicapping is associated with a history of relatively heavy consumption.

In a study ostensibly designed to examine the effects of alcohol on social skills, Higgins and Harris (1989) led heavy and light to moderate social drinkers to anticipate an evaluation of their conversational abilities. After completing a self-report measure of their dating and assertion skills (Levenson & Gottman, 1978), subjects were led to expect a social skills interview with an attractive female assistant (they were shown a picture). Prior to the anticipated interview, subjects were given ad lib access to an "alcoholic beverage" (actually a placebo). Before being allowed to drink, however, the subjects were given either no information or led to believe that intoxication would help, hurt, or have no effect on their performance. The results of the study indicated that heavy social drinkers drank reliably more beverage than did the light to moderate social drinkers. More importantly, however, there was a reliable pattern of consumption among the heavy drinkers such that, relative to non-evaluative controls, alcohol-helps subjects drank *less* beverage, while alcohol-hurts subjects drank *more* (this latter effect represents self-handicapping). Among light to moderate social drinkers, in contrast, those in the alcohol-hurts condition drank the *least* beverage of all the experimental groups. If anything, then, light to moderate social drinkers showed counterhandicapping tendencies.

Such results lend credence to the possibility that alcohol's self-handicapping properties provide a reinforcing outlet for any avoidant tendencies that the abuse-prone individual may harbor. Relatedly, the finding that only heavy drinkers self-handicapped suggests that a history of experiencing the face-saving effects of intoxication may serve to concretize the susceptible individual's view of alcohol as an important instrumental coping aid. To the extent that such use abets the development of abusive drinking patterns, it is surely self-defeating at both the personal and interpersonal levels.

Once again, however, we feel it is important to reiterate our contention that the self-defeating aspects of many self-handicapping behaviors—including strategically timed alcohol abuse—have been shown to serve decidedly self-*protective* functions in limited, but readily identifiable, contexts. Berglas (1986b) presents a number of case studies that conform to a pattern of self-handicapping alcohol abuse designed to preserve a lofty competence image (see also, Berglas, 1986c). Rather than simply leaving an individual in an impaired status, self-handicapping alcohol abuse can protect an individual's self-esteem.

Underachievement*

In the chapter-opening vignette from the life of Mary, we noted that, rather than using her mental block as a temporary face-saving device while working to master problematic tasks, she was more invested in nurturing the illusion that her problem was the fault of others. As Mary's case illustrates, one potential problem with self-handicapping is that it may be used to bolster a pattern of avoidance and, thereby, interfere with the individual's ability to actualize his or her potential. Such avoidance is almost certain to eventuate in the long-range undermining of the individual's self-esteem. This latter point reflects our view that there is an image→control→image cycle in which the individual's ability to exercise control over events is influenced by and, in turn, influences his or her self-image (cf. Higgins & Snyder, 1989; Snyder & Higgins, 1988a).

Although isolated self-handicapping might lead to reduced levels of achievement within specific performance arenas, clinically significant underachievement is likely to result from a pervasive pattern of avoiding esteem- or control-threatening experiences. Moreover, whether this avoidance takes the form of consistently obscuring the meaning of per-

---

*We should acknowledge the distinction between our current use of the term *underachievement* and the manner in which it was used in Jones and Berglas's (1978) initial theoretical presentation of the self-handicapping concept. Jones and Berglas conceptualized underachievement as the withholding of facilitative effort—a subtype of self-handicapping that is distinct from behaviors (e.g., alcohol consumption) that involve "the imposition of inhibitory performance barriers" (p. 202). For our purposes here, however, the term refers to the *consequences* of a self-defeating pattern of self-handicapping, regardless of the specific nature of the handicapping behaviors involved.

formance outcomes (e.g., through drinking, by claiming illness) or the form of invoking handicaps to decline the evaluative "opportunities" altogether (e.g., "I'm too sick [hungover, depressed, tired, unprepared] today."), we believe that it is likely to eventuate in the adoption (or imposition) of some label-based, dispositional attribution for an entire class of problems.

Disposition-Based Self-Handicaps

The reader will, no doubt, have noticed that our discussion of the previous characteristics of self-defeating self-handicaps invariably included the notion that they may eventuate in dispositional attributions. This recurring theme reflects our belief that handicapping-related difficulties that come to the attention of therapists are almost always associated with some "pathological" label. This is consistent with our experience that psychotherapy clients, whether voluntary or involuntary, typically report for treatment because of difficulties that either they or others have characterized as surpassing the ordinary difficulties of life. And, more often than not, they have arrived at, or been given, some shorthand label for their problems. We have deferred our discussion of this final type of self-defeating self-handicap to this point because we also believe that disposition-based self-handicapping is the most likely type to come to the attention of the mental health professional.

Although it is somewhat counterintuitive to hold that a behavior designed to avoid dispositional attributions should, at times, be based on dispositional handicaps, there is growing evidence that such is the case. In order to ward off ability attributions for potential failures, for example, subjects have been shown to inflate their reporting of test anxiety (Smith et al., 1982), hypochondriacal symptoms (Smith et al., 1983), and shyness (Snyder, Smith, Augelli, & Ingram, 1985).

From an attributional perspective, the primary "danger" involved in disposition-based self-handicapping is that, once a handicapping condition comes to be seen as a stable, internal attribute of the individual, audiences (and perhaps the individual) may judge the individual's competence anew (Berglas, 1985). Moreover, once a self-handicapping condition has assumed the proportions of a disposition, judgments about the extent of the individual's limitations may spread beyond the initial, more delimited sphere of concern (cf. Wright, 1983), or result in the imposition of limits on the individual's range of opportunities.

Schouten and Handelsman (1987) examined the excuse value of depressive symptoms. Subjects reacted to case studies in which the protagonists were portrayed as either spouse abusers or as potentially losing their jobs due to poor performance. They were also described as having current depressive symptoms, current depressive symptoms *and* a history of psychiatric involvement, or as having no depression or psychiatric history. The subjects rated the depressed protagonists as being less the cause of their behavior, less responsible for the consequences of their actions, and less blameworthy than the protagonist with no symptoms. They also were less likely to recommend that the depressed protagonists in the work scenario be fired. In addition, the depressed protagonist with a psychiatric history was judged to be less capable of handling job-related duties. On the "positive" side, this study demonstrates that depression can serve as a potent excuse and reveals how social reactions may reinforce its use. *On the other hand*, the depressed individual with a history of psychiatric involvement was judged less able to handle job responsibilities. These latter perceptions could have distinctly adverse consequences in terms of restricting the affected individual's future access to social and tangible rewards. The aborted candidacy of Thomas Eagleton for vice president of the United States in 1972 is a striking case in point. Eagleton was forced to abandon his candidacy after it became known that he had been hospitalized for depression and had received electroconvulsive shock treatments.

Both the excuse value of clinical depression and the associated perceptions of reduced capacity may result from the prevalent view that psychiatric patients are "victims" and that they are not responsible for the symptoms that cause them suffering. In other words, being regarded as "out of control" may be both a blessing and a curse. As Snyder observed in Chapter 4, this volume, the idea that people are in control of their behavior represents an important societal belief (also see Snyder, 1989). Behavior that appears to fly in the face of this belief represents a potential threat to the social order, and freedom-restricting "sanctions" may ensue. Peoples' implicit awareness of this may account for findings such as those of Smith *et al.* (1982), who observed that test-anxious subjects were reluctant to report their symptoms in a self-handicapping manner when the excuse value of doing so was made salient.

The Incorporation of Self-Handicaps. We all have witnessed people proffering disposition-based excuses in lieu of other, more impersonal and situation-bound ones. University advisers, for example, frequently encounter junior-year students who, upon being asked why they haven't taken freshman algebra yet, say that they have "math anxiety." In social arenas, most of us have known (or been) someone who explained his or her unwillingness to get a date by claiming to be "too shy." Such excuses are typically effective in eliciting sympathy rather than criticism, and are usually accepted as adequate explanations. They also provide insight into the way the individual has come to think about himself or herself. In this regard, it is noteworthy that such individuals find proclaiming dispositional impairments to be preferable to facing their fears.

The facility with which the "common person" uses psychological concepts—particularly the complexes identified by Alfred Adler or neuroses that trace their origin to Freudian constructs—reflects the profound impact of the psychological enterprise on modern society (cf. Miller, 1969). It is now so common to hear explanations of behaviors, such as "She's so *defensive*," or "He's *unconsciously* avoiding it," that we fail to take note of the complex psychological phenomena to which they refer. Because the lay public largely accepts the notion that unconscious forces and dispositions formed by age 3 can govern adult behavior, psychological constructs have become convenient tools for shaping desired attributions.

We suspect that the main reason why people eschew situation-bound and time-limited handicaps in favor of disposition-based ones is that their feared situations have recurred with sufficient regularity and intensity that dispositional handicaps ultimately represent a welcome, familiar, and uncomplicating way of dealing with them (cf. Higgins & Snyder, 1989). They are welcome because they "explain" so much *while delimiting the search for causal attributions*. They are uncomplicating because one dispositional excuse serves for many, more externalizing, excuses and obviates the need to find new solutions for similar problems across time. Besides, using a variety of different excuses to accomplish similar goals across times and situations should eventually result in attributions about the individual's *intentions* (Kelley, 1967). Disposition-based handicaps (e.g., math anxiety, shyness) avoid this attributional trap because they imply that the individual "suffers" from them and would certainly want it to be otherwise *if it were possible*.

Once an individual has identified the locus of a handicapping condition within himself or herself, the handicap may be said to be *incorporated* (Snyder & Higgins, 1988b). In a sense, the individual ceases "making" excuses and begins "being" the excuse:

> The excuse is incorporated in the sense that it becomes an ongoing part of who the person is. Thus, the person with an incorporated excuse has an always-available excuse that may serve to weaken the perceived linkage to a nearly endless succession of bad acts. Unlike the anticipatory excuse that is strategically invoked prior to a probable bad performance, the incorporated excuse is simply "there" and available for most failure experiences. (Snyder & Higgins, 1988b, p. 249)

Incorporated Handicaps and Reality Negotiation. Although there are a number of important liabilities associated with dispositional self-handicaps (cf. Berglas, 1985, 1988b; also see above discussion), there may also be a number of important advantages *from the perspective of the excuse maker.* We have noted above, for example, that such handicaps may simplify the individual's efforts to justify repeated avoidance of esteem- and control-threatening experiences (and the associated problem of being perceived as intentionally doing so). A related benefit is the ability of incorporated handicaps to help the individual remain self-deceptively unaware of his or her excuse making.

Imbedded within the typical incorporated self-handicap is a denial of responsibility for the handicap. Most clinicians probably have listened to a client justify a behavior (or defend against engaging in some threatening behavior) by saying something like, "I can't help it. That's just the way I *am.*" Such "genetic" excuses are paradoxical in that they acknowledge *responsibility* for the action (or inaction) while denying *accountability* in the sense of having any choice. Furthermore, therapeutic efforts to increase the individual's level of perceived control over the handicapping condition are, more often than not, met with resistance by the client. In one instance, for example, one of us (Higgins) suggested to a client (who blamed her compulsive ritualizing for her social inactivity) that she willfully enact one of her rituals so that she could observe her reactions to it when she wasn't conflicted. This suggestion was indignantly rejected on the grounds that ritualizing *on purpose* was a sin and against her religion.

We believe that people who have incorporated their handicaps are attempting to "negotiate" a biased view of reality that exempts them from being called to task for their manifest shortcomings and preserves their self-theories of being good/in-control people who are doing the best they can under adverse circumstances. The typical compromise that emerges from this negotiation process not only preserves the individual's self-theory, but it also honors society's need to view outcomes as lawfully related to causes (for further discussion, see Chapter 4, this volume, and Snyder, 1989). In other words, by "splitting" the individual into two parts—the "core," good/in-control part and the more peripheral, negative part—the individual saves face and society has something on which to "pin the rap." As Higgins and Snyder (1989) have observed, "For a world that is enamored with 'medical models' of worrisome things that are poorly understood (e.g., American Psychiatric Association, 1987), the excuse-maker must seem like an excellent negotiator, indeed" (p. 124).

Incorporated Handicaps as Social Contracts. In the preceding section, we have described incorporated self-handicaps as involving a reality-negotiation process in which the individual and "society" attempt to arrive at a compromise agreement that satisfies the basic needs of both. This view of social labeling as often being initiated by the labeled individual differs from the view that has traditionally prevailed in the psychiatric and sociological literature (e.g., Goffman, 1961; Rosenhan, 1973; Scheff, 1971; Szasz, 1963). It more closely resembles the view of psychiatric patients as powerful architects of their social environments (e.g., Braginsky, Braginsky, & Ring, 1969; Coyne, 1976; Kaplan, 1980; Ludwig & Farrelly, 1966, 1967). It would be a mistake, however, to suppose that the primary benefit of incorporated self-handicaps is one of social control. One needs only to listen to agoraphobic (or other) clients describe their extreme relief upon learning that they suffer from an identifiable disorder (and are, therefore, not unique or "crazy") to appreciate the esteem-saving and control-enhancing power of a label (cf. Snyder & Ingram, 1983). To offer a twist on the old saying, "misery loves company," it also may be that "misery loves a label."

The central goal of the social contract that the incorporated self-handicapper attempts to negotiate is a less esteem- and control-threatening interpretation of his or her failures in living. Specifically, the incorporated self-handicapper strives to define his or her problems as resulting from the handicapping condition *and* to define that condition as a relatively peripheral aspect of himself or herself. As Alfred Adler (1913) stated it,

> The patient declares that he is unable to solve his task "on account of the symptoms, and only on account of these." He expects from the others the solution of his problems, or the excuse from all demands, or, at least, the granting of "extenuating circumstances." When he has his extenuating alibi, he feels that his prestige is protected. His line of success, embedded into the life process, can remain uninterrupted—by paying the price. (Adler in Ansbacher & Ansbacher, 1967, p. 266)

The "price" Adler refers to reflects the quid pro quo nature of contracts. For the contract to remain in effect, the individual must "suffer" and, occasionally, demonstrate the handicap's continuing effects. This typically entails some loss of freedom and, perhaps, the assumption of a dependent status. For example, the individual who is labeled "agoraphobic" wishes to retain the privilege of being escorted everywhere, but also must continue to evidence an inability to go it alone. Although the label carries the implication that such an inability is involuntary, the authors have worked with such clients who ultimately acknowledged that they failed to exercise as much autonomy as they could have because doing so might have jeopardized the perceived legitimacy of future demands on their social "safety net." In this vein, it should be recognized that the concern about continuing legitimacy was not only aimed at external audiences—it was of central importance to the individual as well (see above discussion of reality negotiation).

INSTIGATIONS TO INCORPORATED SELF-HANDICAPPING

In previous sections of this chapter we have described self-handicapping as a transaction at both the intra- and interpersonal levels, with both levels involving a form of "reality negotiation" about the meaning that is to be attached to behavior. Moreover, we have characterized self-handicapping as a trade-off between accomplishment and face-saving at the intrapersonal level (cf. Baumeister & Scher, 1988), and as a social contract at the interpersonal level. All of these concepts (i.e., negotiation, trade-off, contract) convey the idea that the self-handicapper is willing to accept certain consequences in return for certain considerations. Our thesis here is that the nature of the deal one can "cut" is related to the strength of one's "hand." Stated differently, the price one is willing to pay for something depends on one's need for it, as well as on the availability of viable, less costly alternatives.

Within the framework of our focus on self-handicapping, the highest prices we can pay in return for having our most cherished self-conceptions (i.e., good/in-control person) exempted from debasement are to play self-handicapping "hard ball" or to sacrifice other, less cherished self-conceptions. In other words, we can invoke such powerful handicaps that they virtually compel that causal attributions be directed to them (and probably guarantee impaired performance), or we can focus causal attributions on dispositional characteristics of ourselves that are less central to our core sense of self-esteem and personal control (see above definition of excuse making). In that we have argued that patterns of truly performance-impairing self-handicapping are likely to eventuate in the adoption (or imposition) of dispositional attributions anyway (see above discussion of Faustian bargains), these two strategies often may be functionally equivalent in the long run.

The individual's willingness to engage in such disposition-based (incorporated) self-handicapping is likely to be a function of three potentially separable but interactive factors: (1) the negativeness of the outcomes to which the individual anticipates being linked; (2) the frequency or regularity with which the threatening arenas occur; and (3) the perceived availability of alternative, more externalizing, face-saving options. We will briefly discuss each of these, in reverse order, in the sections that follow.

The Availability of Other Face-Saving Options

In theory, the "best" excuse is the one that most effectively weakens the individual's causal linkage to a negative outcome. As a general rule, therefore, the excuse maker should elect to employ the most externalizing excuses that are available *and believable* within the prevailing social context.

We have previously cited evidence that "willful" self-handicapping results in negative consequences (i.e., Arkin & Baumgardner, 1985; Springston & Chafe, 1987), and have suggested that this is due to the attributional effects of perceived intentionality (also see Riordan, 1981; Rotenberg, 1980; Tedeschi, Riordan, Gaes, & Kane, 1984). Other research indicates that people are aware of the attributional "rules" governing what excuses will be effective, and tailor their excuses to match the situational needs (e.g., Tetlock, 1981). Along these lines, Weiner *et al.* (1987) reported a series of studies indicating that people systematically offer excuses that elicit attributions of externality, uncontrollability, and unintentionality unless they are specifically asked to make bad excuses. In a similar vein, there is a small body of evidence indicating that people are more willing to engage in potentially negative acts, including self-handicapping (Handelsman *et al.*, 1985), if there is attributional ambiguity regarding their reasons for doing so (Snyder, Kleck, Strenta, & Mentzer, 1979).

The most direct evidence that people forgo self-handicapping when there are more externalizing excuse options available comes from a study of Shepperd and Arkin (1989a). Under the guise of studying the effects of music on intellectual performance, these authors allowed subjects to elect to listen to either performance-enhancing, performance-inhibiting, or performance-neutral music during an anticipated test of intellectual ability. Half of the subjects were told that they would simultaneously listen to performance-disrupting noise, while the other half of the subjects were told nothing about listening to such noise. The subjects were reliably inclined to self-handicap by electing to listen to the performance-inhibiting music, but only if they did not believe they would be listening to distracting noise anyway.

Although it seems likely that people will avoid disposition-based self-handicapping whenever there are viable alternatives, life is not always so generous as to provide us with just what we want, just when we need it. Moreover, even when there are alternatives, our access to

them or their attractiveness may be constrained by their lesser believability (e.g., Carlston & Shovar, 1983), by the presence of potentially
"debunking" audiences (e.g., Mehlman & Snyder, 1985), or by their
violation of role expectations (e.g., Ames, 1975; Beckman, 1973; Ross,
Bierbrauer, & Polly, 1974). In such instances, disposition-based excuse
attributions (or at least relatively internal excuse attributions) may loom
as our primary options.

The Frequency of Threatening Events

To our knowledge, there is no direct research evidence that increasingly frequent or recurring esteem- or control-threatening events
lead to a greater probability of dispositional or incorporated excuse making. Perhaps the closest thing to empirical evidence for this is a group of
studies showing that college students (who constantly face threatening
evaluations) increase their reporting of such "symptoms" as test anxiety
(Smith et al., 1982), hypochondriacal complaints (Smith et al., 1983), and
shyness (Snyder et al., 1985) prior to threatening intellectual evaluations. At best, however, these studies are only suggestive. The weight of
our speculation must be born primarily by the logic that repeated performances in particular evaluation arenas should incrementally raise the
individual's sense of perceived causal linkage to associated outcomes
and lead to an eventual exhaustion of credible, more externalizing excuse
options. A clinical example may serve to illustrate this point.

At the time he sought treatment for his speech phobia, Tom was a
college junior. Dating from a grade school incident when his classmates
ridiculed his nervous mannerisms during a poetry recitation, Tom had
been terrified of public speaking. Throughout the ensuing years, he had
deftly found ways to avoid every public speaking "opportunity" that
came along. He avoided taking particular classes, he failed to prepare,
he got "sick," and he flat-out refused. Finally, while taking a required
college course that involved mandatory presentations, Tom ran out of
options (see above discussion). He had maneuvered to be the last student to present, and he had even managed to drag out the other student's presentations beyond their scheduled dates by asking lots of
questions. But his time was up. At the beginning of the class when he
was to make his presentation, Tom did what he had never done before—
he told his instructor that *he had a speech phobia.*

The point of this clinical illustration is that, due to the nature of
public educational experiences, Tom was repeatedly confronted with
evaluations that threatened his self-esteem and sense of control. Moreover, these same experiences gave him ample opportunity to conclude

that he was somehow "different" (i.e., he formed a dispositional attribution for his difficulties) *and* to exhaust more externalizing excuse strategies. Ultimately, he "went public" with his incorporated handicap because he felt he had no choice. Even here, however, by submitting a meticulously prepared and well-researched written draft of his presentation, Tom delimited the negative implications of his newly avowed speech phobia. This is the reality-negotiation process in action.

The Perceived Negativeness of Potential Outcomes

Tom's case also serves to introduce the final type of instigation to dispositional self-handicapping that we will discuss. That is, conditions that increase the perceived negativeness of potential outcomes will also increase the individual's willingness to pay a high price in order to distance himself or herself from them. In Tom's case, for example, the cruel chiding that his nervousness elicited from his grade school chums led him to conclude that *any* future recurrences would be catastrophic. This conclusion became a "guiding fiction" (cf. Adler in Ansbacher & Ansbacher, 1967) that charted the course of his childhood and adolescent years and that finally eventuated in his emergence as an avowed speech phobic.

Tom's case illustrates the fact that some people become acutely sensitive to potential threats that may leave others unaffected. In terms of their clinical relevance (i.e., their likelihood of becoming the focus of therapy), such "characterological sensitivities" probably represent the most important factor behind the development of dispositional or incorporated self-handicapping. Before discussing these sensitivities, however, we will first examine the notion that highly noxious outcomes may stimulate people to advance dispositional excuse attributions for their behavior and the role that noncontingent positive images may play in the instigation of self-defeating self-handicapping.

Noxious Outcomes. There is growing evidence that the likelihood of self-handicapping is increased when anticipated negative outcomes are highly important to the individual's self-esteem (e.g., Rhodewalt, Saltzman, & Wittmer, 1984; Shepperd & Arkin, 1989a, 1989b). Admittedly, extrapolating from such findings to suggest that *dispositional* self-handicapping should increase prior to expected, highly negative outcomes involves several inferential leaps. Nevertheless, there are several lines of observation that are consistent with this speculation.

Gelles (1972), based on his investigations into the problem of spousal abuse, concluded that the majority of wife beatings are preceded by alcohol use by the husband. Furthermore, he concluded that the husbands often "drink in order to provide an excuse for becoming violent" (p. 116). Consistent with the theorized attributional consequences of such self-handicapping, Gelles also reported that the wives of such problem drinkers typically attribute such abuse to their husbands' drinking problems. Snell, Rosenwald, and Robey (1964) reported similar conclusions based on their examinations of wife abuse. These observations support our conviction that people are willing to "invite" dispositional attributions for highly objectionable outcomes, but they do not indicate that they explicitly offer them as causal attributions. Some interesting work by McCaghy (1968), however, suggests that this happens—especially if the alternative is an even more esteem-threatening dispositional attribution.

In the context of a study of convicted child molesters' attitudes toward other child molesters, McCaghy found that many of his subjects were eager to "trade up" from one dispositional attribution to another, less disparaging one. The central finding of this study was that child molesters who claimed to have been drunk at the time of their offenses expressed more negative attitudes toward other child molesters than did those who either admitted their offense (without claiming intoxication) or who denied committing any offense. These findings have been interpreted as indicating that, because those subjects who claimed to be drunk had "the excuse of intoxication, they could deny their personal membership in the reviled fellowship of child molesters" (Snyder *et al.*, 1983, p. 229). Of more interest here, however, are a number of quotes from McCaghy's subjects indicating their willingness to be regarded as problem drinkers in exchange for relief from being primarily thought of as child molesters:

"If I were sober it never would have happened."

"My trouble is strictly drinking."

"I have an alcohol drinking problem, not a sex problem."

"Drinking is the reason. I could always get a woman. I can't figure it out. A man's mind doesn't function right when he's got liquor on it." (McCaghy, 1968, p. 48).

Similar efforts at reality negotiation (plea bargaining, as it were) can commonly be seen in the legal arenas where the responsibility for truly bad outcomes is often adjudicated. Here we see such "defenses" as insanity (temporary, if possible) and premenstrual syndrome to avoid the more serious consequences of being judged a premeditated murderer, or the admission of alcoholism and drunkenness as a defense against being convicted of hit-and-run driving. A recent, widely publicized example of this latter type of phenomenon was seen following the conviction of Michael Deaver (President Ronald Reagan's former deputy White House chief of staff) for perjuring himself during grand jury and House subcommittee investigations into his lobbying activities. Prior to sentencing, Deaver attributed his failure to "recall" some of his illegal lobbying contacts during testimony to his alcoholism. According to a September 16, 1988, Associated Press article, it was claimed that "The disease clouded Deaver's memory both at the time of the lobbying contacts and when he was later questioned about them under oath," and also that "Deaver's memory might have been impaired because he took a Valium tablet before answering questions" (p. 8).

Obviously, none of these examples of retrospective excuse making are direct support for our hypothesis that disposition-based self-handicapping is more likely in the face of highly negative outcomes. They do indicate, however, that people will pay an extreme price in order to avoid a more extreme loss. In the words of J. L. Austin (1970), "Few excuses get us out of it completely; the average excuse, in a poor situation, gets us only out of the fire into the frying pan—but still, of course, any frying pan in a fire" (p. 177).

Noncontingent Positive Images. As originally conceived, self-handicapping was regarded primarily as a device for preserving precarious esteem gains derived from previous successes (Berglas & Jones, 1978; Jones & Berglas, 1978). On the surface, this perspective differs little from the view of self-handicapping expressed throughout this chapter—that is, as a behavior designed to assuage threats to positive self-theories and a sense of control. However, as operationalized (i.e., Berglas & Jones, 1978) and subsequently elaborated by Berglas (e.g., 1985, 1987a, 1988b), the "original" self-handicapping notion contrasts with the more generalized version presented herein in the sense that it places greater emphasis on a specific situational determinant of the behavior. In other words, Berglas has highlighted the importance of experiencing noncontingent success in particular performance arenas for motivating subsequent self-handicapping in similar arenas. Theoretically, noncontingent success experiences not only contribute to the individual's uncertainty concerning the likelihood of subsequent, successful performances, but they also endow the individual with a fragile, positive image that he or she is motivated to protect against debasement.

In keeping with their theorized importance, noncontingent success experiences have proved to be powerful motivators of self-handicapping. Relative to subjects who have experienced contingent success, subjects who have experienced noncontingent success have been shown to subsequently self-handicap by electing to use performance-impairing drugs (Berglas & Jones, 1978; Kolditz & Arkin, 1982), by drinking alcohol (Higgins & Harris, 1988; Tucker et al., 1981), by electing to take nondiagnostic tests (Slaughter, Shaver, & Arkin, 1988), by increasing their reporting of performance-inhibiting pain (Mayerson & Rhodewalt, 1988), and by electing to perform in the presence of debilitating music (Rhodewalt & Davison, 1986). Two of the above studies (Higgins & Harris, 1988; Rhodewalt & Davison, 1986) included contingent and noncontingent failure groups in addition to contingent and noncontingent success conditions. Neither study observed either contingent or noncontingent failure to stimulate self-handicapping.*

The above findings indicate that having a public success image to protect may be a powerful instigation to self-handicapping. Indeed, those studies that have most successfully attempted to determine whether such handicapping will occur when subjects believe their handicapping and subsequent performance outcomes will be exempted from public scrutiny indicate that the presence of an external audience is critical (Kolditz & Arkin, 1982; Slaughter et al., 1988). In other words, when the external audience that holds the noncontingent positive image of the actor is shielded from potential handicapping behaviors and from subsequent performance outcomes, self-handicapping is eliminated.

In effect, self-handicapping that is designed to preserve noncontingent success images appears to be primarily motivated by impression-management concerns (Kolditz & Arkin, 1982). This means that people who self-handicap in order to preserve noncontingent success images are likely to be doing so under conditions that increase (1) their motivation to use potent (i.e., convincing) self-handicaps and (2) the likelihood that the motivated nature of their handicapping will be detected by themselves and their audiences (Snyder & Higgins, 1988b). With regard to the increased likelihood of using "convincing" handicaps, the most obvious potential problem is that the individual will engage in activities that have a relatively high probability of adversely affecting performance (e.g., drug–alcohol use).

The increased likelihood that such highly motivated (and highly scrutinized) self-handicapping will result in a failure of self- and other-deception may set in motion a dynamic wherein the individual must take steps to avoid perceptions of intentionality and control. As we have

*Weidner (1980) reported a study that has been cited as demonstrating that Type A coronary-prone subjects self-handicapped (through drug selection) following noncontingent failure experiences. Inspection of Weidner's data, however, indicates that, whereas her Type A contingent failure subjects tended to select a performance-enhancing drug, her Type A noncontingent failure subjects tended to avoid both performance-enhancing and performance-inhibiting drugs.

noted above, one effective way of doing this is to invite or invoke dispositional attributions for his or her conduct. In this regard, Berglas's (1985, 1986a, 1987a) discussions of the role of self-handicapping in the genesis of problem-drinker attributions are instructive.

Characterological Sensitivities. In contrast to those extreme circumstances in which virtually everyone would make great sacrifices in order to avoid even greater costs, there are situations that most people take in stride but which cause others great anguish. This is reminiscent of Freud's distinction between "reality anxiety" and "neurotic anxiety" in that the level of experienced threat is less a function of objective circumstances than it is a function of the individual's internal conflicts and needs. Within a phenomenological perspective, the individual responds to the threat as it is perceived. If the individual perceives the threat to be great, and if more externalizing excuse options are unavailable or untenable (see above discussion), then disposition-based handicaps that involve only relative shifts away from more core aspects of the self become likely (Higgins & Snyder, 1989).

Jones and Berglas (1978) hypothesized that self-handicapping is associated with dispositional *overconcern* with competence, and characterized such overconcern as a "competence complex" (p. 204) derived from certain types of learning histories (see Chapters 1 and 5, this volume, for further discussion). Although subsequent research with normal populations has shown self-handicapping to be quite ordinary and often adaptive (see Chapter 4), preexisting research with psychiatric populations has been interpreted as consistent with self-handicapping (e.g., Snyder & Smith, 1982), and self-handicapping has been described as characteristic of certain clinical populations (e.g., Berglas, 1986a, 1987a, 1988a, 1988b, Chapter 5 in present volume; Higgins & Snyder, 1989). Moreover, even research on normal populations shows that extreme scorers on measures of public self-consciousness (Shepperd & Arkin, 1989b), social anxiety (Higgins & Harris, 1989; Shepperd et al., 1986; Snyder et al., 1985), uncertain self-esteem (Harris & Snyder, 1986), and test anxiety (Harris, Snyder, Higgins, & Schrag, 1986; Smith et al., 1982) are especially prone to self-handicapping when their particular concerns are elicited (see Chapter 3 for an extended discussion of individual differences in self-handicapping).

The link between high scores on particular measures of sensitivity and the development of self-defeating self-handicapping may be that the high levels of anxiety engendered by relevant evaluational contexts motivate rapid escape (or avoidance) and, therefore, unfavorable trade-offs between short-term gains and long-term costs (cf. Baumeister &

Scher, 1988). Relatedly, repeated use of particular types of coping responses (e.g., alcohol consumption) may lead to habitual reliance on them when in a jam (cf. Higgins & Harris, 1989). Whatever the specific mechanisms, we propose that people who have developed clinically significant patterns of self-handicapping (especially disposition-based self-handicapping) have fallen into repetitive and rigid patterns.

One focus of Chapter 5 in this volume is the development of self-handicapping behaviors. Accordingly, we will not elaborate here the ways in which people may develop fears and vulnerabilities to the extent that they are motivated to hide them behind characteristic dispositional excuse attributions. Rather, we will close this section by recalling our earlier discussion of the existence of an image→control→image cycle in which the individual's ability to exercise control over important events influences his or her self-image and vice versa. For most of us, the thrust of this cycle is in the direction of the incremental attainment of mastery. For the problematic (especially incorporated) self-handicapper, however,

> it is as if they have incorporated into their self-images (or self-theories) suspicions, beliefs, or outright convictions that they are tragically flawed in some way that is destined to frustrate their strivings for positive efficacy. For these persons, the thrust of the image→control→image cycle becomes one of damage containment rather than one of active mastery. (Higgins & Snyder, 1989, pp. 123–124)

THE TREATMENT OF SELF-HANDICAPPERS

Even clinicians who are familiar with the self-handicapping construct may be confused by our claim that clients like Mary, the protagonist in our chapter-opening clinical vignette, are "incorporated" self-handicappers. Until recently, self-handicapping was thought to involve paradoxical self-presentations, such as binge drinking or test anxiety, that merely *resembled* psychiatric symptoms (e.g., Jones & Berglas, 1978; Smith *et al.*, 1982; see also Snyder & Smith, 1982). Rarely were self-handicapping behaviors thought to be part of a syndrome like depression, or the central component of a disordered interpersonal interaction style such as the one manifested by Mary.

The first systematic examination of why self-handicapping behaviors are an appropriate focus of therapeutic interventions was undertaken by Snyder *et al.* (1983). In their discussion of the inextricable link between excuse making and psychopathology, Snyder *et al.* demonstrated that excuses in general, and self-handicapping in particular, may become quite maladaptive. Yet even Snyder *et al.* focused more on situation-specific instances of self-handicapping than on the dispositional disorders that Mary, and people like her, suffers from. It is only recently that authors (i.e., Higgins & Snyder, 1989; Snyder & Higgins, 1988b; also see above discussion of maintenance) have begun to address the processes that may underly the transition from situational to dispositional (incorporated) excuse making. Moreover, as clinicians familiar with clients like Mary have seen time and again, it *is* possible to use well-entrenched dispositional attributions (e.g., mental blocks) to chronically excuse entire classes of behavior.

According to Berglas (1985, 1987b, 1988b), chronic patterns of self-handicapping comparable to Mary's often dominate the symptom-pictures of people who enter psychotherapy. When self-handicapping becomes an enduring pattern of relating to the interpersonal environment rather than an adaptive response to situational threats to self-esteem, most clinicians would infer either that a habitual self-handicapping "defense mechanism" is in operation or, more probably, that the self-handicapper is suffering from a personality disorder (see Vaillant & Perry, 1985). Although self-handicapping is not a personality disorder recognized in the *Diagnostic and Statistical Manual of Mental Disorders* (American Psychiatric Association, 1987), we believe that it is useful to approach the treatment of self-handicappers with an awareness that their behavior has much in common with certain of the recognized personality disorders.

SELF-HANDICAPPING AS AN "ENDURING PATTERN"

Chronic self-handicappers resemble people diagnosed as suffering from personality disorders in a variety of ways. Chief among these is the "adaptive inflexibility" they reveal in their strategies for relating to others, achieving goals, and coping with stress. According to Millon (1981), people suffering from personality disorders respond to everyday responsibilities in fixed ways without reference to contextual or interpersonal nuances. In essence, they rigidly impose their preferred interactive patterns upon circumstances for which they are often ill-suited.

A major consequence of such adaptive inflexibility is that such people often misconstrue neutral or favorable aspects of the environment as being threatening or stressful. Thus, beyond failing to adapt effectively to authentic environmental or interpersonal demands, these individuals cause themselves unnecessary psychological pain by curtailing opportunities to learn and grow. From the perspective of an outside observer, such people seem caught in "vicious cycles" that exacerbate existing predicaments and set into motion new, self-defeating sequences which further aggravate or intensify existing difficulties (Millon, 1981).

Mary's interaction patterns, as we understand them from the book-case saga and reports of comparable reactions to other situations, reveal her own unique pattern of adaptive inflexibility. As noted above, she fled the task of assembling her bookcase for assistance from a male friend without trying to succeed. When help was provided, she passively rejected the opportunity to learn skills that would enable her to avoid comparable distress and admissions of ineffectuality in the future. Instead, she nursed the pain she experienced from being a victim of forces beyond her control. Most importantly, when pressed to account for the disparity between her generally favorable competence image and her enduring pattern of avoiding mechanical performance demands, Mary acknowledged that she did not try to alter the frustration →dysphoria→help-seeking→relief pattern she had established over the years. Buoyed by the social support she received for her claims that sexist values were the root cause of her failure to achieve an independent lifestyle, Mary spent more time and energy in justifying the existence of her mental block than in attempting to remove it.

The Interpersonal Context

A second noteworthy similarity between chronic self-handicappers and people suffering from APA-recognized personality disorders is the inevitable involvement of other people in their symptomatic expression. Because personality disorders are maladaptive styles of "making peace" with people who pose actual or perceived psychological threats, their "symptoms" are interaction patterns that not only involve other people, but affect them adversely as well (Vaillant & Perry, 1985). Likewise, incorporated self-handicappers' characteristic form of "image insurance policy" provides them with a mechanism for both structuring their interpersonal relationships and for "battling" significant others who may or may not witness the immediate effects of the self-handicapping symptomatology. Indeed, it is the act of *fighting but not winning* these interpersonal battles that legitimizes the individual's subsequent self-handicapping sequences.

Recall that, while one aspect of Mary's self-handicapping disorder involved heaping adulation upon those willing to rescue her from the consequences of her mental block, she afforded less magnanimous treatment to those judged responsible for her being unable to fulfill mechanical performance requirements. During her therapy, Mary angrily laid the blame for her mental block—the raison d'etre for her inability to succeed at mechanical tasks—on her parents and the society that encouraged her to grow up to be a stereotypical, helpless female. It is important here to recognize that the dynamics of Mary's symptomatic self-presentation required her *to sustain, but not win* her struggle against the influence of her parents and society. If she were to successfully surmount the obstacles her upbringing "imposed," it would be tantamount to her eschewing the right to use her mental block as a self-handicap.

Self-Handicapping's Place among the Personality Disorders

In Chapter 5 of this volume, Berglas argued that the etiology of self-handicapping disorders is similar to that thought to account for narcissistic personality disorders (American Psychiatric Association, 1987; see Akhtar & Thomson, 1982, for review). Interestingly, Alfred Adler, whose writings foreshadowed much of the self-handicapping literature, drew similar conclusions about the relatedness of chronic self-handicapping and narcissism.

According to Ansbacher (1985), Adler's concept of the "masculine protest" (later, "will to power" or "striving for superiority") shaped current perspectives on both normal and pathological narcissism by ushering in the era of "ego" psychology. Simply stated, Adler influenced psychiatry's move from a focus on libidinal or "primary" processes to the functioning of the ego (the "self" or "self-concept") by arguing that the supreme law of human life is that the sense of worth of the self shall not be allowed to diminish. According to Adler, *situationally imposed* threats to the sense of self-worth could be defended against by any number of symptoms. In contrast, individuals who experience *self-imposed* threats to self-worth (originating from what Adler called "inferiority complexes") developed dispositional patterns of self-worth protection called "self-centered lifestyles" (e.g., Adler, 1969). Adler's perspective on the manner in which inferiority complexes are hidden by self-centered lifestyles identifies the relationship between incorporated self-handicapping and narcissistic personality disorders:

> Often the inferiority complex may be hidden by a superiority complex, which serves as a compensation. Such persons are arrogant, impertinent, conceited, and snobbish. They lay more weight on appearances than on actions. In the early strivings of a man of this type one may find a certain stage fright, which is *thereafter* used to excuse *all* the person's failures. He says, "If I did not suffer from stage fright, what could I not do!" These sentences with "if" generally hide an inferiority complex. (Adler, 1969, p. 105; emphasis added)

From Adler's perspective, the grandiosity and sense of entitlement that are the hallmarks of narcissistic personality disorders are also the core character traits of the individual who incorporates a disposition-based handicap (stage fright, mental block) early in life and, thereafter, uses it to negotiate a social status superior to that which would be expected were he or she not able to use "sentences with if." Moreover, Adler maintained that all narcissistic disturbances stemmed from faulty patterns of "social interest" (cooperation in interpersonal relationships) that could be attributed to a feeling of weakness that sought "compensation through seemingly making the situation easier" (Ansbacher, 1985, p. 205). If we review Mary's interactive style from this perspective, we find further evidence for a link between narcissistic personality disorder and disposition-based self-handicapping.

Mary's attempt to alleviate the burden of a bookcase that refused to assemble itself had many of the earmarks of a narcissistic disturbance: she was enraged by frustration and the implication of a personal shortcoming, she took advantage of others to achieve personal ends, and she manifested a sense of entitlement when airing her displeasure at her "sexist" parents and the society she held responsible for her "condition." Most importantly, when we closely examine the manner in which Mary responded to interventions that might enable her to ease her "mental block," it is apparent that she behaved in a manner that Adler would find grossly lacking in appropriate levels of social interest. Rather than acquire skills that would make her more independent and a potential aid (rather than a burden) to others, Mary sustained her handicap (and disordered lifestyle) by ignoring her male friend's instructive behaviors.

Bearing in mind that the preceding discussion suggests that chronic self-handicapping is similar, *not* equivalent, to narcissistic personality disorder, we can examine specific therapeutic interventions appropriate to these "lifestyle" disturbances. Although this discussion will, at times, be guided by the literature on the treatment of personality disorders, clinicians should know that most patients with self-handicapping disorders do not experience the severe self-esteem disturbances that are common to individuals with narcissistic personality disorders (cf. G. Adler, 1981). As a consequence, they typically require less intensive and briefer treatments.

GENERAL THERAPEUTIC CONSIDERATIONS

A self-handicapping disorder, like a personality disorder, is often treatment resistant because no single intervention can address the entire syndrome. Furthermore, because all self-handicapping disorders manifest themselves within interpersonal contexts, any modification of a client's interpersonal relationships can create conditions that cause new (or previously unrecognized) symptoms to emerge. Thus, we suggest that therapists who treat self-handicappers vigilantly follow two fundamental rules:

1. Keep therapeutic interventions focused on "target" symptoms as opposed to "global" syndromes.
2. Help clients become cognizant of the manner in which their interpersonal environment influences and is influenced by the course of their disorder.

The basis for proposing rule 1 is self-evident: attempts to address a disordered lifestyle without breaking it down into component "maladaptive parts" is doomed to failure. With regard to our second concern, we have found that clients with self-handicapping disorders rarely recognize that their symptomatic behavior is part of a larger reality-negotiation process.

Reality Negotiation within the Therapeutic Relationship

Self-handicappers usually present for treatment following an actual or threatened major blow to their self-esteem. Consequently, their initial complaint is almost always a concern over meeting behavioral demands. But, as we saw in Mary's case, once psychotherapy is initiated the self-handicapper's focus typically turns from behavioral burdens to a feeling of being "victimized." Although Mary initially railed about the difficulties caused by her "mental block," she ultimately directed her energies against those judged responsible for it. We have observed this "shift of focus" in a number of patients. Accordingly, we have concluded that the treatment of self-handicappers should be guided by an awareness that, at least in the early stages of therapy, the self-handicapping client will view the therapist as a source of evaluative threat and will attempt to inveigle him or her into sharing the client's self-serving view of reality.

In a prior analysis of the relationship between career self-handicapping and individuals suffering from narcissistic personality disorders, Berglas (1987b) suggested that self-handicappers were distinguished by the tendency to use an ego-defensive style marked by "controlling" (i.e., excessive attempts to regulate objects in the environment in the interest of minimizing anxiety). Narcissistically disturbed individuals, it was argued, were marked more by a tendency to act out against others (cf. Meissner, 1980). However, after treating a number of individuals like Mary, we have come to the realization that Berglas's (1987b) distinction was drawn prematurely. Both self-handicappers and individuals suffering from narcissistic personality disorders seem predisposed to use others as devices to maintain their sense of self-worth, substituting "people" for "objects" in the controlling ego defense.

Finally, clinicians must never lose sight of the fact that self-handicappers are exquisitely sensitive to failure—real or imagined. The dynamics of self-handicapping are structured to avoid implications of fundamental inadequacies, or the loss of a lofty status, at all costs. Thus, despite the interpersonal evaluation inherent in all therapeutic contexts, clinicians must realize that when working with self-handicappers it is a "cardinal sin" to impose or convey evaluative demands. Even when therapy seems to have progressed to the point where the self-handicapper no longer appears overly sensitive to evaluative concerns, clinicians should exercise caution. Self-handicappers are adept at inhibiting or masking their achievement–status concerns and, like narcissistically disturbed patients, may *appear to renounce* striving for success as a means of masking their self-esteem concerns (cf. Kernberg, 1975). Thus, clinicians should anticipate the need to manage the self-handicapper's "controlling defenses" throughout the course of treatment.

The Importance of a Supportive Therapist

Stolorow (1976) contends that there is a remarkable degree of similarity between the type of patient he defines as "narcissistically disturbed" and Rogers's (1951) description of the typical client entering client-centered psychotherapy. Rogers describes this individual as feeling that he or she has no real self or not knowing what his or her real self is. Moreover, the self-esteem or self-image of Rogers's prototypic client was derived from external loci—the expectations, judgments, and approval or disapproval of others.

Stolorow (1976) believes that client-centered therapy is an appropriate orientation to adopt when treating narcissistic disturbances, because it seems "ideally suited to promote the development of a narcissistically sustaining mirror transference" (p. 28). In less technical terms, this means that the client-centered therapist responds to the client with an attitude of unconditional positive regard and acceptance in the hope that this will affirm, or help solidify, the client's own self-acceptance and sense of personal value. The "mirroring transference" is so-named because certain clients attempt to maintain favorable but fragile self-images by having others mirror reflections of the self they *wish* was veridical (Kohut, 1971). In essence, client-centered therapy may enable narcissistically disturbed clients to bolster their sagging self-images by having a respected individual treat them as valued human beings, *as they are*.

We believe that a client-centered approach to psychotherapy can help self-handicappers to determine, and ultimately to correct, their conception of how other people "fit" within their world. Because self-handicappers are typically raised by parents grossly lacking in empathy (see Chapter 5), they are unaccustomed to being valued for *who* they are as persons. Instead, they believe that their value comes from *what* they are as "producers" (Berglas, 1986b). Thus, a therapist who can be non-judgmental, supportive, and empathic is essential.

THE FUNDAMENTAL THERAPEUTIC GOAL: COGNITIVE REORIENTATION

Because self-handicappers experience ego-syntonic difficulties and relatively little of the acute anxiety or distressing symptomatology suffered by neurotics (Vaillant & Perry, 1985), they resist most insight-oriented interventions aimed at uncovering or addressing "what's wrong with them." They are more likely to ask their therapist how to get others to treat them as they would like. Moreover, for clients like Mary, behavioral modification or environmental management are, at the outset of treatment, of limited value: self-handicappers first need to change a series of attitudes they hold about their competencies and what constitutes acceptable levels of performance. The process of changing these sorts of attitudes may be best initiated through procedures of cognitive reorientation (Millon, 1981). Only after such techniques have become acceptable should the self-handicapping patient be exposed to more directive or challenging interventions designed to stimulate insights or to produce behavioral change.

A Word about Behavior Therapy

A defining feature of incorporated self-handicappers is their struggle, through symptomatic behavior, to control the implications drawn from evaluative interactions so as to protect their conceptions of themselves as competent, intelligent persons. This symptom presentation almost always involves some "surplus" affective (e.g., mental block, stage fright) or behavioral response (e.g., drinking problem). In reaction to these behavioral difficulties, many clinicians might recommend that self-handicappers strengthen their competencies through some form of skills training, such as that proposed by Kelly (1955) in his fixed- and exaggerated-role training therapy program. However, while well-intentioned, most skills-acquisition interventions, when used in isolation, prove to be inappropriate.

Self-handicappers are typically more concerned with preserving the image of competence they have available for social inspection than in manifesting presumed abilities to self or others (cf. Kolditz & Arkin, 1982). Actually, performing in a competent manner is an ambivalent experience for these individuals. On one hand, every performance, regardless of how well prepared one is, raises the possibility of failure (and the likelihood of symptomatic behavior). On the other hand, should the self-handicapper achieve periodic successes, such "desired" outcomes may serve to inflate the already excessive performance expectations thought to initiate the behavior patterns that evolve into self-handicapping disorders (see Chapter 5).

Skills-acquisition interventions that implicitly promise to increase a self-handicapper's power to perform, simultaneously heighten his or her responsibility to do so as well. Our experience has been that self-handicappers often perceive the obligation to perform in accordance with externally imposed standards in ways that arouse resistances, because these "demands" evoke feelings reminiscent of the struggles for autonomy that lie at the core of their disorder (see Chapter 5). Thus, many skills-acquisition interventions have two paradoxical effects on the self-handicapper: they (1) exacerbate their avoidant tendencies, making it difficult or impossible for them to report for evaluation, and (2) in certain circumstances, make them feel like "pawns" (lacking in autonomy) if they do comply with performance demands (see Berglas, 1985). For these reasons, skills-acquisition approaches to the treatment of self-handicappers should be implemented only within the context of a permissive attitude toward the client's eventual use of the acquired skills. In the words of Alfred Adler,

> The so-called *resistance* is only lack of courage to return to the useful side of life. This causes the patient to put up a defense against treatment, for fear that his relation with the psychologist should force him into some useful activity in which he will be defeated. For this reason we must never force a patient, but guide him very gently towards his easiest approach to usefulness. If we apply force he is certain to escape. (in Ansbacher & Ansbacher, 1967, p. 338)

Many clinicians initially diagnose incorporated self-handicappers as individuals suffering adjustment disorders with work or academic inhibition, given the way these people procrastinate in advance of important projects. In fact, many self-handicappers are introduced to psychotherapy after failing to meet a major deadline, and, because of this "behavioral" presenting complaint, they often find themselves referred to behaviorally oriented clinicians who run the risk of exacerbating the threat imposed by evaluative interactions by providing them with the tools that will enable them to meet performance demands.

One of us (Berglas) treated a 23-year-old male named Scott, who suffered two "misdiagnoses" of this sort while an undergraduate at a prestigious university in the Boston area. Although Scott was able to graduate with a B average, the stress of academic performance was so great that he vowed, upon receiving his diploma, that he would never work again. When a trip to Europe depleted his meagre inheritance, Scott's parents offered him financial support *if* he consented to twice-weekly psychotherapy sessions for one year.

Despite the odds stacked against Scott when he entered therapy, he was able to prevail primarily because he was appropriately diagnosed as suffering a self-handicapping disorder. In stark contrast to the behaviorally oriented therapies that he was exposed to in college, his therapist never once raised the issues of employment, graduate school, or the activities that occupied his day. Instead, the controlling attitudes of his parents that brought him to psychotherapy served as a springboard from which the therapy could focus on the burdensome expectations and performance demands that were the source of his distress.

During the course of psychotherapy, as the affect surrounding his parents' and his university's expectations were discussed and ultimately tolerated, Scott reported that, at the age of 25, he got his first taste of gainful employment. We believe that as a result of not rising to this "bait" and urging him on to success when he first reported working for a living—the therapist actually took pains to *downplay* Scott's job until it was several months old—Scott was able to "claim" it as his own and, in so doing, to derive a range of reinforcers from it.

Cognitive Reorientation Techniques

As noted above, self-handicappers need to change a series of attitudes and beliefs they hold about their competencies and what constitutes acceptable levels of performance. We believe that it is wise to address these concerns, in succession and in the order presented below, in therapeutic programs designed for self-handicappers.

Competencies. Self-handicapping protects a favorable but fragile self-conception from evaluative interactions that threaten to expose it as being either false or undeserved. In operational terms, self-handicappers fear that they will suffer a loss (narcissistic injury) from tests of their competence. From the perspective of self-efficacy theory (Bandura, 1977), self-handicappers suffer from low self-efficacy estimates. One crucial consequence of self-efficacy estimates is that they influence the social settings that people will approach and determine how vigorously and persistently people will pursue goals that are either difficult to attain or blocked by obstacles.

According to Bandura (1977), individuals who have low self-efficacy estimates will fail to persist in pursuing goals following only minimal frustration and, as a consequence, may develop debilitating fears and negative expectations regarding their ability to bring about desired outcomes in the future. Self-handicappers who dispositionally avoid reporting for challenges or, when they do report, refuse to pursue a goal unless encumbered by tangible or "psychological" obstacles, seem caught in a self-perpetuating cycle: low self-efficacy estimates→self-handicapping symptoms→heightened performance anxiety (Berglas, 1986a). One consequence of viewing the world in this debilitating manner is that self-handicappers come to regard a wide range of settings as threatening.

When a clinician evaluates self-handicappers for therapy, it is important to note not only that they have areas of deficient skills, but also that they encode and categorize information from the environment in ways that are guaranteed to sustain low self-efficacy estimates. Called "schema," "automatic thoughts" (Beck, 1976), or "internal dialogue" (Meichenbaum, 1977), these anxiety-exacerbating cognitions should, and often do, become the initial focus of psychotherapy with self-handicappers.

We have found that a variant of Meichenbaum's "stress inoculation training" (1977, pp. 150–162) is particularly effective in enabling self-handicappers to isolate the negative schema that shape their self-efficacy estimates and cause them pain. Originally designed as a coping skills program, the initial stages of stress inoculation training (and similar techniques) are well suited to teach self-handicappers the role that maladaptive cognitive schema play in eliciting and maintaining their symptoms.

We suggest that the following therapeutic strategies be utilized in order to substitute positive "self-statements" for the negative self-referential thoughts (see Meichenbaum, 1977, pp. 155–156) that are common to self-handicappers. Specifically, we feel that self-handicappers should be encouraged to:

1. *Assess the reality of evaluative interactions.* When any entity or setting is feared, it is typically avoided. Self-handicappers are prime examples of this rule, often "avoiding" evaluative interactions via intoxication or other impaired conditions. This avoidant behavior must be addressed as a quasi-phobic response and subjected to "reality testing."

Self-handicappers often begin to understand their avoidant reactions when they learn to think about what they have to do in a given performance setting *prior to acting*. Frequently, when this procedure is followed and the components of evaluative interactions are systematically exposed and explored, self-handicappers begin to see that their anxieties are unrelated to performance requirements. They often discover that the implications of meeting expectations, deviating from role requirements, and the like, are the actual causes of their performance-inhibiting cognitions.

For example, one of us (Berglas) treated an individual who was the son of a wealthy industrialist. Like many children from prominent families, this individual was asked to serve on the boards of prestigious charities and to lecture to business and civic organizations, despite the fact that he had no proven track record of success as a manager or public speaker. Prior to entering treatment, this individual "coped" with these invitations in a stereotypical manner: avoidance→last-minute preparation "aided" by amphetamines→"crashing"→incapacitation→calls for help to one of his uncles. In psychotherapy this individual was able to recognize that his management and communication skills, despite being limited to college course work, were well above average. Ultimately, he also discovered that the dysphoric feelings he experienced prior to board meetings and speaking engagements derived largely from his being used solely for his family name (Berglas, 1986b). These insights would not have been possible had he not been able to analyze the performance demands that confronted him *and* to control his negative thoughts.

2. *Control and replace negative thoughts or "self-talk."* Self-handicappers must learn to inhibit their symptom expression (e.g., drinking, seeking help from neighbors) long enough to identify the thoughts and images that are turning performance challenges into narcissistic threats. Because understanding the meaning of negative "automatic thoughts" (e.g., "I cannot build this bookcase or any case for that matter") is difficult if the self-handicapper "leaves the field" the moment they occur, these individuals must be trained to passively accept their occurrence without seeking symptomatic relief.

The first step in this process might be a self-control and/or relaxation training program (see Goldfried & Davison, 1976; Rehm & Rokke, 1988 for examples) designed to enable self-handicapping patients to monitor their thoughts. Beyond this, however, self-handicappers also need to learn techniques of "cognitive restructuring" (e.g., Beck, Emery, & Greenberg, 1985; Beck, Rush, Shaw, & Emery, 1979; Goldfried & Davison, 1976; Meichenbaum, 1977) so that they may develop a new "attributional logic" for conceptualizing performance expectations and the significance of evaluative interactions. Such procedures enable self-handicappers to "convert" anxiety-exacerbating cognitions (e.g., "I'm terrified that I will be inarticulate when interviewed today") to positive self-statements befitting a healthy orientation toward evaluative interactions (e.g., "I'm so psyched-up to do a great job during this interview that I can feel my heart beating away!").

Although we believe that a number of different "cognitive therapies" can be used to help self-handicappers modify the distorted schema that impede their lives, we are partial to the restructuring techniques of either Ellis (1962) or Beck *et al.* (1979, 1985), owing to their emphasis on training patients to identify faulty information-processing *patterns* that dispositionally rule their lives. In particular, Beck *et al.* (1979, pp. 14–15) describe a number of thinking patterns that distort information received by clients, ultimately causing them distress. By exposing these "thinking errors" and providing opportunities for them to identify their own idiosyncratic data-processing distortions, it is often possible to relieve most of the distress derived from confronting formerly incapacitating situations. Whatever technique the clinician chooses, however, it should include the following elements:

a. A procedure to help identify negative self-statements and the stimuli that trigger them.
b. A procedure to train substituting positive, coping self-statements for negative, maladaptive ones.
c. Feedback from a therapist to reinforce adaptive self-statements when they occur naturally or, in certain procedures, during modeling or rehearsal phases of therapy.

At this point in the treatment process, practitioners of the various cognitive therapies might emphasize training patients to confront their stressors. Because self-handicappers experience paradoxically disruptive reactions to behavioral interventions aimed at facilitating goal acquisition (Berglas, 1985), however, we would advocate a different strategy. Namely, we suggest turning attention to the distorted standards that self-handicappers have about acceptable performances.

Criteria for Success. As noted at the outset of this chapter, self-handicappers grow up as the children of erratically accepting and rejecting parents (cf. Jones & Berglas, 1978; also see Chapter 5, this volume). Consequently, they become more sensitive to the needs and wants of others than to their own needs and wants (Berglas, 1986a) and have difficulty accommodating failure experiences into personally generated standards of acceptable performance. Clinicians attempting to understand the personal construct systems of self-handicappers can assume that, given their inordinate investment in the results of evaluations, there are only three tolerable outcomes: success, postponement due to extraneous factors, or failure attributable to extraneous factors (Berglas, 1986a).

Problems stemming from distorted or unrealistically high criteria for self-reinforcement are not unique to self-handicappers. Bandura (1969), for example, maintained that excessively high performance standards are both widespread in the population *and easily remedied* through rational restructuring techniques:

> Undoubtedly, many competent people do experience a great deal of self-generated distress and many self-imposed constraints as the result of adherence to ill-advised or excessively high standards of self-reinforcement. To the extent that a change agent differentially reinforces realistic standard-setting behavior and elicits emulation of more lenient self-evaluative standards as conveyed through his comments and actions, the client's habitual self-attitudes are likely to undergo change. (p. 614)

Bandura's suggestion that unrealistically high self-reinforcement standards may be rectified through the differential reinforcement of standard setting by change agents deserves to be highlighted. One of the fundamental goals of therapy with self-handicappers is to enable them to achieve a sense of self that is independent of social influence and capable of determining acceptable levels of performance on the basis of internally held standards. It is essential, therefore, to have them substitute personal standards of appropriate performance for the expectations imposed upon them by (or adopted from) others. With the help of an empathic and accepting change agent, self-handicappers can and do learn to recognize and honor their internally generated needs and levels of aspiration (see above; see also Miller, 1981).

Often, despite possessing the requisite skills for success, many self-handicappers have relationships with "standard setters" that all but insure the symptomatic thwarting of their abilities. This often occurs when intrusive parents confront "underachieving" children who find a variety of mechanisms for failing to perform as expected without implicating their assessed—via IQ or comparable testing—potential.

One of us (Berglas), after treating a number of underachieving adolescents who were also self-handicappers, determined that these individuals need a structured form of family therapy to supplement traditional therapeutic interventions. The most important aspect of this adjunct to dyadic psychotherapy is the opportunity to analyze the demand characteristics of parent–child interactions and to actively limit the number of behavioral expectations the child is exposed to.

One patient, a 16-year-old girl with a combined WAIS of 125 who was dismissed from three private high schools for academic failure, had the bulk of her family therapy sessions devoted to inhibiting her parent's discussion of grades. In essence, because she was a dependent and unable to extricate herself from the demands of her parents, as Scott (see above) did, family therapy was used to enable her pursuit of self-generated activities.

One intervention typical of those employed during the 3 years that she sought treatment involved contracting to punish her parents if they mentioned school, grades, or the like, for a 4-month period (essentially one semester). Contingencies for this sanctioned behavior ranged from a mild fine for raising the issue of school performance, to granting the patient access to one of the parents' automobiles (both expensive German sports cars) should they chastise her for a poor performance on an exam. Although this contract was ostensibly awkward and obviously skewed in the patient's favor, the intervention had its desired impact: the parents were forced to modify—in fact, to abandon—an inappropriate set of performance standards. The once underachieving daughter was able to develop an internally generated level of aspiration—graduating from high school with her friends.

How Other People "Fit" within the Self-Handicapper's World

We have argued throughout this treatment section that self-handicappers share similarities with individuals suffering from narcissistic personality disorders. Thus, it is instructive to consider what Stolorow (1975) said about the interpersonal relationships of "narcissists." According to Stolorow, individuals suffering from "narcissistic disturbances" have failed to sufficiently develop "internal structures" necessary for a coherent, stable, and positive self-image. Lacking or deficient in these self-regulatory structures, it is assumed that these people strive to maintain a favorable but fragile competence image through interpersonal relationships. Stolorow (1976) notes that, as a consequence, these individuals are unable to relate to or appreciate separate persons in their own right. Rather, they seek relationships with people who can serve the function of maintaining and regulating their self-esteem (see also, Kohut, 1971).

This description of narcissists' disturbed relations to others is remarkably similar to the interpersonal functioning of career self-handicappers. In fact, as we argued above, a key dynamic of Mary's interpersonal relationships was that she actively sustained an impaired status in certain performance arenas while acknowledging (and fostering) the superiority of others along behavioral dimensions that she could not (or refused to) master. Although a self-handicapper's interpersonal impairment may be less pervasive than that of an individual suffering from a narcissistic personality disorder, both types of clients lack an entrenched sense of positive self-esteem and seek to maintain a favorable "public persona" through their avoidance of authentic relationships with other people. Indeed, career self-handicappers' avoidance of genuine or nonstrategic relationships with other people is one reliable way for clinicians to differentiate them from self-handicapping *strategists*, who typically use objects or contexts to achieve their esteem-protective objectives.

After a self-handicapper has established a sound alliance with a supportive and nonjudgmental therapist (see above discussion of the role of client-centered therapy) and has made significant progress toward the previously discussed goals of cognitive reorganization, it becomes appropriate for the therapist to begin focusing on the patient's pattern of interpersonal relationships. In Adler's (1969) terms, the therapist should attempt to nurture the patient's development of *social interest* (i.e., his or her capacity for cooperating with others toward the achievement of mutually beneficial goals). Perhaps the clinician's greatest asset in this enterprise is his or her own unselfish and noncoercive relationship with the client:

> For the psychologist the first rule is to win the patient; the second is never to worry about his own success; if he does so, he forfeits it. The psychotherapist must lose all thought of himself and all sensitiveness about his assendency, and must never demand anything of the patient. . . . The patient's social interest, which is always present in some degree, finds its best possible expression in the relation with the psychologist. (Adler, in Ansbacher & Ansbacher, 1967, p. 341)

Very often, however, self-handicappers respond favorably to the esteem-supportive aspects of psychotherapy but balk at the "social interest" aspects—that is, at the prospect of approaching other people with a truly cooperative attitude. Having convinced themselves that their avoidance of performance responsibilities is attributable to narcissistic parenting and the like, they often protest that opening themselves up to "unencumbered" encounters with others is likely to lead to further disparagement. Indeed, challenging protests of this sort may be "dangerous" when dealing with self-handicappers. On the one hand, the protests may be authentic—that is, they may be shielding a self-conception that has failed to develop as far as the therapist believes. On the other hand, such challenges are likely to evoke recollections of self-centered parents and, as a consequence, threaten the therapeutic alliance.

When self-handicapping clients resist the prospect of abandoning their claims to "disability compensation" in relation to others, clinicians may often be able to fruitfully combine supportive psychotherapy with the use of paradoxical techniques (or counter projection; e.g., Seltzer, 1986). If, for example, the therapist *accepts the client's resistance and positively reframes it in a manner that is consistent with the client's existing perspectives*, significant gains are often observed in the client's willingness to alter his or her avoidant (interpersonally strategic) behaviors (Coyne, 1987; Tennen & Affleck, in press; Weeks & L'Abate, 1982). Pressuring self-handicappers to relinquish their self-protective symptoms may justifiably arouse psychological reactance and associated efforts to secure the threatened freedom (Brehm, 1976; Brehm & Brehm, 1981). In contrast, accepting the client's need to continue being symptomatic *while simultaneously articulating a positively connoted rational for that need* avoids the reactance "trap" and may provide the client with a palatable opportunity to revise his or her self-defeating way of construing the world of relationships.

Earlier in this chapter, for example, we cited the clinical illustration of Tom, a college junior who developed a "speech phobia." In treating Tom, one of us (Higgins) openly acknowledged Tom's need to continue avoiding presentations and encouraged him to do so *without self-recrimination*, using the rationale that, in doing so, he would discover something important about what lay *behind* his fears. Shortly thereafter, under hypnosis, Tom was asked to imagine himself being invisible in front of a large audience that was listening to another speaker. When asked to describe what he saw in the faces of the audience, Tom characterized them as judgmental and ridiculing. When then asked to describe what he saw *behind* the faces, however, Tom "discovered" that they were sympathetic and accepting. Interestingly, when Tom was next asked to find himself in the audience and to describe what he saw in his own visage, the above sequence was exactly reversed. In *his* face, Tom observed empathy and good will. *Behind* his face, however, Tom encountered a judgmental and distinctly unsympathetic quality that took him quite by surprise. This "insight" marked a pivotal point in therapy for Tom, as he became much more willing to acknowledge his fears to others (e.g., his classmates), he ceased denying that others also experienced anxiety when making presentations, and he willingly embarked on a new assignment to observe as many speakers as he could with an eye toward discovering how they *dealt* with their anxiety—which he now accepted as real.

Given that the "world view" of incorporated or "chronic" self-handicappers typically includes the notion that other people are dangerous and powerful sources of disapproval, attempting to force them into "unprotected" interactions before they are ready invites an exacerbation of their avoidant symptomatology. Rather, the clinician who desires to help self-handicappers to forge a new and positive basis for relating to others must encourage them to negotiate a new reality by introducing positively connoted embellishments upon their existing world views rather than by attempting to supplant them with radically new views that may simply serve to increase the client's burden—and resistance (Coyne, 1987; Shoham-Salomon & Rosenthal, 1987; Tennen & Affleck, in press).

It is important to emphasize here the central role that introducing *positive* connotations for a client's symptomatology has for the success of paradox-based interventions (Shoham-Salomon & Rosenthal, 1987). If a self-handicapper's resistance to forging new, more authentic relationships is simply met with a paradoxical injunction against changing—or a "prescription" to continue the symptomatic behavior—self-handicappers, predictably, are likely to react against the implicit threat to their freedom to behave asymptomatically (Brehm, 1976; Weeks & L'Abate, 1982). However, such a "positive" response may be only short lived—and then only to serve notice that the client will not be controlled by the therapist any more than by other people.

SUMMARY

In this chapter, we have outlined what we believe to be the major factors underlying the maintenance, "incorporation," and successful treatment of self-handicapping. At each step in this progression we have highlighted both the interpersonal and intrapersonal forces hypothesized to be at work. We have, in turn, characterized these forces as being subsumed within a larger, reality-negotiation process wherein the individual and "society" maneuver to achieve a mutual interpretation of events that meets the basic needs of each (Snyder & Higgins, 1988a; see also Chapter 4, this volume).

One of the major paradoxes associated with self-handicapping is that this self-protective strategy, which has many positive consequences when it targets time-limited or situational performance impediments (see Chapter 4), may become distinctly self-defeating once the attributional focus shifts to stable or dispositional aspects of the excuse maker. In its most useful form, self-handicapping facilitates our exploration and overcoming of personal limitations by serving as an ally against the demoralizing consequences of failure (Snyder, 1989; Snyder et al., 1983). In this sense, the use of self-handicaps may embolden us to risk storming the ramparts that define the boundaries of our freedom. In their most destructive form, however, self-handicaps may become self-erected fortifications behind which we cower to save face (Higgins & Snyder, 1989). In this form, they are the instruments of our own embarrassment. We become like the hapless prankster who leans back to enjoy a good smoke while thinking that some other fool has selected the exploding cigar: when the smoke finally clears, the cruel joke is on us. In light of the depth of incorporated self-handicappers' fears of being examined and found to be lacking, it is a tribute to their resilience, and to the psychotherapeutic enterprise, that they often succeed in making the full circuit from risk-taking to face-saving—and back.

REFERENCES

Adler, A. (1969). *The science of living*. New York: Doubleday.

Adler, G. (1981). The borderline-narcissistic personality disorder continuum. *American Journal of Psychiatry, 138*, 46–50.

Akhtar, S., & Thomson, J. A., Jr. (1982). Overview: Narcissistic personality disorder. *American Journal of Psychiatry, 139*, 12–20.

American Psychiatric Association (1987). *Diagnostic and statistical manual of mental disorders* (3rd ed., revised). Washington, DC: Author.

Ames, R. (1975). Teachers' attributions of responsibility: Some unexpected counterdefensive effects. *Journal of Educational Psychology, 67*, 668–676.

Ansbacher, H. L. (1985). The significance of Alfred Adler for the concept of narcissism. *American Journal of Psychiatry, 142*, 203–207.

Ansbacher, H. L., & Ansbacher, R. R. (1967). *The individual psychology of Alfred Adler.* New York: Harper & Row.

Arkin, R. M., & Baumgardner, A. H. (1985). *When self-handicapping fails to serve a purpose: Impressions of the strategic procrastinator.* Unpublished manuscript, University of Missouri, Columbia. Reported in Baumgardner, A. H., & Arkin, R. M. (1987). Coping with the prospect of disapproval: Strategies and sequelae. In C. R. Snyder & C. E. Ford (Eds.), *Coping with negative life events: Clinical and social psychological perspectives* (pp. 323–346). New York: Plenum.

Associated Press. (1988, September 16). Deaver's lawyers cite medical evidence. *The University Daily Kansan* (p. 8). Lawrence: University of Kansas.

Austin, J. L. (1970). *Philosophical papers* (2nd ed.). New York: Oxford University Press.

Bandura, A. (1969). *Principles of behavior modification*. New York: Holt, Rinehart & Winston.

Bandura, A. (1977). Self-efficacy: Toward a unifying theory of behavioral change. *Psychological Review, 84*, 191–215.

Baumeister, R. F., & Scher, S. J. (1988). Self-defeating behavior patterns among normal individuals: Review and analysis of common self-destructive tendencies. *Psychological Bulletin, 104*, 3–22.

Beck, A. T. (1976). *Cognitive therapy and emotional disorders*. New York: International Universities Press.

Beck, A. T., & Emery, G., with Greenberg, R. L. (1985). *Anxiety disorders and phobias: A cognitive perspective*. New York: Basic Books.

Beck, A. T., Rush, A. J., Shaw, B. F., & Emery, G. (1979). *Cognitive therapy of depression*. New York: Guilford.

Beckman, L. (1973). Teachers' and observers' perceptions of causality for a child's performance. *Journal of Educational Psychology, 65*, 198–204.

Berglas, S. (1985). Self-handicapping and self-handicappers: A cognitive/attributional model of interpersonal self-protective behavior. In R. Hogan & W. H. Jones (Eds.), *Perspectives in personality: Theory, measurement and interpersonal dynamics* (pp. 235–270). Greenwich, CT: JAI Press.

Berglas, S. (1986a). A typology of self-handicapping alcohol abusers. In M. J. Saks & L. Saxe (Eds.), *Advances in applied social psychology* (Vol. 3, pp. 29–56). Hillsdale, NJ: Erlbaum.

Berglas, S. (1986b). *The success syndrome: Hitting bottom when you reach the top*. New York: Plenum.

Berglas, S. (1986c). Self-handicapping alcohol abuse. *Alcohol, Health, and Research World, 10* (2), 46–47, 54.

Berglas, S. (1987a). Self-handicapping model. In H. T. Blane & K. E. Leonard (Eds.), *Psychological theories of drinking and alcoholism* (pp. 305–345). New York: Guilford.

Berglas, S. (1987b). Self-handicapping and psychopathology: An integration of social and clinical perspectives. In J. E. Maddux, C. D. Stoltenberg, & R. Rosenwein (Eds.), *Social processes in clinical and counseling psychology* (pp. 113–125). New York: Springer-Verlag.

Berglas, S. (1988a, March). The "self-protective" subtype of the self-defeating personality disorder. *The Psychiatric Times* (Vol. V, No. 3).

Berglas, S. (1988b). The three faces of self-handicapping: Protective self-presentation, a strategy for self-esteem enhancement, and a character disorder. In S. L. Zelen (Ed.), *Self-representation: The second attribution-personality theory conference, CSPP-LA, 1986* (pp. 133–169). New York: Springer-Verlag.

Berglas, S., & Jones, E. E. (1978). Drug choice as a self-handicapping strategy in response to noncontingent success. *Journal of Personality and Social Psychology, 36*, 405–417.

Braginsky, B. M., Braginsky, D. D., & Ring, K. (1969). *Methods of madness: The mental hospital as a last resort*. New York: Holt, Rinehart & Winston.

Brehm, S. S. (1976). *The application of social psychology to clinical practice*. New York: Wiley.

Brehm, S. S., & Brehm, J. W. (1981). *Psychological reactance: A theory of freedom and control*. New York: Academic Press.

Carducci, B. J., & McNeely, J. A. (1981, August). *Alcohol and attributions don't mix: The effect of alcohol on alcoholics' and nonalcoholics' attributions of blame for wife abuse*. Paper presented at the meeting of the American Psychological Association, Los Angeles.

Carlston, D. E., & Shovar, N. (1983). Effects of performance attributions on others' perceptions of the attributer. *Journal of Personality and Social Psychology, 44*, 515–525.

Coyne, J. C. (1976). Toward an interactional description of depression. *Psychiatry, 39*, 28–40.

Coyne, J. C. (1987). The concept of empowerment in strategic therapy. *Psychotherapy, 24*, 539–545.

Critchlow, B. (1985). The blame in the bottle: Attributions about drunken behavior. *Personality and Social Psychology Bulletin, 11*, 258–274.

Darley, J. M., & Fazio, R. H. (1980). Expectancy confirmation processes arising in the social interaction sequence. *American Psychologist, 35*, 867–881.

Darley, J. M., & Zanna, M. P. (1982). Making moral judgments. *American Scientist, 70*, 515–521.

Duval, S., & Wicklund, R. A. (1972). *A theory of objective self-awareness*. New York: Academic Press.

Ellis, A. (1962). *Reason and emotion in psychotherapy.* New York: Lyle Stuart.

Epstein, S. (1980). The self-concept: A review and the proposal of an integrated theory of personality. In E. Staub (Ed.), *Personality: Basic issues and current research* (pp. 82–132). Englewood Cliffs, NJ: Prentice-Hall.

Gelles, R. J. (1972). *The violent home.* Beverly Hills, CA: Sage Publications.

Goffman, E. (1955). On face-work: An analysis of the ritual elements in social interaction. *Psychiatry: Journal for the Study of Interpersonal Processes, 18,* 213–231.

Goffman, E. (1961). *Asylums.* Garden City, NY: Anchor Books.

Goldfried, M. R., & Davison, G. C. (1976). *Clinical behavior therapy.* New York: Holt.

Handelsman, M. M., Kraiger, K., & King, C. S. (1985, April). *Self-handicapping by task choice: An attribute ambiguity analysis.* Paper presented at the meeting of the Rocky Mountain Psychological Association, Tucson, AZ.

Harris, R. N., & Snyder, C. R. (1986). The role of uncertain self-esteem in self-handicapping. *Journal of Personality and Social Psychology, 51,* 451–458.

Harris, R. N., Snyder, C. R., Higgins, R. L., & Schrag, J. L. (1986). Enhancing the prediction of self-handicapping. *Journal of Personality and Social Psychology, 51,* 1191–1199.

Heider, F. (1958). *The psychology of interpersonal relations.* New York: Wiley.

Higgins, R. L., & Harris, R. N. (1988). Strategic "alcohol" use: Drinking to self-handicap. *Journal of Social and Clinical Psychology, 6,* 191–202.

Higgins, R. L., & Harris, R. N. (1989, April 14). *Self-handicapping social performance through "alcohol" use: The interaction of drinker history and expectancy.* Paper presented at the meeting of the Southwestern Psychological Association, Houston, TX.

Higgins, R. L., & Snyder, C. R. (1989). Excuses gone awry: An analysis of self-defeating excuses. In R. C. Curtis (Ed.), *Self-defeating behaviors: Experimental research, clinical impressions, and practical implications* (pp. 99–130). New York: Plenum.

Isleib, R. A., Vuchinich, R. E., & Tucker, J. A. (1988). Performance attributions and changes in self-esteem following self-handicapping with alcohol consumption. *Journal of Social and Clinical Psychology, 6,* 88–103.

Jacobs, L., Berscheid, E., & Walster, E. (1971). Self-esteem and attraction. *Journal of Personality and Social Psychology, 17,* 84–91.

Janoff-Bulman, R., & Timko, C. (1987). Coping with traumatic events: The role of denial in light of people's assumptive worlds. In C. R. Snyder & C. E. Ford (Eds.), *Coping with negative life events: Clinical and social psychological perspectives* (pp. 135–159). New York: Plenum.

Jones, E. E., & Berglas, S. (1978). Control of attributions about the self through self-handicapping strategies: The appeal of alcohol and the role of underachievement. *Personality and Social Psychology Bulletin, 4,* 200–206.

Jones, E. E., & Davis, K. E. (1965). From acts to dispositions: The attribution process in person perception. In L. Berkowitz (Ed.), *Advances in experimental social psychology,* (Vol. 2, pp. 219–266). New York: Academic Press.

Kaplan, H. B. (1980). *Deviant behavior in defense of self.* New York: Academic Press.

Kelley, H. H. (1967). Attribution theory in social psychology. In D. Levine (Ed.), *Nebraska symposium on motivation, 1967* (pp. 192–238). Lincoln: University of Nebraska Press.

Kelley, H. H. (1971). *Attribution in social interaction.* New York: General Learning Press.

Kelly, G. A. (1955). *The psychology of personal constructs* (Vol. 2). New York: W. W. Norton.

Kernberg, O. (1975). *Borderline conditions and pathological narcissism.* New York: Jason Aronson.

Kohut, H. (1971). *The analysis of the self.* New York: International Universities Press.

Kolditz, T. A., & Arkin, R. M. (1982). An impression management interpretation of the self-handicapping strategy. *Journal of Personality and Social Psychology, 43,* 492–502.

Levenson, R. W., & Gottman, J. M. (1978). Toward the assessment of social competence. *Journal of Consulting and Clinical Psychology, 46,* 453–462.

Ludwig, A. M., & Farrelly, F. (1966). The code of chronicity. *Archives of General Psychiatry, 15,* 562–568.

Ludwig, A. M., & Farrelly, F. (1967). The weapons of insanity. *American Journal of Psychotherapy, 21,* 737–749.

MacAndrew, E., & Edgerton, R. B. (1969). *Drunken comportment.* Chicago: Aldine.

Markus, H., & Wurf, E. (1987). The dynamic self-concept: A social psychological perspective. *Annual Review of Psychology, 38,* 299–337.

Mayerson, N. H., & Rhodewalt, F. (1988). The role of self-protective attributions in the experience of pain. *Journal of Social and Clinical Psychology, 6,* 203–218.

McCaghy, C. H. (1968). Drinking and deviance disavowal: The case of child molesters. *Social Problems, 16,* 43–49.

Mehlman, R. C., & Snyder, C. R. (1985). Excuse theory: A test of the self-protective role of attributions. *Journal of Personality and Social Psychology, 49,* 994–1001.

Meichenbaum, D. (1977). *Cognitive-behavior modification: An integrative approach.* New York: Plenum.

Meissner, W. W. (1980). Theories of personality and psychopathology: Classical psychoanalysis. In H. I. Kaplan, A. M. Freedmand, & B. J. Saddock (Eds.), *Comprehensive textbook of psychiatry* (Vol. 3, pp. 631–728). Baltimore: Williams & Wilkins.

Milburn, A. (1978). Sources of bias in the prediction of future events. *Organizational Behavior and Human Performance, 21,* 17–26.

Miller, A. (1981). *The drama of the gifted child.* New York: Basic Books.

Miller, G. (1969). Psychology as a means of promoting human welfare. *American Psychologist, 24,* 1063–1075.

Millon, T. (1981). *Disorders of personality: DSM-III: Axis II.* New York: John Wiley & Sons.

Peters, R. S. (1960). *The concept of motivation.* New York: Humanities Press.

Platt, J. (1973). Social traps. *American Psychologist, 28,* 641–651.

Rehm, L. P., & Rokke, P. (1988). Self-management therapies. In K. S. Dobson (Ed.), *Handbook of cognitive-behavioral therapies* (pp. 136–166). New York: The Guilford Press.

Rhodewalt, F., & Davison, J. (1986). Self-handicapping and subsequent performance: Role of outcome valence and attributional ambiguity. *Basic and Applied Social Psychology, 7,* 307–323.

Rhodewalt, F., Saltzman, A. T., & Wittmer, J. (1984). Self-handicapping among competitive athletes: The role of practice in self-esteem protection. *Basic and Applied Social Psychology, 5,* 197–210.

Richardson, D., & Campbell, J. (1980). Alcohol and wife abuse: The effect of alcohol on attributions of blame for wife abuse. *Personality and Social Psychology Bulletin, 6,* 51–56.

Richardson, D., & Campbell, J. (1982). Alcohol and rape: The effect of alcohol on attributions of blame for rape. *Personality and Social Psychology Bulletin, 8,* 468–476.

Riordan, C. (1981, August). *The effectiveness of post-transgression accounts.* Paper presented at the meeting of the American Psychological Association, Los Angeles.

Rogers, C. (1951). *Client-centered therapy.* Boston: Houghton Mifflin.

Rosenhan, D. L. (1973). On being sane in insane places. *Science, 179,* 250–258.

Ross, L., Bierbrauer, G., & Polly, S. (1974). Attribution of education outcomes by professional and non-professional instructors. *Journal of Personality and Social Psychology, 29,* 609–618.

Rotenberg, K. (1980). Children's use of intentionality in judgments of character and disposition. *Child Development, 51,* 282–284.

Schachter, S. (1964). The interaction of cognitive and physiological determinants of emotional state. In L. Berkowitz (Ed.), *Advances in experimental social psychology* (Vol. 1, pp. 49–80). New York: Academic Press.

Schachter, S., & Singer, J. (1962). Cognitive, social, and physiological determinants of emotional state. *Psychological Review, 69,* 379–399.

Scheff, T. J. (1971). *Being mentally ill: A sociological theory.* Chicago: Aldine. (Originally published 1966)

Schlenker, B. R. (1985). Identity and self-identification. In B. R. Schlenker (Ed.), *The self and social life* (pp. 65–99). New York: McGraw-Hill.

Schlenker, B. R. (1987). Threats to identity: Self-identification and social stress. In C. R. Snyder & C. E. Ford (Eds.), *Coping with negative life events: Clinical and social psychological perspectives* (pp. 323–346). New York: Plenum.

Schlosberg, M. (1985). *Audience evaluation of alcohol intoxication as a retrospective excuse for child abuse.* Unpublished masters thesis, University of Kansas, Lawrence.

Schneider, D. J., Hastorf, A. H., & Ellsworth, P. C. (1979). *Person perception.* Reading, MA: Addison-Wesley.

Schouten, P. G. W., & Handelsman, M. M. (1987). Social basis of self-handicapping: The case of depression. *Personality and Social Psychology Bulletin, 13,* 103–110.

Sears, D. O. (1983). The person-positivity bias. *Journal of Personality and Social Psychology, 44,* 233–250.

Seltzer, L. F. (1986). *Paradoxical strategies in psychotherapy.* New York: John Wiley & Sons.

Sharp, J. A. (1987). *Date rape: Effects of victim/assailant intoxication, observer gender and sex role stereotyping on attributions of responsibility.* Unpublished masters thesis, University of Kansas, Lawrence.

Shaw, M. E. (1968). Attribution of responsibility by adolescents in two cultures. *Adolescence, 3,* 23–32.

Shaw, M. E., & Reitan, H. T. (1969). Attribution of responsibility as a basis for sanctioning behavior. *British Journal of Social and Clinical Psychology, 8,* 217–226.

Shepperd, J. A., & Arkin, R. M. (1989a). Determinants of self-handicapping: Task importance and the effects of preexisting handicaps on self-generated handicaps. *Personality and Social Psychology Bulletin, 15,* 101–112.

Shepperd, J. A., & Arkin, R. M. (1989b). Self-handicapping: The moderating roles of public self-consciousness and task importance. *Personality and Social Psychology Bulletin, 15,* 252–265.

Shepperd, J. A., Miller, P. J., & Arkin, R. M. (1986, May). *Self-handicapping and self-consciousness.* Paper presented at the meeting of the Midwestern Psychological Association, Chicago.

Shoham-Salomon, V., & Rosenthal, R. (1987). Paradoxical interventions: A meta-analysis. *Journal of Consulting and Clinical Psychology, 55,* 22–28.

Slaughter, J. G., Shaver K. G., & Arkin, R. M. (1988). *Self-assessment and self-protection: The roles of uncertainty and response context.* Paper presented at the meeting of the Midwestern Psychological Association, Chicago.

Smith, T. W., Snyder, C. R., & Handelsman, M. M. (1982). On the self-serving function of an academic wooden leg: Test anxiety as a self-handicapping strategy. *Journal of Personality and Social Psychology, 42,* 314–321.

Smith, T. W., Snyder, C. R., & Perkins, S. C. (1983). The self-serving function of hypochondriacal complaints: Physical symptoms as self-handicapping strategies. *Journal of Personality and Social Psychology, 44,* 787–797.

Snell, J. E., Rosenwald, R. J., & Robey, A. (1964). The wifebeater's wife: A study of family interaction. *Archives of General Psychiatry, 11,* 107–113.

Snyder, C. R. (1984). Excuses. *Psychology Today, 18,* 50–55.

Snyder, C. R. (1985). Collaborative companions: The relationship of self-deception and excuse-making. In M. W. Martin (Ed.), *Self-deception and self-understanding* (pp. 35–51). Lawrence, KS: Regents Press of Kansas.

Snyder, C. R. (1989). Reality negotiation: From excuses to hope and beyond. *Journal of Social and Clinical Psychology, 8*, 130–157.

Snyder, C. R., & Higgins, R. L. (1988a). Excuses: Their effective role in the negotiation of reality. *Psychological Bulletin, 104*, 23–35.

Snyder, C. R., & Higgins, R. L. (1988b). From making to being the excuse: An analysis of deception and verbal/nonverbal issues. *Journal of Nonverbal Behavior, 12*, 237–252.

Snyder, C. R., & Higgins, R. L. (1990). Reality negotiation and excuse-making: President Reagan's 4 March 1987 Iran arms scandal speech and other literature. In M. J. Cody & M. L. McLaughlin (Eds.), *Psychology of tactical communication* (pp. 207–228). Clevedon, England: Multilingual Matters.

Snyder, C. R., & Ingram, R. E. (1983). "Company motivates the miserable": The impact of consensus information on help seeking for psychological problems. *Journal of Personality and Social Psychology, 45*, 1118–1126.

Snyder, C. R., & Smith, T. W. (1982). Symptoms as self-handicapping strategies: The virtues of old wine in a new bottle. In G. Weary & H. L. Mirels (Eds.), *Integrations of clinical and social psychology* (pp. 104–127). New York: Oxford University Press.

Snyder, M. L., Kleck, R. E., Strenta, A., & Mentzer, S. J. (1979). Avoidance of the handicapped: An attributional ambiguity analysis. *Journal of Personality and Social Psychology, 37*, 2297–2306.

Snyder, C. R., Higgins, R. L., & Stucky, R. J. (1983). *Excuses: Masquerades in search of grace.* New York: Wiley Interscience.

Snyder, C. R., Smith, T. W., Augelli, R. W., & Ingram, R. E. (1985). On the self-serving function of social anxiety: Shyness as a self-handicapping strategy. *Journal of Personality and Social Psychology, 48*, 970–980.

Sobell, L. C., & Sobell, M. B. (1975). Drunkenness, a "special circumstance" in crimes of violence: Sometimes. *International Journal of Addictions, 10*, 869–882.

Springston, F. J., & Chafe, P. M. (1987, June). *Impressions of fictional protagonists exhibiting self-handicapping behaviors.* Paper presented at the meeting of the Canadian Psychological Association Convention, Vancouver, B.C.

Stolorow, R. D. (1975). Toward a functional definition of narcissism. *International Journal of Psycho-Analysis, 56*, 179–185.

Stolorow, R. D. (1976). Psychoanalytic reflections on client-centered therapy in light of modern conceptions of narcissism. *Psychotherapy: Theory, Research and Practice, 13*, 26–29.

Strack, S., & Coyne, J. C. (1983). Social confirmation of dysphoria: Shared and private reactions to depression. *Journal of Personality and Social Psychology, 44*, 798–806.

Szasz, T. S. (1963). *Law, liberty, and psychiatry.* New York: Macmillan.

Taylor, S. E., & Brown, J. D. (1988). Illusion and well-being: A social psychological perspective on mental health. *Psychological Bulletin, 103*, 193–210.

Tedeschi, J. T., Riordan, C. A., Gaes, G. G., & Kane, T. (1984). *Verbal accounts and attributions of social motives.* Unpublished manuscript, State University of New York, Albany, and University of Missouri, Rolla.

Tennen, H., & Affleck, G. (in press). Paradox-based treatments. In C. R. Snyder & D. R. Forsyth (Eds.), *Handbook of social and clinical psychology: The health perspective.* Pergamon.

Tesser, A., & Rosen, S. (1975). The reluctance to transmit bad news. In L. Berkowitz (Ed.), *Advances in experimental social psychology* (Vol. 8, pp. 193–232). New York: Academic Press.

Tetlock, P. E. (1981). The influence of self-presentation goals in attributional reports. *Social Psychological Quarterly, 44*, 300–311.

Tetlock, P. E., & Manstead, A. S. R. (1985). Impression management versus intrapsychic explanations in social psychology: A useful dichotomy? *Psychological Review, 92*, 59–77.

Tucker, J. A., Vuchinich, R. E., & Sobell, M. (1981). Alcohol consumption as a self-handicapping strategy. *Journal of Abnormal Psychology, 90*, 220–230.

Vaillant, G. E., & Perry, J. C. (1985). Personality disorders. In H. I. Kaplan & B. J. Sadock (Eds.), *Comprehensive textbook of psychiatry* (4th ed., pp. 958–986). Baltimore: Williams & Wilkins.

Wahlroos, S. (1981). *Excuses: How to spot them, deal with them, and stop using them.* New York: Macmillan.

Weeks, G. R., & L'Abate, L. (1982). *Paradoxical psychotherapy: Theory and practice with individuals, couples, and families.* New York: Brunner/Mazel.

Weidner, G. (1980). Self-handicapping following learned helplessness treatment and the Type A coronary-prone behavior pattern. *Journal of Psychosomatic Research, 24*, 319–325.

Weiner, B., Amirkhan, J., Folkes, V. S., & Verette, J. A. (1987). An attributional analysis of excuse-giving: Studies of a naive theory of emotion. *Journal of Personality and Social Psychology, 52*, 316–324.

Wicklund, R. A. (1975). Objective self-awareness. In L. Berkowitz (Ed.), *Advances in experimental social psychology* (Vol. 8, pp. 233–275). New York: Academic Press.

Wright, B. A. (1983). *Physical disability—A psychosocial approach* (2nd ed.). New York: Harper & Row.

Chapter 7

SELF-HANDICAPPING FROM A HEIDERIAN PERSPECTIVE
TAKING STOCK OF "BONDS"

Raymond L. Higgins and C. R. Snyder

INTRODUCTION

To begin this book, Higgins outlined a historical perspective that emphasized the manner in which previous Adlerian views of safeguarding
behavior have contributed to contemporary thinking about self-handicapping. In closing, we return to this historical theme by calling upon
another older vantage point to enhance our understanding of self-handicapping. This time, however, we refer not to the thoughts of Alfred
Adler, but to the insights of Fritz Heider.

Throughout this volume, we have portrayed self-handicapping as a
form of "reality negotiation" in which the individual attempts to manipulate the parameters of causal inference in order to preserve his or her
positive self-theories and sense of control in the face of potential adversity. Although we have not made this point previously, it should be
noted that this is a distinctly Heiderian conception, combining elements
of both maintaining cognitive consistency (i.e., preserving self-theories)
and need-driven subjectivity of perception (e.g., see discussion of moti-

Raymond L. Higgins and C. R. Snyder • Department of Psychology, University of Kansas, Lawrence, Kansas 66045.

vated self-deception in Chapter 6). Also, where we have discussed the self-handicapper's efforts to negotiate self-serving versions of reality with his or her audiences, it is easy to recast those dynamics into Heider's (1958) balance theory. Before illustrating this, however, we shall provide a summary of some of the more basic balance theory concepts. In subsequent sections of this chapter, we will discuss the implications of our balance theory analyses of self-handicapping for a taxonomy of handicapping behaviors, and for our understanding of the manner in which handicaps are involved in the negotiation of reality. Finally, we will examine what our analyses reveal about the importance to the self-handicapper of maintaining "pockets" of negative self-theory, and about the seductive appeal of dispositional self-handicaps.

BALANCE THEORY: A REVIEW

THE NATURE OF RELATIONS

Balance theory (Heider, 1958, pp. 174–217) is predicated on the notion that there are two fundamental types of relations (unit relations and sentiment relations) between potentially distinguishable or separate entities. *Unit relations* denote "belongingness" in the sense that they refer to things that are perceived as being connected or as going together—as forming a unit. Perceptions of belongingness may be based on such things as similarity, spatial and temporal proximity, causality, and ownership. For example, if a person p sees another person o engage in an act x, p is likely to perceive o and x as forming a causally based unit (i.e., o—U—x, where U designates a *unit* relation). Conversely, if p regards o as having no involvement with x, o and x will not be perceived as forming a unit relation (i.e., o—$notU$—x, where $notU$ designates a *nonunit* relation).

Whereas unit relations refer to the connectedness between entities, *sentiment relations* refer to the subjective valuations placed on those entities. At the most basic level, there are two types of sentiment relations: positive and negative. Positive sentiment relations are conveyed by such words as liking, admiring, and approving; while negative sentiment relations are conveyed by such words as disliking, rejecting, and disapproving. Recalling our above example, if p perceives that o approves of his or her act x, this positive sentiment relation would be designated as o—L—x, where L indicates the positive relation. However, if p perceives that o disapproves of x, this would be designated as o—DL—x, where DL signifies the negative sentiment relation.

By way of summarizing, we have adopted the following conventional notations from Heider (1958; see also Wright, 1989):

p	The person whose perceptions are being considered
o	The other person or entity being perceived by *p*
x	A third entity (e.g., an object, act, person)
U	Unit relation—designates things that "belong" together
notU	Nonunit relation—designates things that don't "belong" together
L	Positive sentiment relation (e.g., approval, liking)
DL	Negative sentiment relation (e.g., rejection, disliking)

The Concept of Balance

Heider (1958) defined a balanced state as "one in which the entities comprising the situation and the feelings about them fit together without stress" (p. 180). Moreover, a general assumption underlying balance theory is that "the relationship between sentiments and unit formation tends toward a balanced state" (Heider, 1958, p. 177). To simplify the task of determining when a balanced state exists, Heider designated *U* and *L* relationships as positive, and *notU* and *DL* relationships as negative (although he acknowledged some ambiguity in the *notU* case).

In effect, Heider argued that sentiment relations of a certain value (i.e., positive or negative) will *tend* to be paralleled by unit relations of a similar value (i.e., *U* or *notU*). For example, if *p* likes something she has done (*p—L—x*), she will *tend* to "own" or "claim" the act (*p—U—x*) as well. By the same token, if *p* sees herself as the author of an act (*p—U—x*), she will also *tend* to approve of it (*p—L—x*). When the situation is "balanced" in this fashion, *p* will feel no need to change either her cognitive organization (unit formation) or feelings (sentiment relations) regarding her behavior.

Suppose, however, that *p* perceives she has done something (*p—U—x*) that she doesn't approve of (*p—DL—x*). In this "unbalanced" situation, *p* will feel tension and disharmony, and will experience pressure to move toward a balanced state by either disowning the behavior (i.e., *p—U—x* becomes *p—notU—x*) or changing her sentiment toward it (i.e., *p—DL—x* becomes *p—L—x*).

Balance in Triads

The preceding discussion of dyadic relationships helps more clearly to explicate the concepts we have introduced. Balance theory, however, is also concerned with triadic relationships among *p* (the perceiving individual), *o* (a second person who is perceived by *p*), and *x* (a third entity: person, object, or event, as perceived by *p*). In contrast to his treatment of balance in dyads, where both sentiment and unit relations are operational, Heider's discussion of balance in triads focused on the involvement of *either* sentiment relations *or* unit relations between any two elements of the triad, but *not both*. According to Heider, then, triads are balanced when all three of the relations in the triad are positive (either *L* or *U*), or when one of the relations is positive and the other two are negative (either *DL* or *notU*). Any other combination of positive and negative relations renders an unbalanced triad.

For the purposes of our present extrapolation of balance theory to self-handicapping, we have taken the liberty of extending Heider's principles of balance in dyads to cases involving triads. Accordingly, throughout the remainder of this chapter, we will depict the relations between the elements of triads (i.e., *p* and *o*, *p* and *x*, *o* and *x*) as consisting of *both* unit and sentiment relations. In this extension of Heider's system, triads will be considered balanced *only* when the unit and sentiment relations between elements in the triad are matched in value (i.e., *L* and *U*, or *DL* and *notU*) *and* when all three of the sets of relations in the triad are positive (Figure 1, panel a), *or* when one of the sets of relations is positive and the other two sets are negative (Figure 1, panels b, c, and d).

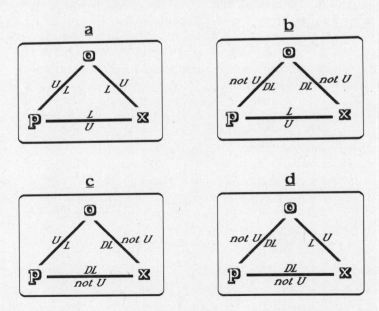

FIGURE 1. Balanced states. *U* and *notU* are positive (*U*) and negative (*notU*) unit relations; *L* and *DL* are positive (*L*) and negative (*DL*) sentiment relations.

Following a logic similar to Heider's we will regard triads as unbalanced when all three sets of relations are negative (Figure 2, panel a), or when two of the sets of relations are positive and only one set is negative (Figure 2, panels b, c, and d). Moreover, recalling our previous discussion of balance in dyadic relationships, we shall also consider that an unbalanced triad results from an imbalance in the sentiment and unit relations between any two of the components of the triad (i.e., between p and o, p and x, or o and x). In Figure 2, panel e, for example, we see an unbalanced dyad involving p and x (i.e., U and DL have different values) which, in turn, creates an unbalanced triad. In this situation, the most economical way for p to balance *both* the dyad and the triad would be for her to change her sentiment relation to x (i.e., p—DL—x should tend to become p—L—x).

In Figure 2, panel f, we see yet another example of a triad that is unbalanced due to an unbalanced dyadic relation. In this case, however,

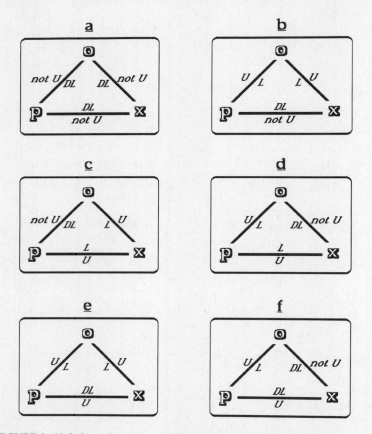

FIGURE 2. Unbalanced states. See Figure 1 for explanation of abbreviations.

the most efficient way for p to balance *both* the dyad and the triad would be for her to alter her unit relation to x (i.e., $p—U—x$ should tend to become $p—notU—x$). To illustrate, suppose that p perceives her good friend, o ($p—L/U—o$), as disliking the policies of and denying any affiliation with a political party, x ($o—DL/notU—x$). Interestingly, p also dislikes the party's policies but is a registered voter with the party ($p—DL/U—x$). Balance theory predicts that p should incline toward changing her voter registration because this would balance both the dyadic and triadic relationships.

BALANCING VIA DIFFERENTIATION ("SPLITTING")

There is one final topic we would like to address before ending this "tutorial" on balance theory. As we shall see later, the process of balancing relationships through "differentiation" (hereafter referred to as "splitting"—see Chapter 6) has special significance for our extrapolation of balance theory to self-handicapping.

Imagine the following situation: p dearly loves his father, o, and admires (L) and identifies with (U) the pleasures o appears to take in

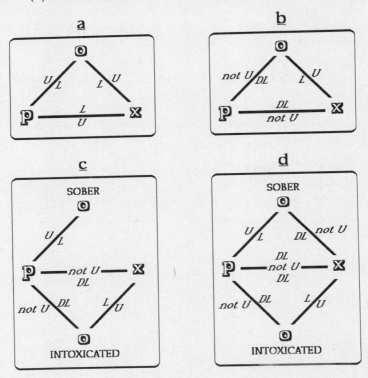

FIGURE 3. Splitting. See Figure 1 for explanation of abbreviations.

treating other people in a respectful manner, x. This balanced situation is depicted in Figure 3, panel a. Now imagine that p is horrified (DL) and feels alienated from ($notU$) o after learning that o seems to relish being abusive after he has been drinking. This new information prompts p to entertain changing his perceptions of o (i.e., p—L/U—o could become p—$DL/notU$—o) and of o's treatment of others (i.e., p—L/U—x could become p—$DL/notU$—x). This potential outcome (see Figure 3, panel b), although balanced, nevertheless clashes with p's admiration for o and for o's behavior when sober. Also, p's relationship to o is based on a very potent unit-forming factor (parenthood) and would be difficult to break cleanly.

Fortunately, balance theory affords p a rather creative solution to his personal clash: p can adopt a more differentiated view of o. In other words, p can "split" o into his sober (good) and intoxicated (bad) parts. Through such "sleight of mind," p can retain his positive (L) identification (U) with the sober part of o while simultaneously condemning (DL) and rejecting ($notU$) the intoxicated part of o with its abusive behavior (see Figure 3, panel c). Although both the resulting dyadic (p—$sober\ o$) and triadic (p—$intoxicated\ o$—x) relationships are balanced, there is, nevertheless, residual imbalance and dysharmony in this solution: p must now reconcile himself with the fact that he perceives o as consisting of both positive and negative parts.

Before leaving this topic, we would like to present a slight embellishment on Heider's treatment of the splitting (differentiating) process. It is nothing more than a logical extension of Heider's presentation of splitting (as depicted in Figure 3, panel c) to embed p's relation to $sober\ o$ within the triadic relationship among p, $sober\ o$, and x (see Figure 3, panel d). The $sober\ o$—$DL/notU$—x relation, for instance, derives from the logic that p should perceive $sober\ o$ as disapproving of and disowning $intoxicated\ o$'s abusive behavior. Similarly, the p—$DL/notU$—x relation depicted in the upper half of Figure 3, panel d simply mirrors p's previously established disaffection with $intoxicated\ o$'s abusive behavior. In all later discussions of splitting, we will adopt the convention of using this modified model.

EXTRAPOLATING BALANCE THEORY TO SELF-HANDICAPPING

REQUIRED ASSUMPTIONS

In order to discuss self-handicapping within a balance theory framework, we ask that the reader grant two assumptions in addition to the basic premises of balance theory presented above.

Assumption 1: The perceiving individual, *p*, is able to adopt both present and future time perspectives.

One of the fundamental features of self-handicapping is its pre-emptive, proactive nature: The individual takes self-protective action in *anticipation* of a *potential* negative outcome. This temporal framework clearly requires a potential self-handicapper who is motivated and able to contemplate future possibilities.

Assumption 2: p is able to adopt a "detached" perspective in the sense of being able to contemplate particular aspects of his or her *self* as if from the point of view of an observer.

Throughout this volume we have expressed our view that self-handicapping is a form of reality negotiation aimed at protecting cherished self-theories and a sense of control. For this view of self-handicapping to be viable, therefore, *p* must have the capacity to appraise the implications of various outcomes for the relevant aspects of his or her self-theory (assumption 2) from within both present-oriented and future-oriented perspectives (assumption 1).

Before leaving this topic, we should note that similar assumptions have been previously articulated by other authors. In Chapter 1 of this volume, for example, Higgins discussed Alfred Adler's (1926) belief that the individual's perception of future obstacles and goals provided direction for his or her ongoing behavior. An even more direct parallel can be found in the work of Hazel Markus and her associates (e.g., Cantor, Markus, Niedenthal, & Nurius, 1986; Markus & Nurius, 1986; Markus & Wurf, 1987) on the construct of "possible selves." To illustrate, in 1986, Cantor *et al.* wrote the following:

> In pursuing particular life tasks, people are likely to be guided by distinct representations of themselves in the future. Within the context of life tasks, we are suggesting that it is "possible selves" that give *personalized* meaning to global motives. Possible selves are the component of self-concept that reflect the individual's perceived potential. They include those selves that individuals *could* become, would *like* to become, or are *afraid* of becoming, including the selves that are hoped for—the successful and accomplished professional self, the witty, creative self, or the loved and admired self—and the selves that are dreaded—the blundering pseudointellectual self or the "bag lady" self. (p. 99)

DEFINITIONS

Our balance theory analysis of self-handicapping incorporates a temporal framework that spans the following sequence of events:

Threat appraisal→Self-handicap→Performance→Review

We shall present balance (i.e., p—o—x) analyses for both the appraisal and review phases of this temporal sequence. However, it is important to note that, because of the changing temporal perspective required of p across the sequence, small but important modifications in the definitions of p, o, and x are required when moving from the appraisal to the review phase. The definitions we will use are indicated in Figure 4.

BALANCING IN THE ABSENCE OF AN EXTERNAL AUDIENCE

As indicated in Chapter 1, early presentations of self-handicapping theory (i.e., Berglas & Jones, 1978; Jones & Berglas, 1978; Snyder & Smith, 1982) emphasized that self-handicapping was motivated primarily by private- rather than social-esteem concerns. Subsequent research, however, has shown that, when external audiences are effectively eliminated from performance arenas, self-handicapping typically does not occur (e.g., Kolditz & Arkin, 1982; Slaughter, Shaver, & Arkin, 1988; Tice & Baumeister, 1984; see Chapter 2 for more extended discussion of this issue).

Snyder, Higgins, and Stucky (1983, pp. 34–38) have argued that the course of individual development may inevitably produce a fusion of public- and self-esteem concerns to the point where they are no longer completely separable. It is possible, however, to create conditions that either enhance or decrease the individual's *awareness* of external audience concerns. Kolditz and Arkin (1982), for example, decreased the

THREAT APPRAISAL PHASE

p = Potential Self-Handicapper

o = p's Imagined Future Self-Theory

x = p's Anticipated Negative Performance

REVIEW PHASE

p = Self-Handicapper

o = p's Current Self-Theory

x = p's Performance Outcome

FIGURE 4. p—o—x definitions. See Figure 1 for explanation of abbreviations.

salience of external audience concerns by purporting to shield both their subjects' handicapping behaviors and subsequent performances from anyone in the subjects' immediate social environment.

The question remains, however, as to why such "private" conditions mitigate self-handicapping. The standard wisdom has followed the lead of Kolditz and Arkin (1982) in holding that self-handicapping is primarily an impression-management strategy. Our analysis of private self-handicapping conditions from within a Heiderian balance theory perspective does not challenge this wisdom. It does, however, yield a somewhat more complex answer to the puzzle.

The key to understanding our analysis of potential self-handicapping situations that are "private" (i.e., low in salience of external audiences) is found in our previous discussion of "splitting." We indicated there that an individual can largely resolve ambivalent reactions toward another person by differentiating that other person into contrasting components (see Figure 3, panels c and d). We shall argue here that the prospective private self-handicapper who is thrown into a state of imbalance by a potential failure may often resolve this imbalance *during the threat-appraisal stage* of the self-handicapping sequence by using a similar form of splitting. In our view, this prehandicapping resolution involves the individual's splitting the *self* into "good" and "bad" components.

Consider the following scenario: p is facing an upcoming evaluation of her typing skills for purposes of applying for an important job advancement. She believes that she has always had difficulty with performing under timed testing conditions and, consequently, has involved herself in a company-sponsored typing-skills program to rectify her problem. Although she has consistently received high praise from her instructor, she does not feel that she has made enough improvement to warrant it. Also, she has noticed that the instructor seems to give everyone high praise—seemingly independent of their actual skill. She is now preparing for the final exercise in her typing-skills program—a timed practice test that is almost identical to the "real thing" that is scheduled for the day following the practice test. The difference is that, for the first test, she will not have to turn in her performance—only she will know how well she did. Even under the informal conditions of the trial run, however, p is very uncertain that she can demonstrate the required level of proficiency.

For our purposes, the central dynamic in p's contemplation of her trial run, can be diagrammed as in Figure 5, panel a (see Figure 4 for threat-appraisal definitions of p, o, and x). As p thinks about how she will feel about herself, o, in the likely event that she does not reach the desired typing proficiency, x, she has the sense of being causally con-

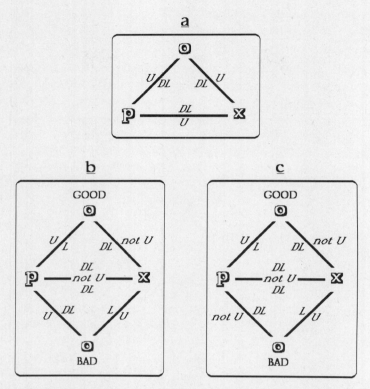

FIGURE 5. Balancing in the absence of salient external audiences. See Figure 1 for explanation of abbreviations.

nected to both o (p—U—o) and x (p—U—x); moreover, she perceives o as being causally connected to x (o—U—x). The reader will notice, however, that each of these three (positive) unit relations is paralleled by negative (i.e., DL) sentiment relations: p doesn't like the notion of failure, the notion of being causally linked to failure, or her perception of how she will feel about herself if/when she fails. Each of the three dyadic relations (and, therefore, the triad) is unbalanced.

In some of our recent writings (e.g., Higgins & Snyder, 1989; Snyder & Higgins, 1988a) we have defined excuse making as including the motivated process of shifting "causal attributions for negative personal outcomes from sources that are relatively more central to the person's sense of self to sources that are relatively less central" (Snyder & Higgins, 1988a, p. 23). The situation we have described above for p affords her the opportunity to solve her balance problem by using a nonhandicapping excuse strategy: p can gain important attributional leverage over her dilemma by splitting her imagined future self, o, into "good" and "bad" components and then shifting her *private* causal attributions for her potential failure from her more encompassing (more central) "good-self" image to a more delimited (less central) "bad-self" image.

Figure 5, panel b portrays such a "splitting" solution for p. In this specific instance, the "bad" component of her now-differentiated future self would probably mirror a self-theory division that had already been formulated within her awareness—that part of her that had difficulty with timed performance tests. Regardless of the specific nature of the split, however, the "good" self-theory has been effectively cut off from any causal connection to the anticipated failure, and the upper (good future self) half of Figure 5, panel b is balanced. The lower (bad future self) half of the figure, however, is unbalanced: The positive unit relation between p and *bad o* (p—U—*bad o*) is paired with a negative sentiment relation (p—DL—*bad o*). In short, this signifies that p "owns" the part of her that has trouble with timed tests, but does not like it.

How might p resolve this remaining imbalance? Changing the sentiment relation would appear to be unlikely because doing so (i.e., p—DL—*bad o* becomes p—L—*bad o*) would be tantamount to "unsplitting" her good and bad selves. In other words, if she were to *like* the part of her that struggles with timed tests, it would remerge with her "good" self and she would lose the attributional leverage she gained from the initial splitting. Also, merely changing her sentiment relation to the *bad o* would leave the lower (*bad o*) half of Figure 5, panel b unbalanced.

More realistically, therefore, the pressure toward balance should be expressed in a changed unit relation—especially if p regards it as possible that timed performance tests will be a continuing feature of her future experience. In this event, p would probably come to increasingly regard the part of her that has difficulty with tests as functioning beyond her voluntary control, thereby negating her sense of *personal* ownership and lending it a "not me" quality (i.e., p—U—*bad o* becomes p—*notU*—*bad o*; see Figure 5, panel c). (We will return to this issue in our later discussion of incorporated self-handicaps.) It should be recognized, however, that, if p does not regard timed performance tests as likely to constitute a continuing threat, she may simply "live with" her imbalance until the impending performance has passed and her awareness of this particular bad aspect of herself recedes as an immediate concern.

Might not p self-handicap *in addition* to splitting? For example, might she make only a half-hearted effort? We regard this as unlikely. There is no additional attributional (or balance) advantage to be gained from doing so. If one again carefully examines Figure 5, panel b, for example, and imagines that p has now self-handicapped, taken her typing test, and failed (refer to Figure 4 for review-phase definitions of p, o, and x), it becomes apparent that the balance diagram should not change as a result of adding the handicap. In other words, both p and *good o* are already in negative sentiment and unit relation to x.

Might not p self-handicap *instead of* splitting? Here we fall back on the empirical evidence that people are apparently very reluctant to self-handicap under private conditions. Logic, however, also comes into play. In p's situation, as we have outlined it, it might well be to her advantage to have accurate (diagnostic) information about her typing skills relative to those required for the job promotion. A behavioral self-handicap could potentially deprive her of the opportunity to gain that information by impairing her performance in what is a relatively benign evaluative context. An avowed (claimed) handicap, on the other hand, is unlikely to secure any advantages beyond what p would gain through the splitting process we have postulated above. In fact, most relevant claimed handicaps (e.g., p's saying to herself, "I have difficulty with timed performance tests" or "I have a *splitting* headache!") would simply replicate that process (see also our discussion below of "internalizing" self-handicaps).

BALANCING IN THE PRESENCE OF AN EXTERNAL AUDIENCE

In our preceding discussion of balancing within private evaluative contexts, we observed that the relative lack of salient external audience concerns in p's awareness afforded her the luxury of using a nonhandicapping form of anticipatory excuse strategy. Suppose, however, that an external audience were salient in p's mind (e.g., suppose that the product of her trial run was to be scored by her typing instructor). To the extent that the audience's opinion of her mattered, p could ill-afford to presume that a split between "good" and "bad" components of her self would be apparent to that audience without her somehow articulating or announcing the split. Her control- and image-maintenance motives should tend to "drive" her concerns in the direction of protecting her internalized vision of the audience's *undifferentiated* view of her as a "good and in-control" person.

Although it is certainly possible that p would proceed through her typing test without self-handicapping and then engage in some form of retrospective excuse making should her performance prove to be unsatisfactory, our interest here is in self-handicapping (see Snyder & Higgins, 1988a; Snyder *et al.*, 1983, for examples and discussion of the effects of retrospective excuses). In the next four sections, we will successively present balance analyses of the four major categories of self-handicaps that p might employ: externalizing/acquired handicaps, externalizing/claimed handicaps, internalizing/acquired handicaps, and internalizing/claimed handicaps. For reasons that will become apparent later (see our subsequent section entitled "Toward a Taxonomy of Self-Handicapping Behavior"), we have organized our balance analyses around the fourfold classification scheme for self-handicapping behaviors described by Arkin and Baumgardner (1985a).

Externalizing/Acquired Self-Handicaps

In our present context, externalizing handicaps are those which shift the causal attributional focus for failure to sources that lie *outside* of the self-handicapper; acquired handicaps are those that involve the active acquisition of actual or likely *impediments* to performance. Imagine, for example, that our typist-trainee has now completed her training course and has reported to the appointed room to take her typing test along with so many other testees that the administrator has to bring an extra typewriter out of storage. As he brings it out, he announces that whoever uses this particular typewriter will be at a disadvantage because it is a manual model that is slower than electric models. If p dawdles long enough that all of the other typewriters have been taken (or volunteers to use it before any other potential self-handicappers can do so), she will have acquired an externalizing handicap. Then, if she fails under such circumstances, she and everyone else in the room will know that it might not have been *her* fault. Our balance analysis of this self-handicapping context begins at the point that p reports to the testing room.

p's contemplation of her potential failure (i.e., during the threat-appraisal stage of the self-handicapping sequence) can be diagrammed as in Figure 5, panel a. In other words, as p imagines her possible failure, x, she perceives both her current, p, and future, o, selves as being causally linked to it, but does not like any of it (i.e., has negative sentiment relations all around). We regard this as the basic self-handicapping frame of mind from a balance perspective, and will dispense with discussing it further in this or subsequent examples of the various forms of self-handicapping.

For our present purposes, the consequences of p's acquisition of her externalizing handicap (i.e., the slow manual typewriter) are of primary interest. To this end, Figure 6 presents our vision of p's balance states following both a successful (panel a) and unsuccessful (panel b) typing performance during the review phase of the self-handicapping sequence (see Figure 4 for review-phase definitions of p, o, and x).

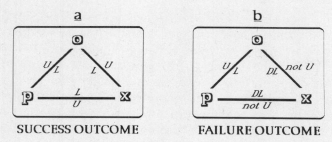

FIGURE 6. Balancing via externalizing handicaps. See Figure 1 for explanation of abbreviations.

Presuming that p's typing performance is successful (see Figure 6, panel a) results in a rather uncomplicated and balanced state: p perceives positive unit (causal) relations with both her current self-theory, o, and her typing performance, x, and also regards the unit relation between o and x as positive. Moreover, each of these positive unit relations is balanced with positive sentiment relations. We regard this as the prototypical balanced pattern following successful handicapped performances and, in subsequent examples, will provide balance diagrams only for unsuccessful outcomes.*

Turning next to the event in which p fails to achieve the required level of typing proficiency (see Figure 6, panel b), we can see that p's externalizing handicap has served her well—just as self-handicapping theory predicts it should. In this instance, for example, the handicap allows p to discount any causal relation between herself and the negative performance outcome (i.e., p—$DL/notU$—x), as well as any link between her self-theory and the performance (i.e., o—$DL/notU$—x). At the same time, she is able to retain her positive identification with her self-theory (i.e., to preserve her self-esteem and sense of control: p—L/U—o). Clearly, this triad is also balanced.

Externalizing/Claimed Handicaps

In the preceding illustration we discussed a handicapping context that afforded our hypothetical protagonist an opportunity to take advan-

*Self-handicapping theory, as articulated by both Jones and Berglas (1978; Berglas & Jones, 1978) and Snyder and Smith (1982), included the notion that succeeding despite the presence of an externalizing handicap might result in self-esteem *enhancement* as opposed to simple self-esteem *preservation*. In the present context, such esteem enhancement might be diagrammed as p—LL/U—o. For ease of presentation, and because Heider's balance theory does not provide for degrees of positiveness or negativeness in either unit or sentiment relations, however, we will not pursue the possibility of esteem enhancement in either this or subsequent examples.

tage of an obvious or "self-evident" (see Snyder *et al.*, 1983) impediment to successful performance. In many evaluative situations, however, the threatened individual is provided only with an opportunity to *claim* that an externalizing handicap exists. The junior faculty member who is facing a tenure decision, for example, may fix his attention on the fact that the university's promotion and tenure committee has adopted a new, more comprehensive and time-consuming form for documenting his research, teaching, and service accomplishments. Although the more rigorous reporting form would not necessarily signify that the standards for actually achieving tenure had risen, it would provide the faculty member with a basis for *believing* (claiming), in advance of the outcome, that the standards were indeed higher. In essence, then, the faculty member could nurture the perception that achieving tenure had become particularly difficult—and perhaps unfairly so, especially in relation to some of the older full professors who may have had to do "little more" than submit a curriculum vitae and a few reprints when they were considered for tenure.

A handicapping context analogous to the one depicted above for the junior faculty member can be easily concocted for our worried typist, *p*. Suppose, for instance, that *p* reports for her typing test to find that she is alone in taking the test that day. After introducing himself, the test administrator informs *p* that the test she will be taking is different from one he ordinarily gives—it involves typing different materials with a longer average word length—and he is curious to find out how it compares with the old test. This simple twist of fate provides *p* with everything she needs to construct an externalizing/claimed self-handicap. She might worry aloud, for example, that if the new test involves typing longer words, it is probably more difficult than the "old" one. If she subsequently fails, neither she nor the examiner will know *for sure* that the test was not particularly difficult, and the true cause for her failure will be obscured.

So long as *p* believes her typing test to have been more difficult than the one she would have taken at an earlier date, the balance dynamics for this claimed handicap are identical to those depicted above for an externalizing/acquired handicap (see Figure 6, panel b). Indeed, *from p's perspective*, there would be no functional difference between taking a more difficult test and taking the standard test with a slower typewriter—both would impair her ability to succeed. In this instance, then, *p* easily achieves balance during the review phase of the handicapping sequence by disclaiming any causal linkage between her ability and the performance outcome. As we will illustrate below, however, *p*'s balancing act becomes somewhat more complicated when we turn to a consideration of the consequences of *internalizing* self-handicaps.

Internalizing/Acquired Handicaps

Imagine once again that our would-be typist has reported to the room where her typing test is to be administered. This time, however, the test administrator fails to provide her with a convenient externalizing handicap either to acquire (i.e., a manual typewriter) or to claim (i.e., novel samples to type). There are many possibilities for acquiring internalizing handicaps (i.e., performance impediments that shift the causal attributional focus to sources *within p*) in this situation. For example, *p* could have a four-martini lunch before the test, she could fail to prepare adequately, or she could fail to try to do her best. Our particular typist, however, was feeling a little nervous about the test and "uncharacteristically" took a couple of extra valiums before arriving. Now she believes she is feeling a little woozy and finds an opportunity to tell the test administrator that she fears her coordination will not be as good as it should be. She tells him that she will do her best, but inquires about the next possible date to take the test—just in case she is unable to overcome the effects of the drug.

Assuming that *p* subsequently fails her typing test, the balance implications of her failure can be represented as in Figure 7, panel a. By now, the reader will recognize that this diagram represents a form of "splitting" (see above discussion of balancing in the absence of external audiences), although, in the present instance, the splitting takes place in the review phase of the self-handicapping sequence. In other words, ingesting the valium enables *p* to deal with her failure by differentiating herself into "normal" and "drugged" components.

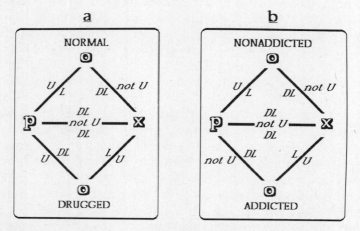

FIGURE 7. Balancing via internalizing handicaps. See Figure 1 for explanation of abbreviations.

In the theater of her own mind, p can retain her positive affiliation with her "normal" (undrugged) self-theory while rejecting any clear causal connection between it and her typing failure. This leaves the upper (normal) half of Figure 7, panel a, in a balanced state, while the lower (drugged) half gets the blame (i.e., *drugged o—L/U—x*). Notice, however, that the drugged half of Figure 7, panel a, is unbalanced: p does not dispute that she is responsible for taking the valium, but she perceives herself as not liking what it did to her (i.e., *p—DL/U—drugged o*). This remaining imbalance or tension, however, is unlikely to cause p much distress. We can readily envision her achieving balance through the simple retrospective excuse strategy of denying having had any intention of taking enough valium to impair her performance (i.e., *p—DL/U—drugged o* becomes *p—DL/notU—drugged o*). As we shall see below, p could have avoided even this minor inconvenience of needing to use a supplementary retrospective excuse strategy had she believed (claimed) she was ill with some incapacitating condition, or had the notion that she was a valium addict been incorporated into her self-theory.

Internalizing/Claimed Handicaps

In contrast to internalizing self-handicaps that are acquired and are, therefore, temporary or situation specific, the notion of claiming an internal handicap often implies that the handicapping condition is a relatively enduring (i.e., dispositional) aspect of the individual. A notable exception to this would be the individual's claim to be suffering from some temporary internal condition such as a cold or the flu. From the vantage point of balance theory, however, the self-handicapping dynamics associated with such illness states and with dispositional aspects of the person are identical—owing to their "involuntary" nature. In our present example, therefore, we will focus on an instance of claiming a dispositional handicap.

In 1982, Snyder and Smith proposed what has been perhaps the most significant, and controversial, revision to date in Jones and Berglas's (1978; Berglas & Jones, 1978) self-handicapping theory. Jones and Berglas had focused almost exclusively on the use of external or temporary (i.e., nondispositional) internal obstacles to performance as self-handicaps. In their analysis of self-handicapping from an Adlerian perspective, however, Snyder and Smith (1982) suggested that *dispositional* barriers to adequate performance may also serve as self-handicaps (see Chapter 1, this volume, for further discussion). Subsequently, Snyder and his associates reported experimental investigations documenting the use of such dispositional handicaps (e.g., DeGree & Snyder, 1985; Smith, Snyder, & Handelsman, 1982; Smith, Snyder, & Perkins, 1983; Snyder, Smith, Augelli, & Ingram, 1985).

Earlier in this chapter (see section on "Balancing in the Absence of External Audiences") we provided a definition of excuse making that focused on the shifting of "causal attributions for negative personal outcomes from sources that are relatively more central to the person's sense of self to sources that are relatively less central" (Snyder & Higgins, 1988a, p. 23). Although incorporated or disposition-based self-handicaps fail to completely sever the individual's causal link to negative outcomes, they may serve well to focus causal attributions on aspects of the self that are relatively peripheral to the individual's core sense of self.

Return for a moment to our preceding example of p's use of valium "intoxication" as an internalizing/acquired self-handicap. This time, however, consider that p has been a longtime abuser of valium and has come to regard herself as an "addict" in the sense that she experiences having lost control over her drug use. Stated otherwise, p has *incorporated* the notion of being an addict into her self-theory. Presume further that p finds occasion to inform the test administrator that she is addicted (or is sick, suffers from test anxiety, etc.).

In this case, the balance implications for p are very similar to those already depicted above for her use of valium as an acquired internalizing handicap (refer again to Figure 7, panel a). There is, however, an important difference: Once p perceives her valium use (illness, test anxiety, etc.) as involuntary and out of her control (see Figure 7, panel b), her splitting solution is balanced for both her "addicted" and "nonaddicted" selves without the need to engage any supplementary excuse strategies. In other words, the unbalanced dyad p—DL/U—*drugged o* (panel a) is transformed "automatically" into a balanced dyad, p—$DL/notU$—*addicted o* (panel b). (See Higgins & Berglas's discussion of incorporated handicaps in Chapter 6.)

In the case of such incorporated or internalizing/claimed self-handicaps, it is likely that the individual has already "initiated" the associated splitting process prior to or, at minimum, during the threat-appraisal phase of the self-handicapping sequence insofar as *internal* audience issues are concerned (see our discussion of balancing in the absence of an external audience and Figure 5 for a related illustration). To the extent that salient external audience concerns are present, however, even the incorporated self-handicapper must somehow manifest his or her handicap if it is to have its desired impression-management effects. For this reason, we have discussed such handicaps *as if* the initiation of the splitting process is temporally located between the threat-appraisal and review phases of the sequence.

The Problem of Deliberate Self-Handicapping

Our next illustration of the application of Heider's balance theory to self-handicapping relates to a problem which we are confident must happen in the "real world," but which has not yet been examined empirically: The problem of failing to convince oneself and/or others that one's self-handicapping efforts are not *intentional* or deliberate. Elsewhere, we have stated our belief that an integral part of successful reality negotiation through excuse making involves the self-handicapper's (excuse maker's) deceiving the self and any external audience re-

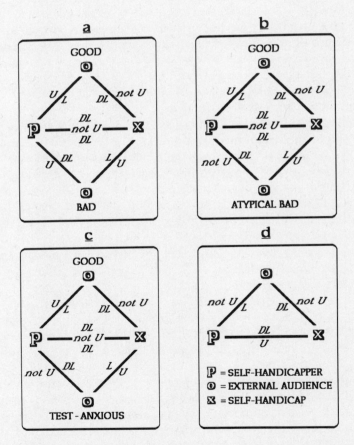

FIGURE 8. Nondeceptive self-handicapping. See Figure 1 for explanation of abbreviations.

garding the possibility that the excuse-making efforts may have been intentionally enacted (see Higgins & Snyder, 1989, in press; Snyder & Higgins, 1988a,b; Snyder *et al.*, 1983; see also Chapter 6, this volume). It is important to ask, then, how the balance theory framework might deal with failure in self- and/or other-deception. For ease of presentation, and because we believe that externalizing handicaps are most subject to detection by external audiences (e.g., Snyder & Higgins, 1988b), we will limit our discussion of nondeceptive self-handicapping to an instance of embracing an externalizing self-handicap.

In our preceding example of an externalizing/acquired self-handicap for our would-be typist, p, we had her managing to get assigned to a manual typewriter that was slower than the electric models being used by the other people being tested. In that example, we presumed that p had no particular difficulty in securing the manual model. Suppose, however, that another examinee had also volunteered to use the manual model and p had "tipped her hand" by being so insistent that *she* be assigned to the typewriter that the examiner had to decide by flipping a coin. Imagine further that, after he had scored p's typing test and told her that she had failed, the examiner commented that he suspected that p had wanted the manual typewriter so badly because it would give her an excuse for doing so poorly. This piece of feedback, combined with her own aggressiveness in getting the typewriter, brings p's self-handicapping motive securely into her conscious awareness.

From a balance perspective, the transparency of p's handicapping motive severely complicates her efforts to negotiate an esteem- and control-saving reality. Now, she not only has to reconcile herself to the performance failure, but she also must gain a face-saving perspective on the handicapping act itself. In other words, to the extent that p and her examiner perceive that p has deliberately self-handicapped, both the handicapping act and the performance failure become distinct objects for p's scrutiny. We turn first to p's performance failure.

Dealing with the Performance Failure

So long as p fails to perceive that her selection of the manual typewriter was motivated by a desire to obfuscate the meaning of potential failure (i.e., she successfully self-deceives), the balance implications of actual failure during the review phase of the self-handicapping sequence are as diagrammed in Figure 6, panel b: p is able to effectively dissociate (*notU*) herself from the failure. Once p recognizes her self-handicapping as motivated, however, we believe that the most probable "balancing act" for p is for her to split off her more enduring "good self-theory" from a more time-delimited and circumscribed "bad self-theory" (see Figure 8, panel a). In effect, this allows p to deny any causal connection between her good self-theory and the negative performance while pointing the finger of blame at the negative or "bad" part.

By now, the reader will no doubt recognize that the lower (bad self) half of Figure 8, panel a, is unbalanced—due to the conflicting unit and sentiment relations between p and *bad o* (i.e., p—DL/U—*bad o*). This recognizes that, although p perceives herself as disliking her "bad" (deliberately self-handicapping) self, she acknowledges her causal linkage to it. To the extent that p regards such testing and self-handicapping experiences as unusual or infrequent in her life, the resulting pressure toward balance will probably be consummated through some retrospective, consistency-lowering excuse strategy (cf. Kelley, 1967) designed to disown the *bad o* part of her. For example, p might come to regard her deliberate self-handicapping as an aberration—as being atypical of her (i.e., p—DL/U—*bad o* becomes p—$DL/notU$—*atypical bad o*; see Figure 8, panel b). If, however, p recognizes that similar self-handicapping has characterized her behavior in the past, or that similar testing experiences are likely to be a continuing feature of her future, she may well move toward disowning her *bad o* by *incorporating* a new element into her self-identify. Specifically, p may come to regard herself as *suffering from* test anxiety. In this instance, p would regard the "test-anxious" part of her as operating beyond her voluntary control—again allowing her to disavow the unit relationship between her and the negative part of her (i.e., p—DL/U—*bad o* becomes p—$DL/notU$—*test-anxious o*; see Figure 8, panel c).

Dealing with the Self-Handicapping Act

In introducing our discussion of deliberate self-handicapping, we noted that failures in self- and other-deception may leave the self-handicapper in the relatively complicated situation of needing to achieve balance not only vis à vis the event of an unsuccessful performance, but also vis à vis the self-handicapping *act*. In the present section, we take up this latter issue.

When we empathically put ourselves in p's shoes and imagine the balance consequences of being told by an important evaluator that he believes that we have deliberately self-handicapped, the resulting state can be represented as in Figure 8, panel d. (Note that the definitions for p, o, and x have now changed: p is the self-handicapper; o, the external audience (evaluator); and x, the self-handicapping act.) From p's per-spective, she (1) wishes to have a positive relation with the test admin-istrator but feels alienated from him (i.e., p—$L/notU$—o); (2) regards the test administrator as rejecting her self-handicapping behavior (i.e., o—$DL/notU$—x); and (3) recognizes that she self-handicapped, but does not like perceiving her behavior in this manner (i.e., p—DL/U—x). This triad is unbalanced due to the asymmetrical unit and sentiment relations between p and o and between p and x.

In this situation, one effective way for p to achieve a balanced state would be for her to find a way to repudiate her unit relation to x (i.e., p—DL/U—x would become p—$DL/notU$—x). Because it is p's unit rela-tion to x that forms the basis for her perception of being alienated from o, breaking that unit relation should also enable her to affirm a sense of being positively connected to o (i.e., p—$L/notU$—o would become p—L/U—o). In our judgment, p can accomplish both of these goals by enacting one of the splitting processes described above for restoring her balance vis à vis the performance failure (i.e., see Figure 8, panels b and c). Stated differently, if p perceives that the test administrator has accept-ed (does not dispute) her claim that her self-handicapping behavior was very uncharacteristic of her (Figure 8, panel b), or her claim that she suffers from test anxiety (Figure 8, panel c), her unit relation with the handicapping act will be broken, and her desire to identify with the test administrator can be fulfilled. In the end, then, p's solutions for the "separate" problems of her negative performance outcome and her de-liberate self-handicapping are one and the same.

SUMMARY

We have now completed our rather lengthy series of examples il-lustrating our vision of how Heider's (1958) balance theory may be ap-plied to various classes of self-handicapping. Given that the roots of Jones and Berglas's (1978) self-handicapping theory can be traced back directly to Heider's innovative thinking about the problems of interper-sonal perception and the processes involved in formulating causal expla-nations for behavior (see Chapter 1), perhaps it is not surprising that self-handicapping behaviors can be recast within a balance theory framework. Although our extrapolations in this regard have been pri-marily "descriptive" to this point, they do appear to have a number of notable implications. In the remaining sections of this chapter, we will turn to a selective review of a few of those implications.

TOWARD A PERSPECTIVISTIC TAXONOMY
OF SELF-HANDICAPPING BEHAVIOR

Arkin and Baumgardner (1985a) presented a two-dimensional tax-onomic matrix of self-handicapping behavior that still represents a com-prehensive framework for conceptualizing the types of self-handicapping behavior that have been discussed in the literature to date. In effect, their taxonomy provided a synthesis of the contrasting views of self-handicapping that had been articulated by Jones and Berglas (1978; Berglas & Jones, 1978) and by Snyder and Smith (1982).

For example, whereas Jones and Berglas had spotlighted the *use of* performance impediments as handicaps, Snyder and Smith had stressed the ability-discounting function of *avowing* that performance impedi-ments existed (see Chapter 1, this volume, for further discussion). Arkin and Baumgardner labeled these contrasting types of handicapping as *acquired* and *claimed*, respectively, to form the "action" dimension of their taxonomy (see also Leary & Shepperd's, 1986, discussion of behav-ioral vs. self-reported self-handicaps). The second, "locus" dimension of Arkin and Baumgardner's taxonomic matrix was conceptually linked to a distinction that was explicitly recognized by both Jones and Berglas (1978) and Snyder and Smith (1982): *external* handicaps focus causal attributions on factors that lie outside of the person, while *internal* hand-icaps implicate nonability aspects of the person himself or herself. Crossing these "action" and "locus" dimensions results in a fourfold classification scheme. In other words, any self-handicap can be classified as either external/acquired, external/claimed, internal/acquired, or inter-nal/claimed. The reader will recall that this taxonomy formed the basis for our selection of self-handicapping behaviors to analyze within a balance framework.

Arkin and Baumgardner's (1985a) classification matrix furnishes us with an extremely useful heuristic for thinking about the nature and variety of self-handicapping behaviors *from the perspective of an external observer*. Once one adopts the (internal) perspective of the self-handicap-per (as we have attempted to do in our balance analyses), however, an interesting thing happens. Specifically, *from the phenomenological perspec-tive of the self-handicapper*, the distinction between acquired and claimed externalizing self-handicaps vanishes (see our above discussions of the balance dynamics associated with these types of handicaps). Our Heiderian balance logic, then, results in only a threefold taxonomy of self-handicapping behaviors: externalizing, internalizing/acquired, and internalizing/claimed.

That there is no functional difference between successful acquired

and claimed externalizing handicaps from the point of view of the excuse-making individual is not surprising once one considers that the
viability of both types depends exclusively upon the individual's belief
that an external handicapping condition exists. Of course, the need for
the individual to claim that a handicapping condition is present may
increase the probability that the handicap will be disputed by a knowledgeable external audience. Even the act of acquiring an externalizing handicap, however, is not without risks. Indeed, in our judgment,
it is in the case of failed externalizing self-handicaps that balance
differences between the claimed and acquired varieties are likely to
emerge.

In our foregoing discussion of the problem of deliberate self-handicapping, we used the illustration of our hypothetical typist's managing
to secure a manual typewriter for her use (an externalizing/acquired
handicap) and detailed some of the complications that might arise if she
were to be accused of wanting to use that typewriter for *strategic* purposes (i.e., if self- and other-deception failed). Specifically, we postulated that our typist would be prompted to reconcile herself to both her
performance failure and her purposeful self-handicapping act. Consider
now the contrasting example presented in the section on externaliz-
ing/claimed handicaps. In this instance, the typist was presented with a
new typing test consisting of novel passages with longer words. The
handicapping act involved the typist's claiming that the new test must
be more difficult than the old one. If, after failing her, the examiner
explained that he had learned that the new test yielded the same average scores as the old test, our erstwhile self-handicapper would be bereft
of an esteem- and control-saving excuse for her poor performance, but
would not suffer the additional affront of being caught in the act of
deliberately self-handicapping.

Perhaps more than any other handicapping context, it is the dilemma of being judged by an external audience to have intentionally self-
handicapped that brings the individual's need to maintain a positive
connection to important others (and to his or her positive self-theories)
into sharp focus. In other words, self-handicappers who have been
found out are confronted with needing to *consciously* distance themselves from their handicapping acts in order to restore balance to their
strained relationships with the external audience(s) and their positive
self-images. Theoretically, of course, pressure to achieve or restore balance in our relations is usually present (Heider, 1958), not just when our
excuse-making tactics go awry. Indeed, as we will argue next, this central fact of our existence not only motivates our self-handicapping, but
also shapes the forms that it takes.

THE TIES (BONDS) THAT BIND

Throughout this book we have conceptualized self-handicapping as an anticipatory excuse-making strategy that is designed to preserve desired aspects of our self-theories. Heider's (1958) balance theory has provided us with a graphic method of illustrating the "bonds" or attachments (i.e., unit and sentiment relations) that link us to those self-theories and which, in turn, link us and our self-theories to potential life outcomes. We have, in effect, proposed that people live out their lives with an eye toward the future, being sensitive to and vigilant for potential threats to their favored self-conceptions. In this process, successful self-handicappers must be capable of making reasonably accurate forecasts of how others will see them, given various potential outcomes, while simultaneously integrating these forecasts with their own, more self-centered, outlook on what the future portends.

Although the individual, his or her relevant self-theories and audiences, and the specific acts or outcomes with which the individual is concerned may evolve and change across time, the bonds that link these components are omnipresent. Until or unless people become so detached or alienated from the life process that they are no longer concerned with meeting the challenges that it poses, they can *never* cease investing in those bonds. Indeed, to a large extent the preceding portions of this book have been devoted not only to documenting the fact that people do make the investment, but also to detailing the situational and personal characteristics that determine the nature and extent of their investment. Moreover, we have characterized self-handicapping as a particular form of "reality negotiation" (see especially Chapters 4 and 6), and have devoted the early portions of the present chapter to demonstrating that it is the *bonds* that are negotiated.

Even though the bonds that tie us to our self-theories and outcomes are negotiable, and the various types of self-handicaps represent different methods of effecting the transactions, there does appear to be a point upon which, if there is compromise, the self-handicapping enterprise fails as an image-protecting strategy. This nonnegotiable bond is the handicapper's link to the handicap itself. If the individual is perceived as willfully self-handicapping, for example, the handicap may "successfully" obscure (discount) nonability attributions for the *specific performance*, but may also result in lowered perceptions of *general competence* (Arkin & Baumgardner, 1985b, reported in Baumgardner & Arkin, 1987).

Snyder (1989b) first suggested applying Heider's balance theory to self-handicapping phenomena. However, in contrast to our foregoing illustrations of balance in self-handicapping (although see our above discussion of deliberate self-handicapping for an exception), Snyder focused his attention on the triadic relationship involving the self-handicapper p, the handicapper's self-theory–audience concerns o, and the self-handicap x as opposed to the handicapped performance outcome. Moreover, he reasoned that there is only one way to balance this triad in a manner that is consistent with self-handicapping theory.

Once one accepts the basic premises that self-handicapping is designed to preserve positive self-theories and images of competence through discounting (Kelley, 1971) ability attributions for negative outcomes (Berglas & Jones, 1978; Jones & Berglas, 1978; Snyder & Smith, 1982), the unit and sentiment relations between the self-handicapper and his or her self-theory–audience concerns (i.e., p and o) and between the audiences and the self-handicap (i.e., o and x) are fixed. In other words, the assumption that the handicapping motive is to preserve positive private and public images "forces" the handicapper–audience relation to be a positive one (i.e., p—L/U—o). By the same token, the assumption that handicaps discount attributions to positive aspects of the public or private image compels negative unit and sentiment relations between the handicapping audience and the handicap (i.e., o—$DL/notU$—x). Simple logic, then, dictates that, for the p—o—x triad to be balanced, the handicapper–handicap relation *must* also be negative (i.e., p—$DL/notU$—x).

On the surface, the above conclusion is not especially remarkable. Lurking just below the surface, however, are far-reaching and potentially disturbing consequences. Consider, for example, the unflexing rigidity of the balancing relations (bonds). In a very real sense, self-handicappers prospectively commit themselves to disowning significant aspects of their behavior (in the case of externalizing self-handicaps) or even themselves (in the case of internalizing self-handicaps). Even before the jury is in with regard to a performance outcome, self-handicappers have compromised their "integrity" in the sense of having relinquished perceived control over personal elements (e.g., choices, symptoms) that they view as guiding their destinies. And, as we have observed above, this self-alienation is required in order for the self-handicapping act to accomplish its theoretical goal.

It is one of the central ironies of self-handicapping that handicappers gain perceived control over their self-theories—as well as others' definitions of them—by perceiving themselves as having no control over parts of themselves or their behavior. For occasional self-handicappers who rely on externalizing or transient internalizing handicaps, this process of surrendering *temporary* control over parts of themselves may be an important and adaptive coping strategy and is unlikely to result in adverse consequences. Indeed, Snyder (Chapter 4, this volume) detailed a number of adaptive benefits deriving from such expedient handicapping. One notable characteristic of occasional self-handicappers, however, is that they discriminate among potential handicapping situations and capitalize on those that are advantageous. The situation may be quite different for "chronic" or "incorporated" handicappers. For these individuals, even the choice to self-handicap may have been effectively forfeited due to their having integrated "ego-alien" or out-of-control components into their self-conceptions. For these individuals, the entire self-handicapping–balance process may be out of their control, especially to the extent that pressures to achieve balance in relations operate outside of awareness, or "automatically."

There is one final topic we would like to address before we leave this section on "bonds." Our belief is that there are a number of forces that operate to entice the individual, over time, to shift his or her self-handicapping increasingly in the direction of internalizing strategies. Even more specifically, we regard these influences as working to encourage the incorporation of handicaps. Each of them is related to our above balance theory-based observation that the success of a self-handicap derives from the ability of the handicapping individual to sustain negative unit and sentiment relations to the handicap.

Perhaps the most fundamental attraction to internalizing self-handicaps is their relative inaccessibility to scrutiny and discovery by skeptical external audiences (Arkin & Baumgardner, 1985a; Higgins & Snyder, 1989; Snyder & Higgins, 1988b). To the extent, then, that especially critical audiences are involved in performance arenas, we might expect self-handicappers to invoke more hidden or internal sources of attributional confusion. In addition, just as external audiences may be motivated to debunk excuses, they may also be involved in judging the acceptability of those that they can not invalidate. For example, behaviors such as ingesting alcohol or claiming that one is not going to try hard prior to an evaluation may elicit severe negative judgments when they violate important role (e.g., job) expectations (cf. Ames, 1975; Beckman, 1973; Ross, Bierbrauer, & Polly, 1974). This may especially be true when such behaviors appear to involve elements of intentionality or controllability (cf. Weiner, Amirkhan, Folkes, & Verette, 1987). To the extent that self-handicappers are attuned to the social consequences of their behaviors, therefore, we might expect them to "adjust" their selection of handicapping strategies to be more appropriate to the setting (cf. Tetlock, 1981).

Also influential in our judgment that there is a tendency to shift toward internalizing–incorporated handicaps across time is our oft-stated view that it is important for the self-handicapper to self-deceive regarding the enactment of such excuses (e.g., Higgins & Snyder, 1989, in press; Snyder, 1985; Snyder & Higgins, 1988a,b, see also Higgins & Berglas, Chapter 6, this volume). Although we may have a distinctive capacity for perceiving our behaviors in ways that are consistent with our positively biased self-perceptions (e.g., Snyder, 1989a; Taylor & Brown, 1988), the accumulated weight of repeated excuse episodes may tend to erode the self-handicapping individual's ability to remain unaware of his or her self-protective behaviors. In that incorporated self-handicaps may offer the "ultimate" level of self-deception (Snyder & Higgins, 1988b), they should become increasingly attractive to the individual who is committed to a self-handicapping style of self-protection.

THE DESIRABILITY OF THE "UNWANTED" SELF

Perhaps one of the most remarkable outcomes of our preceding analyses of self-handicapping behaviors is the emergence of "splitting" (differentiation) as an important dynamic in the individual's efforts to achieve balance. Not only did we propose that individuals who use internalizing self-handicaps split themselves into "good" and "bad" components subsequent to unsuccessful performances, but we also suggested that splitting comes into play when people (1) contemplate performing in the absence of salient external audiences and (2) react to self-handicaps that have failed in the sense that they are perceived to have been intentionally enacted. In effect, our analyses reveal that splitting fails to play a balancing role only in situations involving externalizing self-handicaps wherein the individual successfully self-deceives regarding the purposefulness of his or her handicapping. Among other things, this state of affairs signifies that self-handicappers, to the extent that they engage in internalizing self-handicapping, must have a major investment not only in sustaining their positive self-theories, but also in nurturing relatively circumscribed "pockets" of negative self-theory.

We have previously discussed reality negotiation as a process wherein people attempt to preserve their positive self-theories in the face of negative personal outcomes by seeking a biased compromise between what they would ideally like to be the case and what external audiences will accept as "real" (Snyder, 1989a; Snyder & Higgins, 1988a; see also Chapters 4 and 6, this volume). However, given that we are fallible creatures and given that "society" is occasionally going to insist that we accept *some* level of accountability for "bad" performances, it is inevitable over the course of development that we will need to integrate negative components into our self-theories. Our foregoing balance analyses of self-handicapping suggest that we frequently turn such adversity into advantage. In other words, once we have integrated negative facets into our self-conceptions, we are in the advantageous position of being able to thrust them into the foreground as causal sources for our performance disappointments. When life events threaten, the splitting processes we have described above enable us to preserve our favorable self-conceptions by putting our negative self-conceptions in "harm's way."

This view of negative self-theory components as "good, though damnable, 'friends'" (Higgins & Snyder, 1989, p. 124) carries the implicit suggestion that, whereas self-handicappers are motivated to maintain some elements of negative self-theory, they are also motivated to keep these unsavory elements at a considerable distance from their more "core" self-conceptions. There is some independent support for this idea. Ogilvie and Lutz (1984, reported in Ogilvie, 1987), for example, cited a case study in which a woman appeared to actively construct a negative self-identity in order to provide herself with grounds for assessing the status of her actual self. In a somewhat related vein, Markus and her associates (e.g., Cantor *et al.*, 1986; Markus & Nurius, 1986) have argued that people regularly generate cognitive representations of "possible selves" (including possible negative selves) as motivational guides in their pursuit of life goals.

Although the above lines of thought lend support to our belief that people have a paradoxical positive relationship to their negative self-theories, they do not directly address our supplementary inference that such negative selves are of most use when kept at a distance. Perhaps the best evidence for this idea is found in research by Ogilvie (1987). Ogilvie reported empirical evidence that "the implicit standard individuals use to assess their well-being is how close (or how distant) they are from subjectively being like their most negative images of themselves" (p. 383). Stated differently, the greater the distance Ogilvie's subjects perceived between their real selves and their negative selves, the greater was their life satisfaction—a type of internal downward social comparison (e.g., Wills, 1981). Significantly, Ogilvie, also found that the distance his subjects perceived between their real and undesired selves was a better predictor of life satisfaction than was the distance they perceived between their real and desired, or "ideal," selves.

In summary, we take the above lines of evidence as support for our speculation that people desire to create distance between their "good" selves and their undesired selves, but it may not be particularly functional to eliminate the undesired selves altogether. An irony confronting the internalizing (especially incorporated) self-handicapper in all of this is the logic-driven conclusion that, as the handicapper repeatedly invokes a particular negative self as a splitting solution in the face of performance dilemmas, that negative self-theory *necessarily* becomes increasingly proximal to the "real" self. There are at least two reasons for this conclusion.

The first reason relates to the fact that repeatedly focusing causal attributions on a particular negative aspect of the self should result in that element of the self becoming increasingly cognitively reinforced and elaborated. One means of maintaining psychological distance from a self component is to keep that component only vaguely symbolized and elaborated. The second reason for our presumption that repeated appeals to a negative component of the self-theory should result in that component becoming more central derives from the role that the external audience (i.e., society) plays in the reality-negotiation process.

As Snyder pointed out in Chapter 4, society has a major investment in maintaining a sense of order, predictability, and control. Internalizing–dispositional self-handicaps represent a threat to this societal need in the sense that the individual self-handicapper attempts to distort the rules of causal inference by advancing *internal* attributions in order to avoid personal accountability. To be sure, society has a long history of honoring such appeals, but only after extracting a price: The individual typically will be expected to manifest *evidence* of his or her dispositional handicapping condition (see Higgins & Snyder, 1989, for further discussion). In a sense, then, society's role in the reality-negotiation process is to demand that the individual escalate his or her commitment to the handicapping condition, resulting not only in an increasingly elaborated negative self-theory (see above discussion), but also in the affixing of a "mental illness" label with its consequent loss of freedom. Over time, we are suggesting, the use of a particular incorporated self-handicap probably eventuates in the individual's no longer being able to call upon the handicapping condition as a splitting solution—the negative portion of the individual's self-theory ultimately becomes the embodiment of society's view of the individual.

How might the self-handicapper avoid this trap? The most obvious answer to this important query is for the individual to focus his or her self-handicapping attributions on external or, at minimum, temporary internal conditions. To the extent that the individual does engage in disposition-based self-handicapping, however, it is important to do so in moderation. Moreover, those disposition-based handicaps that are most likely to avoid the pitfall of having the handicapping condition come to

encapsulate society's view of the individual are "domain-specific" strategies (see Rhodewalt's discussion of domain–strategy-specific handicaps in Chapter 3). In other words, some disposition-based self-handicaps (e.g., test anxiety, shyness) are inherently limited in the range of
contexts to which they might reasonably apply (i.e., testing and interpersonal relations, respectively). Other dispositional self-handicaps
(e.g., hypochondriasis, alcoholism, sick-role behavior, etc.), however,
may serve a discounting function across a broad spectrum of evaluative
situations. Although the latter type of dispositional self-handicap may
have the initial appeal of being more broadly applicable (and, therefore,
"simpler"), this very quality increases its likelihood of becoming the
type of "Faustian bargain" (Snyder, 1984) we have described above.

CONCLUDING REMARKS

In this final chapter, we have borrowed upon the genius of Fritz
Heider to present a schematic framework for thinking about the intra-
and interpersonal dynamics associated with the rather peculiar form of
safeguarding behavior that has come to be called self-handicapping.
One of the more appealing (to us) aspects of applying balance theory to
the problem of self-handicapping is the graphic manner in which doing
so highlights the central role of relationships and the individual's perceptions of those relationships in motivating, and negotiating conclusions for, particular handicapping sequences. Indeed, these themes
have coursed throughout this book, lending it an underlying structure.

The preceding chapters on the situational, individual differences,
and developmental influences on self-handicapping have focused
largely on factors affecting individuals' perceptions of and sensitivity to
threats to their relationships (with themselves and others) and their
consequent motivations to self-handicap. Conversely, the chapters relating to sequelae and to maintenance and treatment have primarily emphasized the usefulness of handicaps as navigational aids in negotiating
the narrow passage between self-alienation and social rejection. In keeping with this nautical metaphor, one goal of the present chapter has
been graphically to illustrate that, although self-handicaps may help the
individual to chart a successful course, the individual who uses them
unskillfully or excessively may run aground on social stigma.

Despite the potential hazards associated with self-handicaps, our
balance analyses (and Snyder's review of the effects of self-handicapping in Chapter 4) clearly indicate that they can (theoretically), and do
(empirically), assist the individual in maintaining psychological equi-

librium (balance) in the face of threatening outcomes. But, what is the relationship of equilibrium to growth? Heider (1958) certainly recognized the psychological forces pressing toward the achievement of balance, but he also acknowledged that "balanced situations can have a boring obviousness and a finality of superficial self-evidence," and suggested that "there may also be a tendency to leave the comfortable equilibrium, to seek the new and adventurous" (p. 180).

To the extent to which self-handicaps enable people to catch their breath, gather their forces, and consolidate their gains before venturing forth to face the next challenge along life's road, they may actively contribute to our capacity for change and development. Relatedly, and more likely, they may allow hesitant individuals to *at least* expose themselves to the challenges of living, feeling that, if things go against them, the judgment is not final. Perhaps, in this vein, it is appropriate to return to the conundrum that is inherent in the title of this book and to pose a modern riddle of "When is a handicap not a handicap?" Our answer: When it is a *self*-handicap.

Acknowledgments

We obviously owe a debt of gratitude to our friend and colleague, Fritz Heider, for his seminal thinking and influence on our extrapolation of balance theory to the self-handicapping phenomenon. We would also like to express our thanks to another special colleague, Beatrice A. Wright, Fritz's friend and collaborator on the classic *The Psychology of Interpersonal Relations*. Beatrice has more recently raised our awareness of the relevance of balance theory for self-handicapping and provided insightful feedback on the present chapter. This chapter grew out of initial ideas for applying balance theory to self-handicapping presented by C. R. Snyder at the April, 1989, meeting of the Southwestern Psychological Association, Houston, Texas.

REFERENCES

Adler, A. (1926). *The neurotic constitution*. New York: Dodd, Mead.

Ames, R. (1975). Teachers' attributions of responsibility: Some unexpected counterdefensive effects. *Journal of Educational Psychology, 67,* 668–676.

Arkin, R. M., & Baumgardner, A. H. (1985a). Self-handicapping. In J. H. Harvey & G. W. Weary (Eds.), *Attribution: Basic issues and applications* (pp. 169–202). New York: Academic Press.

Arkin, R. M., & Baumgardner, A. H. (1985b). *When self-handicapping fails to serve a purpose: Impressions of the strategic procrastinator*. Unpublished manuscript, University of Missouri, Columbia, and Virginia Polytechnic Institute and State University, Blacksburg.

Reported in Baumgardner, A. H., & Arkin, R. M. (1987). Coping with the prospect of social disapproval: Strategies and sequelae. In C. R. Snyder & C. E. Ford (Eds.), *Coping with negative life events: Clinical and social psychological perspectives* (pp. 323–346). New York: Plenum.

Baumgardner, A. H., & Arkin, R. M. (1987). Coping with the prospect of social disapproval: Strategies and sequelae. In C. R. Snyder & C. E. Ford (Eds.), *Coping with negative life events: Clinical and social psychological perspectives* (pp. 323–346). New York: Plenum.

Beckman, L. (1973). Teachers' and observers' perceptions of causality for a child's performance. *Journal of Educational Psychology, 65,* 198–204.

Berglas, S., & Jones, E. E. (1978). Drug choice as a self-handicapping strategy in response to noncontingent success. *Journal of Personality and Social Psychology, 36,* 405–417.

Cantor, N., Markus, H., Niedenthal, P., & Nurius, P. (1986). On motivation and the self-concept. In R. M. Sorrentino & E. T. Higgins (Eds.), *Motivation and cognition: Foundations of social behavior* (pp. 96–127). New York: Guilford Press.

DeGree, C. E., & Snyder, C. R. (1985). Adler's psychology (of use) today: Personal history of traumatic life events as a self-handicapping strategy. *Journal of Personality and Social Psychology, 48,* 1512–1519.

Heider, F. (1958). *The psychology of interpersonal relations.* New York: John Wiley & Sons.

Higgins, R. L., & Snyder, C. R. (1989). Excuses gone awry: An analysis of self-defeating excuses. In R. C. Curtis (Ed.), *Self-defeating behaviors: Experimental research, clinical impressions, and practical implications* (pp. 99–130). New York: Plenum.

Higgins, R. L., & Snyder, C. R. (1990). The business of excuses. In R. A. Giacalone & P. Rosenfeld (Eds.), *Impression management in the organization* (pp. 73–85). Hillsdale, NJ: Erlbaum.

Higgins, R. L., & Snyder, C. R. (in press). Reality negotiation and excuse making: The health connection. In C. R. Snyder & D. R. Forsyth (Eds.), *Handbook of social and clinical psychology: The health perspective.* New York: Pergamon.

Jones, E. E., & Berglas, S. (1978). Control of attributions about the self through self-handicapping strategies: The appeal of alcohol and the role of underachievement. *Personality and Social Psychology Bulletin, 4,* 200–206.

Kelley, H. H. (1967). Attribution theory in social psychology. In D. Levine (Ed.), *Nebraska symposium on motivation, 1967* (pp. 192–238). Lincoln: University of Nebraska Press.

Kelley, H. H. (1971). *Attribution in social interaction.* New York: General Learning Press.

Kolditz, T. A., & Arkin, R. M. (1982). An impression management interpretation of the self-handicapping strategy. *Journal of Personality and Social Psychology, 43,* 492–502.

Leary, M. R., & Shepperd, J. A. (1986). Behavioral self-handicapping vs. self-reported handicaps: A conceptual note. *Journal of Personality and Social Psychology, 51,* 1265–1268.

Markus, H., & Nurius, P. (1986). Possible selves. *American Psychologist, 41,* 954–969.

Markus, H., & Wurf, E. (1987). The dynamic self-concept: A social psychological perspective. *Annual Review of Psychology, 38,* 299–337.

Ogilvie, D. M. (1987). The undesired self: A neglected variable in personality research. *Journal of Personality and Social Psychology, 52,* 379–385.

Ogilvie, D. M., & Lutz, M. (1984). *The representation of multiple identities.* Unpublished manuscript. Cited in Ogilvie, D. M. (1987). The undesired self: A neglected variable in personality research. *Journal of Personality and Social Psychology, 52,* 379–385.

Ross, L., Bierbrauer, G., & Polly, S. (1974). Attribution of educational outcomes by professional and non-professional instructors. *Journal of Personality and Social Psychology, 29,* 609–618.

Slaughter, J. G., Shaver, K. G., & Arkin, R. M. (1988, May). *Self-assessment and self-protec-*

tion: The roles of uncertainty and response context. Paper presented at the meeting of the Midwestern Psychological Association, Chicago.

Smith, T. W., Snyder, C. R., & Handelsman, M. M. (1982). On the self-serving function of an academic wooden leg: Test anxiety as a self-handicapping strategy. *Journal of Personality and Social Psychology, 42,* 314–321.

Smith, T. W., Snyder, C. R., & Perkins, S. C. (1983). The self-serving function of hypochondriacal complaints: Physical symptoms as self-handicapping strategies. *Journal of Personality and Social Psychology, 44,* 787–797.

Snyder, C. R. (1984). Excuses. *Psychology Today, 18,* 50–55.

Snyder, C. R. (1985). Collaborative companions: The relationship of self-deception and excuse-making. In M. W. Martin (Ed.), *Self-deception and self-understanding* (pp. 35–51). Lawrence, KS: Regents Press of Kansas.

Snyder, C. R. (1989a). Reality negotiation: From excuses to hope and beyond. *Journal of Social and Clinical Psychology, 8,* 130–157.

Snyder, C. R. (1989b, April 14). *On the taking of a psychological dive.* Paper presented at the meeting of the Southwestern Psychological Association, Houston, TX.

Snyder, C. R., & Higgins, R. L. (1988a). Excuses: Their effective role in the negotiation of reality. *Psychological Bulletin, 104,* 23–35.

Snyder, C. R., & Higgins, R. L. (1988b). From making to being the excuse: An analysis of deception and verbal/nonverbal issues. *Journal of Nonverbal Behavior, 12,* 237–252.

Snyder, C. R., & Smith, T. W. (1982). Symptoms as self-handicapping strategies: The virtues of old wine in a new bottle. In G. Weary & H. L. Mirels (Eds.), *Integrations of clinical and social psychology* (pp. 104–127). New York: Oxford University Press.

Snyder, C. R., Higgins, R. L., & Stucky, R. J. (1983). *Excuses: Masquerades in search of grace.* New York: Wiley/Interscience.

Snyder, C. R., Smith, T. W., Augelli, R. W., & Ingram, R. E. (1985). On the self-serving function of social anxiety: Shyness as a self-handicapping strategy. *Journal of Personality and Social Psychology, 48,* 970–980.

Taylor, S. E., & Brown, J. D. (1988). Illusion and well-being: A social psychological perspective on mental health. *Psychological Bulletin, 103,* 193–210.

Tetlock, P. E. (1981). The influence of self-presentation goals in attributional reports. *Social Psychology Quarterly, 44,* 300–311.

Tice, D. M., & Baumeister, R. F. (1984, May). *Self-handicapping, self-esteem and self-presentation.* Paper presented at the meeting of the Midwestern Psychological Association Convention, Chicago.

Weiner, B., Amirkhan, J., Folkes, V. S., & Verette, J. A. (1987). An attributional analysis of excuse giving: Studies of a naive theory of emotion. *Journal of Personality and Social Psychology, 52,* 316–324.

Wills, T. A. (1981). Downward comparison principles in social psychology. *Psychological Bulletin, 90,* 245–271.

Wright, B. A. (1989). Extension of Heider's ideas to rehabilitation psychology. *American Psychologist, 44,* 525–528.

AUTHOR INDEX

SUBJECT INDEX